Jesus, the Essenes, and Christian Origins

Jesus, the Essenes, and Christian Origins
New Light on Ancient Texts and Communities

Simon J. Joseph

BAYLOR UNIVERSITY PRESS

© 2018 by Baylor University Press
Waco, Texas 76798

All Rights Reserved. No part of this publication may be reproduced, stored in a retrieval system, or transmitted, in any form or by any means, electronic, mechanical, photocopying, recording, or otherwise, without the prior permission in writing of Baylor University Press.

Unless otherwise stated, Scripture quotations are from the New Revised Standard Version Bible, copyright 1989, Division of Christian Education of the National Council of the Churches of Christ in the United States of America. Used by permission. All rights reserved.

Cover design by Daniel Benneworth-Gray
Cover image: mosaic from the floor of an ancient Jericho synagogue (6th to 8th centuries A.D.). Includes Aramaic dedicatory inscription, depiction of the Ark of the Law, seven-branched menorah, lulav, and shofar. The Hebrew inscription reads *shalom al yisrael*, "peace upon Israel." Photo from Todd Bolen/bibleplaces.com.

First published in paperback in 2025 under ISBN 978-1-4813-0777-2

The Library of Congress has cataloged the hardcover as follows:

Names: Joseph, Simon J., 1966– author.
Title: Jesus, the Essenes, and Christian origins : new light on ancient texts and communities / Simon J. Joseph.
Description: Waco, Texas : Baylor University Press, [2018] | Includes bibliographical references and index.
Identifiers: LCCN 2017034038 (print) | LCCN 2017044602 (ebook) | ISBN 9781481308120 (web PDF) | ISBN 9781481308113 (ebook: Mobi/Kindle) | ISBN 9781481307789 (ePub) | ISBN 9781481307765 (cloth : alk. paper) | ISBN 9781481307772 (pbk. : alk. paper)
Subjects: LCSH: Dead Sea scrolls. | Jesus Christ—Jewish interpretations. | Jesus Christ—Historicity. | Essenes.
Classification: LCC BM487 (ebook) | LCC BM487.J67 2018 (print) | DDC 296.8/14—dc23

To the Memory of My Father

CONTENTS

Acknowledgments ix

1 Rediscovering the Essenes in the Study of Christian Origins 1
2 The Community of the New Covenant 27
3 The Anointed Prophet 71
4 The Eschatological Teacher 99
5 Beyond the Essenes 163

Bibliography 171
Index of Authors 229
Index of Subjects 236

ACKNOWLEDGMENTS

The publication of this study—coinciding with the seventieth anniversary of the discovery of the Dead Sea Scrolls in 1947—is part of a long-term research project focused on the relationship between early Judaism and Christian origins. My first book, *Jesus, Q, and the Dead Sea Scrolls: A Judaic Approach to Q*, critically compared the Sayings Source / Gospel Q with passages from the Qumran corpus. My second book, *The Nonviolent Messiah: Jesus, Q, and the Enochic Tradition*, investigated the relationship between the historical Jesus, the Jesus tradition, and early Jewish messianism. My third book, *Jesus and the Temple: The Crucifixion in Its Jewish Context*, proposed that the historical Jesus can be understood in light of his eschatological halakhah—that is, his principled interpretation of the Torah—within early Judaism. In a recent article to be published in the *Harvard Theological Review*, I have further explored the relationship(s) between the early Jesus tradition in Q and Essenic ideas, motifs, and traditions. The present study attempts to advance this discussion by critically reexamining the relationship(s) between the historical Jesus and the Essenes in light of their distinctive Torah interpretation(s), with focused studies on divorce, celibacy, violence, Sabbath, and sacrifice.

    I am grateful and thankful to many scholars, colleagues, and friends who have helped make these studies possible. F. E. Peters and Lawrence H. Schiffman were instrumental in my early graduate studies at New York University. Vincent L. Wimbush facilitated my work in New Testament studies, both at Union Theological Seminary and at Claremont Graduate University. I also had the privilege and honor of working with James M. Robinson on my Ph.D. dissertation on the

Sayings Source / Gospel Q. James A. Sanders, Professor Emeritus at Claremont School of Theology, bringing to bear a lifetime of critical engagement with Scrolls research as the original translator of the Psalms Scroll from Cave 11, read through the entire manuscript, providing numerous helpful suggestions for improvement. I am honored to call him teacher, colleague, and friend. I have also benefited tremendously from the constructive criticism and comments provided by the editors of previous studies, including Loren T. Stuckenbruck, Eibert Tigchelaar, Jörg Frey, Paul Trebilco, and Matthias Konradt. I am grateful to have a warm and supportive environment in which to conduct research at California Lutheran University. I am especially thankful for the Interlibrary Loan Department at CLU, without which I could not possibly have completed this work. Special thanks, in particular, to Monica Kane, Interlibrary Loan Assistant and Melissa Pincus, both of whom provided exceptional assistance in locating and securing obscure sources. In addition to revisiting complex questions about the relationship(s) between Second Temple Judaism, Christian origins, and the Dead Sea Scrolls, I have also taken the present opportunity to address a number of critical responses to my work in the notes. I would like to thank John J. Collins for reading an early draft of the manuscript and providing constructive comments, all of which were very helpful. I would also like to thank the two anonymous Baylor University Press reviewers for their careful reading of the manuscript and constructive criticism. Special thanks to Carey C. Newman for shepherding this project to completion with positive enthusiasm, as well as for making a number of timely recommendations. Above all, this book would not have been possible without the love, support, and constant encouragement of my wife, Jennifer.

Simon J. Joseph
Santa Monica, Calif.
April 2017

Chapter 1

REDISCOVERING THE ESSENES IN THE STUDY OF CHRISTIAN ORIGINS

Was Jesus an Essene? Were the earliest Christians influenced by the Essenes?[1] Since the discovery of the Dead Sea Scrolls in Cave 1—an ancient "library" of Jewish manuscripts composed on parchment, wrapped in linen, sealed with wax, and stored in clay jars—these questions have often been at the forefront of both popular fascination and scholarly discussion.[2] The Dead Sea Scrolls were

---

[1] James H. Charlesworth, "The Dead Sea Scrolls and the Historical Jesus," in *Jesus and the Dead Sea Scrolls*, ed. J. H. Charlesworth (New York: Doubleday, 1992), 1–74; George J. Brooke, "Jesus, the Dead Sea Scrolls, and Scrolls Scholarship," in *The Dead Sea Scrolls and the New Testament* (Minneapolis: Fortress, 2005), 19–26; idem, *Qumran and the Jewish Jesus: Reading the New Testament in the Light of the Scrolls* (Cambridge: Grove Books, 2005); Richard Horsley, "The Dead Sea Scrolls and the Historical Jesus," in *The Scrolls and Christian Origins: The Second Princeton Symposium on Judaism and Christian Origins*, ed. J. H. Charlesworth, vol. 3 of *The Bible and the Dead Sea Scrolls* (Waco, Tex.: Baylor University Press, 2006), 37–60; Herbert Braun, "The Significance of Qumran for the Problem of the Historical Jesus," in *The Historical Jesus and the Kerygmatic Christ: Essays on the New Quest of the Historical Jesus*, ed. C. E. Braaten and R. A. Harrisville (Nashville: Abingdon, 1964), 69–78; William H. Brownlee, "Jesus and Qumran," in *Jesus and the Historian*, ed. F. T. Trotter (Philadelphia: Westminster, 1968), 52–81; Howard Clark Kee, "The Bearing of the Dead Sea Scrolls on Understanding Jesus," in *Jesus in History and Myth*, ed. R. J. Hoffmann and G. A. Larue (Buffalo, N.Y.: Prometheus, 1986), 54–75; Craig A. Evans, "Jesus and the Dead Sea Scrolls," in *The Dead Sea Scrolls after Fifty Years: A Comprehensive Assessment*, ed. P. W. Flint and J. C. VanderKam (Leiden: Brill, 1999), 573–98.

[2] On the use of the term "library" in Qumran Studies, see Sidnie White Crawford, "The Qumran Collection as a Scribal Library," in *The Dead Sea Scrolls at Qumran and the Concept of a Library*, ed. Sidnie White Crawford and Cecilia Wassen, STDJ 116 (Leiden: Brill, 2015), 109–31. On the Scrolls as remnants of an Essene *genizah* and "scroll cemetery," see Joan E.

written during one of the most turbulent eras in world history, while the Temple in Jerusalem was still standing and early Judaism was a complex, multifaceted, and multiregional ancestral religious tradition with several different competing sects, one of which would ultimately become known to us today as "Christianity."

The New Testament Gospels, however, never even mention the Essenes, despite often referring to other Jewish groups like the Pharisees and Sadducees. That is, the Essenes do not even *exist* in the literary-narrative world of the Gospels as Jesus' friends or enemies.[3] Contemporary historians Josephus, Philo, and Pliny wax poetic about their ideals and ethics, but the New Testament writings are conspicuously silent. Did the evangelists intentionally *omit* them from their biographies of Jesus? Or were they so *different* from Jesus and his first followers as to be essentially irrelevant to the study and story of Christian origins? This book, coinciding with the seventieth anniversary of the discovery of the Dead Sea Scrolls, seeks to shed new light on these questions by reexamining and reconsidering the complex relationship(s) between the historical Jesus, the Essenes, and Christian origins within first-century Palestinian Judaism.

The idea that the Essenes influenced early Christianity has a long and colorful history in New Testament scholarship.[4] This exotic history was resurrected by the discovery of the Dead Sea Scrolls in 1947, but many of the earliest critical biographies of Jesus appealed to the Essenes in their reconstructions. As early as 1717, "infidel Deists" were already being criticized for their "wrong use" of the classical sources, particularly when they found "in them an agreement between the Christian religion" and the Essenes.[5] When such "infidels" suggested, "Christ and his followers were no other than a sect branched out from that of the Essenes," their critics countered by challenging them to find "any of the proper doctrines of Christianity in the classical sources."[6] Here the terms of the debate were already being clearly drawn: Christians were so *different* from the Essenes that "almost

---

Taylor, "Buried Manuscripts and Empty Tombs: The Qumran Genizah Theory Revisited," in *"Go Out and Study the Land" (Judges 18:2): Archaeological, Historical and Textual Studies in Honor of Hanan Eshel*, ed. A. M. Maeir, J. Magness, and L. H. Schiffman (Leiden: Brill, 2012), 269–315.

[3] Cf. *Jesus among Friends and Enemies: A Historical and Literary Introduction to Jesus in the Gospels*, ed. C. Keith and L. W. Hurtado (Grand Rapids: Baker Academic, 2011).

[4] See esp. Simon J. Joseph, *Jesus, Q, and the Dead Sea Scrolls: A Judaic Approach to Q*, WUNT 2/333 (Tübingen: Mohr Siebeck, 2012), 22–28; cf. Siegfried Wagner, *Die Essener in der wissenschaftlichen Diskussion: Vom Ausgang des 18. bis zum begin des 20. Jahrhunderts: Eine wissenschaftsgeschichtliche Studie* (Berlin: Alfred Töpelmann, 1960).

[5] Humphrey Prideaux, *The Old and New Testaments Connected in the History of Jews & Neighboring Nations, from the Declensions of the Kingdoms of Israel and Judah to the Time of Christ*, 16th ed., 4 vols. (London: W. Baynes, 1808 [1717]), 3:429–30.

[6] Prideaux, *Old and New Testaments*, 3:429–30.

all that is peculiar in that sect, is *condemned* by Christ and his disciples."[7] That is, the Essenes had *nothing* to do with "Christ and his apostles."[8]

According to one scenario, Christianity began as an Essene plot to transform Jewish society by delivering it from its hopes for a political messiah.[9] According to another, Jesus was secretly trained by the Essenes,[10] but he survived the crucifixion, with Essenes removing his body from the tomb. Despite these fanciful narratives, Albert Schweitzer concluded that "the hypothesis of the [Essene] secret society . . . was in many respects *more historical* than the psychological links of connection which our modernizing historians discover without having any foundation for them in the text."[11] These early appeals to the Essenes sought to propose natural explanations for the events in the Gospels and tended to be characterized by two motifs reflecting their emergence in the Enlightenment: political intrigue and rationalism.[12] Jesus was "the model of rationalism and morality," surrounded by a mysterious secret society and implicated in various political intrigues.[13] These lives provided rational explanations of the miracles while affirming their historicity, preserving a sense of religious mystery "in the face of the threat posed by rationalism."[14] This "odd mixture of the rational and the occult" served several purposes for Christian scholars: the Essenes could be used as a foil for rationalist agendas; identifying Jesus as an Essene also preserved the historical record of Jesus' Jewishness and located him on the margins of Judaism rather than within its "normative," Pharisaic/rabbinical center.[15]

The Essene hypothesis of Christian origins also served several purposes for Jewish scholars: it boosted "Jewish self-esteem in the face of Christianity's success;"[16] destabilized normative self-definitions of Judaism and Christianity;[17]

---

[7] Prideaux, *Old and New Testaments*, 3:430 (emphasis added).

[8] Prideaux, *Old and New Testaments*, 3:431.

[9] Karl Friedrich Bahrdt, *Ausführung des Plans und Zwecks Jesu. In Briefen an Wahrheit suchende Leser*, 11 vols. (Berlin: August Mylius, 1784–1792).

[10] Karl Heinrich Venturini, *Natürliche Geschichte des großen Propheten von Nazareth*, 4 vols. (Copenhagen, 1800–1802); cf. G. O'Collins and D. Kendall, "On Reissuing Venturini," *Gregorianum* 75 (1994): 241–65.

[11] Albert Schweitzer, *The Quest of the Historical Jesus: A Critical Study of Its Progress from Reimarus to Wrede*, trans. W. Montgomery (New York: Macmillan, 1910), 300 (emphasis added).

[12] Susannah Heschel, "The Image of Judaism in Nineteenth-Century Christian New Testament Scholarship in Germany," in *Jewish-Christian Encounters over the Centuries: Symbiosis, Prejudice, Holocaust, Dialogue*, ed. M. Perry and F. M. Schweitzer, AUS 136 (New York: Peter Lang, 1994), 217–20.

[13] Heschel, "Image of Judaism," 219.

[14] Heschel, "Image of Judaism," 220.

[15] Heschel, "Image of Judaism," 134, 141–42, 169.

[16] Susannah Heschel, *Abraham Geiger and the Jewish Jesus*. CSHJ (Chicago: University of Chicago Press, 1998), 134.

[17] Heschel, *Abraham Geiger and the Jewish Jesus*, 239.

supported subversive, revisionist readings of early Christianity in which Jesus was firmly embedded in a Jewish context;[18] and highlighted a Christian "anxiety of influence."[19] For some Orthodox Jewish scholars, Jesus was an Essene who adopted "Essene principles," "a member of the Jewish sect of the Essenes" whose purpose was not to create a new religion but to reform Judaism.[20] That is, Christianity was "an offshoot of the sect of the Essenes, and inherited the aversion of that sect for the Pharisaic laws."[21] Jesus adopted the "fundamental principles" of the Essenes.[22] As a result, Christianity was dependent on Judaism for its existence and its ideas.[23] For some Reform Jews, Jesus' membership in "the Essene party" suggested that Essenes joined the early church.[24] That is, the Essenes "joined the new Church which was ready to acknowledge the crucified Jesus as the expected Messiah and helped in its formation."[25] The reason why the Essenes are not mentioned in the New Testament is simply because they "merged in the early Church."[26]

To be sure, these narratives could be dismissed as conspiracy theories.[27] A seemingly irresistible fascination with "the Essenes" as a "secret society" has spawned many speculative hypotheses.[28] Such proposals have ranged from the assertion that "the identity of many of the precepts and practices of Essenism and Christianity is unquestionable ... [and] that our Saviour himself belonged to this holy brotherhood,"[29] to the recognition that Jesus "repudiated their

---

[18] Heschel, *Abraham Geiger and the Jewish Jesus*, 128, 14.

[19] Harold Bloom, *The Anxiety of Influence* (New York: Oxford University Press, 1973).

[20] Donald A. Hagner, *The Jewish Reclamation of Jesus: An Analysis and Critique of Modern Jewish Study of Jesus* (Grand Rapids: Academie Books, 1984), 62. See Heinrich Hirsch Graetz, *History of the Jews* (Pennsylvania: Jewish Publication Society of America, 1893); Jonathan M. Elukin, "A New Essenism: Heinrich Graetz and Mysticism," *JHI* 59, no. 1 (1998): 135–48.

[21] Hagner, *Jewish Reclamation of Jesus*, 171.

[22] Hagner, *Jewish Reclamation of Jesus*, 150.

[23] Elukin, "A New Essenism," 140.

[24] Kaufmann Kohler, *The Origins of the Synagogue and the Church* (New York: Macmillan, 1929), 205.

[25] Kohler, *Origins of the Synagogue and the Church*, 237.

[26] Kohler, *Origins of the Synagogue and the Church*, 239–40, 133.

[27] See, e.g., Thomas De Quincey, "The Essenes," in *Historical Essays and Researches*, ed. D. Masson, vol. 7 of *The Collected Writings of Thomas De Quincey* (London: A&C Black, 1897), 101–72, here 106 and 109, identifying Josephus' Essenes *as* "Primitive Christians."

[28] De Quincey speculated that early Christians chose a secret society name for themselves based on the "costume" of the high priest's breastplate (חשן/ἐσσὴν), which was called *The Essen* (Josephus, *A.J.* 3.163.216–218). They called themselves *The Society of the Essen* (121–22), "a central Christian Society, secret from necessity, cautious to excess from the extremity of the danger, and surrounding themselves in their outer rings by merely *Jew* pupils" (126).

[29] Christian D. Ginsburg, *The Essenes: Their History and Doctrines; The Kabbalah: Its Doctrines, Development and Literature* (New York: Samuel Weiser, 1974), 22–23, 24–25 (repr. of *The Essenes* [London: Longman & Green, 1864]).

extremes,"[30] being both related to and independent of the Essenes.[31] Indeed, by the end of the nineteenth century, Christianity could casually be described as "an Essenism that has largely succeeded" ("Le christianisme est un essénisme qui a largement réussi").[32] It is not surprising that the relationship between Jesus and the Essenes has long been a prominent feature in Western esotericism.[33] The Essenes have also inspired a series of literary forgeries and mystical speculations. For example, *The Crucifixion by an Eye-Witness*, first published in Leipzig in 1849, was purported to be a "letter" sent from an Essene in Jerusalem to his brothers in Alexandria describing Jesus' crucifixion.[34] Similarly, the *Gospel of the Holy Twelve* (1888)—supposedly an ancient Aramaic Essene manuscript preserved in a Buddhist monastery in Tibet (!)—portrays Jesus as a vegetarian who blesses plants and animals, emphasizes the feminine aspect of God, and travels to India with Mary Magdalene as his partner.[35] The *Essene Gospel of Peace* (1928)—another "Essene gospel" purported to have been hidden in the Secret Archives of the Vatican and the Royal Archives of the Habsburgs in Austria—has Jesus refer to his "Earth Mother" and recommend the health benefits of colonic treatments.[36]

The modern New Age movement tends to recognize the Essenes as the subversive founders of an alternative Christianity. The Theosophical Society promoted the idea that Jesus was secretly trained by the Essenes, received his education from them, but preferred the independent life, leaving their community to become a traveling healer.[37] Jesus was "the last great initiate" of the ancient world and spent a number of years among the Essenes, learning their secrets about

---

[30] Ginsburg, *Essenes*, 25.

[31] For criticism, see J. B. Lightfoot, *Saint Paul's Epistles to the Colossians and to Philemon* (London: Macmillan, 1912). For the assumption that Lightfoot had refuted the Essene theory, see Millar Burrows, *More Light on the Dead Sea Scrolls* (New York: Viking, 1958), 77.

[32] Ernest Renan, *Histoire du Peuple d'Israël* (Paris: Calman-Lévy, 1893), 5:70. On the other hand, A. Regeffe (*La Secte des Esséniens: Essai critique sur son organization, sa doctrine, son origine* [Lyons: Emmanuel Vitte, 1898], 8) denies any relationship between the Essenes and Christianity, claiming that "between Essenism and Christianity" there is "all the distance that separates the divine from the human" ("toute la distance qui sépare le divin de l'humain").

[33] Reender Kranenborg, "The Presentation of the Essenes in Western Esotericism," *JCR* 13, no. 2 (1998): 245–56; Per Beskow, *Strange Tales about Jesus: A Survey of Unfamiliar Gospels* (Philadelphia: Fortress, 1983).

[34] *The Crucifixion, By an Eye-Witness: A Letter, Written Seven Years After the Crucifixion*, Supplemental Harmonic Series, vol. 2 (repr., Chicago: Indo-American Book, 1907).

[35] Gideon Jasper Ouseley, *The Gospel of the Holy Twelve*; repr., E. F. Udny (London: Edson, 1923) [1901].

[36] Edmond Bordeaux Szekely, *The Essene Gospel of Peace* (Nelson, BC: International Biogenic Society, 1981 [1928]).

[37] Helena P. Blavatsky, *Isis Unveiled: A Mastery-Key to the Mysteries of Ancient and Modern Science and Theology*, 2 vols. (Pasadena: Theosophical University Press, 1976 [1877]); idem, *The Secret Doctrine: The Synthesis of Science, Religion, and Philosophy* (Pasadena: Theosophical

nature, prophecy, and healing.[38] He may not have been an Essene "in the strict sense of the word," but he lived as a "lay-brother" of their community, learning their "secret lore." Alternatively, Jesus was an "Aryan Essene" and part of the "Great White Brotherhood" of Egypt. When historical documentation was lacking, various esotericists sought insight from the "Akashic Records," an allegedly interdimensional repository of all human events, thoughts, acts, and knowledge.[39] Helen Schucman, the Jewish author or "scribe" of *A Course in Miracles*—a set of teachings attributed to "Jesus"—even described Qumran as "the holiest place on earth," identifying it with her past-life role as an Essene scribe now buried in the Qumran cemetery.[40]

While such ideas generally tend to be ignored by biblical scholars, their popularity illustrates that the Essenes have long been a controversial subject, a site of fascination for Deists, Jewish and Christian biblical scholars, esotericists, forgers, psychics, and modern New Age groups.[41] At the same time, the Essenes are footnoted in contemporary Judaism and Christianity, where they tend to be regarded either as an historical curiosity or as theologically divergent. The Essenes have thus come to represent the quintessentially "Other Jews" of antiquity—marginalized by both Jews and Christians—and yet continue to haunt the ruined remains of an ancient past long forgotten, a lost people who survive now only in the imaginations of their modern interpreters, a "missing link" in the study of early Christian origins.[42]

University Press, 1963 [1888]); Annie Besant, *Esoteric Christianity: Or the Lesser Mysteries*, 5th ed. (Adyar, Madras: Theosophical Publishing House, 1950 [1901]).

[38] Edouard Schuré, *Jesus: The Last Great Initiate* (Chicago: Yogi, 1917).

[39] Levi Dowling, *The Aquarian Gospel of Jesus the Christ* (Marina del Rey, Calif.: DeVorss, 1972 [1907]); Edgar Cayce, perhaps the most famous psychic of the twentieth century, referred to the "Essenes" in many trance-like "readings" performed between 1939 and 1945. According to Cayce, many of his clients had been Essenes in their past lives. See Jeffrey Furst, ed., *Edgar Cayce's Story of Jesus* (New York: Berkeley, 1968). Anne and Daniel Meurois-Givaudan (*The Way of the Essenes: Christ's Hidden Life Remembered* [Rochester, Vt.: Destiny, 1993]) claim that their work is based on readings from the "Akashic Records" and "does not represent the work of a historian, but is an eye-witness account, the testimony of events truly experienced. As a matter of fact, no documents of any sort have gone into its composition" (vii).

[40] Kenneth Wapnick, *Absence from Felicity: The Story of Helen Schucman and Her Scribing of "A Course in Miracles"* (Temecula, Calif.: FACIM, 1991), 356–57, cf. 124n27.

[41] On the Scrolls as an "open signifier" in popular culture, see Maxine L. Grossman, "Mystery or History: The Dead Sea Scrolls as Pop Phenomenon," *DSD* 12, no. 1 (2005): 68–86, 75–79.

[42] Joan E. Taylor, *The Essenes, the Scrolls, and the Dead Sea* (New York: Oxford University Press, 2012), 11, refers to "the marginalization of the Essenes, their characterization anachronistically as an isolationist 'monastic' order, and their detachment from normative Judaism" prior to the discovery of the Scrolls.

Since the discovery of the Dead Sea Scrolls, the relationship between the Qumran corpus and the New Testament has often been at the forefront of scholarly discussion.[43] Yet despite some highly exaggerated claims to the contrary, the Dead Sea Scrolls do not refer to Jesus, John the Baptist, James, or any other "Christian" character. The Scrolls were written many years *before* the emergence of the Jesus movement and are not the secret writings of early Christians.[44] Qumran was not the original "cradle of Christianity." There was never any Vatican cover-up or conspiracy. The Qumran corpus does not include any texts referring to a "pierced" messiah.[45] And no Greek papyrus fragments of any text from the New Testament have been found at Qumran.[46] Yet such claims have taken their toll on a field already prone to sensationalism. There is no denying that scandals have surrounded the discovery and interpretation of the Scrolls. It also cannot be denied that scholars have sometimes reacted to this speculation by doubting, if not denying, the possibility of contact or influence between the Jesus movement and the Essenes.[47]

---

[43] Jörg Frey, "The Impact of the Dead Sea Scrolls on New Testament Interpretation: Proposals, Problems, and Further Perspectives," in *The Scrolls and Christian Origins: The Second Princeton Symposium on Judaism and Christian Origins*, ed. J. H. Charlesworth, vol. 3 of *The Bible and the Dead Sea Scrolls* (Waco, Tex.: Baylor University Press, 2006), 407–61.

[44] Robert H. Eisenman, *The New Testament Code: The Cup of the Lord, the Damascus Document, and the Blood of Christ* (London: Watkins, 2006); idem, *James the Just in the Habakkuk Pesher* (Leiden: Brill, 1986); idem, *James the Just: The Key to Unlocking the Secrets of Early Christianity and the Dead Sea Scrolls* (New York: Viking, 1996); Barbara Thiering, *The Qumran Origins of the Christian Church* (Sydney: Theological Explorations, 1983); idem, *Jesus & the Riddle of the Dead Sea Scrolls: Unlocking the Secrets of His Story* (New York: HarperSanFrancisco, 1992).

[45] Timothy Lim, *The Dead Sea Scrolls: A Very Short Introduction* (New York: Oxford University Press, 2005), 4–5, 109–10; Geza Vermes, "The Oxford Forum for Qumran Research: Seminar on the Rule of War from Cave 4 (4Q285)," *JJS* 43 (1992): 85–94; M. G. Abegg, "Messianic Hope and 4Q285: A Reassessment," *JBL* 113 (1994): 81–91; Markus Bockmuehl, "A 'Slain Messiah' in 4Q Serek Milḥamah (4Q285)?" *TynBul* 43 (1992): 155–69.

[46] Lim, *Dead Sea Scrolls*, 107–8; referring to Carsten Peter Thiede, *The Earliest Gospel Manuscript? The Qumran Fragment 7Q5 and Its Significance for New Testament Studies* (Carlisle, UK: Paternoster, 1992); idem, *The Dead Sea Scrolls and the Jewish Origins of Christianity* (Oxford: Lion, 2000); José O'Callaghan, *Los papiros griegos de la cueva 7 de Qumrân*, BAC 353 (Madrid: Editorial católica, 1974). For further criticism, see Colin H. Roberts, "On Some Presumed Papyrus Fragments of the New Testament from Qumran," *JTS* 23 (1972): 446–47.

[47] Cf. J. Frey, "Essenes," in *The Eerdmans Dictionary of Early Judaism*, ed. J. J. Collins and D. C. Harlow (Grand Rapids: Eerdmans, 2010), 602: "That the Essenes had a major influence on emerging Christianity, either by direct links between an Essene Quarter and the early Jesus movement or by Essenes joining the messianic Jesus movement after 70 C.E., is highly improbable."

The early Jesus movement and the Dead Sea sect were "very different movements."[48] Yet it is not always entirely clear where the boundaries between these two movements should be drawn, especially given the internal diversity of both movements. It will not do to casually dismiss the Essenes in reconstructing the historical Jesus. The Scrolls may not refer to Jesus of Nazareth or to the Christian church and may not tell us anything about "the vicarious and salvific character of what Jesus accomplished for humanity in his passion, death, and resurrection," but we should not expect them to. The Dead Sea Scrolls are not "Christian" writings.[49]

Today, Qumran Studies is a highly specialized field of interdisciplinary research that focuses on the philological, archaeological, historical, and theological worlds of the Scrolls. The era of sensationalistic speculation is now over. Yet many specialists accept the idea that there was probably *some* kind of direct and/or indirect "influence" between the Essenes and the Jesus movement.[50] The problem is determining the precise nature and extent of that influence. Generally speaking, many similarities between the Essenes and early Christianity can be explained by appealing to "common tradition,"[51] culture, and worldview(s).[52] The question is whether two movements—which share so many distinctive features and coexisted in the same time and place—*should* really be explained as isolated and unrelated social formations. In other words, the fact that the New Testament and Qumran texts represent *different* literary products of Second Temple Judaism should not

[48] John J. Collins, "Qumran, Apocalypticism, and the New Testament," in *The Dead Sea Scrolls—Fifty Years after Their Discovery: Proceedings of the Jerusalem Congress, July 20–25, 1997*, ed. L. H. Schiffman, E. Tov, and J. C. VanderKam (Jerusalem: Israel Exploration Society, 2000), 138.

[49] Joseph A. Fitzmyer, *Responses to 101 Questions on the Dead Sea Scrolls* (New York: Paulist, 1992), 39.

[50] Vermes, "The Qumran Community, the Essenes, and Nascent Christianity," in *The Dead Sea Scrolls—Fifty Years after Their Discovery: Proceedings of the Jerusalem Congress, July 20–25, 1997*, ed. L. H. Schiffman, E. Tov, and J. C. VanderKam (Jerusalem: Israel Exploration Society, 2000), 585–86; James C. VanderKam, "The Dead Sea Scrolls and Christianity," in *Understanding the Dead Sea Scrolls: A Reader from the Biblical Archaeological Review*, ed. H. Shanks (New York: Random House, 1992), 185; Pierre Benoit, "Qumran and the New Testament," in *Paul and Qumran: Studies in New Testament Exegesis*, ed. J. Murphy-O'Connor (Chicago: Priory, 1968), 6; Raymond E. Brown, "The Dead Sea Scrolls and the New Testament," in *John and the Dead Sea Scrolls*, ed. J. H. Charlesworth (New York: Crossroad, 1990), 2.

[51] Lim, *Dead Sea Scrolls*, 112–13; Brooke, *Dead Sea Scrolls and the New Testament*, 13. F. García Martínez, "Qumran between the Old and the New Testament," in *Echoes from the Caves: Qumran and the New Testament*, STDJ 85 (Leiden: Brill, 2009), 5: "different evolutionary phases starting from a common ground."

[52] F. F. Bruce, "Qumran and Early Christianity," *NTS* 2 (1955–1956): 176–90; Raymond E. Brown, "The Qumran Scrolls and the Johannine Gospels and Epistles," *CBQ* 17 (1955): 403–19, 559–74; Joseph A. Fitzmyer, "The Use of Explicit Old Testament Quotations in Qumran Literature and in the New Testament," *NTS* 7 (1961): 297–333.

be confused with the idea that they are *unrelated* and *isolated* phenomena. There are simply too many "parallels" to ignore. The geographical and chronological overlapping and thematic similarities between the two movements makes it virtually inconceivable that Jesus and his followers never encountered—let alone learned from, interacted with, or were "influenced" by—the four thousand Essenes reported to have been living in Judea at the same time.[53]

Nonetheless, a number of methodological caveats are in order. The period under discussion—commonly known as "Christian origins" (30–100 CE)—was a sociologically and politically turbulent time. In less than one century, the Judean population witnessed the ministries of the historical Jesus and John the Baptist, so daily interactions between Essenes and early (Jewish) Christians could have taken place in Jerusalem between 30 CE and 70 CE and intersected with the ministry and death of the historical Jesus. Subsequent events include the early "preaching" (*kerygma*) of the Jerusalem community; the rapid inclusion of non-Judean Jews and Gentiles; the early formation of Pauline communities; the martyrdoms of Stephen, Peter, Paul, and James; the destruction of the Temple in Jerusalem; the "diaspora" of the Jewish Christian "community"; and the composition of the New Testament Gospels. Essene "influence(s)" could theoretically have occurred at any point within this time frame.

The most significant methodological problem in determining the nature of the relationship between Jesus and the Essenes, however, is the assumption that "the Essenes" represent a static, monolithic entity and that the Dead Sea Scrolls are "a homogenous body of literature devoid of any internal tensions and showing no trace of development"[54]—in short, to deny Essenism the possibility of mobility, evolution, development, and transformation as a fluid, adaptable, expansive movement that changed over time. This assumption not only contradicts how religious movements actually function; it also raises rigid and unwarranted boundaries between Essenism and early Christianity and fails to take into account the profoundly (realized) eschatological nature of both movements.[55] We must

---

[53] James H. Charlesworth ("Have the Dead Sea Scrolls Revolutionized Our Understanding of the New Testament?" in *The Dead Sea Scrolls—Fifty Years after Their Discovery: Proceedings of the Jerusalem Congress, July 20–25, 1997*, ed. L. H. Schiffman, E. Tov, and J. C. VanderKam [Jerusalem: Israel Exploration Society, 2000], 123) regards such a perspective as "myopic."

[54] Jerome Murphy-O'Connor, "Qumran and the New Testament," in *The New Testament and Its Modern Interpreters*, ed. J. Epp and G. W. MacRae (Atlanta: Scholars, 1989), 63.

[55] James H. Charlesworth, "Qumran, John and the Odes of Solomon," in *John and the Dead Sea Scrolls*, ed. J. H. Charlesworth (New York: Crossroad, 1990), 123: "An early Christian who borrowed from the Dead Sea Scrolls was dependent upon them regardless of whether he altered these traditions little or greatly . . . as a prism reflects light so the belief in the new dispensation would have altered old traditions."

factor in historical developments *within* Essenism as well as *between* Essenism and early Christianity. If the Essenes expected a new "beginning,"[56] and the conversion of "all the congregation of Israel" (1QSa 1.1–6), we must also be careful about assuming that the Essenes were an essentially "closed" group uninterested in reaching out to their fellow Jews.[57] Moreover, if the Qumran group only regarded its existence as contingent "until the coming of the messiah(s)" (1QS 9.10),[58] we should not be surprised if the group's ideas "underwent a change."[59] Essenism was a more dynamic, diverse, and multifaceted movement than we may realize.

The inherent probability that *some* kind of contact between the Jesus movement and the Essenes—two chronologically concurrent, geographically proximate, and eschatologically oriented renewal movements—can be posited requires the construction of historical models of dynamic relationship and interaction. Direct and indirect influences could theoretically be conceived as a "passive reception," "a transforming reaction," or a sudden "conversion" of Essenes into the Jesus movement,[60] but *that* the Jesus movement was influenced by the Essenes seems to be something of "an emerging consensus."[61] A number of scholars, for example, have suggested that some Essenes "converted" to the Jesus movement, bringing with them their organizational structures, sectarian worldview(s), and scriptural traditions.[62] Some scholars appeal to Josephus' reference to an "Essene Gate" (ἡ Ἐσσηνῶν πύλη, *B.J.* 5.145), and perhaps even an Essene "quarter," in Jerusalem as support for this hypothesis. Indeed, there is no good reason to doubt the existence of Essenes in Jerusalem, since Josephus provides multiple attestations of their presence there. Similarly, there is no good reason to doubt

---

[56] E. P. Sanders, *Paul and Palestinian Judaism: A Comparison of Patterns of Religion* (Philadelphia: Fortress, 1977).

[57] On the Essenes as a "closed" group, see David N. Freedman, "Early Christianity and the Scrolls: An Inquiry," in *Jesus in History and Myth*, ed. R. J. Hoffmann and G. A. Larue (Buffalo, N.Y.: Prometheus, 1986), 97; Kee, "Bearing of the Dead Sea Scrolls on Understanding Jesus," 57.

[58] Nils Alstrup Dahl, "Eschatology and History in the Light of the Dead Sea Scrolls," in *The Future of Our Religious Past: Essays in Honour of Rudolf Bultmann*, ed. J. M. Robinson, trans. C. E. Carlston and R. P. Scharlemann (London: SCM Press, 1971), 14.

[59] Dahl, "Eschatology and History in the Light of the Dead Sea Scrolls," 19–21.

[60] Benoit, "Qumran and the New Testament," 14: "It is not only possible, but very likely, that some zealous and sincere Essenes gradually accepted and joined the infant Church."

[61] Brooke, *Dead Sea Scrolls and the New Testament*, 8; cf. F. F. Bruce, "Qumran and the New Testament," *Faith and Thought* 90 (1958): 92–102.

[62] Otto Betz and Rainer Riesner, *Jesus, Qumran and the Vatican: Clarifications*, trans. J. Bowden (London: SCM Press, 1994), 155; Sherman E. Johnson, "The Dead Sea Manual of Discipline and the Jerusalem Church of Acts," in *The Scrolls and the New Testament*, ed. K. Stendahl (New York: Harper & Brothers, 1958), 129–42; Brooke, *Dead Sea Scrolls and the New Testament*, 4.

the existence of a "Christian" Jerusalem community in relatively close proximity to the Essenes of Jerusalem.[63]

The relationship between the Jesus movement and the Essenes has been understood as a development of Essenism,[64] with the Jesus movement's having "borrowed from the Essenes a repertory of terms and concepts, a certain number of theological schemata, and perhaps also collections of biblical verses."[65] For a number of scholars, especially in the heady days following the first discoveries, there seemed to be no good reason to doubt that Jesus himself knew of and interacted with Essenes,[66] both during and prior to his public ministry.[67] For some, the Scrolls seemed to finally provide us with "a picture of the religious and cultural climate in which ... Jesus was initially reared."[68] It seemed as if Christianity could now be said to have "emerged from an environment close to

---

[63] Paul understood his own ministry in relationship to the "churches in Judea." Richard Bauckham ("The Early Jerusalem Church, Qumran and the Essenes," in *The Dead Sea Scrolls as Background to Postbiblical Judaism and Early Christianity: Papers from an International Conference at St. Andrews in 2001*, ed. J. R. Davila, STDJ 46 [Leiden: Brill, 2003], 63–89, here 72) affirms the presence of the Essenes and "the early Jerusalem church" in the same area.

[64] André Dupont-Sommer, *The Dead Sea Scrolls: A Preliminary Survey*, trans. E. M. Rowley (Oxford: Blackwell, 1952): "The documents from Qumran make it plain that the primitive Christian Church was rooted in the Jewish sect of the New Covenant ... and that it borrowed from it a large part of its organization, rites, doctrines, 'patterns of thought' and its mystical and ethical ideas." Cf. idem, *The Jewish Sect of Qumran and the Essenes: New Studies on the Dead Sea Scrolls*, trans. R. D. Barnett (New York: Macmillan, 1955), 164, 150: "the Jewish sect directly and immediately prepared the way for the Christian Church, and that it helped to shape both the Church's soul and its body.... Christianity is no copy or replica of Essenism. It is, to put it more exactly, a *quasi*-Essene neo-formation" (emphasis original). Cf. Matthew Black, "The Dead Sea Scrolls and Christian Origins," in *The Scrolls and Christianity: Historical and Theological Significance*, ed. M. Black (London: SPCK, 1969), 99: "It is from such an 'Essene-type' of Judaism that Christianity is descended."

[65] Marcel Simon, *Jewish Sects at the Time of Jesus*, trans. J. H. Farley (Philadelphia: Fortress, 1967), 147: "borrowed from the Essenes a repertory of terms and concepts, a certain number of theological schemata, and perhaps also collections of biblical verses, chosen and grouped in accordance with apologetical and catechitical ends."

[66] Simon, *Jewish Sects at the Time of Jesus*, 148: "It appears certain that Jesus knew Essenism, or an environment in which Essenian beliefs were particularly widespread."

[67] Jonathan Campbell, *The Dead Sea Scrolls: The Complete Story* (Berkeley: Ulysses, 1998), 140: "[He] might have had an association with the Essenes before he embarked on his ministry, ceasing to be one of their number only when he began to preach and heal." Cf. Kurt Schubert, "The Sermon on the Mount and the Qumran Texts," in *The Scrolls and the New Testament*, ed. K. Stendahl (New York: Harper, 1957), 131: "It seems practically certain that he (Jesus) was acquainted with the Qumran Essene teachings and that he had come to grips with them. A direct, temporary membership in the Qumran community itself is quite conceivable."

[68] Theodore H. Gaster, *The Dead Sea Scriptures* (New York: Doubleday/Anchor Books, 1964), 13.

that of the Essenes,"[69] and that Essenism represented "the spiritual atmosphere in which lived John the Baptist, the followers of Jesus, and the first members of the primitive church."[70] The Qumran texts provided "an intelligible Palestinian matrix for many of the practices and tenets of the early church."[71] The Scrolls illuminate "an Essenic type of Judaism which . . . almost certainly formed the background of primitive Christianity."[72] An increasingly popular thesis held that the two movements' shared belief in dualism, determinism, election, apocalyptic eschatology, communal property, and the community as a "new covenant" and a spiritual temple could "not be explained away as incidental."[73]

Beginning in the 1950s, many scholars found "parallels" between the Dead Sea Scrolls and the New Testament,[74] the Gospel of John,[75] and the letters of Paul.[76] The relationship between John the Baptist, the Essenes, and/or Qumran,[77] in particular, intrigued New Testament scholars, leading many to conclude that John may have once been a member of the (Qumran) Essene community,[78] or, at the very least, that there must have been some form of direct contact between

[69] Justin Taylor, *Where Did Christianity Come From?* (Collegeville, Minn.: Liturgical, 2001).

[70] Taylor, *Where Did Christianity Come From?* 123.

[71] Joseph A. Fitzmyer, *The Semitic Background of the New Testament* (Grand Rapids: Eerdmans, 1997), 273.

[72] F. F. Bruce, *Second Thoughts on the Dead Sea Scrolls* (Grand Rapids: Eerdmans, 1956), 101.

[73] David Flusser, *Judaism and the Origins of Christianity* (Jerusalem: Magnes, 1988), 72.

[74] Benoit, "Qumran and the New Testament," 1–30; Matthew Black, *The Scrolls and Christian Origins: Studies in the Jewish Background of the New Testament* (New York: Charles Scribner's Sons, 1961); idem, "Dead Sea Scrolls and Christian Origins," 97–106; Brown, "Dead Sea Scrolls and the New Testament," 1–8; Joseph A. Fitzmyer, *The Dead Sea Scrolls and Christian Origins* (Grand Rapids: Eerdmans, 2000); William S. Lasor, *The Dead Sea Scrolls and the New Testament* (Grand Rapids: Eerdmans, 1972); Krister Stendahl, ed., *The Scrolls and the New Testament* (New York: Harper & Brothers, 1957).

[75] M. L. Coloe and T. Thatcher, eds., *John, Qumran, and the Dead Sea Scrolls: Sixty Years of Discovery and Debate*, EJL 32 (Atlanta: Society of Biblical Literature, 2011).

[76] Jerome Murphy-O'Connor, ed., *Paul and Qumran: Studies in New Testament Exegesis* (Chicago: Priory, 1968); Fitzmyer, *Semitic Background of the New Testament*, 213–17.

[77] On the relationship between the Essenes, Qumran, and the Dead Sea Scrolls, see chap. 2.

[78] Daniel R. Schwartz, *Studies in the Jewish Background of Christianity*, WUNT 60 (Tübingen: Mohr Siebeck, 1992), 3; J. M. Oesterreicher, "The Community of Qumran," in *The Bridge* (New York: Pantheon Books, 1956), 91–134; A. S. Geyser, "The Youth of John the Baptist: A Deduction from the Break in the Parallel Account of the Lucan Infancy Story," *NovT* 1 (1956): 70; James D. G. Dunn, *Baptism in the Holy Spirit* (London: SCM Press, 1970). Otto Betz, "Was John the Baptist an Essene?" *BR* 18 (1990): 18; Kurt Schubert, *The Dead Sea Community: Its Origins and Teachings*, trans. J. W. Doberstein (Westport, Conn.: Greenwood, 1959), 126–28; Brown, "Dead Sea Scrolls and the New Testament," 5.

John and the Essenes.[79] Others, more cautiously, concluded that John simply knew *about* the Essenes and may have learned a few things from them.[80] It is helpful, however, to take a closer look at the cogency of these "parallels."

While the social history of the early Jesus movement almost certainly begins with John the Baptist,[81] we actually know very little about the "historical John."[82] Josephus tells us he delivered persuasive "sermons" (A.J. 18.118). In both Josephus and the Synoptics, John is ὁ Βαπτιστής (the Baptist/Baptizer).[83] He is "a good man" (ἀγαθὸς ἀνήρ) who preaches virtue and calls to baptism and righteousness but whose popularity led Herod to put him to death. According to Josephus, John taught that virtue, righteousness, and piety (ἀρετή, δικαιοσύνη, and εὐσέβεια) were prerequisites for baptism's efficacy before God (A.J. 18.117). Baptism was intended for bodily purification (ἀλλ ἐφ' ἁγνείᾳ τοῦ σώματος) after the soul had been purified by righteous living. Josephus also describes the crowds as "aroused to the highest degree by his sayings" (καὶ γὰρ ἤρθησαν ἐπὶ πλεῖστον τῇ ἀκροάσει τῶν λόγων), for he had an "eloquence that had so great an effect on men" (τὸ ἐπὶ τοσόνδε πιθανὸν αὐτοῦ τοῖς ἀνθρώποις, A.J. 18.118).[84] Finally, Josephus portrays John as a political figure whose arrest and execution were political decisions made by Herod Antipas out of fear of John's authority over the people (A.J. 18.5.2).

The geographical site of John's baptism in the Judean desert seems to have been remarkably close to Qumran. According to Luke, John belonged to a priestly family but was raised "in the desert" until his appearance or manifestation in

---

[79] Charles Fritsch, *The Qumran Community* (New York: Macmillan, 1956), 113–14; Raymond E. Brown, "Second Thoughts, the Dead Sea Scrolls and the New Testament," *ExpTim* 10 (1966): 19–23; Leonard F. Badia, *The Qumran Baptism and John the Baptist's Baptism* (Lanham, Md.: University Press of America, 1980), 38; Benoit, "Qumran and the New Testament," 6.

[80] Hermann Lichtenberger, "The Dead Sea Scrolls and John the Baptist: Reflections on Josephus' Account of John the Baptist," in *The Dead Sea Scrolls: Forty Years of Research*, ed. D. Dimant and U. Rappaport, STDJ 10 (Leiden: Brill, 1992), 340–46, here 346.

[81] On Jesus' baptism, see John P. Meier, *A Marginal Jew: Rethinking the Historical Jesus*, vol. 2, *Mentor, Message, and Miracles* (New York: Doubleday, 1994), 7; E. P. Sanders, *Jesus and Judaism* (Philadelphia: Fortress, 1985), 11; idem, *The Historical Figure of Jesus* (London: Penguin, 1993), 92–94; Paul W. Hollenbach, "The Conversion of Jesus: From Jesus the Baptizer to Jesus the Healer," in *ANRW* 2.25.1 (Berlin: de Gruyter, 1982), 198–99.

[82] Ernst Bammel, "The Baptist in Early Christian Tradition," *NTS* 18 (1972): 95–128; Robert L. Webb, *John the Baptizer and Prophet: A Socio-historical Study*, JSNTSup 62 (Sheffield: JSOT, 1991); idem, "John the Baptist and His Relationship to Jesus," in *Studying the Historical Jesus: Evaluations of the State of Current Research*, ed. B. D. Chilton and C. A. Evans (Leiden: Brill, 1994), 179–229.

[83] Matt 3:1; 11:1; 14:2, 8; 16:14; 17:13; Mark 6:25; 8:28; Luke 7:20, 33; 9:19.

[84] See Josephus, *Jewish Antiquities*, books 18–19, trans. L. H. Feldman (Cambridge, Mass.: Harvard University Press, 1996).

Israel.⁸⁵ Similarly, the Qumran group seems to have been a priestly wing of an Essene movement known to adopt orphans and young children (Josephus, *B.J.* 2.120). Each of the Gospels uses Isaiah 40:3 to explain why John was in the desert—that is, to "prepare the way of the Lord" (Mark 1:3; Matt 3:3; Luke 3:3-6; John 1:23).⁸⁶ Similarly, the Qumran group used Isaiah 40:3 to refer to their activity in the desert (1QS 8.12–16).⁸⁷ Like the Essenes, John was not married and seems to have been a priest. He is reported to have eaten locusts and wild honey; the *Damascus Document* (CD) describes how to prepare locusts for consumption (CD 12.13–14). Like Jesus, John criticizes the Pharisees and the Sadducees (Matt 3:4-10; Luke 3:7-14), but not the Essenes. Like the Qumran texts and group, John also anticipates an imminent eschatological judgment.

John and the Qumran group both used immersion as an act of purification accompanied by moral repentance, and both baptisms exceeded merely ritual purification by initiating the repentant into a community of the "true Israel." Josephus describes the Essene baptismal rites as "purification" (ἁγνεία) (*B.J.* 2.129; *A.J.* 18.19). Like the Essenes, John did not offer baptism as a way of gaining forgiveness of sins; rather, he offered water purification *after* repentance.⁸⁸ John was also insisting that his baptism was not only for proselytes but necessary for *all of Israel*, implying that the entire nation needed repentance and purification.⁸⁹ According to 1QS 4.20–21, God is said "to purify him by a holy spirit (ברוח קדושה) from all works of wickedness, and sprinkle upon him the spirit of truth (רוח אמת) like purifying water." Initiates were cleansed "by the holy spirit of the Community (וברוח קדושה ליחד)" (1QS 3.7–8), and then this purification was physically sealed by ritual immersion. The holy spirit itself served as a purifying agent: but it was not only "by a holy spirit (וברוח קדושה)" (1QS 3.7) that cleansing occurred; it was also "*by* the humble submission of his soul" (בענות נפשו, 1QS 3.8)—that is, by "repentance"—that members were purified.⁹⁰

---

⁸⁵ According to Luke 1:80, John "grew up in the desert till the day of his manifestation to Israel."

⁸⁶ Unless otherwise noted, all quotations from the biblical canon are from the NRSV.

⁸⁷ Isaiah 40:3 (MT) seems to refer to a voice of a member of the heavenly council that will proclaim a highway being constructed in the desert, whereas Isa 40:3 (LXX) can be read as referring to the voice in the desert. Special thanks to James A. Sanders for this note (personal communication).

⁸⁸ Burrows (*More Light on the Dead Sea Scrolls*, 59) noted that "John may have been closer to the 'Essenes' of Qumran than the Gospels indicate."

⁸⁹ Badia, *Qumran Baptism and John the Baptist's Baptism*, 37; Bruce D. Chilton, "John the Purifier," in *Judaic Approaches to the Gospels* (Atlanta: Scholars, 1994), 26–27: "Ablutions in Judaism were characteristically repeatable.'"

⁹⁰ Joseph M. Baumgarten, "The Purification Liturgies," in *The Dead Sea Scrolls after Fifty Years: A Comprehensive Assessment*, ed. P. W. Flint and J. C. VanderKam (Leiden: Brill, 1999), 211.

It is not surprising that these "parallels" have led many to associate John and Qumran.[91] Yet the idea that John was an Essene or familiar with the Qumran Essenes is by no means a scholarly consensus. On the contrary, a number of scholars see substantial differences between John and the Essenes and conclude that there was no contact between the two.[92] The Qumran community, after all, was "a priestly, exclusive community," whereas John—notwithstanding his (possibly) priestly line of descent—is identified as "a prophetic, charismatic leader in a public situation."[93] While the geographical proximity of John's baptisms to the Qumran site is significant, physical proximity alone does not require direct influence, contact, or relationship.[94] Moreover, John was a mobile figure and baptized "along the Jordan valley, Samaria, and Perea, not in the wilderness of Judea bordering the Dead Sea."[95] The Baptist has also been identified as a "teacher" (διδάσκαλος) who gathered "disciples" (μαθηταί), only to have been regarded as a "prophet" by some of his contemporaries.[96] It is the Gospels, after all, that re-present John as the one destined to "prepare the way" for the arrival of Jesus. Indeed, there is no compelling evidence that John and the Essenes were ever "linked."[97] It is thus possible to see any perceived similarity between John and the Essenes simply as evidence of "a common milieu."[98]

The central question is whether similarity suggests *contact*. While there is no direct evidence that John lived at Qumran, there is also no way to determine whether John may have been an Essene prior to his public ministry. Many scholars have been struck by the shared use of Isaiah 40:3 to describe John's ministry in the Gospels and the *Rule of the Community* (1QS), yet it is difficult to

---

[91] Schwartz, *Studies in the Jewish Background of Christianity*.

[92] See R. Kenneth Hanson, *The Dead Sea Scrolls* (New York: Harper & Row, 1961), 108–9; Charles H. H., Scobie, *John the Baptist* (London: SCM Press, 1964), 58, 66; Oscar Cullmann, "The Significance of the Qumran Texts for Research into the Beginnings of Christianity," *JBL* 74 (1955): 219; Webb, *John the Baptizer and Prophet*, 351n4; R. L. Webb, "Jesus' Baptism by John: Its Historicity and Significance," in *Key Events in the Life of the Historical Jesus: A Collaborative Exploration of Context and Coherence*, ed. D. L. Bock and R. L. Webb, WUNT 247 (Tübingen: Mohr Siebeck, 2009), 130. Bruce D. Chilton, "John the Purifier," 21, 26.

[93] Adela Yarbro Collins, "The Origin of Christian Baptism," *Studia Liturgica* 19 (1989): 28–46, esp. 52.

[94] Frank Moore Cross, *The Ancient Library of Qumran*, 3rd ed. (Minneapolis: Fortress, 1995), 148; James C. VanderKam, *The Dead Sea Scrolls Today* (Grand Rapids: Eerdmans, 1994), 170; Joan E. Taylor, *The Immerser: John the Baptist within Second Temple Judaism*, SHJ 2 (Grand Rapids: Eerdmans, 1997), 43.

[95] Taylor, *Immerser*, 47.

[96] Taylor, *Immerser*, 8.

[97] Taylor, *Immerser*, 10.

[98] Taylor, *Immerser*, 25.

determine whether this is evidence of direct influence, since John and the Qumran sect use the text in different ways.[99] There may be no compelling evidence of a coherent anti-Temple "Baptist movement" at the time of Jesus,[100] but the Pseudo-Clementine literature does identify baptism as a replacement for animal sacrifice.[101] John may not explicitly state that he regarded the Temple as "defiled and therefore irrelevant to the way of righteousness,"[102] but there is also no evidence in the Gospels that John participated in the Temple cult. John may have known about the Essenes "in general" and may have been "familiar with some of their beliefs," but what that means is that John and the Essenes were *in relationship*.[103] Alleged "parallels" do not need to be precisely the same in order to situate them in ideological proximity; in reality, no two things are ever the same.

To be sure, many alleged parallels now seem more like "parallelomania."[104] For example, the linguistic and theological differences and distinctions between the Qumran terms and similar terms attributed to the Jerusalem community by Paul and the author of Acts are now clearly apparent. The author of Acts may have appealed to Essenic traditions in re-presenting the early Jesus movement's "beginning in Jerusalem,"[105] but it is now far less clear whether such "parallels" can be extended into the actual social history of the Jesus movement or to Jesus himself. Yet insofar as the historical Jesus represents the hypothetical catalyst of the early Jesus movement, it is appropriate to ask: What relationship(s), if any, can be posited between the historical Jesus and the historical Essenes? Here there is no consensus.[106]

---

[99] Taylor, *Immerser*, 25.

[100] On the "Baptist movement," see W. Brandt, *Die jüdischen Baptismen oder das Religiose Waschen und Baden im Judentum mit Einschluss des Judenchristentums* (Giessen: Topelmann, 1910); J. Thomas, *Le mouvement baptiste en Palestine et Syrie (150 av. J.C.–300 ap. J.C.)* (Gembloux, Belgium: Duculot, 1935).

[101] See *Recognitions* 1.39. Taylor does not refer to the Pseudo-Clementine *Homilies* or *Recognitions* in her discussion or to this literature's explicit connection of baptism as a substitute for animal sacrifice.

[102] Taylor, *Immerser*, 29.

[103] Taylor, *Immerser*, 42–43; she adds later: "Even if he did [know of the Essenes] ... this does not mean he was associated with the Qumran group" (47). Taylor suggests that we need only to "look closely" at the differences between John and the Essenes while dismissing and discounting the similarities. It is questionable, however, to propose that "parallels" must be used in "precisely" the same way for them to count when, in reality, *no two things are ever the same*.

[104] Samuel Sandmel, "Parallelomania," *JBL* 81 (1962): 1–13.

[105] Kurt Schubert, *Die Qumran-Essener: Texte der Schriftrollen und Lebensbild der Gemeinde*, UTB 224 (Munich: Basel, 1973), 130; cf. Ernst Haenchen, *The Acts of the Apostles: A Commentary*, trans. B. Noble and G. Shinn (Philadelphia: Westminster, 1971), 98–110; Hans Conzelmann, *Die Apostelgeschichte*, HNT (Tübingen: Mohr Siebeck, 1963), 7, 9–11.

[106] Charlesworth ("Dead Sea Scrolls and the Historical Jesus," 9 [emphases added]) rightly notes that although "many leading New Testament experts have sought to discern what may

The publication of a series of "Beatitudes" from Qumran (4Q525) might appear at first to be reminiscent of the serial Beatitudes in Matthew's Sermon on the Mount, suggesting a tradition common to both,[107] but, even if that *were* true, it would only tell us about the literary composition of serial Beatitudes, not whether they were ever spoken by the historical Jesus or that Jesus was "influenced" by the Essene composition of Beatitudes. Similarly, the so-called "Son of God" text of 4Q246 ii 1—which refers to someone who will be named "Son of God" (ברה די אל) and "Son of the Most High" (בר עליון)—seems to bear a striking resemblance to titles attributed to Jesus in the Gospel of Luke 1:32-35:

> He will be great and will be called the *Son of the Most High* (υἱὸς ὑψίστου)....
> Therefore the child to be born will be holy; *he will be called Son of God* (υἱὸς θεοῦ).

4Q246 and Luke both describe figures predicted to inherit an "eternal kingdom." In 4Q246, "his kingdom will be an eternal kingdom" (מלכותה מלכות עלם); in Luke 1:33, "of his kingdom there will be no end." The similarities are so striking that some scholars think that Luke knew 4Q246 or the tradition from which it emerged.[108] Opinions, however, continue to be divided on the identity of the Son of God,[109] although the consensus seems to be that the figure is "messianic."[110]

---

have been the relation between Jesus and the Essenes. It would be *misleading* to summarize this work as if it leads to a non-debatable consensus." Charlesworth later states that "Jesus was *certainly* not an Essene" (37), adding: "This is *surely* a consensus among scholars" (73).

[107] Émile Puech, "4Q525 et les péricopes des béatitudes en Ben Sira et Matthieu," *RB* 98 (1991): 80–106; idem, "Un Hymne essénien en partie retrouvé et les Béatitudes. 1QH V 12–VI 18 (=col. XIII–XIV 7) et 4QBéat," *RevQ* 13 (1988), 59–88. See also Joseph A. Fitzmyer, "A Palestinian Collection of Beatitudes," in *The Four Gospels. 1992: Festschrift Frans Neirynck*, ed. F. Van Segbroek, BETL 100 (Leuven: Peeters, 1992), 1:509–15.

[108] George J. Brooke, "Qumran: The Cradle of the Christ?" in *The Birth of Jesus: Biblical and Theological Reflections*, ed. G. J. Brooke (Edinburgh: T&T Clark, 2000), 26: "It seems preferable to consider seriously that Luke 1 was dependent on some such tradition as is found in 4Q246." Cf. John J. Collins, *The Scepter and the Star: Messianism in Light of the Dead Sea Scrolls*, 2nd ed. (Grand Rapids: Eerdmans, 2010), 155.

[109] J. T. Milik, *The Books of Enoch: Aramaic Fragments of Qumrân Cave 4* (Oxford: Clarendon, 1976), 60, 213, 261; Joseph A. Fitzmyer, "The Contribution of Qumran Aramaic to the Study of the New Testament," *NTS* 20 (1974): 382–407; David Flusser, "The Hubris of the Antichrist in a Fragment from Qumran," *Imm* 10 (1980): 31–37; Florentino García Martínez ("The Eschatological Figure of 4Q246," in *Qumran and Apocalyptic: Studies on the Aramaic Texts from Qumran*, STDJ 9 [Leiden: Brill, 1992], 162–79) asserts that this is Michael or Melchizedek. Émile Puech now favors the messianic interpretation. See Puech, "246. 4QApocryphe de Daniel ar," in *Qumran Cave 4 XVII. Parabiblical Texts, Part 3*, ed. G. Brooke et al. (Oxford: Clarendon, 1996), 165–84.

[110] James D. G. Dunn, "'Son of God' as 'Son of Man' in the Dead Sea Scrolls? A Response to John Collins on 4Q246," in *The Scrolls and the Scriptures: Qumran Fifty Years After*, ed. S. E. Porter and C. A. Evans (Sheffield: Sheffield Academic, 1997), 209; Seyoon Kim (*The* "Son of

If that is true, then 4Q246 illustrates that the royal messiah could have been understood as the "Son of God" in first-century Palestinian Judaism.[111]

The sheer number of such "parallels"—and their cumulative weight—seem to provide a *prima facie* case for Palestinian Essenism exerting some degree of influence on Palestinian Jewish Christianity. The problem, again, is determining the precise nature and extent of that influence, especially since this is "a triangular issue" involving interrelationships between "Qumran, mainstream Essenism, and the early church."[112] We must avoid both "parallelo-mania" and "parallelo-phobia." That is, we must not confuse parallelomania with the discovery, interpretation, and explanation of genuine "parallels."[113] The relationship(s) between Jesus, the Essenes, and Christian origins needs to be reexamined and explained on the basis of "specific" and "distinctive" parallels that also account for the similarities and differences in both *corpora*.[114]

If proposing direct contact or influence is too speculative an inference for some, it may be that flatly *denying* such possibilities is no less speculative. It will not do, in other words, to casually dismiss the question of John's relationship to

---

Man" as the Son of God, WUNT 30 [Tübingen: Mohr Siebeck, 1983], 22–25) argues that 4Q246 represents a conflation of the "one like a son of man" from Dan 7:13 with a messianic interpretation. Similarly, Collins, *Scepter and the Star*, 167.

[111] L. H. Schiffman, *Reclaiming the Dead Sea Scrolls: The History of Judaism, the Background of Christianity, the Lost Library of Qumran* (Philadelphia: Jewish Publication Society, 1994), 344, 342.

[112] Bauckham, "Early Jerusalem Church," 66.

[113] Sandmel ("Parallelomania," 2 [emphasis added]) describes "parallelomania" as an "extravagance among scholars which first overdoes the supposed similarity in passages and then proceeds to describe source and derivation as if implying literary connection flowing in an inevitable or predetermined direction." Sandmel does not *deny* the existence of "literary parallels and literary influence" and is therefore "not seeking to discourage the study of these parallels" but rather seeking "to encourage them," especially "*in the case of the Qumran documents.*"

[114] Contra Heinz-Wolfgang Kuhn, "Qumran Texts and the Historical Jesus: Parallels in Contrast," in *The Dead Sea Scrolls—Fifty Years after Their Discovery: Proceedings of the Jerusalem Congress, July 20–25, 1997*, ed. L. H. Schiffman, E. Tov, and J. C. VanderKam (Jerusalem: Israel Exploration Society, 2000), 573–80, 573: "A comparison of the Qumran Community with the Jesus movement reveals so many differences that a comparison does not seem very illuminating." Kuhn's methodological procedure—privileging "parallels in contrast"—is inadequately attuned to the complexity of relationship within early Judaism. Cf. idem, "Jesus im Licht der Qumrangemeinde," in *Handbook for the Study of the Historical Jesus*, ed. T. Holmén and S. Porter, 4 vols. (Leiden: Brill, 2011), 2:1245–85, 1246, where the *theological* comparison between the Jesus movement and the Qumran community yields "more dissimilarities than similarities" (*mehr Unterschiede als Gemeinsamkeiten*) and pre-Scrolls era attempts to bring Jesus and the Essenes into relationship are described as "the old absurd speculations" (*Die älteren abwegigen Spekulationen*).

the Essenes as "facile comparison" and "special pleading."[115] Such efforts to deny similarities often suffer from their very own form of "special pleading" by denying that which cannot be disproved.[116] As a result, facile caricatures and misrepresentations of others' views can sometimes become the order of the day.[117] Critical comparison should proceed not by highlighting "differences" and discounting similarities but by creating compelling explanations for why perceived "parallels" appear to form a constellation of possible contact points between two contemporary and geographically proximate Jewish movements. If anything, the history of scholarship on Jesus, the Essenes, and Christian origins remains an open question that continues to illustrate not certainty but the limits of our historical knowledge and the need for the conceptual and terminological expansion of our categories.

The conflicted history of this topic may help explain why the Qumran Essene hypothesis continues to be such a contested site: if the Dead Sea Scrolls and Qumran are identified as *Essenic*—and the Essenes are reified as a movement contemporaneous with Jesus—then the case for Essene influence on early Christianity becomes unavoidable. The history of Scrolls scholarship reflects these ideological concerns. It is widely recognized that the history of Qumran Studies reflects (at least) two broadly construed "eras" of research: the first being dominated by "Christian," the second by predominantly "Jewish" interests.[118]

— ✦ —

Jesus and the Essenes represent historical subjects for which the historical record is fragmentary and incomplete. Our access to the "historical Jesus," for example, is mediated through multiple textual "remembrances" of and theological

---

[115] J. Ian H. McDonald, "What Did You Go Out to See? John the Baptist, the Scrolls and Late Second Temple Judaism," in *The Dead Sea Scrolls in Their Historical Context*, ed. T. H. Lim (Edinburgh: T&T Clark, 2000), 61, 59, 54.

[116] Taylor, *Essenes, the Scrolls, and the Dead Sea*, 20–21.

[117] Clare K. Rothschild (review of Simon J. Joseph, *Jesus, Q, and the Dead Sea Scrolls*, *DSD* 22, no. 1 [2015]: 129–31) claims that I argue that the Baptist was "an Essene raised at Qumran" and that my goal is to "escort readers" into the world of my "imagination" where the Baptist "comes of age at Khirbet Qumran," "mastering the texts of Cave 4," and "flouting apprenticeship to his father, a Zadokite priest" before he decides "to peddle a version of atonement." These caricaturistic flourishes are simply off the mark: my study does *not* claim that John was an "Essene" or *ever* lived at Qumran, let alone "mastered" the "texts of Cave 4." Rothschild suggests that my study is "a well-constructed house ... for those willing to entertain such theses" (as Q and the Qumran/Essene hypothesis) but is "moot" for those who "reject the existence of Q" and the "Essene authorship of the sectarian scrolls." This is a surprising statement given that Q and the Qumran/Essene hypothesis are not fringe theories and that the reviewer has written a monograph on "Baptist traditions and Q"!

[118] Edna Ullmann-Margalit, *Out of the Cave: A Philosophical Inquiry into the Dead Sea Scrolls Research* (Cambridge, Mass.: Harvard University Press, 2006), 137, 17–18.

narratives about Jesus. Contemporary Jesus Research has become an increasingly complex discourse, with recent critiques of the traditional "criteria of authenticity" undermining their reliability as historiographical tools,[119] and source-critical solutions remaining in a state of near-perpetual debate.[120] Yet Jesus Research does not depend on source-critical solutions to the complex literary relationships between the Synoptic Gospels. Jesus Research does not depend on the existence of Q. There were multiple "sources" circulating in the early Jesus movement (cf. Luke 1:1) and it does not *always* matter which particular Synoptic solution we adopt when reconstructing Jesus.[121] It is sometimes sufficient simply to affirm the *general* reliability of the "Early Palestinian" (Jesus) tradition.[122] Specific aspects of this "Palestinian Tradition" may indeed go back to Jesus, but it is the *general* contours of the tradition that tend to be the most reliable: the historical Jesus was a man who taught in Galilee, "attracted followers, clashed with people over interpretation of the Law, gained a reputation as a (sometimes) successful healer and exorcist, preached the coming of the kingdom, often spoke in parables, and went to Jerusalem where he died."[123] None of this data depends on the specific source-critical solution one adopts.[124]

On the Two-Source/Document Hypothesis, Q represents an early Palestinian Jewish representation of Jesus that provides a theoretical window into early Jewish/Christian reflection on Jesus' life and teaching, a window which also reflects chronological shifts within the Jesus movement itself. That is why it is necessary to continue attending to the "difference" Q makes and the discursive "trouble" Q causes.[125] A world without Q represents a very different theoretical

---

[119] Chris Keith, "The Indebtedness of the Criteria Approach to Form Criticism and Recent Attempts to Rehabilitate the Search for an Authentic Jesus," in *Jesus, Criteria, and the Demise of Authenticity*, ed. C. Keith and A. Le Donne (New York: T&T Clark, 2012), 25–48.

[120] Mark S. Goodacre, *The Case against Q: Studies in Markan Priority and the Synoptic Problem* (Harrisburg, Pa.: Trinity International, 2002).

[121] James G. Crossley, *Jesus and the Chaos of History: Redirecting the Life of the Historical Jesus* (London: Oxford University Press, 2015), 35.

[122] Cf. Dale C. Allison, *Constructing Jesus: Memory, Imagination, and History* (Grand Rapids: Baker Academic, 2010).

[123] Crossley, *Jesus and the Chaos of History*, 47.

[124] Cf. Crossley, *Jesus and the Chaos of History*, 44, 45, 70, 82.

[125] John S. Kloppenborg, "The Sayings Gospel Q and the Quest of the Historical Jesus," *HTR* 89 (1996): 307–44; idem, *Q, The Earliest Gospel: An Introduction to the Original Stories and Sayings of Jesus* (Louisville, Ky.: Westminster John Knox, 2008), 62–97; William E. Arnal, "The Trouble with Q," *Forum: Foundations and Facets* 3 (2013): 7–79; cf. Daniel A. Smith, "What Difference Does Difference Make? Assessing Q's Place in Christian Origins," in *Scribal Practices and Social Structures Among Jesus Adherents: Essays in Honour of John S. Kloppenborg*, ed. W. E. Arnal, R. S. Ascough, R. A. Derrenbacker, Jr., and P. A. Harland; BETL 285 (Leuven: Peeters, 2016), 183–211.

trajectory of literary development(s), transferring Q-material to Matthew's now more expanded and chronologically *later* body of material (M+).[126] Nonetheless, both models presuppose the circulation of sources representing the compositional impetus to transmit Jesus-sayings within a Judean/Jewish context. So while this study presupposes the priority of Mark—that is, the dominant consensus in Synoptic studies—the point is not to argue for the Two-Document Hypothesis,[127] but rather to work with the broadest possible agreement of what constitutes reliable historical Jesus data as *comparanda* with what can be known about the Essenes of early Judaism.

This is not, of course, to suggest that the Essenes were Jesus' only conversation partners. Jesus interacted with a wide range of contemporary Jews, most of whom were probably non-sectarians. Nonetheless, it is within Jesus' sectarian halakhic conflicts that we can most clearly identify and delineate his distinctive profile within Judaism. Indeed, many of Jesus' most heated interactions in the Gospels were with "Pharisees." The Pharisees (φαρισαῖος/פרושים) are referred to in the Gospels, the book of Acts, and Josephus, but we do not have any of their own literary productions.[128] According to Josephus, this "sect" or "philosophy" had its origins in the second century BCE and represented one of the three major "philosophical schools" active at the time of Jesus. Josephus himself claimed to be a Pharisee (*Vita* 2 §§10–12),[129] as did Paul (Phil 3:5), although in Josephus' case this may have had as much to do with political posturing as it did with genuine affiliation. The New Testament Gospels, written between 70 and 100 CE, paint the Pharisees in a particularly negative light, although these writings also reflect the sociopolitical conditions of the time of their composition—that is, when Pharisaic opposition to the nascent Jesus movement involved sectarian rivalries. "Jesus'" attacks on the Pharisees as "hypocrites" reflect these later circumstances—when Jesus' followers were interacting more frequently with Pharisaic leaders in the

---

[126] Alan Kirk, *Ancient Media, Memory, and Early Scribal Transmission of the Jesus Tradition*, LNTS 564 (New York: T&T Clark, 2016), 308, argues that the "Mark-Without-Q" hypothesis's allegedly "greater economy is a sham: its claims for parsimony at one end must always be paid for by complicated accounts of Luke's utilization at the other end."

[127] Giovanni Bazzana, *Kingdom of Bureaucracy: The Political Theology of Village Scribes in the Sayings Gospel Q*, BETL 274 (Leuven: Peeters, 2015), 2–3, rightly argues, in any case, that "appealing to the undeniably hypothetical nature of the Sayings Gospel is not a sufficient reason to reject in principle the possibility of deriving historical results from a sound analysis of Q."

[128] Cf. Jacob Neusner and B. Chilton, eds., *In Quest of the Historical Pharisees* (Waco, Tex.: Baylor University Press, 2007). The word "Pharisee" is commonly derived from *Perushim* or "separatists," signifying a tendency to separate from others for the purposes of purity. On the Pharisees, see *B.J.* 1.52–3 §§110–114; 2.8.14 §§162–166; *A.J.* 13.5.9 §§171–172; 18.1.3 §§4–23.

[129] Cf. Steve Mason, "Was Josephus a Pharisee? A Re-examination of *Life* 10–12," *JJS* 40 (1989): 31–45.

post-70 CE period (cf. Matt 23:1-39)—and are not accurate representations of Jesus' historical relationship to the sect. The Gospels portray them as strict observers of the Law who avoided eating with the unclean or impure, yet fasted, made vows, tithed, observed the Sabbath, and adhered to priestly purity regulations outside the cultic context of the Temple, trying to extend the ritual purity laws of the Temple into everyday life. Above all, they are known for adhering to "the traditions of the fathers," a collection of oral laws and practices (Mark 7:3; Acts 23:8), which represent the ideological foundations of rabbinical Judaism. The rabbis held that the Oral Law, later the Mishnah, was given by Moses along with the Written Law, but they never refer to themselves as "Pharisees."[130] This silence on the part of the rabbis can be explained by positing that the post-70 CE rabbis sought to distance themselves from earlier sectarian identities. Nonetheless, the doctrinal positions of many of the rabbis, as well as their loyalty to a traditional body of Oral Law, suggests that the Pharisees were indeed the lineal ancestors of rabbinical Judaism. It is unlikely, however, that the "historical" Pharisees represented the dominant or most authoritative voice in pre-70 CE Palestinian Jewish society.[131] It was the destruction of the Temple and the subsequent disappearance of the priesthood and Sadducees that created the sociopolitical circumstances that allowed the rabbis to emerge as the dominant religious authorities within post-70 CE Judaism.

Like the New Testament Gospels, the rabbis did not remember the Essenes. This erasure of the Essenes from Jewish memory (already in antiquity!) involved suppressing the evidence of sectarian conflict and the halakhic opinions of a radically different ideology and worldview. Halakhic disagreements were a major catalytic factor in Jewish sectarianism, and Pharisees were rival legal authorities. Qumran texts seem to identify the Pharisees as "seekers of smooth things" (דורשי חלקות, 1QH^a 10.15, 32), a derogatory title signifiying that they wanted to exchange the demands of the Torah "for smooth things" (בחלקות).[132] Most

---

[130] Cf. Jacob Neusner, *The Rabbinic Traditions about the Pharisees before 70* (Leiden: Brill, 1971); E. Rivkin, "Defining the Pharisees: The Tannaitic Sources," *HUCA* 43 (1972): 205–40.

[131] On the Pharisees, see Lester L. Grabbe, *Judaism from Cyrus to Hadrian*, 2 vols. (Minneapolis: Fortress, 1992), 467–87; Steve Mason, *Flavius Josephus on the Pharisees: A Composition-Critical Study* (Leiden: Brill, 1991); Anthony J. Saldarini, *Pharisees, Scribes and Sadducees in Palestinian Society: A Sociological Approach* (Wilmington: Michael Glazier, 1998).

[132] The designation דורשי חלקות (cf. Isa 30:10) is found in a number of sectarian texts (CD1.18; 4Q163 23 iii 10; 4Q169 3–4 i 2, 7; 3–4 ii 2, 4; 2–4 iii 3, 7). On this designation, see Albert I. Baumgarten, "Seekers after Smooth Things," in *The Encyclopedia of the Dead Sea Scrolls*, ed. L. H. Schiffman and J. C. VanderKam (New York: Oxford University Press, 2000), 2:857–58; James C. VanderKam, "Those Who Look for Smooth Things, Pharisees, and Oral Law," in *Emanuel: Studies in Hebrew Bible, Septuagint and Dead Sea Scrolls in Honor of Emanuel Tov*, ed. S. M. Paul et al., VTSup 94 (Leiden: Brill, 2003), 465–77.

scholars regard this unnamed group as the Pharisees, noting the use of the term חלקות as a verbal pun on הלבות (*halakhot*).[133] Qumranic sectarian opposition and/or hostility toward the Pharisees, however, is yet another apparent correspondence or "parallel" between the Jesus movement and the Essenes.[134]

In sum, our ability to establish clear relationships between Jesus and the Essenes—and/or the Dead Sea Scrolls and the New Testament—is complicated by the paucity of evidence, the ambiguity of the data, and their remoteness in time. Moreover, any exploration of this problem intersects with questions about social, cultural, ethnic, and religious identities. The comparative study of the Dead Sea Scrolls and the New Testament—like that of Jesus and the Essenes—involves crossing textual border lines and ideological boundaries, many of which have been raised precisely in order to resist, refute, and/or prevent such probing questions.

Our methodological problems, then, involve (1) reassessing the fragmentary remains of the past in order to retrace lost relationships between movements already prone to rapid social change (that is, we must resist assuming that "the Essenes" represent a static monolithic community-structure over the two hundred years of their existence in order to provide a contrasting foil for "Jesus" or early Christianity); (2) navigating the ancient theological, social, and religious identity formations inscribed in our texts, many of which were hard won and labored to efface their origins, relationships, and matrices; (3) reckoning with the challenge of trying to peer into the inner lives and thoughts of self-consciously secretive and esoteric groups and individuals; and (4) translating our findings into the most appropriate conceptual categories and discourses without reinscribing ancient or modern ideologies of constructed difference.

There is power, after all, in *naming* things. All too often, defining terms is linked to the politics of authority and identity, and to discourses of inclusion and exclusion. The identification of "heretical" categories in antiquity, for example, led to the marginalization and erasure of unorthodox traditions and practices. Today, such categorizations continue to affect how scholars understand ancient phenomena.[135] Judaism and Christianity are now commonly recognized as distinct categories, yet the relationship between Judaism and Christianity remains complex and paradoxical. The critical study of the relationship between

---

[133] William H. Brownlee, "Biblical Interpretation among the Sectaries of the Dead Sea Scrolls," *BA* 14 (1951): 59–60; L. H. Schiffman, *Reclaiming the Dead Sea Scrolls*, 251; idem, "The Pharisees and Their Legal Traditions according to the Dead Sea Scrolls," *DSD* 8 (2001): 266; VanderKam, "Those Who Look for Smooth Things," 477.

[134] Cf. CD 8.12; 19.25; Matt 23:27-28; 1QH^a 4.6–8; Matt 23:3; 1QH^a 4.11; Matt 23:13.

[135] Steve Mason (*Josephus, Judea, and Christian Origins: Methods and Categories* [Peabody, Mass.: Hendrickson, 2009], 1) questions "the appropriateness of our standard categories ... when we set out to compare two very different kinds of phenomena as if they belonged in comparable categories."

Judaism and Christianity in antiquity is thus a particularly pertinent example and potential illustration of how *difference* is constructed and maintained. Christianity began within Judaism, but it is still not quite so easy to understand or reconstruct where ancient Judaism ends and early Christianity begins.[136]

Our desire for firm, fixed categories reflects our anxieties about influence, improper mixings, and the shadowy world of blurred boundaries. Constructing difference may be a nearly universal phenomenon, but biblical studies continue to reinscribe difference by reifying categories.[137] That is why the continual interrogation of categories—whether by introducing new models of the "parting(s) of the ways," "new perspective(s)" on Paul, or (re)emphases of Jesus' Jewishness—helps us pay more attention to the various ways that our categories actually function. Ancient data sometimes demand from us new categories and better models to explain the origin, development, and eventual separation of Christianity from Judaism.[138] The discovery of the Dead Sea Scrolls in the Judean desert—often acclaimed as the single greatest archaeological discovery of the twentieth century—continues to play a central role in these redescriptions.[139]

It may seem relatively easy today to draw up a quick list of "parallels" and "differences" between Jesus and the Essenes, with categorical contrasts ranging from the Mosaic Law and Sabbath observance to prophecy, Temple worship, table fellowship, social boundaries, ritual immersion, messianism, and apocalyptic militancy. Yet assembling such lists is methodologically problematic. First, we do not have a stable, secure, or complete body of knowledge from which such "differences" can be safely isolated and identified. Second, the identification of difference(s) does not and need not signify nonrelationship.[140] Family members can be both different and intimately related, being born and raised within the same household, community, and environment. It is this combination of similarity and difference that makes complex comparative and/or relational pictures both possible and

---

[136] Cf. Daniel Boyarin, *Border Lines: The Partition of Judaeo-Christianity*, Divinations (Philadelphia: University of Pennsylvania Press, 2004).

[137] Cf. Karen L. King, "Factions, Variety, Diversity, Multiplicity: Representing Early Christian Differences for the 21st Century," *MTSR* 23 (2011): 217–37.

[138] On the problematic category of "the Bible" to describe Second Temple texts, see Eva Mroczek, *The Literary Imagination in Jewish Antiquity* (New York: Oxford University Press, 2016).

[139] Alison Schofield, *From Qumran to the Yahad: A New Paradigm of Textual Development for The Community Rule*, STDJ 77 (Leiden: Brill, 2009), 22.

[140] David M. Freidenreich ("Comparisons Compared: A Methodological Survey of Comparisons of Religion from 'A Magic Dwells' to *A Magic Still Dwells*," *MTSR* 16 [2004]: 83) cautions against comparative approaches that seek to explain similarity as the "*reflection of an historical relationship*" (emphasis in original), but he admits that this can be done "credibly to demonstrate the existence of 'borrowing' across religious lines."

necessary.[141] The idea, therefore, that the historical Jesus was an incomparably "unique" human being is historically problematic not only since every human being is "unique" (rendering the concept meaningless) but also because it deploys *difference* as a rhetorical-ideological device to construct boundaries by denying relationship. Here difference obscures more than it reveals, confuses more than it clarifies. Again, differences need not be denied in order to affirm relationship.

The study of Christian origins is a discourse identifying and explaining the origins and development of a very particular kind of difference-in-process: Christianity's emergence within Judaism. This discipline continues to be challenged by the need to develop the conceptual, critical, and categorical language and tools that can best articulate the tensions inherent within the ancient realities of an early Christianity being different-from-Judaism while simultaneously affirming early Christianity *as* Jewish. The present study attempts to make a modest methodological contribution to this ongoing challenge by revisiting the characterization of the historical Jesus—in particular, his eschatological halakhah, the quintessential identity marker of Jesus' "Jewish" ethnicity and *praxis*—in light of the Dead Sea Scrolls.

The evidence from antiquity is too fragmentary to reconnect the many ancient pathways of relationship between Jesus and the Essenes, but the Dead Sea Scrolls nonetheless illustrate that the Jesus of history cannot be isolated as an incomparably "unique" creative agent that can somehow be set apart from his Jewish context and matrix. On the contrary, the quest for Jesus' "distinctiveness"—that is, the Holy Grail of Jesus Research—now leads inexorably to locating Jesus *within* his early Jewish context, in dialogue with contemporary Jews, *including the Essenes*.

---

[141] Jeffrey Carter, "Comparison in the History of Religions: Reflections and Critiques," *MTSR* 16 (2004): 3–11. Cf. Jonathan Z. Smith, "In Comparison a Magic Dwells," in *Imagining Religion: From Babylon to Jonestown* (Chicago: University of Chicago Press, 1982), 19–35; idem, *Drudgery Divine: On the Comparison of Early Christianities and the Religions of Late Antiquity* (Chicago: University of Chicago Press, 1990).

CHAPTER 2

THE COMMUNITY OF THE NEW COVENANT

Hidden for almost two thousand years, the Dead Sea Scrolls were discovered in a remote corner of the Judean desert, the lowest place on the face of the earth, by a young man named Muhammed edh-Dhib of the *Ta'amireh* Bedouin tribe. The general consensus today is that they were copied and/or collected by a group of Essenes living at the Qumran site.[1] While some scholars deny that the Dead Sea Scrolls were collected by Essenes or that the Scrolls accurately reflect their beliefs, with a few going as far as to deny the historical *existence* of the Essenes

---

[1] Frank M. Cross, *Canaanite Myth and Hebrew Epic* (Cambridge, Mass.: Harvard University Press, 1973), 331–32; E. L. Sukenik, *Megillot Genuzot I* (Jerusalem: Mosad Bialik, 1948), 16–17; J. T. Milik, *Ten Years of Discovery in the Wilderness of Judaea*, trans. J. Strugnell, 2nd ed. (London: SCM Press, 1963), 80–98; André Dupont-Sommer, *The Essene Writings from Qumran*, trans. G. Vermes (Oxford: Blackwell, 1961); Millar Burrows, *The Dead Sea Scrolls* (New York: Viking, 1955); Theodore H. Gaster, *The Dead Sea Scriptures* (New York: Doubleday/Anchor, 1964); Florentino García Martínez, "Qumran Origins and Early History: A 'Groningen Hypothesis,'" *FO* 25 (1989); H. Stegemann, "The Qumran Essenes: Local Members of the Main Jewish Union in Late Second Temple Times," in *The Madrid Qumran Congress*, ed. J. Trebolle Barrera and L. Vegas Montaner (Leiden: Brill, 1992), 83–166; Gabriele Boccaccini, *Beyond the Essene Hypothesis: The Parting of the Ways between Qumran and Enochic Judaism* (Grand Rapids: Eerdmans, 1998), 191; Todd S. Beall, *Josephus' Description of the Essenes Illustrated by the Dead Sea Scrolls* (Cambridge: Cambridge University Press, 1988); Joseph Fitzmyer, "The Dead Sea Scrolls and Christian Origins: General Methodological Considerations," in *The Dead Sea Scrolls and Christian Faith: In Celebration of the Jubilee Year of the Discovery of Qumran Cave 1*, ed. J. H. Charlesworth and W. P. Weaver (Harrisburg, Pa.: Trinity International, 1998), 16. James C. VanderKam, *The Dead Sea Scrolls Today* (Grand Rapids: Eerdmans, 1994).

altogether,[2] the identification of the Scrolls as an "Essenic" library remains the dominant consensus.[3] There are indeed differences between the contents of some of the Scrolls and the historical accounts of the Essenes by Josephus, Philo, and Pliny, but specialists now know that most of the Scrolls found at Qumran were not written there, nor are they all "Essene" compositions reflecting "Essene" beliefs. Different documents were also written at different times and reflect different phases of the movement's development.[4] It is not always possible, or even advisable, to drive sharp wedges between the allegedly "sectarian" and "non-sectarian" texts found at Qumran.[5] Many apparent differences between the Essenes as described by Josephus and Philo and the groups portrayed in the Scrolls can also be understood as reflecting the difference between viewing the Scrolls as primary sources and relying on Josephus and Philo as secondary sources, as well as the complex multiregionalism of the Essene movement, and its development over time.[6] The

---

[2] John C. Reeves, "Complicating the Notion of an 'Enochic Judaism,'" in *Enoch and Qumran Origins: New Light on a Forgotten Connection*, ed. G. Boccaccini (Grand Rapids: Eerdmans, 2005), 380; Rachel Elior, זיכרון ונשייה סודן של מגילות מדבר יהודה [*Memory and Oblivion: The Mystery of the Dead Sea Scrolls*] (Jerusalem: Hakibbutz Hameuchad–Van Leer Institute, 2009); Henri E. Del Medico, *Le Mythe des Esséniens: Des Origines a la Fin du Moyen Age* (Paris: Librarie Plon, 1958). For criticism, see Devorah Dimant, "On Remembering and Forgetting Research," *Katharsis* 13 (2010): 22–53; Edna Ullmann-Margalit, "The Identity, Identification and Existence of the Sects: The 'Zadokite Priests,' the Essenes, and the Scrolls," *Cathedra* 139 (2011): 31–54; Joan E. Taylor, *The Essenes, the Scrolls, and the Dead Sea* (New York: Oxford University Press, 2012), 20.

[3] Jonathan Klawans, "The Essene Hypothesis: Insights from Religion 101," *DSD* 23 (2016): 51–78.

[4] Philip R. Davies ("The Birthplace of the Essenes: Where Is 'Damascus?'" *RevQ* 14, no. 56 [1990]: 505) points out that CD "claims some antiquity for its community" (512). Michael A. Knibb, "The Place of the Damascus Document in Recent Scholarship," in *The Provo International Conference on Methods of Investigation of the Dead Sea Scrolls and the Khirbet Qumran Site: Present Realities and Future Prospects*, ed. M. O. Wise, N. Golb, J. J. Collins, and D. G. Pardee (New York: New York Academy of Sciences, 1994), 153; Charlotte Hempel, "Community Origins in the *Damascus Document* in the Light of Recent Scholarship," in *The Provo International Conference on the Dead Sea Scrolls: Technological Innovations, New Texts, and Reformulated Issues*, ed. D. W. Parry and E. Ulrich, STDJ 30 (Leiden: Brill, 1999), 328.

[5] Aaron Glaim, "Reciprocity, Sacrifice, and Salvation in Judean Religion At the Turn of the Era," Ph.D. diss., Brown University, 2014, 108n2, notes that texts like 1 Enoch and *Jubilees* were "kept and copied by the social formation(s) associated with Qumran," were "held in high regard there," "appear to have been cited in texts that scholars consider securely 'sectarian,'" and contain "many points of theological continuity" with sectarian texts. Glaim concludes, "scholars of the Dead Sea Scrolls are sometimes overly hasty in positing non-sectarian authorship when they do not detect certain identifying characteristics or complete ideological consistency in a text."

[6] Devorah Dimant, *History, Ideology and Bible Interpretation in the Dead Sea Scrolls: Collected Studies*, FAT 90 (Tübingen: Mohr Siebeck, 2014), 9.

Essenes seem to have been much more widespread than is commonly recognized.[7] The Qumran site, therefore, does not represent the origins of the *Essenes* as much as the origins of the *Qumran* Essenes, meaning that the Qumran group was related to and part of, if not supported by, a larger movement, commonly referred to as the *Yahad* or "the Community."[8]

Biblical scholars and specialists in Second Temple Judaism are now in wide agreement that the *Yahad* not only developed distinctive traditions but also *inherited* earlier esoteric traditions.[9] This esoteric tradition taught about a group of fallen angels identified in the book of Genesis as the "Sons of God" who took human sexual partners and thereby perverted the divine order (1 En. 15:3-7), infecting humanity with evil, violence, and disease. This tradition—and the authors who developed it—also maintained that God would restore the original creation, inaugurate a new age, and reverse the earlier fallen state of humanity. Biblical scholars call this the "Enoch(ic) tradition," after a collection of five books dated from the fourth to the first century BCE (the *Book of the Watchers*, the

---

[7] Taylor, *Essenes, the Scrolls, and the Dead Sea*, 200; Brian J. Capper, "The New Covenant in Southern Palestine at the Arrest of Jesus," in *The Dead Sea Scrolls as Background to Postbiblical Judaism and Early Christianity: Papers from an International Conference at St. Andrews in 2001*, ed. J. R. Davila, STDJ 46 (Leiden: Brill, 2003), 99.

[8] James C. VanderKam ("Sinai Revisited," in *Biblical Interpretation at Qumran*, ed. M. Henze [Grand Rapids: Eerdmans, 2005], 44–66, 52), proposes Exod 19:8 as the inspiration behind the Essenic use of the term. Alternatively, Deut 33:5 may have influenced the development of the term as a noun. See, e.g., Shermaryahu Talmon, "The Sectarian יחד—A Biblical Noun," *VT* 3 (1953): 133–40. Arie van der Kooij ("The *Yahad*—What is in a Name?," *DSD* 18 [2011]: 109–28, 112) suggests that 11QT^a 57.13 inspired its usage in 1QS. Moshe Weinfeld (*The Organizational Pattern and the Penal Code of the Qumran Sect: A Comparison with Guilds and Religious Associations of the Hellenistic-Roman Period*, NTOA 2 [Göttingen: Vandenhoeck & Ruprecht, 1986], 13–14) notes that Josephus and Philo both use the Greek term κοινωνία—a term used of Greco-Roman voluntary associations—in their descriptions of the Essenes (cf. Philo, *Prob.* 84.91; Josephus, *B.J.* 2.122, 123). On the Therapeutae as an Egyptian branch or "wing" of the wider Palestinian Essene movement, see F. García Martínez and J. T. Barrera, *The People of the Dead Sea Scrolls*, trans. W. G. E. Watson (Leiden: Brill, 1995), 93; Per Bilde, "The Essenes in Philo and Josephus," in *Qumran between the Old and New Testaments*, ed. F. H. Cryer and T. L. Thompson, JSOTSup 290 (Sheffield: Sheffield Academic, 1998), 65; Geza Vermes and Martin Goodman, eds., *The Essenes according to the Classical Sources*, OCT 1 (Sheffield: JSOT, 1989), 17; Jean Riaud, "Les Thérapeutes d'Alexandrie dans la tradition et dans la recherche critique jusqu'aux découvertes de Qumran," in *ANRW* 2.20.2 (Berlin: de Gruyter, 1987), 1189–295; Otto Betz, "Essener und Therapeuten," *TRE* 10 (1982): 386–91; Geza Vermes, "Essenes and Therapeutae," *RevQ* 3 (1962): 495–504; idem, "Essenes-Therapeutae-Qumran," *DUJ* 21 (1960): 97–115.

[9] Devorah Dimant, "The Library of Qumran: Its Contents and Character," in *The Dead Sea Scrolls—Fifty Years after Their Discovery: Proceedings of the Jerusalem Congress, July 20–25, 1997*, ed. L. H. Schiffman, E. Tov, and J. C. VanderKam (Jerusalem: Israel Exploration Society, 2000), 173–76.

Astronomical Book, the *Dream Visions*, the *Epistle of Enoch*, and the *Parables* or *Similitudes*), together known as the *Book of Enoch*.[10]

Rediscovered in Ethiopia in 1773, the *Book of Enoch* is named after the biblical figure of Enoch who appears in Genesis 5:24 as Noah's grandfather but who does not die, because he was "taken" by God. The biblical text is terse:

ויתהלך חנוך את האלהים ואיננו כי לקח אתו אלהים

Enoch walked with God; then he was no more, because God took him.

Jewish speculation on the figure of Enoch continued well into the early rabbinic period.[11] The ambiguity inherent in the biblical text directly contributed to early Jewish apocalyptic identification(s) of Enoch as one who knew the secrets of heaven and facilitated the production of Enochic literature, since the word used to describe Enoch being "taken" (לקח) was also used to describe Elijah's disappearance from the earth (2 Kgs 2:9) and suggested heavenly ascent.

Many experts in Second Temple Judaism now regard these writings as the most important textual production of this period. Most of the Aramaic books of Enoch were found at Qumran, many in multiple copies, illustrating the importance of these texts. Enoch traditions and the Qumran texts are both characterized by cosmic dualism, a 364-day solar calendar, and a distinctive focus on revelation and eschatology. The Enochic texts were not only ideologically compatible with Qumranic religious thought, but the Enochic calendar also informed community life and observances. The Qumran community developed its own distinctive worldview, placing greater emphasis on the prophets, the covenant, and the Mosaic Torah, but their intellectual, ideological, and theological debts to the earlier Enochic tradition are undeniable.[12]

---

[10] George W. E. Nickelsburg, "The Books of Enoch at Qumran: What We Know and What We Need to Think About," in *Antikes Judentum und Frühes Christentum: Festschrift für Hartmut Stegemann zum 65. Geburtstag*, ed. B. Kollmann, W. Reinbold, and A. Steudel, BZNW 97 (Berlin: de Gruyter, 1999), 99–113; Gabriele Boccaccini, "Enochians, Urban Essenes, Qumranites: Three Social Groups, One Intellectual Movement," in *The Early Enoch Literature*, ed. G. Boccaccini and J. J. Collins, JSJSup 121 (Leiden: Brill, 2007), 320; G. W. E. Nickelsburg, *1 Enoch: A Commentary on the Book of 1 Enoch*, Hermeneia (Philadelphia: Fortress, 2001), 82–100; James C. VanderKam, "1 Enoch, Enochic Motifs, and Enoch in Early Christian Literature," in *The Jewish Apocalyptic Heritage in Early Christianity*, ed. J. C. VanderKam and W. Adler, CRINT 3/4 (Minneapolis: Fortress, 1996), 32–101.

[11] Christopher Rowland, "Enoch in Jewish and Early Christian Tradition," in *The Mystery of God: Early Jewish Mysticism and the New Testament*, ed. C. Rowland and C. R. A. Morray-Jones, CRINT 12 (Leiden: Brill, 2009), 33–61.

[12] The term "Enochic Judaism" was coined by Paolo Sacchi in 1990. Sacchi envisioned 1 Enoch as "the core of a distinct variety" of Second Temple Judaism. Yet we have no ancient record of any group who self-identified as "Enochic Jews" and the *"Book of Enoch"* is itself a construct, a Christian composition preserved only within the Ethiopian Orthodox Church. Cf.

There are a number of similarities between the Essenes and the Enochic books.[13] Enochic traditions describe a pre-Mosaic priesthood, with a lineage of great antiquity, which is reminiscent of Pliny's description of the Essenes existing for thousands of years (*Nat.* 5.17.4). Enochic traditions and the Essenes also share distinctive traits like angelology and exorcism. Josephus reports that the Essenes studied the "works of the ancients" and "in them they study the healing of diseases, the roots offering protection and the properties of stones" (*B.J.* 2.137; cf. 1 En. 7:1).[14] The Essenes possessed books that contained secret teachings on prophecy and healing. Josephus refers to their prophetic powers in reference to these books (*B.J.* 2.159). "They are described as 'zealous in the writing of the ancients,' and 'educated in holy books' and the 'books of their sect'" (*B.J.* 2.136; 159; 142). An Essene will "swear that he will transmit their teachings to no one in a way other than as he received them . . . and that he will preserve in like manner both the books of their sect and the names of the angels" (*B.J.* 2.142).[15]

The New Testament letter of Jude also shows familiarity with and respect for the *Book of Enoch*.[16] The author describes how "the angels who did not keep their own position, but left their proper dwelling" in heaven, have been "kept" in "eternal chains in deepest darkness for the judgment of the great day" (Jude 1:6). The reference to "eternal chains," which is found in many passages in the *Book of Enoch* (1 En. 13:1; 14:5; 54:3-5; 56:1-4; 88:1; 4QEnGiants^a 8:14; as well as in 2 Apoc. Bar. 56:13; Jub. 5:6), indicates that the early Jesus movement regarded the Enoch tradition as authoritative, if not as "Scripture." By the end of Late Antiquity, however, most Jews and Christians seem to have rejected the *Book of Enoch*, presumably either because heretics used it or because it proposed an alternative explanation of evil, which Jews and Christians attributed to the so-called fall of Adam and Eve. The modern rediscovery of the Ethiopic *Book of Enoch* and the Aramaic Enoch tradition among the Dead Sea Scrolls has revitalized the study of this ancient literary tradition, which was clearly a major intellectual influence on the pre-sectarian formation of the early Qumran community.

Annette Yoshiko Reed, *Fallen Angels and the History of Judaism and Christianity: The Reception of Enochic Literature* (New York: Cambridge University Press, 2005).

[13] See Phillip R. Davies (*Behind the Essenes: History and Ideology in the Dead Sea Scrolls*, BJS 84 [Atlanta: Scholars, 1987], 109) identifies the authors of the Enochic texts as "Essenes."

[14] This list correlates to the arts and sciences revealed by the fallen angels (1 En. 7:1). Translations of Josphus here are from Vermes and Goodman, *Essenes according to the Classical Sources*, 43.

[15] James C. VanderKam ("The Book of Enoch and the Qumran Scrolls," in *The Oxford Handbook of the Dead Sea Scrolls*, ed. T. H. Lim and J. J. Collins [New York: Oxford University Press, 2010], 254–80) cautions against identifying the Enochic tradition with Essenism.

[16] Simon J. Joseph, "'Seventh from Adam' (Jude 1:14-15): Re-examining Enoch Traditions and the Christology of Jude," *JTS* (2013): 463–81.

The Qumran Essene Hypothesis

The Qumran Essene hypothesis is based on two interrelated components: (1) the similarities between the Essenes as described in the classical sources and the community described in the Dead Sea Scrolls; and (2) Pliny the Elder's description of the Essenes living west of the Dead Sea (*Nat.* 5.17.4 [73]).[17] It is methodologically imperative, however, not to conflate the classical sources with the Dead Sea Scrolls and the Qumran site until the contents of each corpus are analyzed independently. We will proceed, therefore, by first reviewing the classical sources on the Essenes in antiquity and *then* reassessing whether the Scrolls and the Qumran site represent sufficient evidence to warrant reaffirming the hypothesis.

The historical origin of the Essenes remains a mystery. The word "Essene" itself continues to perplex. Although various solutions have been proposed, the etymology remains elusive. The most popular explanation is that "Essene" can be derived from חסי, חסיא, or חסין, the Aramaic word for "pious" or "holy."[18] According to Josephus and Philo, the Essenes were known above all for their holiness. Philo calls them "Essenes or holy ones" (Ἐσσαίων ἤ ὁσίων, *Prob.* 91). He suggests that they "are called Essenes (Ἐσσαῖοι), having merited this title, I think, because of their holiness (ὁσιότητά)" (*Hypoth.* 1). Josephus also notes that the Essenes "have a reputation for cultivating a particularly holy (σεμνότητα) life" (*B.J.* 2.119). Accordingly, most scholars have sought to explain the origin of the term from the Hebrew *Hasidim* (חסידים) ("pious" or "holy ones"), especially as this name was used to describe a Jewish group in the Maccabean era (1 Macc 7:13), although the name is never explicitly used in the Dead Sea Scrolls as a group self-designation.[19]

---

[17] Lester L. Grabbe, *Judaism from Cyrus to Hadrian*, 2 vols. (Minneapolis: Fortress, 1992), 492, 494; Jodi Magness, *The Archaeology of Qumran and the Dead Sea Scrolls* (Grand Rapids: Eerdmans, 2002), 41.

[18] Emil Schürer, *A History of the Jewish People in the Time of Jesus Christ*, vol. 2 (Edinburgh, 1893), 2:191. Milik, *Ten Years of Discovery*, 80–81; Frank Cross, *The Ancient Library of Qumran*, 3rd ed. (Minneapolis: Fortress, 1995), 183; André Dupont-Sommer, *Dead Sea Scrolls: A Preliminary Survey*, trans. E. M. Rowley (Oxford: Blackwell, 1952), 86–87.

[19] In 1 Maccabees the Hasidim are "mighty men of Israel who willingly offered themselves for the Law (1 Macc. 2:42)." See Henry A. Fischel, *The First Book of Maccabees* (New York: Schocken, 1948), 30. The text of 1 Macc 7:13 describes them as a "company of scribes"; 2 Macc 14:6 calls them "war-mongers and revolutionaries." F. M. Cross ("The Early History of the Qumran Community," in *New Directions in Biblical Archaeology*, ed. D. Freedman and J. Greenfield [Garden City, N.Y.: Doubleday, 1976], 70–89) suggested an Essenes = *Hasidim* model. Neither Josephus nor Philo refers to the Essenes *as* Hasidim, nor do the classical authors describe the Essenes as militant. On the contrary, Philo and Josephus explicitly describe the Essenes as *pacifists*. So unless the Hasidim (who refused to fight on the Sabbath) renounced their militancy (as described in

Another suggestion is that "Essene" can be derived from אסיא, the Aramaic word for "healers" (θεραπευταί).[20] There are similarities between the Egyptian Therapeutae as "healers" and Josephus' description of the Essenes as healers (similarities that many see as justifiable grounds for identifying the Therapeutae as an Egyptian branch of Essenism), but this suggestion does not concur with Philo's opinion that the correct etymology for "Essene" stems from the word "holy," nor does it ever occur in the Qumran scrolls as a self-designation.

Alternatively, an etymology from the word עשה has been proposed.[21] The "Essenes," then, would be "The Doers [or 'Followers'] of the Law" (עושי התורה). This proposal has some support from the Dead Sea Scrolls since the *Yahad* seems to have identified itself as "Doers" (עושין) of the Law" and "Doers of His will" (1QpHab 7:10–12; 1QpHab 8:1–3). Yet the Scrolls do not contain any references to "Doers" being used as an explicit self-designation for a group.[22]

Another possibility is that the word "Essene" is derived from the movement's profound interest in the Urim and Thummim of Exodus 28:22-30. According to Josephus (*A.J.* 3.215–217), twelve precious stones were attached to the breastplate, the "Essen" (ἐσσὴν). Josephus uses the word ἐσσὴν as a Greek transliteration (ἐσσὴν) of the Hebrew word for the breastplate (חשן) worn by the high priest (3.185; 218).[23] Josephus tells us that some Greeks "called that breastplate the oracle" (τὸν ἐσσῆνα λόγιον καλοῦσιν, *A.J.* 3.163.216–218). Since the Essenes had a reputation for prophetic powers and knowing "the properties of stones," the name *Essenes* may have been given to the movement because of their interest with these priestly oracles.[24] Finally, the Greek word *essēn* was also a name for the priests of

---

1 Macc) and transformed themselves into a peaceful sect of "holy ones" as a result of their political misfortunes (and thus no longer actually were Hasidim), identifying the Essenes with the Hasidim remains problematic. For criticism, see Philip R. Davies, "Hasidim in the Maccabean Period," *JJS* 28 (1977): 127–40; John J. Collins, *The Apocalyptic Vision of the Book of Daniel*, HSM 16 (Atlanta: Scholars, 1977), 201; Lester L. Grabbe, "Digging among the Roots of the Groningen Hypothesis," in *Enoch and Qumran Origins*, 280–85, esp. 281.

[20] Geza Vermes, "The Etymology of 'Essenes,'" *RevQ* 7 (1960): 427–43; Étienne Nodet, "*Asidaioi* and Essenes," in *Flores Florentino: Dead Sea Scrolls and Other Early Jewish Studies in Honour of Florentino García Martínez*, ed. A. Hilhorst, É. Puech, and E. Tigchelaar, JSJSup 122 (Leiden: Brill, 2007), 87.

[21] William Brownlee, *The Midrash Pesher of Habakkuk* (Missoula, Mont.: Scholars, 1979), 119; Stephen Goranson, "'Essenes': Etymology from עשה," *RevQ* 44 (1984): 483–98; James C. VanderKam, "Identity and History of the Community," in *The Dead Sea Scrolls after Fifty Years: A Comprehensive Assessment*, ed. P. W. Flint and J. C. VanderKam (Leiden: Brill, 1999), 498.

[22] John J. Collins, *Beyond the Qumran Community: The Sectarian Movement of the Dead Sea Scrolls* (Grand Rapids: Eerdmans, 2010), 158.

[23] Collins, *Beyond the Qumran Community*, 157.

[24] Crispin H. T. Fletcher-Louis, *All the Glory of Adam: Liturgical Anthropology in the Dead Sea Scrolls* (Leiden: Brill, 2002), 248–51. But see Vermes, "Etymology of 'Essenes,'" 249.

Artemis in Ephesus (Pausanias 8.13.1). The name *Essēnes* could thus refer both to cultic officials of Artemis as well as to the Jewish group of priests.[25] Some scholars have even attempted to identify the Essenes as the "Herodians" (Ἡρῳδιανοί) of the Gospels, although this proposal has not persuaded many.[26] While the debate over the precise etymological origin of the word "Essene" continues, the derivation from חסיא, signifying the Essenes as "holy ones," seems to be the most popular explanation, especially since an Aramaic fragment (4QLevi[b] ar) published in 1996 mentions a "holy/righteous one" (חסיה) in Palestinian Aramaic,[27] confirming its use at Qumran.[28] Nonetheless, it is certainly possible that different authors at different times and places may have had their own particular understandings of the etymological derivation and meaning of the term.

— ♦ —

The earliest historical evidence for the Essenes is found in the writings of a contemporary of Jesus, the Jewish Alexandrian philosopher Philo (15 BCE–50 CE), who probably composed his work between 20 and 40 CE.[29] He refers to them in two different works: *Quod omnis probus liber sit* (*That Every Good*

---

[25] John Kampen, "A Reconsideration of the Name Essene," *HUCA* 57 (1986): 61–81; Allen H. Jones, *Essenes: The Elect of Israel and Priests of Artemis* (Lanham, Md.: University Press of America, 1985).

[26] On the "Herodians" of the Gospels as "Essenes" (Mark 3:6; 12:13; 8:15; and Matt 22:16), see Constantin Daniel, "Nouveaux arguments in faveur de l'identification des Hérodiens et des Esséniens," *RevQ* 7 (1969–1971): 397–402; Taylor, *Essenes, the Scrolls, and the Dead Sea*, 109–31. For criticism, see Willi Braun, "Were New Testament Herodians Essenes? A Critique of an Hypothesis," *RQ* 14 (1989): 75–88; John P. Meier, "The Historical Jesus and the Historical Herodians," *JBL* 119 (2000): 740–46.

[27] Frank M. Cross suggested, "The common derivation from *hasen, hasayya*, the standard East Aramaic equivalent of Hebrew *qedosim*, 'holy ones,' is thoroughly suitable." Cross, *Ancient Library of Qumran*, 54. As M. E. Stone and J. C. Greenfield, the editors of the Levi fragment, note, "The main objection in the past to this etymology was that this word is attested only in Syriac.... Its occurrence in the present text shows that it was also used in the literary Aramaic attested at Qumran." *Discoveries in the Judaean Desert XXII, Qumran Cave 4 XVII: Parabiblical Texts, Part 3*, ed. G. Brooke, J. Collins, T. Elgvin, P. Flint, J. Greenfield, E. Larson, C. Newsom, E. Puech, L. H. Schiffman, M. Stone, and J. T. Barrera, with J. C. VanderKam (Oxford: Clarendon, 1996), 33.

[28] *Aramaic Levi* (4Q213a frgs. 3–4 line 6). J. C. Greenfield, M. E. Stone, and E. Eshel (*The Aramaic Levi Document: Edition, Translation, Commentary*, SVTP 19 [Leiden: Brill, 2004], 219–22, 222) read חסיה and note: "Its occurrence in the present texts shows that is [sic] was also used in the literary Aramaic attested at Qumran." Collins, *Beyond the Qumran Community*, 157, notes that חסיא "is in fact the Semitic word that corresponds most closely to *Essaioi*."

[29] Steve Mason ("The Historical Problem of the Essenes," in *Celebrating the Dead Sea Scrolls: A Canadian Constribution*, ed. P. W. Flint, J. Duhaime, and K. S. Baek, SBLEJL 30 [Atlanta: Society of Biblical Literature, 2011], 211) notes, "A historical inquiry into the Essenes must begin with the surviving evidence that describes this group."

Person Is Free) 75–91, and *Hypothetica* (*Apology for the Jews*) 11.1–8 (Eusebius' *Preparation of the Gospel* 8.11). Philo claims that they were Moses' disciples and lived according to his original instructions (*Hypoth.* 1). He states, "Our lawgiver encouraged the multitude of his disciples to live in community (κοινωνία): these are called Essaeans" (*Hypoth.* 1).[30] Philo tells us that the Essenes numbered over four thousand men and women located in numerous villages and towns (*Prob.* 75).[31] He locates them in Παλαιστίνη Συρία (Palestinian Syria, *Prob.* 75–76) and does *not* limit them to Judea (*Hypoth.* 1G).[32] He reports:

οἰκοῦσι δὲ πολλὰς μὲν πόλεις τῆς Ἰουδαίας,
πολλὰς δὲ κώμας καὶ μεγάλους καὶ πολυανθρώπους ὁμίλους.

On one hand they live in many towns in Judea;
on the other hand, they *also* live in many villages and large groups. (*Hypoth.* 1)[33]

According to Philo, the Essenes lived in many villages (κωμηδὸν) but avoided the cities (πόλεις) (*Prob.* 76), their principal occupation being agriculture (*Hypoth.* 11.8; Josephus, *A.J.* 18.19). They also practiced various trades, including sowing, planting, grazing herds, and keeping bees (Philo, *Hypoth.* 8.11.8). Philo called them "servants of God" and "holy ones" (*Prob.* 91), exemplary Jews known for their "moral excellence" (*Prob.* 75–91), devout observance of the Sabbath, and voluntary poverty (76–78). He claims that they do not offer (animal) sacrifices in the Temple (75), because they prefer "to render their minds truly holy" (75).[34] They also condemn slavery (79) and avoid marriage (*Hypoth.* 8.11.14). What is also noteworthy about Philo's report is that Essenes frequently travelled to other Essene communities (*Prob.* 12.85).[35]

Josephus is our most extensive source of information about the Essenes and refers to them in three works: the *Bellum judaicum* (*Jewish/Judean War*) 2.8, 2–13, 119–161 (c. 75 CE); *Antiquitates judaicae* (*Jewish Antiquities*) 18.1, 2, 5, 11, 18–22 (c. 93 CE); and *Vita* (*The Life*) 1.2.10–12.[36] Unfortunately, Josephus is also our most problematic source of information since he was a Jewish apologist

---

[30] Vermes and Goodman, *Essenes according to the Classical Sources*, 27.
[31] Cf. *A.J.* 18.1.5, 20–21.
[32] Philo's use of a μέν/δέ clause suggests that the Essenes could be found *not only* in Judean towns but also in many villages and communities *elsewhere*.
[33] Cf. Eusebius, *Praep. ev.* 8.6–7.
[34] Vermes and Goodman, *Essenes according to the Classical Sources*, 21.
[35] Cf. *B.J.* 2.124–125.
[36] Josephus devotes two passages to the Essenes—one in *B.J.* 2.119–1161, the other in *A.J.* 18.18–22. The earlier one does not mention the number four thousand, refusal to own slaves, agricultural pursuits, or exclusion from the Temple's common court. The later passage introduces these elements that were not in *B.J.* 2 but that are found in Philo's *Quod omnis probus liber sit*.

who surrendered to the Romans during the Revolt. Josephus is often guilty not only of overexaggeration but of outright deception.[37] Josephus' descriptions of the Essenes have been shaped by his own rhetorical aims, themes, and goals, namely to characterize them as idealized representatives of Judean character.[38] Josephus' (and Philo's) reports should therefore be understood in the context of Greco-Roman apologetics, which can account for their appeal to the exotic as well as familiar elements amenable to Greco-Roman readers.[39] Josephus uses language reminiscent of Spartan virtues and shapes his account to conform to Hellenistic expectations of manly virtue, aretē, courage, and asceticism.[40] Josephus' Essenes bathe in frigid water. Their common meals are sacred and solemn events. They have a reputation as "fair administrators of anger, able to restrain temper, masters of fidelity, servants of peace" (*B.J.* 1.135). They follow a disciplined regimen (δίαιτα) as a τάγμα ("order") (2.122, 125, 143, 160, 161), and their initiation rites are intended to produce "endurance" (καρτερία) (2.138). Their resistance toward the Romans during the Jewish Revolt exemplifies a "Greek-like view of immortality and post-mortem rewards,"[41] echoing common Greco-Roman philosophical ideas of facing death with courage. Similarly, Josephus' description of the Essenes as "avoiding oil" is best explained as an appeal to Greco-Roman ascetic virtues.[42] Essene reverence for the sun as a god also seems to be a Hellenistic embellishment (2.128, 148).[43] Since Jews did not "worship" the sun—but Greco-Romans *did*—Josephus has clearly shaped his account to conform to Greco-Roman consumption here.[44]

---

[37] For exaggeration, see *B.J.* 2.135, 143, 145, 147; for "Hellenization," see *B.J.* 2.119, 154–158, 128; *A.J.* 15.10; 4.371; for deception, see Josephus' claim that he joined the Essenes (*Vita* 1.2.10–12).

[38] Steve Mason, "Essenes and Lurking Spartans in Josephus' Judean War: From Story to History," in *Making History: Josephus and Historical Method*, ed. Z. Rodgers, JSJ 110 (Leiden: Brill, 2007), 219–61; idem, "What Josephus Says about the Essenes in His *Judean War*," in *Text and Artifact in the Religions of Mediterranean Antiquity: Essays in Honour of Peter Richardson*, ed. S. G. Wilson and M. Desjardins (Waterloo: Wilfrid Laurier University Press, 2000), 434–67. See also idem, *Josephus, Judea, and Christian Origins: Methods and Categories* (Peabody, Mass.: Hendrickson, 2009), 239–79. For an earlier "Spartan-influenced Essene" theory, see F. C. Conybeare, "Essenes," in *A Dictionary of the Bible*, ed. J. Hastings, 5 vols. (New York: Scribner, 1902–1904), 1:771.

[39] Doron Mendels, "Hellenistic Utopia and the Essenes," *HTR* 72, nos. 3–4 (1979): 207–22.

[40] Mason, "Historical Problem," 248, 246.

[41] Mason, *Josephus, Judea, and Christian Origins*, 264.

[42] Mason, *Josephus, Judea, and Christian Origins*, 267–68.

[43] Mason, *Josephus, Judea, and Christian Origins*, 270–71.

[44] Mason, *Josephus, Judea, and Christian Origins*, 270. Josephus' reference to Essenes' avoiding spitting in the middle is also to be harmonized not with 1QS or to rigorous Sabbath observance (2.147) but rather to "behaviors popularly thought to prevent or cure illness" in the

Despite the fact that Josephus' description of the Essenes has been shaped by rhetorical aims and goals,[45] this does not undermine the historical *existence* of a Palestinian Jewish movement between 100 BCE and 70 CE—that is, within the time frame of the Palestinian Jesus movement.[46] Moreover, there is no good reason to doubt the existence of a group of "marrying Essenes" (*B.J.* 2.160–161).[47] The fact that Josephus does not mention the Qumran settlement does not mean the Qumran community was not associated with the Essene movement, especially considering that Pliny does mention the site and the Essenes lived in many places (2.124).[48] Many scholars find evidence of source material in Josephus' account of the Essenes.[49] Josephus' reference to "four thousand" Essenes, for example, is remarkably similar to the number given by Philo, which leads many to suspect either that Josephus knew Philo or, alternatively, that Josephus knew Philo's source.[50] The most likely explanation is that Josephus knew *about* the Essenes and relied on literary sources in his own literary works.[51]

Greco-Roman world "grounded in a belief in the curative powers of human saliva" (273). Cf. Kenneth Atkinson and Jodi Magness, "Josephus's Essenes and the Qumran Community," *JBL* 129, no. 2 (2010): 317–42, esp. 326–29 on "spitting" (*B.J.* 2.147; 1QS 7:13) and the transmission of impurity via "oil" (*B.J.* 2.123; CD 12.15–17; 11QT 49.11).

[45] Mason, *Josephus, Judea, and Christian Origins*, 274. On Josephus' "rhetorical" interests, see also Douglas P. Finkbeiner, "The Essenes according to Josephus: Exploring the Contribution of Josephus' Portrait of the Essenes to His Larger Literary Agenda," Ph.D. diss., University of Pennsylvania, 2010.

[46] Mason, "Historical Problem," 244.

[47] Collins, *Beyond the Qumran Community*, 138; Jodi Magness, "The Essenes and the Qumran Settlement," review of Joan Taylor, *The Essenes, the Scrolls, and the Dead Sea*, *Marginalia*, May 1, 2014, http://marginalia.lareviewofbooks.org/the-essenes-and-the-qumran-settlement-by-jodi-magness/ (accessed April 23, 2016).

[48] Contra Mason, *Josephus, Judea, and Christian Origins*, 269. Mason contrasts Josephus' Essenes with the Qumran *Yahad* by pointing out that Josephus' Essenes have no center or main settlement, taking this to be "one of the clearest casualties of the Qumran-Essene hypothesis."

[49] On Josephus' use of sources, see also Bilde, "Essenes in Philo and Josephus," 64–65; Catherine M. Murphy, *Wealth in the Dead Sea Scrolls and the Qumran Community*, STDJ 40 (Leiden: Brill, 2002), 408–9; Jörg Frey, "Zur historischen Auswertung der antiken Essenerberichte: Ein beitrag zum Gespräch mit Roland Bergmeier," in *Qumran Kontrovers: Beiträge zu den Textfunden vom Toten Meer* (Paderborn: Bonifatius, 2003), 34–46; Collins, *Beyond the Qumran Community*, 132.

[50] On Josephus and Philo as evidence of literary dependence (*A.J.* 18.18–22; *Prob.* 75–91), see Randall A. Argall, "A Hellenistic Jewish Source on the Essenes," in *For a Later Generation: The Transformation of Tradition in Israel, Early Judaism, and Early Christianity*, ed. R. A. Argall, B. A. Bow, and R. A. Werline (Harrisburg, Pa.: Trinity International, 2000), 22–23. Mason, "Historical Problem," 239.

[51] Roland Bergmeier, *Die Essener-Berichte des Flavius Josephus: Quellenstudien zu den Essenertexten im Werk des Jüdischen Historiographen* (Kampen: Kok Pharos, 1993), 51–52; idem, "Zum historischen Wert der Essenerberichte von Philo und Josephus," in *Qumran kontrovers:*

Josephus introduces the Essenes during the reign of Jonathan (c. 150 BCE), but he does not claim that the Essenes as a group or movement *originated* during the Maccabean period (A.J. 13; 18.11). The Essenes are an αἵρεσις—that is, a "sect," party, or "heresy" as well as a distinctive γένος, or "race."[52] This "philosophy" has "existed since ancient times" (A.J. 13; 18.11). Like Philo, Josephus tells us that the Essenes were located in many places, including Jerusalem (A.J. 13.31.1; 15.373; B.J. 2.124). Josephus even refers to an "Essene Gate" in Jerusalem:

> This wall began in the north at the so-called Hippicus Tower and went on to the Xystos, and reaching Council House ended at the western Colonnade of the Temple. On the other side facing west, it began at the same starting point, extended through a placed called Bethso to the Essene Gate and turned thereafter facing south towards the Pool of Siloam. (B.J. 5.145)

In 1977 the remains of this ancient Essene gate as well as an Essene "quarter" on Mount Zion were reported.[53] This identification continues to be contested,[54] but there is no question that the identification is supported by the Josephan passage. Josephus tells us of several Essenes (in Jerusalem) who used their prophetic

Beiträge zu den Textfunden vom Toten Meer, ed. J. Frey and H. Stegemann (Bonifatius: Paderborn, 2003), 11–22; idem, "Die drei jüdischen Schulrichtungen nach Josephus und Hippolyt von Rom: Zu den Paralleltexten Josephus, B.J.2, 119–6 und Hippolyt, Haer. IX 18, 2–29,4," *JSJ* 34, no. 4 (2003): 443–70. Bergmeier, *Die Essener-Berichte des Flavius Josephus*, 79.

[52] For "sect," see B.J. 2.119, 122, 124, 137, 141, 142; A.J. 13.171. For "race," see B.J. 2.113, 199; A.J. 13.172; 15.371.

[53] See Bargil Pixner, "An Essene Quarter on Mount Zion?" in *Studi Archeologici*, ed. G. C. Bittini, vol. 1 of *Studia Hierosolymitana in onore del P. Bellarmino Bagatti*, SBFCM 22 (Jerusalem: Franciscan Printing, 1976), 245–86; Bargil Pixner, Doron Chen, and Shlomo Margalit, "Mount Zion: The Gate of the Essenes Reexcavated," *ZPV* 105 (1989): 85–95; Bargil Pixner, "Das Essener-Quarter in Jerusalem," in *Wege des Messias und Stätten der Urkirche*, ed. R. Riesner (Giessen: Brunnen, 1991), 180–207; idem, "Das letzte Abendmahl Jesu," in *Wege des Messias und Stätten der Urkirche*, ed. R. Riesner (Giessen: Brunnen, 1991), 219–28; idem, "Essener-Viertel und Urgemeinde," in *Wege des Messias*, 327–34; idem, "Archäologische Beobachtungen zum Jerusalemer Essener-Viertel und zur Urgemeinde," in *Christen und Christliches in Qumran?* ed. B. Mayer, ES 32 (Regensburg: F. Pustet, 1992), 89–113; idem, "Jerusalem's Essene Gateway: Where the Community Lived in Jesus' Time," *BAR* 23 (1997): 23–31. See also Rainer Riesner, "Josephus' Gate of the Essenes in Modern Discussion," *ZPV* 105 (1989): 105–9; idem, "Jesus, the Primitive Community, and the Essene Quarter of Jerusalem," in *Jesus and the Dead Sea Scrolls*, ed. J. H. Charlesworth (New York: Doubleday, 1991), 198–234; idem, "Essene Gate," in *ABD*, ed. D. N. Freedman et al., 3 vols. (New York: Doubleday, 1992), 2:618–19.

[54] The "Gate of the Essenes" has also been identified as the stone courtyard or "judgment seat" of the *Praetorium* near Herod's palace. See Shimon Gibson, *The Final Days of Jesus: The Archaeological Evidence* (New York: HarperOne, 2009), 96–106; idem, "Suggested Identifications for 'Bethso' and the 'Gate of the Essenes' in the Light of Magen Broshi's Excavations on Mount Zion," in *New Studies in the Archaeology of Jerusalem and Its Region: Collected Papers*, ed. J. Patrich and D. Amit (Jerusalem: Israel Antiquities Authority, 2007), 25–33.

powers in a political context: Judah in the time of the Hasmonean Antigonus (B.J. 1.78–80; A.J. 13.311–313); Menachem during the time of Herod the Great (A.J. 15.372–379); and Simon the Essene during Archelaus' reign (B.J. 2.111; A.J. 17.345–348). The Essenes, then, live "in every town" in Palestine (B.J. 2.124). Like Philo, Josephus does not isolate the Essenes in Judea. In fact, he indicates that "Judea" is the name for the entire land of Israel, including the district Galilee, and the specific district, Judea.[55] It follows that Essenes may have lived anywhere in greater Judea, including Galilee. "Judea" was a geographical location intended to include Galilee. Pliny also reports, "the part of Judaea adjoining Syria is called Galilee" (Nat. 5.70). It follows, therefore, that *some* Essenes may have lived in Galilee.[56]

Josephus describes them as "the noblest men in their way of life . . . some among them profess to foreknow the future, being educated in holy books and various rites of purification and sayings of prophets." They had "a reputation for cultivating a particularly holy life." They study the "works of the ancients," and "in them they study the healing of diseases, the roots offering protection and the properties of stones" (B.J. 2.137). They are "educated in holy books" and the "books of their sect" (B.J. 2.136, 159, 142). These books contain teachings on prophecy, healing, and the names of angels. Josephus also refers to their prophetic powers in reference to these books (B.J. 2.159). The Essenes "search out medicinal roots and the properties of stones for the healing of diseases" (B.J. 2.36; 1 En. 7:1). They "swear that he [they] will transmit their teachings to no one in a way other than as he received them . . . and that he will preserve in like manner both the books of their sect and the names of the angels" (B.J. 2.142).

Finally, Pliny the Elder (23–79 CE), a Roman historian who visited Judea in the late first century, tells us that the Essenes lived near the Dead Sea. In his work *Natural History* (c. 77 CE), Pliny reports:

> On the west side of the Dead Sea, but out of range of the noxious exhalations of the coast, is the solitary tribe (*gens*) of the Essenes, which is remarkable beyond all the other tribes in the whole world, as it has no women (*sine ulla femina*) and has renounced all sexual desire, has no money, and has only palm-trees for company. Day by day the throng of refugees (*convenarum turba*) is recruited to an equal number by numerous accessions of persons tired of life and driven thither by the waves of fortune to adopt their manners. Thus through thousands of years (*saeculorum milia*) (incredible to relate)

---

[55] Shaye J. D. Cohen, *The Beginnings of Jewishness: Boundaries, Varieties, Uncertainties*, HCS 31 (Berkeley: University of California Press, 1999), 72. See Josephus, A.J. 11.173.

[56] James H. Charlesworth, "The Dead Sea Scrolls and the Historical Jesus," in *Jesus and the Dead Sea Scrolls*, ed. J. H. Charlesworth (New York: Doubleday, 1992), 6; Thiede, *Dead Sea Scrolls*, 33.

a race (*gens*) in which no one is born lives on forever: so prolific
for their advantage is other men's weariness of life! (*Nat.* 5.17.4 [73] [Rackham, LCL])[57]

Pliny's account locates the Essenes on the western shore of the Dead Sea and serves as the cornerstone of the Qumran Essene hypothesis. According to Pliny,

> Below the Essenes was the town of Ein-gedi, second only to Jerusalem
> in its fertility and palm-groves but now another ash-heap.
> From there, one comes to the fortress of Masada,
> located on a rock, and itself near the sea of Asphalt. (*Nat.* 5.17.4 [73] [Rackham, LCL])

The Greek orator and philosopher Dio Chrysostom (40–115 CE), a contemporary of Pliny, is reported to have referred to the Essenes

> "who form a whole and prosperous *city* near the Dead Sea,
> in the middle of Palestine, in the vicinity of Sodom."[58]

While Dio Chrysostom's testimony supports identifying the inhabitants of Qumran with the Essenes, there is still some debate regarding Pliny's use of the phrase "*infra hos*," the question of Pliny's sources, and his geographical knowledge of Judea. It is generally recognized that Pliny used a number of sources in composing his *Natural History*.[59] This would explain a number of problems, namely the description of Ein-Gedi lying "downstream," "south of," or "below" the Essenes, and being able to proceed from there, further south, to Masada. Second, it would account for the fact that although Pliny's account was written after 70 CE, and apparently refers to the destruction of Jerusalem, he does not mention the Roman destruction of Qumran or Masada. This omission is best explained not only by positing an earlier source but by proposing that at some point in its transmission, "Jerusalem" was substituted for "Jericho," a far more likely candidate for Pliny's description of a fertile location of palm groves, especially since both place names begin with Hier.[60] Moreover, Pliny's description of Jerusalem's destruction (*nunc alterum bustum*) does not require a second destroyed place. Consequently, there is no reason to assume that Pliny is actually referring to the destruction of Jerusalem

---

[57] On the location of the Essenes north of Ein-gedi, see Christian Burchard, "Pline et les Esséniens: À propos d'un article récent," *RB* 69 (1962): 533–69; Magen Broshi, "Essenes at Qumran? A Rejoinder to Albert Baumgarten," *DSD* 14 (2007): 25–33.

[58] Dio Chrysostom, preserved in Synesius of Cyrene, *Dion or Of Life after His Example*, 3, 2 (ca. 400 CE). See Vermes and Goodman, *Essenes according to the Classical Sources*, 58–59.

[59] Stephen Goranson, "Rereading Pliny on the Essenes," Orion Center for the Dead Sea Scrolls, 1998, http://orion.mscc.huji.ac.il/orion/programs/Goranson98.shtml (accessed December 21, 2016).

[60] Théodore Reinach, *Textes d'auteurs grecs et romains relatifs au Judäisme* (Paris: Ernest Laroux, 1895), 273n2.

after 70 CE. Pliny's account, therefore, remains a reliable early first-century CE description of the Essenes. Despite suggestions that Essenes lived in the Ein-Gedi area, no site other than Qumran/Ein-Feshka qualifies.[61]

The Qumran site is in fact very close to the caves, and identical pottery has been found in both the site and the caves. Moreover, Pliny's description of the Ein-Gedi lying "below" or "south" of the Essenes, with Masada further "below," seems to be relatively accurate geographical knowledge. Pliny refers to Ein-Gedi lying "below" the Essenes, and "from there" one comes to Masada, suggesting a north-south movement. Pliny's Essenes therefore seem to have been located at the northernmost part of this description, especially if Pliny used sources and consulted a map of the Dead Sea area. In any case, Pliny refers to a group of Essenes living near the western shore of the Dead Sea north of Masada. Yet no suitable Essene settlements have been found in the hills "above" Ein-Gedi. Nonetheless, Pliny's Essenes must still be accounted for, and identifying the Qumran site as an Essenic group is still the most satisfying explanation.[62]

Some scholars have suggested that the site better resembles a Roman manor house than a sectarian community center.[63] It has also been suggested that the Qumran site originated as a Hasmonean fortress (c. 140 BCE) subsequently abandoned and inhabited by sectarians.[64] Others have sought to identify the

---

[61] Yizhar Hirschfeld, *Qumran in Context: Reassessing the Archaeological Evidence* (Peabody, Mass.: Hendrickson, 2004).

[62] Mason, *Josephus, Judea, and Christian Origins*, 241–49.

[63] Yizhar Hirschfeld, "Early Roman Manor Houses in Judea and the Site of Khirbet Qumran," *JNES* 57 (1998): 161–89. But see Jodi Magness, "A Villa at Khirbet Qumran?" *RevQ* 16 (1994): 397–419; idem, "Qumran: Not a Country Villa," *BAR* 22, no. 6 (1996): 38, 40–47, 72–73. Robert Donceel and Pauline Donceel-Voûte, "The Archaeology of Khirbet Qumran," in *Methods of Investigation of the Dead Sea Scrolls and the Khirbet Qumran Site: Present Realities and Future Prospects*, ed. M. O. WisenGolb, J. J. Collins, and D. G. Pardee, ANYAS 722 (New York: New York Academy of Sciences, 1994), 1–38. Rachel Bar-Nathan ("Qumran and the Hasmonean and Herodian Winter Palaces of Jericho: The Implication of the Pottery Finds on the Interpretation of the Settlement at Qumran," in *Qumran: The Site of the Dead Sea Scrolls: Archaeological Interpretations and Debates: Proceedings of a Conference Held at Brown University, November 17–19, 2002*, ed. K. Galor, J.-B. Humbert, and J. K. Zangenberg [Leiden: Brill, 2006], 263–77) holds that the dishware found at Qumran resembles that found at Masada and Jericho.

[64] Robert R. Cargill, *Qumran through (Real) Time: A Virtual Reconstruction of Qumran and the Dead Sea Scrolls*, Bible in Technology 1 (Piscataway: Gorgias, 2009); idem, "The Qumran Digital Model: An Argument for Archaeological Reconstruction in Virtual Reality," *NEA* 72 (2009): 28–41, 44–47; cf. Jodi Magness, "The Qumran Digital Model: A Response," *NEA* 72 (2009): 42–45; idem, "Digital Qumran: Virtual Reality or Virtual Fantasy?" in *A Teacher for All Generations: Essays in Honor of James C. VanderKam*, ed. E. F. Mason et al., JSJSup 153 (Leiden: Brill, 2012), 275–84.

Qumran site as a manufacturing center for hide-tanning or pottery production.[65] Yet the idea that Qumran was a manor house, villa, or manufacturing site is hard to reconcile with the sectarian texts, the shape and style of the pottery found in the caves being identical to the pottery found at the site[66] (with many of them using the same local clay),[67] the footpaths to the caves, the cemetery, numerous ink-wells, Pliny's description of the Essene community, and Dio's secondary reference to the Essenes' "city" by the Dead Sea. Such theories also tend to disregard the presence of carefully buried animal bones, the *miqvaot*, and the lack of any equipment for commerce. Furthermore, Qumran does not lie on a major trade route. There are a number of reasons, therefore, why alternative proposals have not been very convincing. Pliny explicitly mentions a community of Essenes living on the west shore of the Dead Sea. Eleven caves containing manuscripts were found in the immediate vicinity of the site, some of which can be accessed only by entering the settlement, inextricably linking the Scrolls and the caves. There are well-worn paths from the site to the caves, many of which contained pottery identical to that found at the site. The internal evidence of the Scrolls attests to a sectarian establishment, and no pro-Hasmonean or Sadducean texts were found in the caves. This hypothesis is also supported by several *mikvaot*, which are also referred to in the sectarian texts. The ink used in the Hodayot scroll even seems to have used water from the Dead Sea.[68]

The paleographical evidence dates the handwriting between 150 BCE and 70 CE, which corresponds to the historical existence of the Essenes. This confluence of archaeological, paleographical, geographical, and internal evidence is sufficient to warrant and defend the Qumran Essene hypothesis.[69] This does

---

[65] David Stacey ("Some Archaeological Observations on the Aqueducts of Qumran," *DSD* 14, no. 2 [2007]: 222–43) associates Qumran with the estate at Jericho as a tannery and pottery production facility. See also idem, "A Reassessment of the Stratigraphy of Qumran," in *Qumran Revisited: A Reassessment of the Archaeology of the Site and Its Texts*, ed. David Stacey and Gregory Doudna, BARIS 2520 (Oxford: Archaeopress, 2013), 53–61. For critique, see Jodi Magness, "A Response to D. Stacey, 'Some Archaeological Observations on the Aqueducts of Qumran,'" *DSD* 14, no. 2 (2007): 244–53; Yizhak Magen and Yuval Peleg (*The Qumran Excavations 1993–2004: Preliminary Report*, JSP 6 [Jerusalem: Israel Antiquities Authority, 2007]) propose that Qumran was a pottery production plant.

[66] Magness, *Archaeology of Qumran*, 44.

[67] Jan Gunnweg and Marta Balla, "Neutron Activation Analysis: Scroll Jars and Common Ware," in *Khirbet Qumrân et 'Ain Feshkha II: Études d'anthropologie, de physique et de chimie*, ed. J.-B. Humbert and J. Gunneweg (Fribourg: Academic, 2003), 3–53.

[68] Ira Rabin, Oliver Hahn, Timo Wolff, and Admir Masic, "On the Origin of the Ink of the Thanksgiving Scroll (1QHodayota)," *DSD* 16, no. 1 (2009): 97–106.

[69] For the Qumran site as a sectarian Jewish community center and/or Essene site, see Jean-Baptiste Humbert, "L'espace sacré á Qumrân: Propositions pour l'archéologie (Planches I–III)," *Revue Biblique* 101 (1994): 161–214; Humbert argues that Qumran was an Essene site. See also Minna Lönnqvist and Kenneth Lönnqvist (*Archaeology of the Hidden Qumran: The*

not mean, of course, that all of the Scrolls found at Qumran were written there or that they were all sectarian compositions. Different documents written at different times also reflect different phases of the Yahad's development.[70] Yet the Qumran community was economically supported by and related to a larger Essene movement.[71]

Despite many converging lines of evidence supporting the Qumran Essene hypothesis, some scholars maintain that the differences between the Scrolls and the classical sources undermine it enough to cast doubt on its sustainability. Methodological objections have thus been raised about the *use* of the classical sources in Qumran Studies.[72] Others continue to maintain rigid methodological boundaries between the classically described Essenes and the Qumran group.[73] It has been suggested, for example, that although the Qumran Essene hypothesis is based on "geographical proximity," "similar activity," and "similar Halakhot," those who affirm the Qumran Essene hypothesis tend to "ignore some serious difficulties with this identification."[74] These "difficulties" include the fact that "no Qumran-like site has been found" in other ancient cities, that the Qumran cemetery includes women and children, and that the Qumran site seems to represent "clear evidence of private property." Essene pacifism also seems to be irreconcilable with Qumranic "aggression."[75] It has also been suggested that the

---

New Paradigm [Helsinki: Helsinki University Press, 2002]), who see Qumran as the site of an Essene-like or Therapeutae-like group. Cargill (*Qumran through [Real] Time*) sees Qumran as both a Hasmonean fortress and a sectarian Jewish settlement. Ada Yardeni ("A Note on a Qumran Scribe," in *New Seals and Inscriptions: Hebrew, Idumean, and Cuneiform*, ed. M. Lubetski, HBM 8 [Sheffield: Sheffield Phoenix, 2007], 287–98) argues that manuscripts from Caves 1, 2, 3, 4, 6, 8, and 11 can be assigned to a single "Qumran scribe."

[70] Magness (*Archaeology of Qumran*, 65) argues that the Qumran site was settled between 100 and 50 BCE—that is, *after* the copying of Yahad texts like 1QS (c. 125 BCE). Magness no longer thinks, however, that the Qumran site was "abandoned" during this period.

[71] Mark A. Elliott, "Sealing Some Cracks in the Groningen Foundation," in *Enoch and Qumran Origins*, ed. G. Boccaccini (Grand Rapids: Eerdmans, 2005), 263–72, esp. 271–72.

[72] Curtis Hutt, "Qumran and the Ancient Sources," in *The Provo International Conference on the Dead Sea Scrolls: Technological Innovation, New Texts, and Reformulated Issues*, ed. D. W. Parry and E. Ulrich, STDJ 30 (Leiden: Brill, 1999), 274–93; Ian Hutchesson, "The Essene Hypothesis after Fifty Years: An Assessment," *Qumran Chronicle* 9 (2000), 17–34, here 28–34; Eyal Regev (*Sectarianism in Qumran: A Cross-Cultural Perspective*, RS 45 [New York: de Gruyter, 2007], 264) concludes that "the Essenes were a later development of the Qumran movement" but does not explain how Josephus (A.J. 13, 171–172) could claim that the Essenes existed c. 150 BCE or how "Judah the Essene" lived around 104 BCE in Jerusalem.

[73] Hillel Newman, *Proximity to Power and Jewish Sectarian Groups of the Ancient Period: A Review of Lifestyle, Values, and Halacha in the Pharisees, Sadducees, Essenes, and Qumran*, BRLJ 25 (Leiden: Brill, 2006),

[74] Newman, *Proximity to Power*, 46.

[75] Newman, *Proximity to Power*, 45.

Scrolls belonged to the Jerusalem Temple library and were brought there circa 66–73 CE.[76] Another theory posits that the Dead Sea Scrolls and/or the Qumran site represents a "Sadduccean" priestly group.[77] According to this theory, a group of Sadducees "underwent a gradual process of development and radicalization" as the "Dead Sea sect."[78] Consequently, the term "Essene" refers either to "the originally Saducean sectarians" or to "a wide variety of similar groups, of which the Dead Sea sect might be one."[79]

It is one thing, however, to reject the Qumran Essene hypothesis.[80] It is quite another to produce a more compelling explanation for the full range of data.[81] Biblical scholars are methodologically justified in studying different *corpora* in isolation, and there certainly are significant differences between the Essenes as described by Josephus, Philo, and Pliny and the groups presupposed in the Dead Sea Scrolls.[82] The question is whether the differences compel positing nonrelationship. True, the names and geographical locations of the movements appear

---

[76] Norman Golb, *Who Wrote the Dead Sea Scrolls? The Search for the Secret of Qumran* (New York: Scribner, 1995). Golb identifies the Qumran site as a fortress.

[77] Lawrence H. Schiffman, *Reclaiming the Dead Sea Scrolls: The History of Judaism, the Background of Christianity, the Lost Library of Qumran* (Philadelphia: Jewish Publication Society, 1994); Louis Ginzberg, *An Unknown Jewish Sect* (New York: Jewish Theological Seminary of America, 1976); Cecil Roth, *The Historical Background of the Dead Sea Scrolls* (Oxford: Blackwell, 1958). For criticism, see Geza Vermes, *The Complete Dead Sea Scrolls* (New York: Penguin, 1997), 42; Philip R. Davies, *Sects and Scrolls: Essays on Qumran and Related Topics* (Atlanta: Scholars, 1996), 131–38; Joseph Fitzmyer, *Dead Sea Scrolls and Christian Origins* (Grand Rapids: Eerdmans, 2000), 16; James C. VanderKam, "The People of the Dead Sea Scrolls: Essenes or Sadducees?" in *Understanding the Dead Sea Scrolls*, ed. H. Shanks (New York: Vintage, 1993), 51–61.

[78] Schiffman, *Reclaiming the Dead Sea Scrolls*, 89: "Its origins and the roots of its halakhic tradition lie in the Sadducean Zadokite priesthood."

[79] Schiffman, *Reclaiming the Dead Sea Scrolls*, 129. Gregory Doudna ("The Sect of the Qumran Texts and Its Leading Role in the Temple in Jerusalem during Much of the First Century BCE: Toward a New Framework for Understanding," in *Qumran Revisited: A Reassessment of the Archaeology of the Site and Its Texts*. BARIS 2520 [Oxford: Archaeopress, 2013], 75–124) suggests that the sect was a group of Hasmonean "Zadokite" high priests and that Josephus' "Essenes" is "a label fictitiously applied to some existing Jewish phenomenon, ordinarily known under other names" (87).

[80] See M. H. Gottstein, "Anti-Essene Traits in the Dead Sea Scrolls," *VT* 4 (1954): 141–47; Cecil Roth, "Why the Qumran Sect Cannot Have Been Essenes," *RevQ* 3 (1959): 417–22; G. R. Driver, *The Judaean Scrolls: The Problem and a Solution* (Oxford: Blackwell, 1965).

[81] Jonathan Klawans, *Josephus and the Theologies of Ancient Judaism* (New York: Oxford University Press, 2013), 35: "There is little of substance that the critics agree on other than their opposition to the Essene hypothesis. Indeed, many, if not most, of the alternatives to the Essene hypothesis are, literally, *idiosyncratic*" (emphasis in original).

[82] Alan David Crown and Lena Cansdale, "Focus on Qumran: Was It an Essene Settlement?" *BAR* 20 (1994): 24–35, 73; Lena Cansdale, *Qumran and the Essenes: A Re-evaluation of the Evidence*, TSAJ 60 (Tübingen: Mohr Siebeck, 1997).

to be different.[83] According to Josephus, the Essenes were "sun-worshippers" (*B.J.* 2.128, 148), while, according to 11QTemple, sun worship was prohibited and a capital offense (11QT 55.15–21). According to Philo, the Essenes did not sacrifice (Philo, *Prob.* 75; Josephus, *A.J.* 18.19), but several Qumran texts seem to presuppose sacrifice.[84] Josephus reports that new members swore oaths only at the end of their probation period (*B.J.* 2.139–142), yet 1QS's new members swear an oath to God and are then instructed by priests and Levites (1QS 1.16–17, 5.1–11). Josephus reports that new members were admitted to the common meal after their final vows and admittance to the community (*B.J.* 2.139), whereas 1QS has new members being admitted after two years of probation (1QS 6.16–17). Philo claims that only older men could join the order (*Hypoth.* 3), yet 1QSa indicates that women and children were part of the community (1QSa 1.4–20). Josephus and Philo claim that all property was handed over to the community for safekeeping (*B.J.* 2.122; *Hypoth.* 4; *Prob.* 86), yet CD appears to allow for private property.[85] Both Josephus and Philo claim that the Essenes did not use oaths (*B.J.* 2.135; *Prob.* 84) except for admittance oaths (*B.J.* 2.139–140), yet several Qumran texts presuppose oath taking.[86] Both Josephus and Philo claim that the Essenes did not possess slaves (*A.J.* 18.21; *Prob.* 79), yet CD presupposes the existence of slaves (CD 11.12; 12.10). Josephus refers to Essene determinism (*A.J.* 13.171–173 §5.9) and immortality of the soul (*B.J.* 2.154–158 §8.11) but to nothing about their dualism and eschatology."[87]

Nonetheless, the differences between the Essenes and the Qumran community as represented in the sectarian texts can also be explained in a number of ways:[88] 1QS and CD may refer to different groups and different stages within the movement's history;[89] the classical authors, being "outsiders," may not have had

---

[83] The term "Essene" is never mentioned in the Qumran texts. Pliny and Dio mention the Dead Sea. CD describes "camps" (13.7) and cities (11.5–6), including Jerusalem (1/4QM 7.4).

[84] 11QT and 1/4QM describe burnt offerings; CD 4.2 presupposes sacrifice; 1QS does not mention sacrifice and regards the ascetic life of the community as an "acceptable" offering in lieu of animal sacrifice.

[85] CD 9.10–16, 14.12–13 may allow for private property, but 1QS 6.19, 22 does seem to agree with Josephus and Philo's testimony, although 7.6–8, paradoxically, also seems to allow for private property.

[86] 1QS 5.8 presupposes an oath entering the community, and both CD 15.5–11 and 11QT 53.9–54.5 presuppose oaths.

[87] George W. E. Nickelsburg, *Ancient Judaism and Christian Origins: Diversity, Continuity, and Transformation* (Minneapolis: Fortress, 2003), 167–75, esp. 171.

[88] Martin Goodman, "A Note on the Qumran Sectarians, the Essenes and Josephus," *JJS* 46 (1995): 161–66, esp.161.

[89] Beall (*Josephus' Description of the Essenes*, 11) points out that 1QS and CD are inconsistent and may reflect the two divisions of the movement mentioned by Josephus. Josephus clearly describes the Essenes as including a secondary, "lay," or marrying group (*B.J.* 2.160–161),

access to specific rules and practices. Since neither Josephus nor Philo were fully initiated members, we should not expect them to have fully accurate information on the initiation rules and probation periods of the Essenes. Furthermore, a major literary-rhetorical qualification of the two bodies of literature is that of projected audience. The classical authors were writing to and for Greco-Roman readers, whereas the Scrolls were written by and for sectarian Jews. The projected audiences are different and determine the purpose, style, content, and intent of discourse. Josephus', Philo's, and Pliny's accounts should be understood in the context of Greco-Roman apologetics. Hence, the focus on the exotic and peculiar—elements amenable to Greco-Roman cultural comprehension. It is to be expected, therefore, that various aspects of the Essenes were altered, shaped, modified, and perhaps even omitted. It is telling that even scholars who might regard the Qumran Essene hypothesis as "much less probable than is usually proposed" also concede that the evidence makes it "overwhelmingly likely that the site at Qumran was used by ascetic Jews" and that the Essenes match the description of the sectarians in 1QS better than any other group.[90]

There is a high degree of correlation between the details mentioned by Philo, Pliny, and Josephus and the contents of the Scrolls.[91] At the risk of some oversimplification and harmonization, it is still noteworthy that both communities practiced ascetic self-control (B.J. 2.120; 1QS 4.9–11), despised riches (B.J. 2.122; 1QS 9.21–24; 10.18–19; 11.1–2), and performed purificatory washings (B.J. 2.129; 1QS 3.4–5; 5.13–14). Both held common meals (B.J. 2.129; 1QS 6.2–5), ate in silence (B.J. 2.132–133; 1QS 6.10–13), and had priests perform prayers before the meal (B.J. 2.131; 1QS 6.4–5; 1QSa 2.17–21). Both communities required an extensive probationary period for new members (B.J. 2.137–138; 1QS 6.13–23), demanded obedience to overseers (B.J. 2.134; 1QS 5.2–3; 6.11–13; 7.17), and expelled members for certain offenses (B.J. 2.143–144; 1QS 7.1–2, 16–17). Both communities required extensive entrance oaths (B.J. 2.139; 1QS 5.8–9), and both were against stealing (B.J. 2.141; 1QS 4.10; 10.19) and disclosing community secrets to outsiders while concealing nothing from fellow members (B.J. 2.141; 1QS 8.11–12; 4.5–6; 7.22–24). Both studied ancient writings (B.J. 2.136; 2.159; 1QS 6.6–8; CD 16.1–5), as well as their own sectarian books (B.J. 2.142; 1QS; 1QSa; CD; 1QM; 11QTemple; 11QMelchizedek), and professed to know the future (B.J. 2.159; *pesharim*). Both appear to have held to a belief in predestination. Both appear to have been comprised of a network of various "camps."

---

which suggests "the entire Essene movement was more fluid than Josephus presents." Similarly, there is evidence in CD that the Essenes lived in a number of locations.

[90] Goodman, "Note on the Qumran Sectarians," 164; Shemaryahu Talmon, "Qumran Studies: Past, Present and Future," *JQR* 85 (1994): 11.

[91] Beall, *Josephus' Description of the Essenes*.

The cumulative weight is impressive. The correspondences are compelling.[92] Moreover, models that identify the Qumran group as affiliated with the "Essenes" are capable of reconciling most problems. For example, at least three differences between Qumran and the Essenes involve discrepancies between 1QS and CD that describe different positions on private property, oaths, and slavery. Yet the classical sources do not mention in any significant detail the different practices of the lay and married Essene communities.[93] The significance of Khirbet Qumran has also often been exaggerated relative to the number of its possible occupants. The Qumran site could have supported only about 150 people.[94] Yet the Qumran texts refer to its members living in many "camps," indicating a movement with groups in multiple locations.

Despite its limitations, this hypothesis is still the best solution to the data.[95] The Dead Sea Scrolls were collected by a sectarian group loosely identifiable as *Essenic*. The Qumran site was part of an Essene movement.[96] The Essenes should not be equated with the Qumran group,[97] but the term "Essene" is still the best categorical reference to this network of multiregional groups.[98] In other words, the "Essenes" of Philo, Josephus, and Pliny are different, but related to the authors, scribes, and collectors of the Dead Sea Scrolls.

---

[92] Collins, *Beyond the Qumran Community*, 156; Bilde, "Essenes in Philo and Josephus," 67.

[93] Josephus (*B.J.* 2.160–161) mentions the marrying Essenes almost as an afterthought.

[94] Roland de Vaux, *Archaeology and the Dead Sea Scrolls* (London: Oxford University Press, 1973), 86; Magen Broshi and Hanan Eshel, "How and Where Did the Qumranites Live?" in *The Provo International Conference on the Dead Sea Scrolls: Technological Innovations, New Texts, and Reformulated Issues*, ed. D. W. Parry and E. Ulrich (Leiden: Brill, 1999), 272.

[95] Daniel R. Schwartz, *Studies in the Jewish Background of Christianity*, WUNT 60 (Tübingen: Mohr Siebeck, 1992), 35n19; Beall, *Josephus' Description of the Essenes*, 11.

[96] Talmon, "Qumran Studies," 6; John J. Collins, "Forms of Community in the Dead Sea Scrolls," in *Emanuel: Studies in Hebrew Bible, Septuagint and Dead Sea Scrolls in Honor of Emanuel Tov*, ed. S. M. Paul et al., VTSup 94 (Leiden: Brill, 2003), 97–111; Murphy, *Wealth in the Dead Sea Scrolls*, 3.

[97] Charlotte Hempel, "The Essenes," in *Religious Diversity in the Graeco-Roman World: A Survey of Recent Scholarship*, ed. D. Cohn-Sherbok and J. M. Court (Sheffield: Sheffield Academic, 2001), 75. Boccaccini, *Beyond the Essene Hypothesis*, 192; Richard Bauckham, "The Early Jerusalem Church, Qumran, and the Essenes," in *The Dead Sea Scrolls as Background to Postbiblical Judaism and Early Christianity: Papers from an International Conference at St. Andrews in 2001*, ed. J. R. Davila, STDJ 46 (Leiden: Brill, 2003), 65–66; Stegemann, "Qumran Essenes," 90–92; Jerome Murphy-O'Connor, "Qumran and the New Testament," in *The New Testament and Its Modern Interpreters*, ed. J. Epp and G. W. MacRae (Atlanta: Scholars, 1989), 63.

[98] Hempel, "Essenes," 67; Cross, *Canaanite Myth and Hebrew Epic*, 332.

The *Yahad*

Since the discovery of the Dead Sea Scrolls, the general scholarly consensus has been that the Qumran library—a collection of biblical, nonbiblical, and sectarian texts copied and/or composed between 200 BCE and 70 CE—belonged to a group of Essenes living at the Khirbet Qumran site in the Judean desert. The most significant recent methodological clarification in Qumran Studies, however, is the recognition that the Essene movement was far more widespread and multifaceted than previously recognized.[99] This clarification—that the Essenes were a multiregional movement—is key to (re)constructing their significance in early Judaism and their possible relationship(s) to the early Jesus movement.

The most compelling reason to posit a multiregional Essene movement comes from the Qumran corpus itself. The *Damascus Document* (CD) uses language suggesting that there were a number of places where its members lived. The word for "camp" occurs fifteen times in CD (7.6–7; 19.2; 12.23; 13.20; 14.3; 14.9). The *Damascus Document* also contains the term (עיר) six times (CD 12.1–2; 20.22; 10.21; 11.5–6; 12.19). These terms point to different groups of Essenes living outside of Qumran and Jerusalem. The "new covenant" thus seems to have been a "family-based" renewal movement in early Judaism that sought to reaffirm its loyalty to and observance of Mosaic Law in and through following a "new covenant":[100]

> ... a new covenant with the house of Israel, and with the house of Judah.
> It will not be like the covenant that I made with their ancestors....
> A covenant that they broke ... But this is the covenant
> that I will make with the house of Israel after those days, says the Lord,
> I will put my law within them, and I will write it on their hearts;
> and I will be their God, and they shall be my people. (Jer 31:31-33)

---

[99] On Qumran as a "fringe phenomenon," see Charlotte Hempel, "Qumran Communities: Beyond the Fringes of Second Temple Society," in *The Scrolls and the Scriptures: Qumran Fifty Years After*, ed. S. E. Porter and C. A. Evans (Sheffield: Sheffield Academic, 1997), 43–53. Alison Schofield ("Between Center and Periphery: The Yahad in Context," *DSD* 16, no. 3 [2009]: 330–50, 336) refers to a "radial-dialogic" exchange of traditions with Jerusalem and between the groups responsible for 1/4QS and CD, illustrating that the *Yahad* was not limited to Qumran. John J. Collins ("Beyond the Qumran Community: Social Organization in the Dead Sea Scrolls," *DSD* 16, no. 3 [2009]: 351–69, 360, 369) sees the *Yahad* as "an association dispersed in multiple settlements ... spread widely throughout the land." Michael A. Knibb, "The Community of the Dead Sea Scrolls: Introduction," *DSD* 16, no. 3 (2009): 297–308, 306: "The view ... that the *yahad* was not confined to one settlement in the wilderness, but was a broader phenomenon ... seems to me right."

[100] Collins, *Beyond the Qumran Community*, 24.

The "new covenant" would be written in the hearts and minds of the people. Yet this "new covenant" was also the renewal of the "eternal covenant" (ברית עולם) (CD 3.4; cf. 1QS 4.22, 5.5; 1QSb 1.2, 2.25; 1QM 17.3). The *Damascus Document* traces the spiritual history of the community from Noah and Abraham to Moses, suggesting that they believed they were fulfilling the original covenantal relationship that God made with Adam (CD 2.14–5.12).[101] This new relationship would require unswerving loyalty, discipline, and commitment. The word "covenant" (ברית) occurs over 150 times in the sectarian Scrolls, illustrating that the community believed they were the true "remnant of Israel" destined to inherit the "new covenant" that God was making with them (CD 6.19, 8.21, 19.33–34, 20.12). This covenant was being divinely revealed to the community (CD 15.8–10) and required a covenant oath (CD 15.5–8).[102] This "new covenant," however, would only be made between God and those who correctly understood, interpreted, and observed the Law.

The *Damascus Document* refers to an annual "assembly of all the camps" (CD 14.3–6) or "Feast of the Renewal of the Covenant" (4QD 266, 270), which was presumably a gathering of the entire movement when everyone renewed their commitment to the community. Each "camp" was supervised by a *mevaquer* or Guardian, but the camp does not seem to be supported by an elaborate Council (CD 13.9–10). The Guardian examined newcomers and decided on their admission to the community (4Q265), and was responsible for maintaining the social and ritual boundaries between the members of the camp and outsiders or nonmembers. The "towns" (ערים) and "camps" (מחנות) had tribunals for legal cases and "judges" that were experts in "the constitutions of the Covenant."

The members of the "new covenant" "live in camps . . . marry and have children" (CD 7.6–7). CD discusses marriage and divorce (13.16–17), the instruction of children (4Q266 fr. 9 iii 6), and sexual relations (4Q267 fr. 9 vi 4–5; 4Q270 fr. 7 i 12–13). The movement was "family-based in the sense that members joined as families," meaning that children would have been born into the movement.[103] Those who lived in the villages, "camps," and towns (CD 12.19, 23) contributed to their fellow members' welfare when and where needed as part of a monthly tithe to the orphans, the poor, the old, and the sick (CD 14.12–16). Members engaged in commerce and trade, tending cattle and laboring as farmers, but do not seem to have engaged in any particular ascetic practices or study.

---

[101] On CD's view of history, see Maxine L. Grossman, *Reading for History in the Damascus Document: A Methodological Method*, STDJ 45 (Leiden: Brill, 2002).

[102] The *Rule of the Community* refers to a covenant-ceremony (1QS 1.18–3.12), and new members were expected to "enter," "cross over," and "hold fast to" the covenant. In short, the community itself *was* "the community of the covenant" (1QS 5.5).

[103] Collins, *Beyond the Qumran Community*, 31.

At some point in its development, this movement seems to have been led and instructed by a "Teacher of Righteousness." The Teacher interpreted the Law in a distinctively authoritative way and produced an early set of sectarian rules and codes.[104] The community laws referred to in the *Damascus Document* represent a tradition *predating* the Qumran community.[105] Here the origins of the Essene movement are traced back to the exile "in the land of Damascus." In CD the exile is followed by the "plant root" that sprang from Israel and Aaron (CD 1.5–8) and "the new covenant" that was enacted "in the land of Damascus" (CD A 6.19, 8.21). Referring to "the converts (or returnees) of Israel, who left the land of Judah and lived in the land of Damascus" (CD A 6.5), CD also mentions "an Interpreter of the Law who came to Damascus" (8.17).

There is no consensus as to what "Damascus" signifies. One explanation is that the phrase should be understood literally, with the group returning to Judea following the Maccabean war.[106] Another explanation identifies the "Damascus" of CD as a code name for Qumran,[107] yet this hypothesis has neither archaeological nor textual support; Qumran was in "the land of *Judah*," not "the land of Damascus." A third explanation suggests that "Damascus" refers to the place of exile in which the movement originated—that is, the city of Babylon.[108] According to this model, the community originated during the Babylonian exile and formed a "new covenant" consisting of sectarian law, returning to Israel after the Maccabean revolt. Upon arrival, they were joined by a group of Zadokite priests, including

---

[104] John J. Collins (*Beyond the Qumran Community*, 50) claims that "there is little or no basis for referring to the movement described in the *Damascus Rule* as Essene," but the Essenes (as described by Josephus) included marrying groups, just as the *Damascus Document* suggests. Collins describes the *Yahad* as "identical with the Essenes" (151) and affirms the textual relationship between 1QS and CD, concluding, "the *yahad* is a more developed form of the association described in the *Damascus Rule*" (65). See also idem, "The Yahad and 'The Qumran Community,'" in *Biblical Traditions in Transmission: Essays in Honour of Michael A. Knibb*, ed. C. Hempel and J. Lieu (Leiden: Brill, 2006), 81–96; Eyal Regev, "The 'Yahad' and the 'Damascus Covenant': Structure, Organization, and Relationship," *RevQ* 21 (2003): 233–62.

[105] Davies, "Birthplace of the Essenes," 505; idem, *Damascus Covenant: An Interpretation of the "Damascus Document"* (Sheffield: Sheffield Academic, 1983), 39. Knibb, "Place of the Damascus Document," 153; Hempel, "Community Origins," 328.

[106] Stegemann, "Qumran Essenes"; David Flusser, *The Spiritual History of the Dead Sea Sect*, trans. C. Glucker. (Tel Aviv: MOD Books, 1989), 11; John H. Hayes and Sara R. Mandell, *The Jewish People in Classical Antiquity: From Alexander to Bar Kochba* (Louisville, Ky.: Westminster John Knox, 1998), 92; Philip R. Callaway, "Qumran Origins: From the *Doresh* to the *Moreh*," *RevQ* 14, no. 56 (1990): 644.

[107] Gaster, *Dead Sea Scriptures*, 4, 24. Cross, *Ancient Library of Qumran*.

[108] Jerome Murphy-O'Connor, "The Essenes and their History," *RB* 81 (1974): 219–23; Davies, "Birthplace of the Essenes," 503–19; Isaac Rabinowitz, "A Reconsideration of Damascus," *JBL* 73 (1954): 11–35; Annie Jaubert, "Le pays de Damas," *RB* 65 (1958): 214–48; E. Wiesenberg, "Chronological Data in the Zadokite Fragments," *VT* 5 (1955): 284–308.

the Teacher of Righteousness, who founded the Qumran community. The Admonition of CD does refer to an exilic origin for the community,[109] suggesting both an exilic origin and a second-century reconstitution of the community.[110] Various sectarian collections of law (like the *Damascus Document*) may have been in existence long before they were copied and stored at Qumran. If that is the case, then the community may have existed long *before* the arrival of the Teacher of Righteousness, only to be transformed by the Teacher's arrival, which led to a new phase of development in Palestine, where they envisioned themselves as the true "remnant of Israel."

Since the discovery of the Scrolls, efforts have been made to (re)construct the many notable social, textual, and chronological relationship(s) between the *Damascus Document* and the *Rule of the Community* as well as the relationships between the many different versions of the *Rule of the Community* (1QS/4QS).[111] The *Damascus Document* and the *Rule of the Community* share organizational structures, administration, community language, and penal codes.[112] The Qumran versions of the *Damascus Document* seem to preserve an "older and more original form of the communal legislation," and the *Rule of the Community* "can be seen to have developed from it at various points."[113] Nonetheless, CD and 1QS/4QS represent concurrent groups within a larger, wider movement.[114] While the *Damascus Document* represents the "family-based" wing, the *Rule of the Community* represents the more halakhically rigorous, priestly, and perhaps even

---

[109] William F. Albright and C. S. Mann, "Qumran and the Essenes: Geography, Chronology, and Identification of the Sect," in *The Scrolls and Christianity: Historical and Theological Significance*, ed. M. Black (London: SPCK, 1969), 16; Hempel, "Community Origins," 329.

[110] Jonathan Campbell, "Essene-Qumran Origins in the Exile: A Scriptural Basis?" *JJS* 46 (1995): 143–56.

[111] For the latter, see Sarianna Metso, *The Textual Development of the Community Rule* (Leiden: Brill, 1997). Metso suggests that the Cave 4 versions of the *Rule of the Community* are earlier than 1QS but were copied later (89–90) and that 1QS represents the latest version of the Rule. Alison Schofield (*From Qumran to the Yahad: A New Paradigm of Textual Development for The Community Rule*, STDJ 77 [Leiden: Brill, 2009], 7) suggests that different versions "share a common core of material" as "diverging traditions" in and through a process of "semi-independent development."

[112] Schofield (*From Qumran to the Yahad*, 171–72) points to "the overlapping roles of the Overseer (1QS 6.12, 20; CD 14.3, 9; 4Q266 10 i, 2; 4Q267 9 v, 6, 13; etc.), and the Sage (1QS 3.13; 9.12, 21; CD 12.21; 13.22), their similar rules for meetings (1QS 2.19–23; 5.23–24; CD 14.9b–10a), and admission procedure (1QS 5.7c–9a; CD 15.5b–15.6a)."

[113] Collins, *Beyond the Qumran Community*, 6. See also Charlotte Hempel, *The Laws of the Damascus Document: Sources, Traditions and Redaction*, STDJ 29 (Leiden: Brill, 1998), 191; Stephen Hultgren, *From the Damascus Covenant to the Covenant of the Community: Literary, Historical, and Theological Studies in the Dead Sea Scrolls*, STDJ 66 (Leiden: Brill, 2007); Knibb, "Place of the Damascus Document," 153–60.

[114] Collins, *Beyond the Qumran Community*, 73.

male celibate "inner circle,"¹¹⁵ an inner core of *twelve* described in 1QS 8.10–11 perhaps representing "the most dedicated and highest form of community life... an expression of its highest potential and its telos."¹¹⁶ It is this latter "temple-like" community *within* the larger movement, or *Yahad*, that settled at Qumran.

Extant in twelve different manuscripts, including the Cairo *Genizah* texts (CD A and B) and ten from Qumran (4Q266–273, 5Q12, and 6Q15), the *Damascus Document* rarely mentions the *Yahad*.¹¹⁷ The married members of the Damascus Covenant would think that their children were included within the community (cf. CD 7.4–6). On the other hand, the *Yahad* was entered by voluntary submission to the community's rules, not by birth (1QS 6.13; cf. CD 13.11; 15.5).¹¹⁸ 1QS and CD thus seem to represent two different but overlapping branches of the same movement, corresponding to Josephus' description of the Essenes' two "branches" (*B.J.* 2.160–161). While there are differences between 1/4QS and CD,¹¹⁹ the *Damascus Document* almost certainly preceded the composition of the *Community Rule*.¹²⁰

---

¹¹⁵ Collins, *Beyond the Qumran Community*, 73.

¹¹⁶ Carol A. Newsom, *Self as Symbolic Space: Constructing Identity and Community at Qumran*, STDJ 52 (Leiden: Brill, 2004), 153.

¹¹⁷ The two *possibilities* are CD 20.1, which refers either to "the unique teacher" (מורה היחיד) or (emended) to the "teacher of the *Yahad*" (מורה היחד), and CD 20.31–32, which may refer to "the men of the community" (אנשי היחיד). On the relationship between CD and 1QS, see further Charlotte Hempel, "CD Manuscript B and the *Rule of the Community*—Reflections on a Literary Relationship," *DSD* 16, no. 3 (2009): 370–87.

¹¹⁸ Jutta Jokiranta (review of John J. Collins, *Beyond the Qumran Community*, *DSD* 20 [2013]: 314–17, 316) rejects the view that "The *yahad* cannot be described as a family-based organization."

¹¹⁹ Regev ("'Yahad' and the 'Damascus Document,'" 258) argues that the communities behind 1QS and CD were not connected ("entirely distinct groups with almost no common characteristics"), and that 1QS represents the *original* stage of the community that preceded the composition of the *Damascus Document*. Regev (*Sectarianism in Qumran*, 264) also suggests that the Essenes of Josephus and Philo were an "outgrowth" of the Damascus Covenant and *Yahad*, although Josephus refers to the Essenes in the context of the Maccabean period ca. 150 BCE (*A.J.* 13.171–172) and to an individual Essene ca. 105 BCE (*B.J.* 1.78–80). That is, the Essenes already existed during the occupation/settlement of the Qumran site. Regev's facile appeal to the first-century setting of Josephus and Philo's accounts ("the scrolls are more ancient than descriptions of the Essenes") simply does not demonstrate a middle- to late-first-century origin of the Essenes. Regev's second argument, that the Essenes "appear to be a more complex social phenomenon" than the Qumran groups, and thus require more time to develop, is equally unconvincing given the high degree of sociological complexity already in the sectarian texts. For further criticism, see John J. Collins, review of Eyal Revev, *Sectarianism in Qumran*, *DSD* 16 (2009): 150–54.

¹²⁰ Hilary Evans Kapfer, "The Relationship Between the Damascus Document and the Community Rule: Attitudes toward the Temple as a Test Case," *DSD* 14, no. 2 (2007): 152–77. Cf. Davies, *Damascus Covenant*; Michael A. Knibb, "Exile in the Damascus Document," *JSOT*

The relationship between the Essenes, sacrifice, and the Temple, for example, provides an illuminating test case for understanding the development of the sectarian rule books (1/4QS; CD) as well as the social history of the Essene movement.[121] While the *Damascus Document* assumes an ongoing participation in the Temple cult,[122] it also criticizes its current administration, but has not yet envisioned the community as substituting for the Temple or the community's prayer as efficacious "sacrifice." Yet these themes are presupposed in 1QS, which seems to have severed ties with the Jerusalem Temple and envisions the community itself as a temple with prayer as sacrifice (1QS 9.4–5). 1QS does not mention the Temple cult's impurity, which seems to represent further indication that its author/community was now disaffiliated from the Temple/cult, which may also be why Philo almost casually describes the Essenes as not participating in the Temple cult in Jerusalem in the mid-first century CE.

Many scholars think that the Qumran group originated and developed as a result of conflicts about the hereditary legitimacy, moral purity, and ritual integrity of the priests serving in the Jerusalem Temple.[123] Beginning in the early second century BCE, the high priesthood became the center of political, economic, and military conflict. The founder(s) concluded that the priesthood was illegitimate and corrupt, which meant that the sacrificial system was illegitimate and corrupt, the Temple defiled, and the sacrifices taking place there inefficacious. It is within this atmosphere of conflict that the *Yahad*'s "Teacher of Righteousness" seems to have appeared. According to some scholars, a group of Zadokite priests were led by the Teacher to form a new community that saw itself as the true Temple of Israel that could offer pure atonement for the people (1QS 8.5–6, 8–9). It is not clear, however, that there ever really was an exodus of Zadokite priests from the Jerusalem Temple.[124] It is possible that the *Yahad* incorporated Zadokite priests,[125] but it is not clear whether Zadokite ideology refers to actual Zadokite

---

25 (1983): 99–117. Hempel (*Laws of the Damascus Document*, 150), refers to the community of the *Damascus Document* as "the parent group of the *yahad*." See also Hultgren, *From the Damascus Covenant to the Covenant of the Community*, 233–318.

[121] Kapfer, "Relationship Between the Damascus Document and the Community Rule."

[122] Kapfer, "Relationship Between the Damascus Document and the Community Rule," 164.

[123] Robert A. Kugler, "Priesthood at Qumran," in *The Dead Sea Scrolls after Fifty Years: A Comprehensive Assessment*, ed. P. W. Flint and J. C. VanderKam, 2 vols. (Leiden: Brill, 1999), 2:113. Rachel Elior (*The Three Temples: On the Emergence of Jewish Mysticism* trans. D. Louvish [Portland, Ore.: Littman Library of Jewish Civilization, 2004], 15) suggests that "the majority of the Judaean Desert Scrolls were writtten by these deposed priests" unable to participate in the Temple cult.

[124] Metso, *Textual Development of the Community Rule*.

[125] Kugler, "Priesthood at Qumran," 114.

priests.[126] The *Yaḥad* included priests,[127] but they were not its only members. It is therefore not certain that the priestly members of the *Yaḥad* ever actually enjoyed power in the Temple or developed ideological differences in order to challenge the authority of the Temple priesthood.[128] The benefits of sectarian religious practices (eternal life, freedom from evil spirits, salvation from divine wrath) do not seem to correspond with or replace the benefits of the Temple cult. The *Yaḥad* may have concluded that the terms and conditions of right relationship with God had changed.[129] If the eschatological era had begun, and divine wrath was imminent, it is possible that God was no longer accepting Temple sacrifices.[130] The fact that most of the nation was not aware of this dire situation could only have further exasperated those sectarians convinced of it.

— ♦ —

The *Yaḥad* (יחד) was the *union-of-communities* living in "all of their residences" (מגוריהם, 1QS 6.1b–8) in Judea.[131] The *Yaḥad*, however, is not to be understood as synonymous with the *Qumran* settlement.[132] The *Yaḥad* is modeled after the revelation of the Law to the twelve tribes at Sinai.[133] Just as Israel was a nation of God's holy people composed of twelve tribes, so a council of twelve men is envisioned (1QS 8.1). At Sinai, the people camped in the wilderness and waited for the appearance of God, purifying themselves in preparation (Exod 19:1) with ritual baths and sexual abstinence (Exod 19:15). They would be "God's holy possession

---

[126] Jacob Liver, "The Sons of Zadok the Priests' in the Dead Sea Sect," *RevQ* 6, no. 21 (1967): 3–32; Joseph Baumgarten, "The Heavenly Tribunal and the Personification of *Sedeq* in Jewish Apocalyptic," in *ANRW* 2.19 (Berlin: de Gruyter, 1979), 233–36; Brownlee, *Midrash Pesher of Habakkuk*.

[127] Schiffman, *Reclaiming the Dead Sea Scrolls*, 72–73; Davies, *Sects and Scrolls*, 132.

[128] Glaim, "Reciprocity, Sacrifice, and Salvation in Judean Religion," 159.

[129] Glaim, "Reciprocity, Sacrifice, and Salvation in Judean Religion," 113.

[130] Glaim, "Reciprocity, Sacrifice, and Salvation in Judean Religion," 15.

[131] Collins, "Yahad and 'The Qumran Community,'" 85–88; Regev, "'Yahad' and the 'Damascus Covenant,'" 233–62. Sarianna Metso ("Whom Does the Term *Yahad* Identify?" in *Biblical Traditions in Transmission: Essays in Honour of Michael A. Knibb*, ed. C. Hempel and J. M. Lieu [Leiden: Brill, 2006], 213–35) suggests that this passage is an interpolation. See also idem, "Methodological Problems in Reconstructing History from Rule Texts Found at Qumran," *DSD* 11 (2004): 315–35, esp. 324. Yet Schofield (*From Qumran to the Yahad*, 134) points out that the term appears in 4QS^g (4Q261), 4QS^d, and 4QS^i (4Q263). See also Shemaryahu Talmon, "The Community of the Renewed Covenant: Between Judaism and Christianity," in *The Community of the Renewed Covenant: The Notre Dame Symposium on the Dead Sea Scrolls (1993)*, ed. E. C. Ulrich and J. C. VanderKam, CJA 10 (Notre Dame, Ind.: University of Notre Dame Press, 1994), 3–24; idem, "Sectarian יחד," 133–40.

[132] Torleif Elgvin, "The *Yahad* Is More than Qumran," in *Enoch and Qumran Origins: New Light on a Forgotten Connection*, ed. G. Boccaccini (Grand Rapids: Eerdmans, 2005), 273–79.

[133] VanderKam, "Sinai Revisited," 44–66, here 52.

and a kingdom of priests" (Exod 19:5). Similarly, the *Yahad* is envisioned as a "kingdom of priests" living in atonement for the land (1QS 8.8). Its members were to "conceal" their "knowledge" (1QS 10.24) and "the counsel of the law among the men of iniquity" (1QS 9.17).

According to 1QS 8.9, the *Yahad* is a "House of Perfection," and its members were to walk "along the path of perfection" (8.21). New members were to "walk with perfection" (1QS 3.9–10; 8.20–26) and be tested in "the perfection of their path" (1QS 5.24).[134] The *Yahad* represents the "men of perfect holiness" (1QS 8.20; CD 20.2, 5, 7). They are "to walk in perfection of way" (1QS 2.2; 3.9; 8.18) and be "perfect of way" (1QS 4.22; 9.2, 5). "Perfection" seems to have been the goal, only possible with divine assistance (1QS 11.2, 11, 17). This would be fully realized in the eschatological future (1QS 3.18; 2.20–21; CD 3.20; 1QH 11.19–21, 22), when God would eliminate the forces of darkness and inaugurate a "new creation" (1QS 4.25) and "the glory of Adam" (1QS 4.23; CD 3.20; 1QH 4.13–15; 4Q171 3.12).

Initiation at Qumran

Initiation was a complex, multitiered process involving a probationary period of two or three years.[135] One joined the *Yahad* to "be united in the counsel of God and walk in perfection in his sight" (1QS 1.8), but this was a rigorous and demanding process. New members appeared before the Guardian "at the head of the congregation" during an annual session in order to determine whether or not they were suitable. If the Guardian and others were satisfied, the new member "entered the covenant" (1QS 6.13–15) and swore to adhere to the (Mosaic) Law as revealed to and interpreted by the community (1QS 5.7–11). The new member then underwent a year of training and instruction in "the rules of the Community," after which he appeared before the congregation again, to be either confirmed as a member or dismissed. If accepted, he would now be a new member of the Council but was still not admitted to the "pure food" for another year. Similarly, during this first probationary year, the new initiate could not share the community's property. At another Community Council, the new member was examined and tested, and, if accepted again, he would hand over his money and belongings, but neither his money nor his possessions were used yet or even considered the property of the community. For another full year the new member could not

---

[134] Alex R. G. Deasley, *The Shape of Qumran Theology* (Carlisle, UK: Paternoster, 2000), 210–54. On "perfection" as ritual purity, see Michael Newton, *The Concept of Purity at Qumran and in the Letters of Paul*, SNTSMS 53 (Cambridge: Cambridge University Press, 1985), 39.

[135] On entry into the *Yahad* as "initiation," see Susan Haber and Adele Reinhartz, *They Shall Purify Themselves: Essays on Purity in Early Judaism* (Atlanta: Society of Biblical Literature, 2008), 47–71.

touch the pure liquids and "drink of the congregation" (1QS 6.20–21). At the end of this second year, the initiate was once again examined and was either finally accepted as a full member or rejected. If accepted, his property was also accepted and assimilated into the community's holdings, and the new member was then allowed to speak during the annual Council meetings (1QS 6.13–23).

The *Yahad* seems to have been divided into priests and lay people (Aaron and Israel), with the people further subdivided into twelve tribes (1QM 11.1–3). Everyone was placed "in the order of his rank" (1QS 6.22). The leadership fell to the Guardian, the Bursar, and the priests. The priests were in charge of doctrinal matters, discipline, and ritual purity of the community. They needed to be present during meetings, study and prayer sessions, and meals to recite grace and pronounce blessings. The priests were known as "the men of holiness." They lived together, ate together, and deliberated and studied together (1QS 6.2–3; 1.11; 8.6–10). They were trained in the secret teachings of the Two Spirits (1QS 3) by the Guardian (מבקר) or Master (משכיל).

Once admitted into the *Yahad*, new members were taught various forms of secret knowledge. The Master instructed new members in "the nature of all the sons of humankind" (1QS 3.13–4.26). One of the first levels of instruction was the Two Spirits. According to 1QS 3.17–18, "God created humankind to have dominion over the world and designed for him Two Spirits in which to walk until the time of His visitation." These Two Spirits struggled for supremacy. Human nature was determined by an individual's discernment between the Two Spirits (1QS 4.15) and depended on their particular individual allotments of "light" or "darkness," an inheritance predetermined by God before they were born.[136] The Masters identified their members' "allotments" or "portions" of light and darkness and determined their character and destiny. These predictions seem to have been the result of individual astrological horoscopes and physiognomies. According to 4Q186, for example, one man's spirit is said to have "six parts in the house of light and three in the pit of darkness" (4Q186 1.2 and 2.1). This text seems to suggest that one man's natal chart was studied in order to evaluate the amount of "light" and "darkness" his spirit possessed.[137]

According to 1QS, God created both the Spirit of Light and the Spirit of Darkness. Truth originated "in a place of Light" and deceit in a place of

---

[136] P. S. Alexander, "Physiognomy, Initiation and Rank in the Qumran Community," in *Geschichte—Tradition—Reflexion 1, Festschrift Martin Hengel*, ed. P. Schaeffer et al. (Tübingen: Mohr Siebeck, 1996), 385–94; F. Schmidt, "Astrologie juive ancienne: Essai d'interpretation de 4QCriptique (4Q186)," *RevQ* 18 (1997): 125–41; J. Licht, "Legs as Signs of Election," *Tarbiz* 35 (1965–1966): 18–26.

[137] M. Albani, "Horoscopes in the Qumran Scrolls," in *The Dead Sea Scrolls after Fifty Years: A Comprehensive Assessment*, ed. P. W. Flint and J. C. VanderKam, 2 vols. (Leiden: Brill, 1999). 2:283.

darkness (1QS 3.19). These Two Spirits were represented by two opposing forces, the Prince of Light and the Angel of Darkness. The Prince of Light, also known as the "Spirit of Truth," is most likely to be identified with Michael, the "Prince of Light" in the *War Scroll* (1QM).[138] The Angel of Darkness (1QS 3.20–21) was also known as the "Spirit of Darkness" or "Belial" (1QS 1.18; 2.5; 10.21, 19).

The members of the *Yahad* were the "Sons of Light." According to 1QS 4.2–6, the nature of the "Spirit of Light" was

> to shine in the heart of man, and to make straight before him
> all the ways of true righteousness . . . and to induce a spirit
> of humility, and slowness to anger, and great compassion,
> and eternal goodness, and understanding and insight,
> and mighty wisdom, which is supported by all the works of God
> and leans upon the abundance of his steadfast love,
> and a spirit of knowledge in every thought of action,
> and zeal for righteous judgments, and holy thought
> with sustained purpose, and abundance of steadfast love
> for all the sons of truth, and glorious purity, abhoring all unclean
> idols, and walking humbly with prudence in all things,
> and concealing the truth of the mysteries of knowledge.[139]

While new members were called the "sons of dawn," after their probationary period was complete, they became the "Sons of Light." The author of 1QS 11.5–7 praises God, giving thanks for "illumining" his heart:

> A light is in my heart from His marvelous mysteries.
> My eyes have gazed upon that which is eternal, on wisdom hidden
> from mankind, knowledge and wise discretion (hidden) from the sons of Adam,
> a fountain of righteousness and a well of strength together with a spring
> of glory (hidden) from the assembly of flesh.

The inheritance of the Sons of Light would be "great peace in a long life, and fruitfulness, together with all eternal blessings and eternal joy in eternal life, and a crown of glory together with robes of majesty in eternal light" (1QS 4.7–8).

Once instructed in the Two Spirits, new initiates were to be cleansed from sin, pledging to remove themselves from impurity, falsehood, and wickedness. The new initiate would be cleansed "by the holy spirit of the Community" (1QS 3.7). In 1QS 4.20–21 God is said "to purify him by the holy spirit from all

---

[138] Yigael Yadin, *The Scroll of the War of the Sons of Light against the Sons of Darkness: Edited with Commentary and Introduction* (Oxford: Oxford University Press, 1962), 235–36.
[139] Burrows, *Dead Sea Scrolls*, 374–75.

works of wickedness, and sprinkle upon him the Spirit of Truth like purifying water."[140] Daily life at Qumran seems to have involved three major ritual components: common meals (preceded by purification baths), the study of the Law, and community prayer services (1QS 6.3–8). Life at Qumran was designed to be one of incessant prayer and devotion, with a cycle of three daily hours of prayer: morning, midday, and evening (1QS 10.1–7; 1QH 12.3–9; 1QM 14.12–14).

The Qumran community was envisioned as the earthly reflection of the heavenly hierarchy. The Scrolls repeatedly refer to archangels Michael (1QS 3.20; CD 5.18), Sariel, Raphael, and Gabriel (1QM 9.15), the "sons of heaven" (1QS 4.22; 1QH 3.22), the "host of heaven," and "holy ones" (1QM 12.1). The angels are God's servants: holy beings filled with knowledge and wisdom. They are called "gods" (1QM 1.10, 11; 14.15, 16; 15.14; 17.7; 1QH 7.28; 19.3; *Songs of the Sabbath Sacrifice*), "holy ones" (1QS 11.5; 11.8; 1QM 10.2; 12.1, 4, 7, 8; 18.2; *Songs of the Sabbath Sacrifice*), "the sons of heaven," "Angels of the Presence," angels who serve before God in heaven (1QH 6.12–13; 1QH 3.20–23; CD 15.15–17; 1QM 7.6; 1QSa 2.8–9), "mighty ones" (1QH 5.21; 1QM 15.14), "lofty ones," "priests" that serve in the heavenly temple, "ministers of the presence," "spiritual beings," "cherubim" (4Q403; 4Q405), and "Angels of His Glory" (4QShir).

The *Yahad* lived in a world of angels and demons in perpetual conflict. They believed that their secret knowledge, ascetic ritual purity, and rigorous adherence to the Law provided them with an especially close and intimate relationship with the heavenly realm. That is, they enjoyed the fellowship of angels (1QS 11.7; 1QH 3.21; 4.24; 6.11, 13; 1QS 11.7; 1QSa 2.3–11).[141] The Qumran community believed that they were united to the heavenly community of angels.[142] Angels were said to be present in the midst of the community (CD 15.17; 1QSa). The *Songs of the Sabbath Sacrifice* further suggest a liturgical correspondence between the *Yahad*'s worship and angelic worship in heaven.[143] This text (4Q400–407), found in eight different manuscript copies in Cave 4, describes the praise offered by the angels—the heavenly priesthood—in God's temple before God's heavenly throne.[144] While the angels praise God in the heavenly temple, the community—as an

---

[140] Baumgarten, "Purification Liturgies," 211, noting that it is not the water that cleanses, but the holy spirit.

[141] Christopher Rowland, *Christian Origins: From Messianic Movement to Christian Religion* (Minneapolis: Augsburg, 1985), 36; H. Ringgren, *The Faith of Qumran: Theology of the Dead Sea Scrolls*, trans. E. T. Sander (New York: Crossroad, 1995), 85.

[142] M. J. Davidson, *Angels at Qumran: A Comparative Study of 1 Enoch 1–36, 72–108 and Sectarian Writings from Qumran* (Sheffield: Sheffield Academic, 1992), 167.

[143] Carol A. Newsom, *Songs of the Sabbath Sacrifice: A Critical Edition* (Atlanta: Scholars, 1985).

[144] Bilhah Nitzan, *Qumran Prayer and Religious Poetry* (Leiden: Brill, 1994), 274.

earthly temple—offers its praise on earth.[145] The *Songs* thus seem to have served a liturgical purpose in the community.[146]

The *Yahad* anticipated the eschatological restoration of the "glory of Adam" (כבוד אדם; 1QS 4.22–23; CD 3.20; and 1QH 4.15).[147] In 4Q171 3.1–2 the "inheritance of Adam" (נחלת אדם) will be made available to the community. It is "a crown of glory with majestic raiment in eternal light" (1QS 4.7–8), "some kind of metamorphosis"[148] (1QS 4.25). Initiation—with its rigorous purification rituals, holiness, esoteric knowledge, and communion with angels—had as its highest goal the transformation of its members.[149] The idea that human beings could be transformed into angels or angel-like divine human beings developed in pre-Christian Jewish circles.[150] A number of texts found at Qumran further attest to this growing tradition;[151] 4Q491 1, in particular, describes what appears to be the heavenly enthronement of an individual:

> [El Elyon gave me a seat among] those perfect forever,
> a mighty throne in the congregation of the gods.
> None of the kings of the east shall sit in it
> and their nobles shall not [come near it].
> No Edomite shall be like me in glory,
> and none shall be exalted save men, nor shall come against me.
> For I have taken my seat in the [congregation] in the heavens,
> and none [find fault with me].
> I shall be reckoned with the gods
> and established in the holy congregation.
> I do not desire [gold], as would a man of flesh;
> everything precious to me is in the glory of [my God].[152]

---

[145] Nitzan, *Qumran Prayer*, 273.

[146] Nitzan, *Qumran Prayer*, 292–93.

[147] Cf. Oscar Cullmann, *The Christology of the New Testament* (London: SCM Press, 1963), 141; Geza Vermes, *Discovery in the Judean Desert* (New York: Desclee, 1956).

[148] Vermes, *Complete Dead Sea Scrolls*, 87.

[149] James H. Charlesworth, "The Portrayal of the Righteous as an Angel," in *Ideal Figures in Ancient Judaism: Profiles and Paradigms*, ed. J. J. Collins and G. W. E. Nickelsburg (Chico, Calif.: Scholars, 1980), 136; Elliott R. Wolfson, "Mysticism and the Poetic-Liturgical Compositions from Qumran: A Response to Bilhah Nitzan," *JQR* 85 (1994): 185–202, here 200.

[150] Martha Himmelfarb, *Ascent to Heaven in Jewish and Christian Apocalypses* (New York: Oxford University Press, 1993); Wolfson, "Mysticism," 194.

[151] Morton Smith, "Two Ascended to Heaven—Jesus and the Author of 4Q491," in *Jesus and the Dead Sea Scrolls*, ed. J. H. Charlesworth (New York: Doubleday, 1992), 298; Eileen Schuller, "A Hymn from a Cave Four Hodayot Manuscript: 4Q427 7 i + II," *JBL* 112 (1993): 605–28; Wolfson, "Mysticism," 185–202.

[152] Cited in Smith, "Two Ascended to Heaven," 296.

Although this text was originally published as part of the *War Scroll* (1QM) and called a "canticle of Michael,"[153] this figure cannot be Michael, as the archangel is never mentioned in this text, and the figure is quite unlike Michael, being indifferent to money and a teacher. The assertions of the speaker, who claims to be reckoned with the gods, but was not originally one of them, resemble those contained in the hymns attributed to the Teacher of Righteousness. Indeed, a direct relationship between this fragment and the *Hodayot*—much of which has been ascribed to the Teacher of Righteousness—seems likely considering the parallels between 4Q491 and other fragments.[154] In the *Hodayot* the speaker claims to be "among the angels." Similarly, the figure of 4Q491 claims to have been "taken up" and seated in heaven like one of the angels. This claim to heavenly enthronement suggests a kind of "angelification" process.[155] Similar enthronement themes emerge in the Enochic literature.[156]

The Dead Sea Scrolls contain "the only written collections of established prayer texts from the period before the destruction of the Temple."[157] In the Hebrew Bible, "prayer" (תפילה) includes a variety of forms such as "petition, praise, confession, and thanksgiving."[158] During this period, prayers were typically spontaneous, circumstantial, and occasional,[159] reflecting what seems to

---

[153] DJD 7:26.

[154] Schuller, "Hymn from a Cave Four Hodayot Manuscript," 605–28.

[155] Fletcher-Louis, *All the Glory of Adam*, 130. Wolfson ("Mysticism," 186–87) suggests that 4Q491 may describe "the 'angelification' of the human being who crosses the boundary of space and time and becomes part of the heavenly realm" through the process of enthronement that "represents the fullest expression of the mystical experience, an eschatological ideal of deification," "the ascension to heaven and transformation into an angelic being who occupies a throne alongside the throne of glory" (193).

[156] Cf. 1 En. 62:5; 69:27, 29; 45:3; 47:3; 51:3; 55:4; 60:2. In 1 Enoch 17:36, Enoch is described as "a fit companion for angels." In 1 En. 71:14, Enoch is portrayed as an angelic being. Similarly, in 2 and 3 Enoch, Enoch is transformed into an exalted angel. Cf. Dan 12:3; 1 En. 104:2.

[157] E. M. Schuller, "Some Reflections on the Function and Use of Poetical Texts among the Dead Sea Scrolls," in *Liturgical Perspectives: Prayer and Poetry in Light of the Dead Sea Scrolls: Proceedings of the Fifth International Symposium of the Orion Center for the Study of the Dead Sea Scrolls and Associated Literature, 19–23 January, 2000*, ed. E. G. Chazon, STDJ 48 (Leiden: Brill, 2003), 173–89, here 174.

[158] Emmanuel O. Tukasi, *Determinism and Petitionary Prayer in John and the Dead Sea Scrolls: An Ideological Reading of John and the Rule of the Community (1QS)*, LNTS/LSTS 66 (New York: T&T Clark, 2008), 19. Bruce Malina ("What Is Prayer," *Bible Today* 18 [1980]: 214–20) classifies seven types of Jewish prayer: (1) petitionary; (2) regulatory; (3) interactional; (4) self-focused; (5) heuristic; (6) contemplative; and (7) thanksgiving.

[159] Tukasi, *Determinism and Petitionary Prayer*, 23.

be pre-"scripturalized" and pre-"institutionalized" modes of prayer.[160] Today, many biblical scholars see links between the Scrolls and later Jewish liturgical practices.[161] Some scholars also seek to trace such continuities between pre- and post-70 CE forms of Judaism without the Temple,[162] suggesting that the Scrolls represent a point along a spectrum or "trajectory" from spontaneous prayer to standardized liturgical prayer.[163]

In early Judaism, the Temple was highly regarded and revered as the house of God by both Judeans and Galileans.[164] For most Jews, most of the time, prayer was *praxis* associated with and oriented toward the Temple's institutionalized, ritualized sacrifices. It follows that if a certain marginal subgroup (or "sect") within the body of Palestinian Judaism departed from these cultural codes and disaffiliated with the Jerusalem-based Temple-cult complex, and no longer regarded the sacrifices as efficacious, the pivotal question would be: What are we to do now about *replacing* the Temple's sacrificial system?[165] A "lost" or "imperiled" Temple allegiance requires the construction of alternative approaches to prayer.[166] Here, prayers emerge from the suffering and alienation of *present*-day earthly experience transferred, projected, and "transcribed" onto the "heavenly" sphere.

---

[160] Judith Hood Newman, *Praying by the Book: The Scripturalization of Prayer in Second Temple Judaism* (Atlanta: Scholars, 1999); Shemaryahu Talmon ("The Emergence of Institutionalized Prayer in Israel in Light of Qumran Literature," in *The World of Qumran from Within* [Jerusalem: Magnes, 1989], 201) refers to this as progressive "institutionalization."

[161] M. Weinfeld, "Prayer and Liturgical Practice in the Qumran Sect," in *The Dead Sea Scrolls: Forty Years of Research (University of Haifa, March 20–24, 1988)*, ed. D. Dimant and U. Rappaport (Leiden: Brill, 1992), 241–58; Esther G. Chazon, "On the Special Character of the Sabbath Prayer: New Data from Qumran," *JJML* 15 (1993): 1–21; idem, "Prayers from Qumran and Their Historical Implications," *DSD* 1, no. 3 (1994): 265–84. Esther Eshel, "Prayer in Qumran and the Synagogue," in *Community Without Temple*, ed. B. Ego, A. Lange, and P. Pilhofer (Tübingen: Mohr Siebeck, 1999), 323–34, here 323.

[162] Nitzan, *Qumran Prayer*; Lawrence H. Schiffman, "Jewish Law at Qumran," in *The Judaism of Qumran: A Systemic Reading of the Dead Sea Scrolls*, vol. 1: *Theory of Israel*, JLA 5/1, HOS 56 (Leiden: Brill, 2001), 85–88.

[163] E. M. Schuller, "Petitionary Prayer and the Religion of Qumran," in *Religion in the Dead Sea Scrolls*, ed. J. J. Collins and R. A. Kugler (Grand Rapids: Eerdmans, 2000), 29–45, here 45.

[164] S. Freyne, *Galilee, Jesus and the Gospels: Literary Approaches and Historical Investigations* (Philadelphia: Fortress, 1988), 178–87; idem, *Galilee and Gospel: Collected Essays*, WUNT 125 (Tübingen: Mohr Siebeck, 2000), 130, 154; Jonathan L. Reed, *Archaeology and the Galilean Jesus: A Re-examination of the Evidence* (Harrisburg, Pa.: Trinity International, 2000), 57–58; cf. Josephus, *A.J.* 2.280; 17.254–258; 20.118, 123; *B.J.* 2.237.

[165] Elior (*Three Temples*) sees the Qumran writings and "mystical" prayers as representing the writings of alienated priest-scribes unable to participate in the temple rites.

[166] For this terminology, see Kyu Sam Han, *Jerusalem and the Early Jesus Movement: The Q Community's Attitude Toward the Temple*, JSNTSup 207 (Sheffield: Sheffield Academic, 2002).

The Dead Sea Scrolls reflect an extended period of legal and exegetical experimentation, as well as esoteric divinatory practices resulting from this group's ongoing alienation from the Temple cult. Many texts represent daily prayers for morning and evening, for festivals, and for the Sabbath, paralleling the ritual cultic calendar in Jerusalem,[167] where prayers are generally associated with rituals of sacrificial worship.[168] Although we do not know the "daily liturgical schedule" of the *Yahad*,[169] or precisely what texts they used, the group does seem to have participated in daily prayers (1QS 10.5–11.22), although 1QS seems to refer more to cosmological cycles than to the times of sacrifices in the Jerusalem Temple.

The *Yahad* regarded itself as a *substitute* for the Temple cult; prayer served as a substitute for sacrifices.[170] As a covenantal scribal community, the Qumran sect's library reflects many of the prayer forms also found in the Hebrew Bible. Special emphases, however, fall on *thanksgiving*[171] and *penitential* prayer,[172] defined as "direct address to God in which an individual, group, or individual on behalf of the group confesses sins and petitions for forgiveness as an act of repentance."[173]

---

[167] Daniel K. Falk, *Daily, Sabbath, and Festival Prayers in the Dead Sea Scrolls*, STDJ 27 (Leiden: Brill, 1998); cf. idem, "The Contribution of the Qumran Scrolls to the Study of Ancient Jewish Liturgy," in *The Oxford Handbook of the Dead Sea Scrolls*, ed. T. H. Lim and J. J. Collins (New York: Oxford University Press, 2010), 618.

[168] Jeremy Penner, *Patterns of Daily Prayer in Second Temple Period Judaism*, STDJ 104 (Leiden: Brill, 2012); Weinfeld, "Prayer and Liturgical Practice in the Qumran Sect," 53–67; Mark J. Boda, Daniel K. Falk, and Rodney A. Werline, eds., *Seeking the Favor of God*, vol. 1, *The Origins of Penitential Prayer in Second Temple Judaism*, EJL (Atlanta: Society of Biblical Literature, 2006).

[169] John J. Collins, "Prayer and the Meaning of Ritual in the Dead Sea Scrolls," in *Prayer and Poetry in the Dead Sea Scrolls and Related Literature: Essays in Honor of Eileen Schuller on the Occasion of Her 65th Birthday*, ed J. Penner, K. M. Penner, and C. Wassen, STDJ 98 (Leiden: Brill, 2011), 69–86, here 74.

[170] Shemaryahu Talmon, "The 'Manual of Benedictions' of the Sect of the Judaean Desert," *RevQ* 2 (1960): 475–500; idem, "Emergence of Institutionalized Prayer in Israel," 200–243. See also Daniel K. Falk, "Qumran Prayer Texts and the Temple," in *Sapiential, Liturgical and Poetical Texts from Qumran*, ed. D. K. Falk, F. García Martínez, and E. M. Schuller, STDJ 35 (Leiden: Brill, 2000), 106–26.

[171] Newsom, *Self as Symbolic Space*, 206–8.

[172] Lorenzo DiTommaso, "Penitential Prayer and Apocalyptic Eschatology in Second Temple Judaism," in *Prayer and Poetry in the Dead Sea Scrolls and Related Literature: Essays in Honor of Eileen Schuller on the Occasion of Her 65th Birthday*, STDJ 98, ed. J. Penner, K. M. Penner, and C. Wassen (Leiden: Brill, 2011), 115–33, here 115: "Penitential prayers . . . presume that human action can influence the future."

[173] R. A. Werline, "Defining Penitential Prayer," in *Seeking the Favor of God*, vol. 1, *The Origins of Penitential Prayer in the Second Temple Period*, ed. M. Boda, D. K. Falk, and R. A. Werline, 3 vols., SBLEJL 22 (Leiden: Brill, 2007), xiii–xvii, here xv.

The community also employed various *petitionary* forms of prayer.[174] The *Rule of the Community* (1QS 1.24–2.18) contains an extended section of various forms of petitionary prayers, including a "Prayer of Confession" (1.24–2.1), "Petitionary Blessings" (2.2–4), and "Imprecatory Petitions" or curses (2.5–18).[175] These "Blessings" in 1QS reflect the divine gifts and rewards for fulfilling the (sectarian) covenantal obligations:

> May he bless you with everything good (יברככה בכול טוב)
> May he protect you against everything evil (ישמורכה מכול רע)
> May he enlighten your heart with insight for living (יאר לבכה בשכל חיים)
> May he favor you with eternal knowledge (יחונכה בדעת עולמים)
> May he lift his kind countenance toward you for eternal peace (ישא פני חסין לבה לשלום עולמים)

Here we find a prayer of protection against "evil" (רע). We also find a petitionary prayer for "enlightenment" and "insight for living," with the noun אור ("light") being a central theme of the *Rule*.[176] We also find a petition for "knowledge" (דעת) and for "everything good" (כול טוב), climaxing with the request for the (divine) "countenance for peace" (שלום). At the same time, we also find—in the section on curses—an eschatological drama reminiscent of both the Deuteronomistic curses,[177] as well as the harrowing scenes of hell envisioned in the Enochic literature and the book of Jubilees.[178] Salvation and judgment were two sides of the same divine coin.[179] The *Yahad* is characterized by an intensity of devotion manifesting as "complete and total dependence on God."[180] This dependence on God is evident in the group's many "prayers of praise and thanksgiving," their emphasis on the

---

[174] Daniel K. Falk, "Petition and Ideology in the Dead Sea Scrolls," in *Prayer and Poetry in the Dead Sea Scrolls*, 135–59.

[175] Tukasi, *Determinism and Petitionary Prayer*, 65–82.

[176] The *Rule* also uses the verb יאר in 1QS 4.2, where it describes the work of the Spirit of Truth: "to *illuminate* the heart of (a) man" (להאיר בלבב איש).

[177] Stephen D. Fraade, "Rhetoric and Hermeneutics in Miqsat Ma'ase ha-Torah (4QMMT): The Case of the Blessings and Curses," *DSD* 10 (2003): 150–61.

[178] Rodney A. Werline, "The Curses of the Covenant Renewal Ceremony in 1QS 1:16–2:19," in *For a Later Generation: The Transformation of Tradition in Israel, Early Judaism, and Early Christianity*, ed. R. A. Argall, B. A. Bow, and R. A. Werline (Harrisburg, Pa.: Trinity International, 2000), 280–88.

[179] Johann Maier, "Die Mittel der Darstellung der Geschichte Israels in Texten aus Qumran und ähnlichen Schriften: Zwischen Protologie und Eschatologie," in *Q in Context I: The Separation between the Just and the Unjust in Early Judaism and in the Sayings Source*, ed. M. Tiwald, BBB 172 (Bonn: Bonn University Press, 2015), 19–42. For similar themes, see also Loren T. Stuckenbruck, "Eschatologie und Zeit im *1 Henoch*," in *Q in Context I*, 43–60.

[180] George J. Brooke, "Aspects of the Theological Significance of Prayer and Worship in the Qumran Scrolls," in *Prayer and Poetry in the Dead Sea Scrolls*, 35–54, here 50.

"covenant," their willingness to withdraw from the Temple cult and live in "exile" without any "dependence on cultic machinery," and their alignment with "the cultic activity of heaven." The members of the *Yahad* envisioned themselves as the privileged recipients of divine revelation of judgment and salvation.

The Mystery (That Is to Come)

The *Yahad* believed that they were living before or during the "End of Days" (אחרית הימים).[181] This term occurs over thirty times in Qumran texts in reference to prophetic scriptural interpretation; 4QMMT announces that "this is the End of Days" (4Q394–399), while 4Q174 and 4Q177 4.1 associate the "End of Days" with a time period known as "the time of refining that has come," indicating a period of preparation that has already begun. On the other hand, 1QS describes the *Yahad's* laws as remaining in effect "until the time of his visitation" (1QS 3.18) and "until the appointed time and the new creation" (1QS 4.25). Yet its addendum (1QSa) is described as a rule "for the End of Days," signifying an imminent shift in the community's organization. Furthermore, both 11QMelch and 4Q174 predict the arrival of messianic figures "at the End of Days," which is also known as "the age of visitation" (CD 19.10).

The "End of Days" (1QpHab 2.5) is a central theme of the Qumranic worldview: God created the world by divine design, fixed the courses of the heavenly bodies, set the stars in motion, and allowed the Two Spirits to remain in conflict until the predetermined *end* of this conflict. The "End of Days" was this last period in a series of divinely determined periods of time.[182] All of world history was leading up to this period of time.[183] History was seen as a series of "ages" (קצים)

---

[181] Annette Steudel, "The Development of Essenic Eschatology," in *Eschatology in the Bible and in Jewish and Christian Tradition*, ed. H. G. Reventlow (Sheffield: Sheffield Academic, 1997), 241; L. H. Schiffman, *The Eschatological Community of the Dead Sea Scrolls: A Study of the Rule of the Congregation*, SBLMS 38 (Atlanta: Scholars, 1989); Bilhah Nitzan, "Eschatological Motives in Qumran Literature: The Messianic Concept," in *Eschatology in the Bible and in Jewish and Christian Tradition*, ed. H. G. Reventlow (Sheffield: Sheffield Academic, 1997), 133.

[182] Steudel, "Development of Essenic Eschatology," 231. See also idem, *Der Midrasch zur Eschatologie aus der Qumrangemeinde (4QmidrEschata–b)*, STDJ 13 (Leiden: Brill, 1994); idem, "4QMidr Esch: 'A Midrash on Eschatology' (4Q174 + 4Q177)," in *The Madrid Qumran Congress: Proceedings of the International Congress on the Dead Sea Scrolls, Madrid, 18–21 March 1991*, 2 vols., ed. J. Trebolle Barrera and L. Vegas Montaner (Leiden: Brill, 1992), 2:531–41; Jean Carmignac, "La Notion d'Eschatologie dans la Bible et à Qumrân," *RevQ* 7 (1969): 17–31; Jacob Licht, "Time and Eschatology in Apocalyptic Literature and in Qumran," *JJS* 16 (1965): 177.

[183] Shemaryahu Talmon, "Waiting for the Messiah: The Spiritual Universe of the Qumran Covenanters," in *Judaisms and Their Messiahs at the Turn of the Christian Era*, ed. J. Neusner, W. Scott-Green, and E. S. Frerichs (New York: Cambridge University Press, 1987), 126.

ending with "the decreed epoch of new things" (קץ נחרצה ועשות חדשה) (1QS 4.25). This comprehensive periodization of history from creation to the "End of Days" includes all "the ages made by God.... Before ever He created them, He determined the works of ... age by age. And it was engraved on tablets ... the ages of their domination."[184] Time was part of God's divine design: "All things are graven ... on a written Reminder for everlasting ages, and for the numbered cycles of the eternal years in all their seasons" (*Hodayot* IX, formerly I).[185] God's creation included "the sacred seasons ... the cycles of the years and of time everlasting" (1QM 10.15).[186] The natural world, with its rhythms and cycles, the "turning-points" of sunrise, sunset, and the changing seasons were designed "according to a statute engraved forever: at the heads of years and at the turning points of the seasons" (1QS 10.1–6).[187]

The *Yahad* understood that time moved in cycles. That is why they understood their community as the "*new* covenant," not because the covenant was being annulled, but because it was being *renewed*. God's revelations were ongoing, and the *Yahad* was already (partly) living in the "new age."[188] The End of Days was not the end of time but a turning point *in* time, a turning point of cosmological proportions, a universally new beginning.[189]

The *Yahad*'s interest in secrecy, esoteric knowledge, and "mystery" (רז) language served as a vehicle of ideological power and rival authority in the Second Temple period.[190] The *Yahad*'s *scribal* interests also reflect wider parallels in ancient Near Eastern (especially Babylonian) society, where such appeals to

---

[184] Vermes, *Complete Dead Sea Scrolls*, 520.

[185] Vermes, *Complete Dead Sea Scrolls*, 254.

[186] Vermes, *Complete Dead Sea Scrolls*, 174.

[187] Quoted from J. H. Charlesworth et al., eds., *The Dead Sea Scrolls: Hebrew, Aramaic, and Greek Texts with English Translations*, vol. 1, *The Rule of the Community and Related Documents* (Louisville, Ky.: Westminster John Knox, 1994), 43.

[188] William S. Lasor, *The Dead Sea Scrolls and the New Testament* (Grand Rapids: Eerdmans, 1972), 93; Alfred C. Leaney, *The Rule of Qumran and Its Meaning* (London: SCM Press, 1966), 152; John J. Collins, *The Scepter and the Star: Messianism in Light of the Dead Sea Scrolls*, 2nd ed. (Grand Rapids: Eerdmans, 2010), 105; Gaster, *Dead Sea Scriptures*, 8; Davies, *Meaning of the Dead Sea Scrolls*, 43; Henning Graf Reventlow, "The Eschatologization of the Prophetic Books: A Comparative Study," in *Eschatology in the Bible and in Jewish and Christian Tradition*, ed. H. G. Reventlow (Sheffield: Sheffield Academic, 1997), 170–71; Schiffman, *Eschatological Community of the Dead Sea Scrolls*, 7; Talmon, "Waiting for the Messiah," 126.

[189] E. P. Sanders, *Paul and Palestinian Judaism: A Comparison of Patterns of Religion* (Philadelphia: Fortress, 1977).

[190] Samuel I. Thomas, *The "Mysteries" at Qumran: Mystery, Secrecy, and Esotericism in the Dead Sea Scrolls*, EJL 25 (Atlanta: Society of Biblical Literature, 2009), 52.

secrecy and divine knowledge were the special province of scribal elites.[191] The *Yahad* seems to have inherited and further developed similar forms and practices of divination.[192] The appearance of the Persian loan word רז in the pre-sectarian Aramaic literature at Qumran points, in particular, to the origin of the *Yahad*'s "esoteric discourse"—and perhaps the *Yahad* itself—among Aramaic-speaking Jewish scribes familiar with the scribal and divinatory practices of the ancient Near East. This "esoteric discourse" not only facilitated the construction of the *Yahad*'s self-understanding but implicitly challenged the official knowledge presupposed by public representatives of the Torah and Temple in Jerusalem.[193] A prominent example of the *Yahad*'s penchant for esoteric speculation can be found in 4QInstruction, a wisdom text found in multiple copies at Qumran.

The sense of an imminent and profound eschatological mystery is a frequent motif in the Dead Sea Scrolls. The *Book of Mysteries* (1Q27, 4Q299–301), for example, refers to "mysteries of eternity" (4Q299 2b.5) and "mysteries of light" (4Q299 5.2). The most common expression for God's "mysteries" is "the mystery that is to be/come" (רז נהיה), referred to several times in the *Book of Mysteries* (1Q27, 4Q299–301) and the *Rule of the Community* (1QS 11.3–4).[194] Unfortunately, it is not clear exactly what this "mystery" refers to.[195] In 1Q27, it is contrasted with "the things of the past," which suggests it has a future character. People outside the *Yahad* "know not the mystery to be/come."[196] It seems to be "a body of teaching" known only to those able to understand its true interpretation,[197] "a comprehensive word for God's mysterious plan for creation and history, his plan for man and for redemption of the elect."[198]

---

[191] Alan Lenzi, *Secrecy and the Gods: Secret Knowledge in Ancient Mesopotamia and Biblical Israel*, SAAS 19 (Winona Lake, Ind.: Eisenbrauns, 2008), 149.

[192] Armin Lange, "The Essene Position on Magic and Divination," in *Legal Texts and Legal Issues: Proceedings of the Second Meeting of the International Organization for Qumran Studies, Cambridge, 1995: Published in Honour of Joseph M. Baumgarten*, ed. F. García Martínez, M. J. Bernstein, and J. Kampen, STDJ 23 (Leiden: Brill, 1997), 377–433.

[193] Thomas, *"Mysteries" at Qumran*, 48, 67–68.

[194] John J. Collins, "Wisdom Reconsidered, in Light of the Scrolls," *DSD* 4, no. 3 (1997): 265–81.

[195] Alex P. Jassen, *Mediating the Divine: Prophecy and Revelation in the Dead Sea Scrolls and Second Temple Judaism*, STDJ 68 (Leiden: Brill, 2007), 321–22.

[196] Vermes, *Complete Dead Sea Scrolls*, 389.

[197] Daniel J. Harrington, *Wisdom Texts from Qumran* (London: Routledge, 1996), 41; idem, "The *Raz Nihyeh* in a Qumran Wisdom Text (1Q26, 4Q415–418, 4Q243)," *RevQ* 17 (1996): 552; Schiffman, *Reclaiming the Dead Sea Scrolls*, 114.

[198] Torleif Elgvin, "The Mystery to Come: Early Essene Theology of Revelation," in *Qumran Between the Old and New Testaments*, ed. F. H. Cryer and T. L. Thompson (Sheffield: Sheffield Academic, 1998), 135; Matthew J. Goff, "The Mystery of Creation in 4QInstruction," *DSD* 10, no. 2 (2003): 163–86.

The רז נהיה is a major theme in 4QInstruction.[199] The expression is used over thirty times;[200] 4QInstruction is an early Jewish wisdom Instruction, an example of the most common wisdom genre found at Qumran.[201] Both 1QS and CD are manuals of instruction, the latter *beginning* with an exhortation, references to personified Wisdom (CD 1.1; 2.2, 14), and sapiential expressions (CD 2.3). Josephus and Philo both extol the Essenes for their wisdom (Philo, *Prob.* 11–13; Josephus, *B.J.* 2.158). The Qumran community was intimately familiar with the wisdom traditions of Israel.[202] Qumran itself was a kind of "Wisdom community" founded by a *"Teacher* of Righteousness."[203] A prominent figure was the maskil (משביל), "he who imparts wisdom," and this teacher's function was to provide instruction to members of the community. Based on the number of copies found at Qumran, 4QInstruction was evidently important to the Qumran community,[204] illustrating that wisdom and apocalyptic material coexisted in the same text and community.[205] 4QInstruction presupposes family life and addresses those engaged in regular society and traditional occupations such as farmers,

---

[199] Daniel J. Harrington and John Strugnell, "Qumran Cave 4 Texts: A New Publication," *JBL* 112 (1993): 490–99, esp. 492–94; Daniel J. Harrington, "Wisdom at Qumran," in *The Community of the Renewed Covenant: The Notre Dame Symposium on the Dead Sea Scrolls,* ed. E. Ulrich and J. VanderKam (Notre Dame, Ind.: University of Notre Dame Press, 1994), 137–52; Torleif Elgvin, "Admonition Texts from Qumran Cave 4," in *Methods of Investigation of the Dead Sea Scrolls and the Khirbet Qumran Site: Present Realities and Future Prospects,* ed. M. O. Wise et al. (New York: Academy of Arts and Sciences, 1993), 137–52; idem, "Wisdom, Revelation, and Eschatology in an Early Essene Writing," in *Society of Biblical Literature 1995 Seminar Papers,* ed. E. H. Lovering (Atlanta: Scholars, 1995), 440–63; Matthew J. Goff, *The Worldly and Heavenly Wisdom of 4QInstruction,* STDJ 50 (Leiden: Brill, 2003).

[200] 1Q26 1 i 1.4; 4Q415 6.4, 24.1, 25.1; 4Q416 2 i 5; 4Q416 2 iii 1.9, 14, 18, 21, 17; 4Q417 1 i 6, 8, 18, 21; 4Q417 1 ii 1.3; 4Q417 2 i 10–11; 4Q418 10.1, 43.4, 43.14, 43.16, 77.2, 77.4, 123.4, 148 i 4, 172.9, 179/5, 184/2; 4Q418a 1 2; 4Q418 c 1.8; 4Q423 1 i 5.

[201] Harrington, *Wisdom Texts from Qumran,* 81–82: "The most prominent literary genre among the Qumran wisdom texts is the instruction or admonition in which the sage instructs either an individual or a group—and sometimes both."

[202] John J. Collins, Gregory E. Sterling, and Ruth A. Clements, eds., *Sapiential Perspectives: Wisdom Literature in Light of the Dead Sea Scrolls: Proceedings of the Sixth International Symposium of the Orion Center for the Study of the Dead Sea Scrolls and Associated Literature, 20–22 May, 2001,* STDJ 51 (Leiden: Brill, 2004).

[203] John E. Worrell, "Concepts of Wisdom in the Dead Sea Scrolls," Ph.D. diss., Claremont Graduate School, 1968, 121, 383.

[204] 4Q415; 4Q415; 4Q417; 4Q418; 4Q418a; 4Q423; and 1Q26. John Strugnell, Daniel J. Harrington, and Torleif Elgvin (*Qumran Cave 4.XXIV: 4QInstruction [Musar leMevin]:* 4Q415ff., DJD 34 [Oxford: Clarendon, 1999], 2) designated the fragments of seven manuscripts (4Q415; 4Q415; 4Q417; 4Q418; 4Q418a; 4Q423; and 1Q26). Vermes (*Complete Dead Sea Scrolls,* 402) asserts, "the work is unquestionably sectarian."

[205] Matthew J. Goff, "Discerning Trajectories: 4QInstruction and the Sapiential Background of the Sayings Source Q," *JBL* 124, no. 4 (2005): 657–73, 669, 659.

herders, and craftsmen while disclosing eschatological mysteries, wisdom, and knowledge. 4QInstruction may be a nonsectarian text, although several terminological affinities with 1 Enoch are apparent.[206] The esoteric wisdom provided by 4QInstruction may have been known among those living in the "camps" (the villages and towns referred to in CD) where its agricultural, legal, and marital instruction would have been practical.[207] It would seem that 4QInstruction was used as a guidebook, providing advice and guidance.[208] 4QInstruction begins with "a cosmic and eschatological theological framework,"[209] contains several sections that use agricultural imagery,[210] and refers to plowmen, baskets, barns, fruits, trees, gardens, and the harvest (4Q418 103.2–5). Here a teacher gives instruction to those pursuing a number of professions. Yet the "elect" are also given insight into mysteries and knowledge hidden from others.[211]

Since 4QInstruction contains both practical and cosmological ideas,[212] and presupposes a teacher/student context, it may have been used as part of the "curriculum" in a "school" setting. 4Q417 2 i advises the student (מבין) to meditate on the *raz nihyeh* so the student will know "truth and injustice" and "the difference between good and evil." 4QInstruction begins with "a cosmic and eschatological framework,"[213] describing how "the host of the Heavens He has established" (17) and how "From Heaven He shall pronounce judgment upon the *work* of wickedness, But all his faithful Children will be accepted with favor."[214] 4Q417 2 i 10–11 mentions "the mystery that is to be/come" as a prerequisite for understanding "the birth time of salvation." 4Q416 2 iii line 9 encourages the student to study the "origins" of the "mystery" to know what is "allotted" to it. By studying the "mystery," one comes to understand "all the ways of truth and all the roots of

---

[206] 1 En. 5:7; 4Q418 81.14; 1 En. 10:16; 84:6; 93:5, 10; 4Q418 81.13; 4Q423 1–2.7.

[207] 4QInstruction refers to the "instruction for a maven" or student (מוסר למבין).

[208] For a compositional theory, see Torleif Elgvin, "Wisdom and Apocalypticism in the Early Second Century BCE—The Evidence of 4QInstruction," in *The Dead Sea Scrolls—Fifty Years after Their Discovery: Proceedings of the Jerusalem Congress, July 20–25, 1997*, ed. L. H. Schiffman, E. Tov, and J. C. VanderKam (Jerusalem: Israel Exploration Society, 2000), 226–47.

[209] Harrington, *Wisdom Texts from Qumran*, 41. See also Harrington and Strugnell, "Qumran Cave 4 Texts"; Harrington, "Wisdom at Qumran," 137–52.

[210] Harrington, *Wisdom Texts from Qumran*, 58. See 4Q418 103; 4Q423 2, 5.

[211] Alexander Rofé, "Revealed Wisdom: From the Bible to Qumran," in *Sapiential Perspectives: Wisdom Literature in Light of the Dead Sea Scrolls: Proceedings of the Sixth International Symposium of the Orion Center for the Study of the Dead Sea Scrolls and Associated Literature, 20–22 May, 2001*, ed. J. J. Collins, G. E. Sterling, and R. A. Clements, STDJ 51 (Leiden: Brill, 2004), 1–11, here 1: "A central tenet of Qumran theology is the notion of 'revealed wisdom.'"

[212] Elgvin, "Mystery to Come," 114.

[213] Harrington, *Wisdom Texts from Qumran*, 41. The precise beginning of the text is unknown, as there is an extensive margin before the beginning of 4Q416.

[214] Strugnell, Harrington, and Elgvin, *Qumran Cave 4.XXIV*, 83.

iniquity" (4Q416 2 iii 14). Meditating on the *raz nihyeh* will help one to understand "the generations of humankind" (4Q418 77.2) and "the inheritance of all that lives" (4Q418 2 i 18). 4Q417 2 i 8 urges the student to meditate "day and night" on "the mystery that is to be/come" and "you will know truth." According to 4Q418 123 ii.2–8, meditating on the רז נהיה enables one to understand the cosmological cycles of *creation*.

In sum, the *Yahad* could only be entered via an elaborate process of initiation. To divulge any of the movement's secrets would result in expulsion. Community members regarded themselves as "the new covenant" and believed that the revelations of God were ongoing. They sought to embody the highest possible degree of purity and holiness and implemented a rigorous process of initiation, purification, and consecration. New members were instructed in the Two Spirits, purified by the holy spirit (or the spirit of holiness), believed they enjoyed the fellowship of angels, and strove to become transformed into angelic or divine-like human beings. The Scrolls provide only fragmentary evidence, but they nonetheless represent a relatively coherent soteriological system, a divine plan in which God's promise to renew the covenant, restore Israel, and regenerate creation would be achieved by the members of the *Yahad* living lives of perfection in anticipation of the imminent arrival of the End of Days, the messianic age.

CHAPTER 3

THE ANOINTED PROPHET

The historical and theological origins of Jewish Davidic messianism have been traced back to the ancient Near Eastern royal ideal of divine kingship.[1] Yet "messiah language" came to be expressed in remarkably different ways in the political, religious, and literary landscape of Second Temple Judaism.[2] This variety of different eschatological-textual scenarios makes it difficult to speak of any such thing as "messianic expectations" in pre-Christian Judaism.[3] Monolithic categorical approaches to this topic tend to conflate different eschatological figures in an effort to classify and systematize the data, but it is better "to deal with each

---

[1] Sigmund Mowinckel, *He That Cometh*, trans. G. W. Anderson (New York: Abingdon, 1954); Nils Alstrup Dahl, "Messianic Ideas and the Crucifixion of Jesus," in *The Messiah: Developments in Earliest Judaism and Christianity. The First Princeton Symposium on Judaism and Christian Origins*, ed. J. H. Charlesworth (Minneapolis: Fortress, 1992), 384.

[2] Jacob Neusner and William Scott Green, eds., *Judaisms and Their Messiahs at the Turn of the Christian Era* (New York: Cambridge University Press, 1987); John J. Collins, *The Scepter and the Star: Messianism in Light of the Dead Sea Scrolls*, 2nd ed. (Grand Rapids: Eerdmans, 2010); Joseph A. Fitzmyer, *The Dead Sea Scrolls and Christian Origins* (Grand Rapids: Eerdmans, 2000), 78; Gerbern S. Oegema, *The Anointed and His People: Messianic Expectations from the Maccabees to Bar Kochba*, JSPSup 27 (Sheffield: Sheffield Academic, 1998), 303; Kenneth E. Pomykala, *The Davidic Dynasty Tradition in Early Judaism: Its History and Significance for Messianism*, SBLEJL 7 (Atlanta: Scholars, 1995), 271; Marinus de Jonge, "The Use of the Word 'Anointed' in the Time of Jesus," *NovT* 8 (1966): 132–48. On "messiah language," see Matthew V. Novenson, *Christ Among the Messiahs: Christ Language in Paul and Messiah Language in Ancient Judaism* (New York: Oxford University Press, 2012).

[3] Géza G. Xeravits, *King, Priest, Prophet: Positive Eschatological Protagonists of the Qumran Library*, STDJ 47 (Leiden: Brill, 2003), 2.

type of positive eschatological individual present . . . in their own right." The term "messiah" is fraught with problematic assumptions.[4] Scholars of early Judaism and Christianity now recognize a plurality of "messianic" figures, ideas, texts, traditions, and templates.[5] Nonetheless, textual variation was still somewhat limited because such ideas were widely shared based on a common allegiance to the Jewish Scriptures.[6] That is why—despite the diversity in the many different first-century Jewish groups—royal Davidic ideas continued to play a major role in eschatological hopes and dreams.[7] The Hasmonean era, for example, with its politico-military struggles and territorial expansion, gave rise to the resurgence of royal Davidic hopes.[8] By the turn of the century, the messiah—envisioned as a Davidic king who would "destroy the enemies of Israel and institute an era of unending peace"—seems to have become the most common model.[9]

The messianic texts from Qumran attest to the creative diversity of early Jewish messianic speculation. Some scholars claim that the small number of messianic texts discovered at Qumran indicates that messianism was relatively unimportant to them. This argument is undermined by the sheer diversity of messianic texts discovered at Qumran and the fact that messianism played a significant role in the earliest formation of the Qumran community and remained a major feature of its religious ideology. Messianism plays a significant role in many of the *Yahad*'s central documents of self-definition (1QS; 1QSa; 1QSb; CD) and is inseparable from its apocalyptic and eschatological worldview.

According to the *Rule of the Community* (1QS), the men of the *Yahad* (היחד אנשי) are to set themselves apart as "a holy house for Aaron" (בית קודש לאהרון, 9.5–6) and live according to the rules of the *Yahad* "until the coming of a/the prophet and the messiahs of Aaron and Israel" (עד בוא נביא ומשיחי אהרון וישראל, 9.11).[10] The *Rule of the Congregation* (1QSa) describes the time when God "begets"

---

[4] Xeravits, *King, Priest, Prophet*, 9.
[5] Collins, *Scepter and the Star*, 237.
[6] Collins, *Scepter and the Star*, 18, 21.
[7] Sarah E. Rollens (review of Simon J. Joseph, *The Nonviolent Messiah: Jesus, Q, and the Enochic Tradition*, RBL [June 2015], http://www.bookreviews.org/pdf/9811_10841.pdf [accessed January 3, 2016]) detects an "odd tension" in my study between the diversity of messianic ideas in early Judaism and Q's subversion of "traditional" Davidic expectations ("How is it subversive . . . if its portrait is just another among many understandings of messianism?"), yet fails to recognize that this "odd tension" is part of Q's conceptual universe, reflecting both diversity and royal Davidic ideas within early Judaism.
[8] Collins, *Scepter and the Star*, 52.
[9] Collins, *Scepter and the Star*, 78.
[10] 1QS 9.5b–11 appears to be a later insertion. The Cave 4 texts 4Q258 (4QS^d) and 4Q259 (4QS^e) do not include it, although in the former case the text is fragmentary.

(יו[ל]יד) the messiah (המשיח) "among them" (אתם),[11] confirming that the royal messiah could indeed be regarded as the "son of God" in pre-Christian Judaism (1QSa 2.11–12).[12] This idea seems to be derived from Psalm 2:7, where God declares, "You are my son; today I have begotten you." 1QSa 2.12–21 describes a time when the "messiah of Israel" will appear and extend "his hands toward the bread" (ידיו בלחם, 12.20–21) during what appears to be a kind of eschatological or "messianic" banquet. The *Rule of Blessings* (1QSb 5.20) refers to the "Prince of the Congregation" (נשיא העדה), using language reminiscent of Isaiah 11:1-5. The "Prince" will "renew the covenant of Da[v]id" (ברית דו[י]ד יחדש, 5.20), establish "the kingdom of his people" (מלכות עמו), rule with the "scepter," and "kill the wicked" (24–25).

The Qumran messianic texts tend to typify what many first-century Jews would have expected from a political king or "royal messiah." He will be a great warrior.[13] He will "smite the nations, slay the wicked with the breath of his lips, and restore the Davidic dynasty."[14] In 1QSa 2.11–22, he presides over the community's eschatological banquet. In 1QSb, he is the "Prince of the Congregation" (נשיא העדה). In CD 19.10–11, 1QSb 5.20–29, and 1QM 11.6–13, he executes judgment on those who oppress God's people, subduing the Kittim and the nations. In 1QM 11.9–12 he leads a new exodus. The *Damascus Document* (CD) refers to the arrival of the "anointed one of Aaron and Israel" (משיח אהרן וישראל) "in the age of the visitation" (בקץ הפקדה), when the group's opponents will be

---

[11] John F. Priest, "The Messiah and the Meal in 1QSa," *JBL* 82 (1963): 95–100; H. Neil Richardson, "Some Notes on 1QSa," *JBL* 76 (1957): 108–22; Robert Gordis, "The 'Begotten' Messiah in the Qumran Scrolls," *VT* 7 (1957): 191–94; Philip Sigal, "Further Reflections on the 'Begotten' Messiah," *HAR* 7 (1983): 221–33.

[12] Shemaryahu Talmon, "The Concepts of *Mashiah* and Messianism in Early Judaism," in *The Messiah: Developments in Earliest Judaism and Christianity. The First Princeton Symposium on Judaism and Christian Origins*, ed. J. H. Charlesworth (Minneapolis: Fortress, 1992), 110n73; Frank Moore Cross, *The Ancient Library of Qumran*, 3rd ed. (Minneapolis: Fortress, 1995), 87; Lawrence H. Schiffman, *The Eschatological Community of the Dead Sea Scrolls: A Study of the Rule of the Congregation*, SBLMS 38 (Atlanta: Scholars, 1989), 53–54; Richardson, "Some Notes on 1QSa," 108–22; Joseph Fitzmyer, *The Semitic Background of the New Testament* (Grand Rapids: Eerdmans, 1997), 153n27; John J. Collins, "The Son of God Text," in *From Jesus to John: Essays on Jesus and New Testament Christology*, ed. M. C. De Boer (Sheffield: JSOT, 1993), 78–79; Martin Hengel, *The Son of God* (Philadelphia: Fortress, 1976), 44; Gordis, "'Begotten' Messiah in the Qumran Scrolls," 191–94; Morton Smith, "'God's Begetting the Messiah' in 1QSa," *NTS* 5 (1958–1959): 218–24; Sigal, "Further Reflections on the 'Begotten' Messiah," 221–33. J. T. Milik proposed יוליד ("will bring"), followed by D. Barthélemy, DJD 1:117.

[13] Craig A. Evans, "Qumran's Messiah: How Important Is He?" in *Religion in the Dead Sea Scrolls*, ed. J. J. Collins and R. A. Kugler, SDSSRL (Grand Rapids: Eerdmans, 2000), 146.

[14] Collins, *Scepter and the Star*, 67.

"delivered up to the sword" (ימסרו לחרב) (19.10–11).[15] The Davidic messiah's job description seems fairly consistent.

The Qumran *pesharim* also contain multiple references to an eschatological Davidic figure. The *Pesher on Isaiah* (4Q161) interprets Isaianic passages between Isaiah 10:21 and 11:5 and refers to the "Branch of David" (צמח] דויד) who will appear at the "End of Days" (ב]אח[רית הימים]) to wage war (frgs. 7–10, 18–25).[16] He will receive a "throne of glory" (כ]סא כבוד]), a "crown" (נזר), and will carry a "sword" (חרב). The *pesher* interprets Isaiah 11:3 ("he will not judge by what his eyes see or pass sentence by what his ears hear") to mean that

כאשר יורוהו כן ישפוט ועל פיהם

> according to what they teach him, he will judge, and upon their authority. (4Q161 frgs. 7–10, 24)[17]

The *Eschatological Midrash* (4Q174 and 4Q177), also known as the *Florilegium*, interprets the Psalms and the Nathan oracle (2 Sam 7:11) ("I will be his father and he will be my son") as referring to the "Branch of David" (צמח דויד) who will appear "[in the e]nd of days" (ב]אחרית הימים], 4Q174 1–2 i 11–12). In *A Commentary on Genesis* (4Q252), the "Branch of David" (צמח דויד) is explicitly identified as the "Messiah of Righteousness" (משיח הצדק, 5.3). He has been given "the covenant of royalty of his people, for all everlasting generations" (ברית מלכות עמו עד דורות עולם).[18] 4Q252 5.5 also refers to the "Branch" observing the Torah "with the men of the *Yahad*" (עם אנשי היחד).

The fragment commonly known as the "Pierced Messiah" text, but more properly identified as *Sefer ha-Milhamah* (4Q285), also refers to the "Branch of David" (צמח דויד) and the "Prince of the Congregation" (נשיא העדה), but, contrary to those who interpret the text as referring to the Prince's death,[19] the overwhelming consensus on this text reads the controversial passage in precisely the opposite way: it is the "Prince of the Congregation" who "will kill him" (המיתו, 4Q285 frg. 7, 4), presumably the enemy's leader.[20]

---

[15] See also CD 12.22–13.2; 14.18–19; 19.33–20.1.

[16] The title צמח דויד is fragmentary, but it is also found in 4Q174; 4Q252; and 4Q285.

[17] Florentino García Martínez, *The Dead Sea Scrolls Translated: The Qumran Texts in English*, 2nd ed. (Grand Rapids: Eerdmans, 1996), 186.

[18] García Martínez, *Dead Sea Scrolls Translated*, 215.

[19] Robert Eisenman and Michael O. Wise, *Dead Sea Scrolls Uncovered* (Shaftesbury: Element, 1992), 24–29.

[20] Geza Vermes, "The Oxford Forum for Qumran Research: Seminar on the Rule of War from Cave 4 (4Q285)," *JJS* 43 (1992): 85–90. The line in question (4Q285 frg. 7, 4) has a lacuna prior to צמ]ח העדה נשיא והמיתו [ ]. Xeravits, *King, Priest, Prophet*, 66.

The identification of the royal messiah as the "Branch of David" in 4Q161, 4Q174, 4Q252, 4Q285—a title derived from Isaiah 11:1 ("a branch shall grow")—represents a remarkably consistent portrait of military prowess.[21]

4Q161 (75–50 BCE)	Branch	[צמח] דויד
4Q174 (100–75 BCE)	Branch	צמח דויד
4Q252 (50–20 BCE)	Branch/Messiah	משיח הצדק צמח דויד
4Q285 (75–50 BCE)	Branch/Prince	נשיא העדה צמח דויד

These texts were all composed in Herodian script and can be paleographically dated to the mid-first century BCE. It is reasonable to suppose that this pronounced emphasis on the royal messiah can be attributed in part to the political turbulence following the Roman invasion of Judea. The overthrow of the Hasmonean dynasty following the invasion of 63 BCE would have led to even greater emphasis on the political role of the royal messiah. Yet despite the impressive consistency of this portrait, this collection does not exhaust the full range and variety of the *Yahad*'s eschatological expectations and convictions.

Moreover, our surveys of "Qumran Messianism" tend to reflect disciplinary emphases that privilege "Christian" interests and thus run the risk of emphasizing aspects of eschatological conviction that were not necessarily foregrounded within the daily life of the *Yahad*. Indeed, the current consensus in Qumran Studies is that it was the *Torah*, not "The Messiah," that served as the soteriological center of gravity in the *Yahad*'s self-understanding. According to 1QS 9.11, the *Yahad* was to live by the original laws in which it was first instructed "until the coming of a/the prophet and the messiahs of Aaron and Israel" (עד בוא נביא ומשיחי אהרון וישראל).[22] Those laws were to give "guidance to the sect within the current 'period of wickedness,'"[23] but they would change when the Prophet reinterpreted the Torah.

— ♦ —

The central importance of the Law at Qumran has increasingly been recognized in recent years.[24] This discursive shift in Qumran Studies can be traced back

---

[21] See George J. Brooke, "Kingship and Messianism in the Dead Sea Scrolls," in *King and Messiah in Israel and the Ancient Near East: Proceedings of the Oxford Old Testament Seminar*, ed. J. Day (Sheffield: Sheffield Academic, 1998), 447–54.

[22] Evans, "Qumran's Messiah," 147; Talmon, "Concepts of the *Mashiah*," 112.

[23] Lawrence H. Schiffman, *The Halakhah at Qumran*, SJLA 16 (Leiden: Brill, 1975), 78.

[24] Cf. Lawrence H. Schiffman, "Halakhah and Sectarianism in the Dead Sea Scrolls," in *The Dead Sea Scrolls in their Historical Context*, ed. T. H. Lim et al. (Edinburgh: T&T Clark, 2000), 124. On "halakhah," see John P. Meier, "Is There *Halaka* (the Noun) at Qumran?" *JBL*

to the realization that the *Yahad* appealed to ongoing *revelation* as the source of its distinctive halakhah.[25] Since the publication of 4QMMT, with its concerns regarding Temple law, the calendar, and ritual purity, there has been a growing awareness that legal disagreements played a major role in the *Yahad*'s separation from the Temple and its difference from its contemporaries.[26] This discursive shift has led to a noticeable increase in "Jewish" topics and interests and an attempt to correct what has been perceived as an overemphasis on "crypto-Christian" concerns like "messianic expectations," "monastic" life, and "baptism." There is, of course, always the danger of *over*-correction, but this new emphasis does seem to be leading to a positive rebalancing of a field in which *both* "Jewish" and "Christian" interests can be mutually illuminated.

The *Yahad* believed that they were receiving a renewed revelation of the Law. They did not interpret the Law like other Jews, accepting neither the Pharisaic oral law nor the Sadducean assumption that the Law was fixed. God's revelations were ongoing, and the Law could be renewed through prophetic revelation. The Law was both eternal and subject to change, both hidden and revealed; it needed to be continually reinterpreted and clarified. Accordingly, the Law at Qumran consisted of both "revealed things" (נגלות) and "hidden things" (נסתרות) (CD 3.14; cf. 1QS 5.7–12). The revealed Law was known to all Israel; the hidden Law was the *Yahad*'s esoteric interpretation received through divine inspiration.[27]

The Qumran corpus includes many halakhic texts whose central concerns are priestly law. The *Yahad* used a different calendar from the one currently used

---

122 (2003): 150–55; Philip R. Davies, "Halakhah at Qumran," in *A Tribute to Geza Vermes: Essays on Jewish and Christian Literature and History*, ed. P. R. Davies and R. T. White, JSOTSup 100 (Sheffield: JSOT, 1990), 37–50; Dennis Green, "Halakhah at Qumran? The Use of 'h.l.k' in the Dead Sea Scrolls," *RevQ* 22 (2005): 235–51. On the question of comparison, see Lutz Doering, "Parallels without 'Parallelomania': Methodological Reflections on Comparative Analysis of Halakhah in the Dead Sea Scrolls," in *Rabbinic Perspectives*, ed. S. Fraade, A. Shemesh, and R. A. Clements, STDJ 62 (Leiden: Brill, 2006), 87–112; Aharon Shemesh, *Halakhah in the Making: The Development of Jewish Law from Qumran* (Berkeley: University of California Press, 2009).

[25] Joseph M. Baumgarten, "The Unwritten Law in the Pre-rabbinic Period," in *Studies in Qumran Law*, SJLA 24 (Leiden: Brill, 1977), 29–31; Schiffman, *Halakhah at Qumran*.

[26] J. Strugnell and E. Qimron, eds., *Qumran Cave 4, V, Miqsat Ma'aśe Ha–Torah*, DJD 10 (Oxford: Clarendon, 1994); L. H. Schiffman, "The Place of 4QMMT in the Corpus of Qumran Manuscripts," in *Reading 4QMMT, New Perspectives on Qumran Law and History*, ed. J. Kampen and M. J. Bernstein, SBLSS 2 (Atlanta: Scholars, 1996), 81–98.

[27] Cf. Schiffman, *Halakhah at Qumran*, 48.

in Jerusalem.[28] The publication of the *Temple Scroll* (11QT^a) in 1977,[29] followed by the publication of 4QMMT (*Miqsat Ma'aśe ha-Torah*) in 1994, indicated that halakhic conflicts were a major factor in the *Yaḥad*'s worldview. The Qumran copies of the *Damascus Document* (4Q266–4Q273), published in 1996, only further confirmed this finding.[30] More recently, it has been suggested that Qumran halakhah was "realistic," meaning that it understood the Torah as deriving from the natural order of creation.[31] According to 1QS 9.11, the *Yaḥad* was to live by the laws in which it was first instructed "*until* the coming of a/the prophet and the messiahs of Aaron and Israel" (עד בוא נביא ומשיחי אהרון וישראל). Qumran law was a *temporary* legal code.[32] The laws described in CD apply to observing the Sabbath during the *current* age of wickedness.[33] The messianic age could thus significantly alter how the *Yaḥad* interpreted the Law.

— ♦ —

The *Yaḥad* adapted the concept of "biblical prophecy" into new mediums of mediation, especially inspired "revelatory exegesis" of Scripture.[34] The Scrolls attest to two "nascent models of revelation": the "inspired exegesis of prophetic Scripture

---

[28] See Shemaryahu Talmon, "The Calendar Reckoning of the Sect from the Judaean Desert," in *Aspects of the Dead Sea Scrolls*, ed. C. Rabin and Y. Yadin, ScrHier 4 (Jerusalem: Magnes, 1965 [1958]), 162–99.

[29] Yigael Yadin, *The Temple Scroll*, 3 vols. (Jerusalem: Israel Exploration Society, 1977) (Hebrew); L. H. Schiffman (*Reclaiming the Dead Sea Scrolls: The History of Judaism, the Background of Christianity, the Lost Library of Qumran* [Philadelphia: Jewish Publication Society, 1994], 257–71) holds that the *Temple Scroll* is pre-sectarian. More recently, see idem, *The Courtyards of the House of the Lord: Studies on the Temple Scroll*, STDJ 75 (Leiden: Brill, 2008), 10–11.

[30] Joseph M. Baumgarten, *Qumran Cave 4.XIII: The Damascus Document (4Q266–273)*, DJD 18 (Oxford: Clarendon, 1996); idem et al., eds., *Qumran Cave 4.XXV: Halakhic Texts*, DJD 35 (Oxford: Clarendon, 1999).

[31] Daniel R. Schwartz, "Law and Truth: On Qumran-Sadducean and Rabbinic Views of the Law," in *The Dead Sea Scrolls: Forty Years of Research*, ed. D. Dimant and U. Rappaport, STDJ 10 (Leiden: Brill, 1992), 229–40; idem, "Arguments *a minore ad majore* (*qal waḥomer*)—Sadducean Realism," *Massekhet* 5 (2006), 145–56 (Hebrew).

[32] Nils Alstrup Dahl, "Eschatology and History in the Light of the Dead Sea Scrolls," in *The Future of Our Religious Past: Essays in Honour of Rudolf Bultmann*, ed. J. M. Robinson, trans. C. E. Carlston and R. P. Scharlemann (London: SCM Press, 1971), 14; Schiffman, *Halakhah at Qumran*, 78.

[33] Schiffman, *Halakhah at Qumran*, 78.

[34] Alex P. Jassen, *Mediating the Divine: Prophecy and Revelation in the Dead Sea Scrolls and Second Temple Judaism*, STDJ 68 (Leiden: Brill, 2007); George J. Brooke, "Prophecy and Prophets in the Dead Sea Scrolls: Looking Backwards and Forwards," in *Prophets, Prophecy, and Prophetic Texts in Second Temple Judaism*, ed. M. H. Floyd and R. D. Haak, LHB/OTS 427 (New York: T&T Clark, 2006), 151–65.

(revelatory exegesis) and the cultivation of divine wisdom (sapiential revelation)."[35] The biblical prophets (נביאים) were understood to have received and transmitted "hidden secrets concerning the end time" and "foretold events concerning the sectarians themselves."[36] The ancient prophets were also believed to have mediated divine law.[37] In the Hebrew Bible, "prophets commonly exhort Israel to observe the covenantal laws properly. At the same time, prophets sometimes appear as independent mediators of revealed law, whereby they either transmit new law or reinterpret older law."[38] This relatively "non-juridical role ... is dramatically transformed" in the Scrolls so that the ancient prophets "become active mediators of divinely revealed law."[39]

The *Rule of the Community*'s imperative is that its members seek to do what is good and right "as he commanded *through* Moses and *through* all his servants the prophets" (כאשר צוה ביד מושה וביד כול עבדיו הנבאים, 1QS 1.2–3), thereby directly associating Moses—*and* the prophets—as "mediators" of divine will. Moreover, the *Rule of the Community* also clarifies how the *Yahad* envisioned the prophets' role in the "revelation" of Law, since the Torah was "commanded through Moses to do, according to everything which has been revealed time to time, *and according to that which the prophets have revealed by his holy spirit*" (ובאשר גלו הנבאים ברוח קודשו, 1QS 8.15–16). The Torah study of the *Yahad*—the hidden meaning of Isaiah's call to "prepare the way of the Lord" (פנו דרך יהוה, Isa 40:3)—links Mosaic Torah with prophetic revelation. 1QS 1.1–3 even seems to envision Moses and the prophets sharing the role of "transmitters of the Torah" (52), whereas 1QS 8.15–16 envisions that being "the exclusive domain of Moses," with the prophets "entrusted with a secondary task." In this second passage, the prophets were "to illuminate the performance" of the Torah and "provide instruction on how to carry out this directive properly" (52). Nonetheless, the "revelatory experience at Sinai ... was incomplete with respect to the future legislative needs of Israel" and led to "the introduction of legislation that stands outside of the immediate framework of Mosaic law."[40]

---

[35] Jassen, *Mediating the Divine*, 20.

[36] Jassen, *Mediating the Divine*, 29; William H. Brownlee, "Biblical Interpretation among the Sectaries of the Dead Sea Scrolls," *BA* 14 (1951): 54–76, here 60.

[37] Jassen, *Mediating the Divine*, 19, 37–63.

[38] Jassen, *Mediating the Divine*, 40.

[39] Jassen, *Mediating the Divine*, 40–41; citing 1QS 1.1–3; 8.14–16; 4Q166 2.1–6 (*Pesher Hosea*); CD 5.21–6.1; 4Q390 2 i 4–5 (Apocryphon of Jeremiah); 4Q375 1 i 1–2 (Apocryphon of Moses); 4Q381 69 1–5. For Jassen, 1QS 8.15–16, 4Q381 69, and 4Q390 1 present the prophets as "amplifying Mosaic law and actively engaged in the formation of non-Mosaic law" (61).

[40] Jassen, *Mediating the Divine*, 52, 61. See also Hindy Najman, *Seconding Sinai: The Development of Mosaic Discourse in Second Temple Judaism*, JSJSup 77 (Leiden: Brill, 2004).

Envisioning the prophetic role as mediator of divine law (1QS 1.2–3; 8.14–16; 4QpHosa [4Q166] 2.1–6), the *Yaḥad* viewed their legal interpretation as prophetic revelation, a continuation of the revelations received and "mediated" by the prophets.[41] The holy spirit was the mediating agent of divine knowledge, making the prophets "anointed ones."[42] The identification of the prophet as "anointed" is presupposed in Isaiah 61:1a, where the speaker announces that

> the spirit (רוח) of the Lord God is upon me,
> because the Lord has anointed (משח) me.

This passage envisions the descent of the spirit onto the prophet. This "anointing" symbolizes "the idea of full and permanent authorization to carry out the prophet's God-given assignment."[43] Indeed, the Targum of Isaiah explicitly identifies the "spirit" as a "spirit of prophecy."[44]

While the Hebrew Bible rarely refers to prophets as "anointed" (1 Kgs 19:16; Isa 61:1; Ps 105:15; cf. 1 Chr 16:22), the Qumran corpus attests to a significant increase in identifying prophets as "anointed ones," reflecting "a widening belief in the important role played by the holy spirit in the prophetic experience."[45] Isaiah 61 seems to have been the fountainhead of this development, as it was for early Jewish speculation on the eschatological Jubilee and for early Christian reflection on the ministry and person of Jesus.

One example of this development at Qumran can be found in 11QMelchizedek, a *pesher* drawing from Leviticus, Deuteronomy, Isaiah, and the Psalms, and announcing the arrival of an eschatological Jubilee, the "day of [peace]" (יו[ם ה]שלום).[46] Melchizedek appears as a heavenly or (arch)angelic figure

---

[41] Jassen, *Mediating the Divine*, 22–23.

[42] Jassen (*Mediating the Divine*, 85) notes that the Scrolls "reflect a widening use of 'anointed' as a prophetic title," citing nine texts: 1Q30 1 2; CD 2.12, 6.1 (cf. 4Q267 2 6; 6Q15 3 4); 1QM 11.7–8; 4Q270 2 ii 14; 4Q287 10 13; 4Q377 2 ii 5; 4Q521 2 ii + 4 I; [8 9]; 11Q13 2.18.

[43] Joseph Blenkinsopp, *Isaiah 56–66*, AB 19B (Garden City, N.Y.: Doubleday, 2003), 223.

[44] Bruce D. Chilton, *The Isaiah Targum: Introduction, Translation, Apparatus, and Notes* (Wilmington: Michael Glazier, 1987), 118.

[45] Jassen, *Mediating the Divine*, 96; citing John R. Levison, *The Spirit in First-Century Judaism*, AGJU 29 (Leiden: Brill, 1997).

[46] For bibliography, see Adam S. van der Woude, "Melchisedek als himmlische Erlösergestalt in den neugefundenen eschatologischen Midraschim aus Qumran Höhle XI," *Oudtestamentische Studien* 14 (1965): 354–73; idem, "11QMelchizedek and the New Testament," *NTS* 12 (1966): 301–26; Joseph A. Fitzmyer, "Further Light on Melchizedek from Qumran Cave 11," *JBL* 86 (1967): 25–41; David Flusser, "Melchizedek and the Son of Man," *Christian News from Israel* 17 (1966): 23–29; Yigael Yadin, "A Note on Melchizedek and Qumran," *IEJ* 15 (1965): 152–54; Merrill P. Miller, "The Function of Isa 61:1–2 in

inaugurating the liberation of the "captives." The text also conflates Isaiah 52:7 and Isaiah 61:1-2 in its depiction of a "messenger . . . anointed of the spirit" (המבשר הואה משיח הרוח) who will announce "salvation" (ישועה).⁴⁷

> Isa 52:7: How beautiful upon the mountains
> are the feet of the messenger (מבשר) who announces peace (שלום/εἰρήνης),
> who brings good news (εὐαγγελιζομένου),
> who announces salvation (ישועה/σωτηρίαν),
> who says to Zion, "Your God reigns" (מלך אלהיך/βασιλεύσει σου ὁ Θεός).
>
> Isa 61:1b: The LORD has anointed me (משח/ἔχρισέ) to proclaim
> good news to the poor (לבשר ענוים/εὐαγγελίσασθαι πτωχοῖς).⁴⁸

While Isaiah 61:1 refers to one "anointed" by the "spirit" of God, Isaiah 52:7 envisions a coming age of peace and salvation to be inaugurated by a divinely authorized (prophetic) "herald" or "messenger."⁴⁹ 11QMelchizedek interprets Isaiah 52:7, which speaks of a prophetic "messenger" (מבשר) whose feet are on the mountains, by interpreting the "mountains" (הרים) as the "prophets" (הנביאים) and the "messenger" as "the anointed of the spirit" (משיח הרוח]).⁵⁰ In 11QMelchizedek, Melchizedek is said "to atone" (לכפר, 2.7-8), presumably fulfilling the role of a heavenly high priest on the Day of Atonement (*Yom Kippur*). This eschatological atonement will coincide with the tenth Jubilee:

> And the "D[ay of Aton]ement" i[s] the e[nd] of the tenth [ju]bilee,
> to atone on that for all the sons [of light and] men of the lot of Mel[chi]zedek.

In this text, however, the "year of the LORD's favor" (Isa 61:2) is now "the time of *Melchizedek's* year of favor" (הואה הקץ לשנת הרצון למלכי צדק, 2.9). Melchizedek

---

11QMelchizedek," *JBL* 88, no. 4 (1969): 467–69; Daniel F. Miner, "A Suggested Reading for 11QMelchizedek 17," *JSJ* 2 (1971): 144–48; J. T. Milik, "Milkî-Sedeq et Milkî-Reš' dans les anciens écrits juifs et chrétiens," *JJS* 23 (1972): 95–112, 124–26; James A. Sanders, "The Old Testament in 11QMelchizedek," *Janes* 5 (1973): 373–82; Émile Puech, "Notes sur le manuscrit de XIMelkîsédeq," *RevQ* 12 (1987): 483–513.

⁴⁷ 11QMelch 2.18–19. Bruce D. Chilton and Craig A. Evans, "Jesus and Israel's Scriptures," in *Studying the Historical Jesus: Evaluations of the State of Current Research*, ed. B. Chilton and C. Evans, NTTS 19 (Leiden: Brill, 1994), 283–335, here 325.

⁴⁸ Cf. Luke 4; Isa 40:9; 52:7. Isaiah 61 is generally dated to ca. 530 BCE.

⁴⁹ Peter Stuhlmacher, "The Theme: The Gospel and the Gospels," in *The Gospel and the Gospels*, ed. P. Stuhlmacher, trans. J. Vriend (Grand Rapids: Eerdmans, 1991), 1–25; William Horbury, "'Gospel' in Herodian Judaea," in *The Written Gospel*, ed. M. Bockmuehl and D. Hagner (Cambridge: Cambridge University Press, 2005), 7–30; Hubert Frankemölle, "Jesus als deuterojesajanische Freudenbote? Zur Rezeption von Jes 52,7 und 61,1 im Neuen Testament, durch Jesus und in den Targumim," in *Vom Christentum zu Jesus. Festschrift für Joachim Gnilka*, ed. Hubert Frankemölle (Freiberg: Herder, 1989), 34–67.

⁵⁰ Xeravits, *King, Priest, Prophet*, 182.

also seems to be identified with the אלוהים of Psalm 82:1. He will precipitate "the vengeance of God's (אל) judgment" (2.13).[51] Here, Melchizedek seems to fulfill the functions of archangel Michael while the "herald" of Isaiah 52:7 is the one "anointed with the spirit" (משיח הרוח). The prophet is *anointed*.[52] 11QMelchizedek 2.15–20 interprets Isaiah 52:7 and 61:1-3, identifying the "mountains" as the "prophets" and the "messenger" as the "anointed of the spirit."

The *Yahad* believed that they were living in the end time and were soon to be attended by the arrival of the Eschatological Prophet. Accordingly, the *Yahad* was to live by the original laws or "precepts" in which it was first instructed

עד בוא נביא ומשיחי אהרון וישראל

until the coming of a prophet and the messiahs of Aaron and Israel. (1QS 9.11)

The Prophet, however, is "a shadowy figure" in the Dead Sea Scrolls and early Judaism.[53] In the book of Deuteronomy (18:18-19), God assures Israel:

> I will raise up for them a Prophet like you from among their brethren.
> I will put my words into his mouth and he shall tell them all
> that I command him. And I will require a reckoning of whoever
> will not listen to the words which the Prophet shall speak in my name.[54]

While the extant literature on the role of the Eschatological Prophet is limited,[55] 1QS, 4Q175, and 11QMelchizedek all seem to expect "the same figure,"[56] a kind

---

[51] Fitzmyer, "Further Light," 253.

[52] Jassen, *Mediating the Divine*, 93. See also Yadin, "A Note," 153; M. de Jonge and A. S. van der Woude, "11QMelchizedek and the New Testament," *NTS* 12 (1965): 301–26; Xeravits, *King, Priest, Prophet*, 74, 182–83. F. García Martínez ("Two Messianic Figures in the Qumran Texts," in *Qumranica Minora II: Thematic Studies on the Dead Sea Scrolls*, ed. E. J. C. Tigchelaar, STDJ 64 [Leiden: Brill, 2006], 13–32, esp. 24–32) notes that the Prophet is "not termed *anointed*" in 1QS 9.11 (25), but other texts do "enable us to determine that this expected prophet was at times considered a messianic figure" (26). 11QMelchizedek 2.18 identifies the messenger of Isa 52:7 as "anointed of the spirit," a reference "to *a* prophet, an anointed one, or messiah, who is expected at the time of Melchizedek" (25). 4QTestimonia (4Q175), 11QMelchizedek, and 1QS 9.11 make it seem "justifiable to consider this Prophet . . . as a true messianic figure" (26).

[53] Collins, *Scepter and the Star*, 128.

[54] Geza Vermes, *The Complete Dead Sea Scrolls* (New York: Penguin, 1997), 495.

[55] Jassen (*Mediating the Divine*, 155) discusses the "eschatological prophet," looking at Malachi; Ben Sira; 1 Macc 4:42-46; 14:41; 4Q521; 4Q558; 1QS 9.11; 4QTestimonia (4Q175); and 11QMelchizedek.

[56] Jassen, *Mediating the Divine*, 185.

of Moses *redivivus*, a future Teacher of Righteousness, and/or "revealer" of Torah. The Prophet's role will be "transforming law at the end of days."[57] It follows, therefore, that the *Yahad*'s halakhah was a *temporary* legal code expected to change during the messianic age.[58] Here, however, we must make a critical distinction between the historical Teacher of Righteousness' possible identification as *a* prophet and *the* future "Eschatological Prophet."

A number of scholars have suggested that the historical Teacher of Righteousness *was* the "Prophet" foretold by Moses and expected by the *Yahad*.[59] If the historical Teacher of Righteousness was viewed by the sect not only as *a* prophet but as "a prophet like Moses," then the *Yahad* might have "believed that the prophecy had been fulfilled in the past" and that their Teacher was "the Prophet anticipated in 1QS 9:11." In other words, "for the Qumran Essenes the *Teacher of Righteousness* was this expected last prophet."[60] There is some justification for this view. In 1QpHab, we are told that the historical Teacher received words "from the mouth of God" (2.2b–3a) and that the true meaning of the prophets regarding the end time was revealed to him (1QpHab 2.6b–10a) for "God made known to him all the mysteries of the words of his servants the prophets" (7.4). If the Teacher understood the true, but hidden, meaning of the prophets, then he too may have been regarded as *a* prophet. While there may be good reason to suspect that the historical Teacher displayed "prophet qualities" and may have achieved a kind of "quasi-prophetic status" in the community,[61] the historical Teacher is *never* explicitly identified as *the* "Eschatological Prophet" expected by the *Yahad*. The identification of the historical Teacher with the Eschatological Prophet anticipated in 1QS 9.11 would require that any passage

---

[57] Jassen, *Mediating the Divine*, 175, based on 4QTestimonia.

[58] Schiffman, *Halakhah at Qumran*, 78.

[59] Vermes, *Complete Dead Sea Scrolls*, 87. See also N. Wieder, "The 'Law Interpreter' of the Sect of the Dead Sea Scrolls: The Second Moses," *JJS* 4 (1953): 158–75; A. S. van der Woude, *Die messianischen Vorstellungen der Gemeinde von Qumran* (Assen: Van Gorcum, 1957), 186.

[60] Howard M. Teeple, *The Mosaic Eschatological Prophet* (Philadelphia: Society of Biblical Literature, 1957), 54–56. So also Frederick M. Strickert, "Damascus Document VII, 10–20 and Qumran Messianic Expectation," *RevQ* 47 (1986): 344; Kurt Schubert, *The Dead Sea Community: Its Origins and Teachings*, trans. J. W. Doberstein (Westport, Conn.: Greenwood, 1959), 114. W. H. Brownlee, "John the Baptist in the New Light of Ancient Scrolls," in *The Scrolls and the New Testament*, ed. K. Stendahl (New York: Harper, 1957), 44; H. Ringgren, *The Faith of Qumran: Theology of the Dead Sea Scrolls*, trans. E. T. Sander (New York: Crossroad, 1995), 198; E. Puech, "Messianism, Resurrection, and Eschatology at Qumran and in the New Testament," in *The Community of the Renewed Covenant: The Notre Dame Symposium on the Dead Sea Scrolls*, ed. E. Ulrich and J. VanderKam (Notre Dame, Ind.: University of Notre Dame Press, 1994), 240–41.

[61] D. Petersen, *Late Israelite Prophecy*, SBLMS 23 (Missoula, Mont.: Scholars, 1977), 101–2.

referring to the *future* arrival of the Prophet *predate* the historical Teacher's actual arrival.[62] That, however, cannot be established, since 1QS 9.11 may belong to a later period in the community's history. In other words, the *Yahad* seems to have expected "a more definitive Teacher to come" after the historical Teacher of Righteousness.[63] According to the *Damascus Document*—and 1QS 9.11—the Eschatological Prophet will be the "one who *will* teach righteousness at the end of days" (יורה צדק באחרית הימים, CD 6.11).[64] The Prophet will "continue the mission" of the historical Teacher of Righteousness.[65]

The Eschatological Prophet is sometimes identified with Elijah or an Elijah-like figure. Two passages in Malachi would seem to suggest this identification:

Mal 3:1: "See, I am sending my messenger to prepare the way before me."

Mal 4:5: "Lo, I will send you the prophet Elijah before the great and terrible day of the Lord comes."

The first book of Maccabees looks forward to a future time when "a trustworthy prophet should arise" (1 Macc 14:41). The New Testament suggests that some Jews believed that Elijah would return before the messiah arrived. It is not clear, however, whether the New Testament reflects early Jewish belief or Christian innovation.[66] The appearance of Elijah as the forerunner of the messiah was later developed in rabbinic Judaism, but it is not widely attested in first-century Judaism.[67] It seems more likely that the Eschatological Prophet expected by the *Yahad* should be seen as "a prophet 'like Moses,' a Moses *redivivus*."[68] This conclusion is supported by the fact that 4Q377, an apparently nonsectarian text from Qumran, identifies Moses as an "anointed one" (משיח) and a "messenger" (מבש[ר]), titles found in 11QMelchizedek to denote the Eschatological ("Anointed") Prophet.[69]

---

[62] Jassen, *Mediating the Divine*, 189: "The text of 1QS 9:11, however, possibly dates, on both a paleographic and redactional basis, to a later period in the sect's history."

[63] Collins, *Scepter and the Star*, 128.

[64] Jassen, *Mediating the Divine*, 192–93.

[65] Jassen, *Mediating the Divine*, 188.

[66] On Elijah's appearance before the messiah as a Christian innovation, see Morris M. Faierstein, "Why Do the Scribes Say that Elijah Must Come First?" *JBL* 100 (1981): 75–86; Joseph A. Fitzmyer, "More about Elijah Coming First," *JBL* 104 (1985): 295–96. Cf. Dale C. Allison, "Elijah Must Come First," *JBL* 103 (1984): 256–58. Mark 9:11 affirms that John was Elijah, but John's Gospel has the Baptist *deny* that he is "Elijah" or "the prophet" (John 1:19-21).

[67] Collins, *Scepter and the Star*, 130. One fragment from Cave 4 reads, "therefore I will send Elijah be[fore . . .]" (4Q558), but "the context is unclear."

[68] Jassen, *Mediating the Divine*, 188; citing Xeravits (*King, Priest, Prophet*, 183), who notes that 4Q377 (4QApocryphal Pentateuch B) uses both מבשר and משיח to describe Moses (2 ii 5, 11), which "suggests that the anointed prophetic herald of 11QMelchizedek is a new Moses."

[69] Xeravits, *King, Priest, Prophet*, 126, 177, 182–83.

This identification of Moses as "his anointed one" (משה משיחו), "man of God" (איש האלוהים), and "like an angel" (כמלאך) (4Q377 frg. 2 ii 5, 9, 11) confirms Moses' status as an *"anointed* prophet" and suggests that the Eschatological Prophet will be similarly "anointed." The *Yahad* associated Moses in parallelism to the biblical prophets.[70] There is no question that the *Yahad* anticipated the arrival of a "Prophet-like Moses" (4Q175; cf. Deut 18:15). This future Prophet is not the return of "Elijah" but a prophet "whose task will be to resume the work of Moses as authoritative teacher of the Law."[71] And since the *Yahad* regarded the *biblical* prophets as "anointed ones," so too would the Eschatological Prophet also be "anointed."[72]

Jesus and 4Q521

Since its publication in 1992, the Dead Sea Scroll fragment 4Q521 has generated a significant amount of discussion, providing scholars of early Judaism and Christian origins with a remarkable description of what God would do when "his messiah" arrived.[73] Paleographically dated to the first quarter of the first century BCE,[74] 4Q521 is a copy, not an autograph, with its original composition dated to the second half of the second century BCE (c. 150–100 BCE).[75] The genre of the text has been identified as an eschatological psalm.[76] Due to the fragmentary nature of the text, it is difficult to determine its provenance. The original editor,

---

[70] See, e.g., 4QMMT (4Q397 fr. 14–21, 10) (בספר מושה [ו]בספר[י הנ[ביאים); cf. 1QS 1.3; CD 4.21–5.1.

[71] Wieder, "'Law-Interpreter' of the Sect of the Dead Sea Scrolls," 170–71.

[72] Schiffman, *Reclaiming the Dead Sea Scrolls*, 322; Florentino García Martínez, "Messianic Hopes in the Qumran Writings," in *The People of the Dead Sea Scrolls*, ed. F. García Martínez and J. Trebolle Barrera (Leiden: Brill, 1995), 186.

[73] Fitzmyer, *Dead Sea Scrolls and Christian Origins*, 37; Émile Puech, "Une Apocalypse Messianique (4Q521)," *RevQ* 15 (1992): 475–519; idem, *Qumran Grotte 4 XVIII: Textes Hebreux (4Q521–4Q528, 4Q576–4Q579)*, DJD 25 (Oxford: Clarendon, 1998), 1–38; Robert Eisenman, "A Messianic Vision," *BAR* 17, no. 6 (1991): 65; James D. Tabor and Michael O. Wise, "4Q521 'On Resurrection' and the Synoptic Gospel Tradition: A Preliminary Study," in *Qumran Questions*, ed. J. H. Charlesworth (Sheffield: Sheffield Academic, 1995), 151–63; Geza Vermes, "Qumran Forum Miscellanea I," *JJS* 43 (1992): 299–305; Schiffman, *Reclaiming the Dead Sea Scrolls*, 347–50; John J. Collins, "The Works of the Messiah," *DSD* 1 (1994): 98–112.

[74] See Puech, *Qumran Grotte 4 XVIII*, 5.

[75] Émile Puech, "Some Remarks on 4Q246 and 4Q521 and Qumran Messianism," in *The Provo International Conference on the Dead Sea Scrolls: Technological Innovations, New Texts, and Reformulated Issues*, ed. D. W. Parry and E. Ulrich, STDJ 30 (Leiden: Brill, 1999), 552.

[76] Karl Wilhelm Niebuhr, "4Q521, 2 II—Ein eschatologischer Psalm," in *Mogilany 1995: Papers on the Dead Sea Scrolls Offered in Memory of Aleksy Klawek*, ed. Z. J. Kapera (Krakow: Enigma, 1996), 151–68.

Émile Puech, argued that 4Q521 is a sectarian text.[77] There are a number of indications that 4Q521 may have originated within the *Yaḥad*. First, the use of the terms צדיקים, חסידים, and ענוים is noteworthy in their implicit relationship to the theory that the Qumran Essenes had Hasidean and Zadokite origins and referred to themselves as "the Poor."[78] References to the חסידים are also striking, considering that the word "Essene" can be etymologically derived from the Aramaic חסא ("holy"). Second, the word לוא on line 2, with its additional *waw*, is a distinctive feature characteristic of Qumran orthography.[79] Its presence here, as well as on line 10, confirms that 4Q521 is at least a Qumran *copy* of a text. In addition, the presence of a scribal correction on line 11 also indicates that this text is a copy produced at Qumran. Third, 4Q521 was discovered in Cave 4 and is otherwise unknown in early Jewish literature, which also supports a Qumranic/Essenic provenance. Fourth, 4Q521 envisions the messianic age as involving the *healing* of the wounded, the sick, the bent, the lame, and the blind. 1QS 4.6 also describes the "visitation" as being an age of *healing*. These factors (the references to the "poor," "righteous," and "pious"; the orthographic features; the text's presence in the Qumran library; and its focus on eschatological healing) are consistent with Qumran compositions. None of these factors, however, are decisive or compel a sectarian identification of this fragmentary text.

Some scholars have argued that 4Q521 is not a "sectarian" text at all, citing the absence of any explicit "sectarian" terminology.[80] This position is consistent with the prevailing methodological orientation in Qumran Studies: that previously unknown texts are not necessarily sectarian documents. Sectarian texts are characterized by cosmic dualism, predestination, and the equation of evil and impurity (1QS 3.13–4.26), with 1QS, 1QSa, 1QSb, 1QH, 1QM, 4Q400–407, 1QpHab, and 4QpNah being regarded as representative of sectarian texts.[81]

---

[77] Puech, *Qumran Grotte 4 XVIII*, 25:36–38. Evans, "Qumran's Messiah," 135–49, esp. 137n17; Tabor and Wise, "4Q521 'On Resurrection,'" 162; James H. Charlesworth, "Have the Dead Sea Scrolls Revolutionized Our Understanding of the New Testament?" in *The Dead Sea Scrolls—Fifty Years after Their Discovery: Proceedings of the Jerusalem Congress, July 20–25, 1997*, ed. L. H. Schiffman, E. Tov, and J. C. VanderKam (Jerusalem: Israel Exploration Society, 2000), 129. George J. Brooke ("The Pre-sectarian Jesus," in *Echoes from the Caves: Qumran and the New Testament*, ed. F. García Martínez, STDJ 85 [Leiden: Brill, 2009], 46) identifies it as a "pre-sectarian" or "quasi-sectarian" text.

[78] E.g., 4Q171 2.11; 3.10; 1QHab 12.3; 12.6; 12.10.

[79] Emanuel Tov, "The Orthography and Language of the Hebrew Scrolls Found at Qumran and the Origins of These Scrolls," *Textus* 13 (1986): 31.

[80] Vermes, "Qumran Forum Miscellanea I," 303–4; Schiffman, *Reclaiming the Dead Sea Scrolls*, 347; Roland Bergmeier, "Beobachtungen zu 4Q521 f2, II, 1–13," *ZDMG* 145 (1995): 44–45.

[81] Gabriele Boccaccini, *Beyond the Essene Hypothesis: The Parting of the Ways between Qumran and Enochic Judaism* (Grand Rapids: Eerdmans, 1998), 59.

4Q521 does not refer to the *Yahad* or to "sectarian" rules. Yet this is to be expected of a work in this literary *genre*. Moreover, the text is clearly a copy of an unknown work, which limits its known circulation to *Qumran*. At the very least, 4Q521 is *compatible* with Qumran ideology and eschatology.

The largest and most significant fragment (2 ii) describes how:

כי השמים והארץ ישמעו למשיחו
וכל אשר בם לוא יסוג ממצוות קדושים
כי אדני חסידים יבקר וצדיקים בשם יקרא
ועל ענוים רוחו תרחף ואמונים יחליף בכחו
כי יכבד את חסידים על כסא מלכות עד
מתיר אסורים פוקח עורים זוקף כפופים
ונכבדות שלוא היו יעשה אדני כאשר דבר
כי ירפא חללים ומתים יחיה ענוים יבשר

1. The heavens and the earth will listen to his anointed/messiah
2. and all that is in them will not turn away from the commandments of the holy ones...
5. For the Lord will visit the pious and call the righteous by name
6. And upon the poor his spirit will hover and the faithful he will renew with his force
7. He will honor the pious on a throne of an eternal kingdom,
8. liberating the captives, giving sight to the blind, straightening the bent...
11. And glorious deeds that never were the Lord will perform as he said
12. For he will heal the wounded, revive the dead, and proclaim good news to the poor. (4Q521 2 ii 1–2, 5–8, 11–12)

There is no consensus on the identity, number, or type of "messianic" figure(s) present in 4Q521. Some scholars have explored the possibility that משיחו can be read as a defective plural paralleling the reference to the "holy ones" (קדושים) in the next line.[82] The text could therefore be understood as related to other Qumran references to prophets as "anointed ones," especially since we know that the *Yahad* regarded the prophets as "anointed ones." Yet such references are usually in the plural, not the singular.[83] It would seem then that משיחו is paral-

---

[82] Michael Becker, "4Q521 und die Gesalbten," *RevQ* 18 (1997): 73–96, esp. 74–78; H. Stegemann, *The Library of Qumran: On the Essenes, Qumran, John the Baptist, and Jesus* (Grand Rapids: Eerdmans, 1998), 206; idem, *Die Essener, Qumran, Johannes der Täufer und Jesus: Ein Sachbuch* (Freiburg: Herder, 1993), 49; Niebuhr, "4Q521, 2 II," 153; idem, "Die Werke des eschatologischen Freudenboten (4Q521 und die Jesusüberlieferung)," in *The Scriptures in the Gospels*, ed. C. M. Tuckett, BETL 131 (Leuven: Leuven University Press, 1997), 638.

[83] 4Q521 fr. 8 has a reference to "all her anointed ones" (ובל משיחיה), which may refer to "prophets" in the plural, as in CD 2.12; 6.1; 1QM 11.7.

leled or accompanied by "holy ones," which are typically understood as angels.[84] Although 4Q521 8.9 does contain an instance of the plural form with a feminine suffix (וכל משיחיה),[85] this plural form has a feminine pronominal suffix, unlike the masculine suffix of למשיחו.[86] Moreover, the plural משיחיה in fragment 8, line 9, is far from column 2, II, and it is found in an entirely different literary context. The general consensus, therefore, reads משיחו as a singular referent.[87]

If the "messianic" figure in 4Q521 is arguably singular, there is still considerable debate on what *kind* of "messiah" is being described. One interpretation identifies the figure as a royal messiah.[88] The fact that the figure seems to be invested with a high degree of authority, in that both "heaven and earth" are said to listen to him or obey him, seems reminiscent of royalty.[89] The Psalms of Solomon, for example, describe "his words ... as the words of holy ones in the midst of sanctified peoples" (17:43).[90] Some scholars have also considered the possibility of the figure being a priestly messiah, but this proposal has not been well received.[91] A stronger case has been made for reading the figure as a "prophetic messiah."[92] Since the fragment does not contain a "clear reference ... to a royal figure,"[93] and the *Yahad* regarded prophets as "anointed,"[94] there is nothing a priori

---

[84] John J. Collins, "Jesus, Messianism and the Dead Sea Scrolls," in *Qumran Messianism: Studies in the Messianic Expectations in the Dead Sea Scrolls*, ed. J. H. Charlesworth, H. Lichtenberger, and G. S. Oegema (Tübingen: Mohr Siebeck, 1998), 115.

[85] Becker, "4Q521," 89n76.

[86] Lidija Novakovic, "4Q521: The Works of the Messiah or the Signs of the Messianic Time?" in *Qumran Studies: New Approaches, New Questions*, ed. M. T. Davis and B. A. Strawn (Grand Rapids: Eerdmans, 2007), 211n11.

[87] Bergmeier, "Beobachtungen," 44–45; Novakovic, "4Q521," 208–31, esp. 212; Collins, "Works of the Messiah," 98–112.

[88] García Martínez ("Messianic Hopes," 169) argues that the word "scepter" appears in fr. 2 3.6; Puech, "Une apocalypse messianique," 498–99; idem, DJD 25:18–19. This reference to "scepter" in 4Q521, however, while arguably "messianic" in Num 24:15-17 (and CD MS A 7.19–20), is uncertain. Cf. F. García Martínez, "Messianische Erwartungen in den Qumranschriften," in *Der Messias*, vol. 8 of *Jahrbuch für Biblische Theologie* (Neukirchen-Vluyn: Neukirchener, 1993), 183; Collins, "Works of the Messiah," 103.

[89] Puech, DJD 25:37.

[90] Stephen Hultgren, "4Q521, the Second Benediction of the Tefilla, the Hasidim, and the Development of Royal Messianism," *RevQ* 23 (2008): 313–40, 337; idem, "4Q521 and Luke's *Magnificat* and *Benedictus*," in *Echoes from the Caves: Qumran and the New Testament*, ed. F. García Martínez, STDJ 85 (Leiden: Brill, 2009), 119–32. Hultgren affirms the Davidic reading.

[91] Niebuhr, "4Q521, 2 II," 151–68; idem, "Die Werke des eschatologischen Freudenboten," 636–46. See also Puech, "Some Remarks on 4Q246 and 4Q521," 551–58.

[92] Collins, "Works of the Messiah," 98–99; idem, "Jesus, Messianism and the Dead Sea Scrolls," 100–120; idem, *Scepter and the Star*, 117–22.

[93] Collins, "Works of the Messiah," 103.

[94] E.g., CD MS A 2.12, 6.1; 1QM 11.7.

incompatible about a prophet being "anointed." Indeed, the speaker in Isaiah 61 explicitly claims to be "anointed" (משיח) and speaks on God's behalf. It is this "anointing" that allows the prophet-messenger to proclaim the "good news."[95] Similarly, the "anointed one" of 4Q521 seems to be envisioned as one who will preach "good news" to the poor.[96] The similarities between the proclamation of "good news" to the poor (ענוים יבשר) mentioned in 4Q521 1 ii 12 and the "herald" or "messenger . . . anointed of the spir[it]" (המבשר הואה משיח הרוח) referred to in 11QMelchezedek ii 18 further support this thesis.[97] The proclamation of "good news" in 4Q521 does not explicitly refer to a "herald," since it is the *Lord* who is identified as the agent of the eschatological blessings,[98] but it is highly likely that the Lord will use an agent.[99] It is furthermore likely that the implicit "herald" of "good news" is the "anointed" (משיחו) of line 1.[100]

If the "anointed one" of 4Q521 is God's agent, it is remarkable that one of the blessings said to be performed is the raising of the dead, since that is not usually part of the job description of the *royal* messiah.[101] Yet that *is* an act attributed to the prophet Elijah.[102] The "anointed" figure of 4Q521 might best be understood as "a prophet like Elijah."[103] Further support for this reading may be found in

---

[95] Collins, *Scepter and the Star*, 133.

[96] Collins, "Jesus, Messianism and the Dead Sea Scrolls," 118–19.

[97] Chilton and Evans ("Jesus and Israel's Scriptures," 325) note, "We are told that the 'Anointed of the Spirit' of Isa 61:1 is the herald of glad tidings of Isa 52:7 (11QMelch 2.18). He will proclaim liberty for them [ויקרא להמה דרר]" and "make atonement for their sins" (2.6–8). It will be the "acceptable year" (שנת הרצון, 2.9). The "tenor" of 4Q521 "coheres with that of 11QMelchizedek: A messianic figure, in fulfillment of Isa 61:1-2 and other related prophetic texts, is anticipated who will appear in the 'acceptable' time, vindicate the righteous of Israel, and vanquish Israel's enemies." The day of judgment is said to be the day of which Isaiah spoke, proclaiming the arrival of the messenger (מבשר) who announces peace and salvation, the herald here identified as "anointed of the spirit" (משיח הרוח).

[98] Becker, "4Q521," 92.

[99] Lidija Novakovic, *Messiah, the Healer of the Sick: A Study of Jesus as the Son of David in the Gospel of Matthew*, WUNT 2/70 (Tübingen: Mohr Siebeck, 2003), 173.

[100] Collins, *Scepter and the Star*, 133.

[101] Collins, *Scepter and the Star*, 134.

[102] Collins (*Scepter and the Star*, 134) notes that (general) resurrection and the messianic age were associated in early Judaism (2 Bar 30:2; 4 Ezra 7; 1 Cor 15; *j.Ketubot* 12.3; *m.Sota* 9; *j.Sheqalim* 3.3), but he rightly points out that "Elijah was credited with raising the dead during his historical career" (1 Kgs 17; 2 Kgs 4). Elijah's "command of the heavens was legendary" (135), as "by the word of the Lord he shut up the heavens and also three times brought down fire" (Sir 48:3). Rev 11 refers to "two olive trees" that have power over the heavens.

[103] Collins, *Scepter and the Star*, 135. See also Albert I. A. Hogeterp, *Expectations of the End: A Comparative Traditio-historical Study of Eschatological, Apocalyptic and Messianic Ideas in the Dead Sea Scrolls and the New Testament*, STDJ 83 (Leiden: Brill, 2009), 448; Brooke, "Kingship and Messianism in the Dead Sea Scrolls," 449; Xeravits, *King, Priest, Prophet*, 110; J. Zimmermann, *Messianische Texte aus Qumran: Königliche, priesterliche und prophetische*

4Q521 fr. 2 iii, which cites Malachi 3:24 ("the fathers will return to the sons" [באים אבות על בנים]). The reading and interpretation are contested,[104] hinging on the implied speaker, but there is a first-person line ("and I will liberate them" [ואתה אותם]) that can be read as the (implied) author in 2 ii + 4 ("forever will I cleave to [those who] hope").[105] If we take God as the speaker in 4Q521 fr. 2 iii, then God would be predicting the arrival of Elijah or an Elijah-like figure.[106] Although the "anointed one" of 4Q521 is nowhere explicitly identified as an agent,[107] this can be inferred since the acts described require a human agent. Given the fragmentary nature of the text, it is impossible to be more precise about the identification,[108] but 4Q521 nonetheless sheds considerable new light on the "messianic" identification of the historical Jesus.[109]

The relationship between 4Q521 and the New Testament was first publicized in 1992, prior to its official publication. Moreover, the grammatical subject of line 12—which refers to the dead being raised and the poor having "good news" preached to them—was initially (mis)identified as the "messiah" mentioned in line 1.[110] This suggestion, in conjunction with scholarly disapproval of the text's unauthorized publication and translation, has led many authorities to shy away

---

Messiasvorstellungen in den Schriftfunden von Qumran, WUNT 2/104 (Tübingen: Mohr Siebeck, 1998), 386; Andrew Chester, *Messiah and Exaltation: Jewish Messianic and Visionary Traditions and New Testament Christology*, WUNT 207 (Tübingen: Mohr Siebeck, 2007), 253 (tentative, but probable).

[104] Puech concludes that the speaker is the new Elijah/Moses *but distinguishes this figure from the messiah* who is referred to in the third person in other fragments. See Puech, "Une apocalypse messianique," 497. Puech insists that the messiah in 4Q521 is "clearly the kingly messiah, whom the prophet announces" (497); Joel Marcus, "John the Baptist and Jesus," in *When Judaism and Christianity Began: Essays in Memory of Anthony J. Saldarini*, ed. A. J. Avery-Peck et al., JSJSup 85 (Leiden: Brill, 2004), 194n56.

[105] Collins, *Scepter and the Star*, 136.

[106] Collins, *Scepter and the Star*, 137.

[107] Hans Kvalbein, "Die Wunder der Endzeit. Beobachtungen zu 4Q521 und Matth 11,5f.," NTS 43 (1997): 111–25; Bergmeier, "Beobachtungen," 44; Michael Becker, "4Q521," 73–96; idem, "Die 'messianische Apokalypse' 4Q521 und der Interpretationsrahmen der Taten Jesu," in *Apokalyptik und Qumran*, ed. J. Frey and M. Becker (Paderborn: Bonifatius, 2007), 237–303.

[108] Novakovic, *Messiah*, 175n220.

[109] See also John J. Collins, "The Scrolls and Christianity in American Scholarship," in *The Dead Sea Scrolls in Scholarly Perspective: A History of Research*, ed. D. Dimant, STDJ 99 (Leiden: Brill, 2012), 197–215, esp. 210–11: noting how 4Q521 "may indeed throw light on the question how Jesus came to be regarded as a messiah."

[110] Michael O. Wise and James D. Tabor, "The Messiah at Qumran," BAR 18, no. 6 (1992): 60–65; Tabor and Wise, "4Q521 'On Resurrection.'" For critique, see Otto Betz and Rainer Riesner, *Jesus, Qumran und der Vatikan: Klarstellungen* (Giessen: Brunnen, 1993), 111–15; Peter Stuhlmacher, *Wie treibt man Biblische Theologie*, Biblisch-theologische Studie 24 (Neukirchen-Vluyn: Neukirchener, 1995), 32; Niebuhr, "Die Werke des eschatologischen,"

from reading too much into this fragmentary passage. Nonetheless, the text clearly describes what *God* will do when "his messiah" (משיחו) arrives, utilizing a number of scriptural passages from Isaiah:

> ... liberating the captives, giving sight to the blind,
> straightening the bent ...
> For he will heal the wounded, revive the dead,
> and proclaim *good news* to the poor.

The Gospels of Matthew and Luke also describe Jesus citing a number of the same Isaianic passages in order to confirm his identity as "the one who is to come":

> "The blind see, and the lame walk, the lepers are cleansed,
> and the deaf hear, and the dead are raised,
> and the poor have *good news* preached to them (καὶ πτωχοὶ εὐαγγελίζονται)."
> (Matt 11:4-5 // Luke 7:22)

Are these two texts related?[111] Both texts "juxtapose an allusion to Isa 61,1 with a reference to giving life to the dead,"[112] and in "the whole of Jewish literature between the Bible and the Mishnah, it is only in 4Q521 and the Jesus saying" in Matthew 11:4-5 // Luke 7:22 that Isaiah 61 is expanded with a statement about the raising of the dead.[113] These relationships between Jesus, Matthew 11:4-5 // Luke 7:22, and Isaiah 61 are significant, not only because Isaiah 61 provided the semantic anchor for the Greek gospel genre (LXX: εὐαγγελίσασθαι),[114] but also because 4Q521 may be a missing link in the compositional history of the Beatitudes. 4Q521 links language from Isaiah 61 with language from Psalm 146 set in an eschatological context.[115] A "similar exegetical tradition ... lies behind the Q tradition,"[116] so much so that "the language and form of the Q beatitudes may thus be significantly influenced ... by an exegetical tradition in which Isa 61 and Ps 146 had already been allowed to influence and interpret each other." Finally, Isaiah 61 is here being used as an exegetical key "to inform and delineate the teaching of Jesus ... and his own interpretation of his work."[117]

637–46; Hans Kvalbein,"The Wonders of the End-Time: Metaphoric Language in 4Q521 and the Interpretation of Matt 11.5 par.," *JSP* 18 (1998): 87–110.

[111] Tabor and Wise ("4Q521 'On Resurrection,'" 163) describe this as "a pre-Synoptic formula for identifying the Messiah."

[112] Christopher M. Tuckett, "Scripture and Q," in *The Scriptures in the Gospels*, ed. C. M. Tuckett, BETL 131 (Leuven: Leuven University Press, 1997), Q, 22.

[113] George J. Brooke, *The Dead Sea Scrolls and the New Testament* (Minneapolis: Fortress, 2005), 262.

[114] Chilton and Evans, "Jesus and Israel's Scriptures," 322.

[115] Tuckett, "Scripture and Q," 3–26, esp. 24.

[116] Christopher M. Tuckett, "Introduction," in *Scriptures in the Gospels*, xiii–xiv.

[117] Tuckett, "Scripture and Q," 21.

Jesus' "good news" was part of an exegetical tradition in which Isaiah 61 was understood as heralding an eschatological new age of peace, salvation, healing, and debt forgiveness: the Jubilee year.[118] According to Leviticus 25:10 and Deuteronomy 15, God commanded that a Jubilee year be held every forty-nine years for the release of slaves, the remission of debts, and the restoration of property. The Jubilee year was a "day" of physical and spiritual release and restoration.[119] The socioeconomic difficulties associated with the Jubilee motivated the Pharisees to invent a legal compromise (the *Prosbul*) in order to avoid implementing the Jubilee. The authority to proclaim the Jubilee shifted from the king to the priests to God and the eschatological age. This last Jubilee tradition was developed by the *Yahad*, for whom eschatological redemption and salvation—the time when the poor, oppressed, and imprisoned would hear the "good news" of God's favor and release—was an imminent reality. Jesus also seems to announce his ministry as the arrival of the Jubilee year.[120]

Jesus' reply to John seems to be an indirect claim to be "anointed."[121] Both Matthew and Luke portray this response as Jesus' messianic qualifications or credentials. Yet Jesus' affirmation of his identity does not quite tally with John's expectations.[122] Jesus' credentials do not reflect "traditional Jewish expectations about the messiah."[123] Jesus' response is remarkably similar, however, to the eschatological events anticipated by the author of 4Q521. Although 4Q521 affirms

---

[118] James A. Sanders, "From Isaiah 61 to Luke 4," in *Christianity, Judaism and Other Greco-Roman Cults: Studies for Morton Smith at Sixty*, ed. J. Neusner (Leiden: Brill, 1975), 1:75–106; idem, "Isaiah in Luke," in *Interpreting the Prophets*, ed. J. L. Mays and P. J. Achtemeier (Philadelphia: Fortress, 1987), 75–85.

[119] John Sietze Bergsma, *The Jubilee from Leviticus to Qumran: A History of Interpretation*, VTSup 115 (Leiden: Brill, 2007), 20. See also James C. VanderKam, "Sabbatical Chronologies in the Dead Sea Scrolls and Related Literature," in *The Dead Sea Scrolls in Their Historical Context*, ed. Timothy H. Lim (Edinburgh: T&T Clark, 2000), 159–79; Robert G. North, *Sociology of the Biblical Jubilee*, AnBib 4 (Rome: Pontificio Instituto Biblico, 1954); Jean-François Lefebvre, *Le jubilé biblique: Lv 25—exégèse et théologie*, OBO 194 (Göttingen: Vandenhoeck & Ruprecht, 2003).

[120] Robert B. Sloan Jr., *The Favorable Year of the Lord: A Study of Jubilary Theology in the Gospel of Luke* (Austin: Scholars, 1977).

[121] Graham Stanton, "On the Christology of Q," in *Christ and Spirit in the New Testament*, ed. B. Lindars and S. S. Smalley (Cambridge: Cambridge University Press, 1973), 32; Charles K. Barrett, *The Holy Spirit and the Gospel Tradition* (London: SPCK, 1947), 118; Werner G. Kümmel, *Heilsgeschehen und Geschichte. Gesammelte Aufsätze, 1933–1964*, ed. E. Grässer, O. Merk, and A. Fritz, MTS 3 (Marburg: N. G. Elwert, 1965), 434. Joan E. Taylor, *The Immerser: John the Baptist within Second Temple Judaism*, SHJ 2 (Grand Rapids: Eerdmans, 1997), 293.

[122] Christopher M. Tuckett, *Q and the History of Early Christianity: Studies on Q* (Edinburgh: T&T Clark, 1996), 126.

[123] John S. Kloppenborg, *The Formation of Q: Trajectories in Ancient Christian Wisdom Collections* (Philadelphia: Fortress, 1987), 107.

that it is the *Lord* who performs the deeds as causal agent, there is nonetheless an implicit relationship between the deeds performed and the appearance of the "anointed" figure. Similarly, Jesus does not explicitly claim to have performed the miracles as much as report their occurrence. Jesus does not claim to have performed the deeds himself, as his response is composed in the passive ("the blind see, the lame walk, and the poor have good news . . .").

Whether or not the historical Jesus ever said such things in response to John the Baptist,[124] Jesus' healings and exorcisms are widely acknowledged as historical. It would seem, then, that Jesus' response represents how "traditional" messianic expectations were being reconfigured in light of Jesus' ministry.

Since its publication in 1992, the literary relationship between 4Q521 and the Jesus tradition has been a topic of considerable discussion. Most scholars have concluded that the evidence does not support the case for direct literary dependence.[125] After all, 4Q521 is composed in Hebrew, and Matthew 11:4-5 // Luke 7:22 is composed in Greek. Moreover, the use of Isaiah is sufficiently different as to preclude obvious literary dependence. 4Q521 looks to the future, for example, while Q narrates the *past* deeds of Jesus. While such grammatical and philological differences are easily noted, these differences do not really get to the heart of the matter: addressing the distinctive combination of several selected references to particular passages appearing in two chronologically and geographically proximate locations.

---

[124] As a genuine Jesus saying, see Rudolf Bultmann, *The History of the Synoptic Tradition* (Oxford: Blackwell, 1968), 110, 126; P. Maurice Casey, *An Aramaic Approach to Q: Sources for the Gospels of Matthew and Luke*, SNTSMS 122 (Cambridge: Cambridge University Press, 2002), 114, 144: "We have an authentic report of John's uncertain question to Jesus, and of Jesus' reply." See also John P. Meier, *A Marginal Jew: Rethinking the Historical Jesus*, vol. 2, *Mentor, Message, and Miracles* (New York: Doubleday, 1994), 131–37; R. L. Webb, *John the Baptizer and Prophet: A Socio-historical Study*, JSNTSup 62 (Sheffield: JSOT, 1991), 278–82; Walter Wink, "Jesus' Reply to John: Matt 11:2-6 // Luke 7:18-23," *Forum* 5 (1989): 121–28; Werner G. Kümmel, *Promise and Fulfillment: The Eschatological Message of Jesus*, trans. D. M. Barton (London: SCM Press, 1958), 110–11; Martin Dibelius, *Die urchristliche Überlieferung von Johannes dem Täufer*, FRLANT 15 (Göttingen: Vandenhoeck & Ruprecht, 1911), 313–19; James D. G. Dunn, *Jesus and the Spirit: A Study of the Religious and Charismatic Experience of Jesus and the First Christians as Reflected in the New Testament* (London: SCM Press, 1975), 55–60; Joseph A. Fitzmyer, *The Gospel according to Luke I–IX*, AB 28 (Garden City, N.Y.: Doubleday, 1981), 662–64. As nonhistorical, see A. Polag, *Die Christologie der Logienquelle*, WMANT 45 (Neukirchen-Vluyn: Neukirchener, 1977), 35, 38, 145; H. Schürmann, *Das Lukasevangelium* (Freiburg: Herder, 1969), 414; Siegfried Schulz, *Q: Spruchquelle der Evangelisten* (Zurich: Theologischer Verlag, 1972), 195; Paul Hoffmann, *Studien zur Theologie der Logienquelle*, NTAbh n. F. 8 (Münster: Aschendorff, 1972), 200–214; Kloppenborg, *Formation*, 107; Maurice Goguel, *Au seuil de l'Évangile: Jean-Baptiste* (Paris: Payot, 1928), 60–63.

[125] Dale C. Allison, *The Intertextual Jesus: Scripture in Q* (Harrisburg, Pa.: Trinity International, 2000), 112. Brooke, *Dead Sea Scrolls and the New Testament*, 82.

Attempting to address this question, some scholars suggest that Matthew 11:4-5 // Luke 7:22 and 4Q521 both drew from a "common tradition."[126] This conclusion is problematic, since it essentially means that an *additional* undocumented Jewish author/community and textual tradition (separate and distinct from Qumran) produced the *earlier* "common tradition" from which both the Qumran text and the Jesus tradition drew. This appeal to "common tradition" cannot be proved (because the common ancestor is lost) or disproved. Although it continues to bear the burden of proof, it actually avoids dealing with the literary problem altogether.[127]

Hypotheses alleging literary dependence face formidable burdens of proof. It is, of course, theoretically possible that the author(s) of Matthew 11:4-5 // Luke 7:22 independently combed through Isaiah and the Psalms looking for suitable miraculous deeds to ascribe to Jesus, but the author(s) would have had to combine at least three different passages to do so.[128] In contrast, 4Q521 represents a scribal tradition that had already combined four of Matthew 11:4-5 // Luke 7:22's six Isaianic miracles in a single text. It seems more likely therefore that the author of Matthew 11:4-5 // Luke 7:22 had access to traditions in which such deeds were already ascribed to a coming messianic age and/or figure.[129] The reference to resurrection, for example, "invite[s] speculation as to a shared source."[130] The two texts betray "an uncanny resemblance."[131] It has even been suggested that "the author of the Sayings source knew 4Q521; at least he drew on a common

---

[126] Tabor and Wise, "4Q521 'On Resurrection,'" 161; Novakovic, "4Q521," 225.

[127] Thomas L. Brodie (*The Birthing of the New Testament: The Intertextual Development of the New Testament Writings* [Sheffield: Sheffield University Press, 2004], 47) argues that appeals to common tradition posit documents "or traditions for which there is no reliable evidence."

[128] Isa 26:19; Isa 29:18-19; Isa 35:5-6; Isa 61:1.

[129] Michael Labahn (review of Simon J. Joseph, *Jesus, Q, and the Dead Sea Scrolls: A Judaic Approach to Q*, *RBL*, February 13, 2015, http://www.bookreviews.org/pdf/8811_9701.pdf [accessed September 28, 2015]) suggests that positing contact may be "too far reaching" ("zu weit reichenden Urteilen") since the relationship(s) can be understood as "parallel phenomena" ("parallele Phanomene"). The question, however, is not whether these texts *can* be understood as "parallel" developments but whether they *should* be.

[130] James M. Robinson, "The Sayings Gospel Q," REL 484. Unpublished class notes, Claremont Graduate School, Fall 1992, 5; referring to Matt 11:4-5 // Luke 7:22 as "a mosaic put together in some other context and just taken over (and perhaps adapted) by Q to its redactional purposes ... dependence on an erudition shared with Qumran."

[131] John S. Kloppenborg, "The Sayings Gospel Q and the Quest of the Historical Jesus," HTR 89 (1996): 330n101; cf. John S. Kloppenborg Verbin, *Excavating Q: The History and Setting of the Sayings Gospel* (Edinburgh: T&T Clark, 2000), 405n72 (emphasis in original): "It would appear that a synthesis of Isaian texts was *already* in circulation by the time of the composition of Q (and certainly, Matthew) and that Q 7:22 reflects this exegetical development."

tradition."[132] In both texts, Isaiah 61 and the eschatological raising of the dead are combined. Nowhere else in extant Jewish literature is this creative combination to be found. The two texts share a density of themes: the blind receiving their sight, the lame being healed, the dead being raised, and the poor having good news preached to them. Furthermore, where Matthew 11:4-5 // Luke 7:22 and 4Q521 *share* Isaianic motifs, the order is identical.

The argument from order, in addition to the high density of parallels, and the complex exegetical decisions involved with combining several passages from different texts, strongly suggests familiarity and dependence. The author of Matthew 11:4-5 // Luke 7:22—a Jewish follower of Jesus familiar with (accounts of) his teachings and healings and conversant with the wider cultural context(s) in which they both lived—seems to have inherited traditions that looked forward to very similar specific eschatological blessings during the "messianic" age.

There is no need here to posit *sameness*. The two traditions represent two different authors in two very different sociological settings. More significantly, one text looks toward the future for fulfillment; the other recalls the recent past. Yet in order for Jesus' reply to John to make rhetorical sense, Jesus' reply must be presumed to have been intelligible within a cultural and literary context where these allusive cues and codes would invite assent and agreement. Jesus, in other words, must be able to presuppose the correct recognition of these signs. Since John appears to have predicted a powerful figure whose imminent arrival would vindicate the righteous and condemn the wicked in judgment,[133] it is understandable that John could have had some doubts about Jesus. Accordingly, John is portrayed as unsure of Jesus' identity. In response, Matthew 11:4-5 // Luke 7:22 affirms that Jesus, despite appearances, is the fulfillment of John's expectation, although perhaps not in the way he may have hoped.

Jesus' reply to John reconfigures "messianic" expectations by appealing to *an earlier exegetical tradition* that recognized healing, raising the dead, and preaching good news to the poor as "messianic" events, with the result being that Jesus is scripturally authorized as "Messiah" in light of both his ministry and his apparent failure to fulfill "Davidic" expectations. This apparent "failure" is mitigated by the fact that Jesus' acts of healing restore the socially outcast to wholeness, signifying the inauguration of the messianic age.[134] The *Yahad* excluded lepers,

---

[132] Collins, "Works of the Messiah," 107; cf. Gaye Strathearn, "4Q521 and What It Might Mean for Q 3–7," in *Bountiful Harvest: Essays in Honor of S. Kent Brown*, ed. A. C. Skinner, D. Morgan Davis, and C. W. Griffin (Chicago: University of Chicago Press, 2012), 397: "The Q community knew of 4Q521."

[133] John J. Hughes, "John the Baptist: Forerunner of God," *NovT* 14 (1972): 190–218; Webb, *John the Baptizer and Prophet*, 221–27, 259, 283.

[134] Jodi Magness, "'They Shall See the Glory of the Lord' (Isa 35:2): Eschatological Purity at Qumran and in Jesus' Movement," in *Q in Context II: Social Setting and Archeological*

the blind, the sick, and the lame as ostracized (1QSa 2.4–10). The *Temple Scroll* explicitly identifies lepers as outcasts (11QT 45–47; cf. CD 15.15). Yet the *Yahad* also anticipated an eschatological age of miraculous "healing" (1QS 4.6). Jesus' acts of healing are represented as "signs" of a new "messianic" age being fulfilled through the ministry of Jesus.[135] It is difficult not to come to the conclusion that the author of Matthew 11:4-5 // Luke 7:22 is reconfiguring an *inherited* exegetical tradition—already present within the Qumran/Essene library—which associated Isaianic blessings with the arrival of an "anointed" figure.

— ♦ —

The Synoptic Gospels clearly portray Jesus as a prophet. In Mark, Jesus is reported to have said, "Prophets are not without honor, except in their hometown," seemingly referring to himself.[136] In most passages, however, the prophetic identification is given *to* Jesus by others. In Mark 8:28 / Matthew 16:14, the crowds regard him as "one of the prophets." In Matthew 21:11 the pilgrim crowds in Jerusalem say, "This is the prophet Jesus from Nazareth of Galilee." In Matthew 21:46 the Jerusalem crowd is reported as having "held him to be a prophet." In Luke 7:16, the crowds proclaim, "A great prophet has arisen among us." In Luke 7:39-50 the Pharisees are aware of Jesus' reputation as a prophet. In John 4:19, the healed blind man proclaims Jesus as prophet. In Mark 14:65 / Matthew 26:68 / Luke 22:64, the Roman guards mock Jesus by asking him to "prophesy" who struck him. In Luke 24:19, the disciples refer to Jesus as "a prophet mighty in word and deed." Jesus may not seem to display the typical signs of a prophetic mission insofar as he does not use the prophetic formula "Thus sayeth the Lord,"[137] but Jesus is portrayed as making predictions about the fate of Israel and forms a school of disciples. He proclaims (Isaianic) "good news" to the poor. He announces himself to be God's "anointed" and authorized agent. He develops a reputation for miracle-working and healing. He criticizes the Temple's administration. He

Background of the Sayings Source, ed. M. Tiwald, BBB 173 (Bonn: Bonn University Press, 2015), 179–94.

[135] Chilton and Evans ("Jesus and Israel's Scriptures," 322, 325) refer to Jesus' allusions to Isa 61:1-2 as the fulfillment of "what the members of Qumran longed for."

[136] Jesus indirectly refers to himself as "prophet" in Mark 6:4 and Luke 13:33 ("it is impossible for a prophet to be killed outside of Jerusalem").

[137] Helmut Koester, *Introduction to the New Testament*, vol. 2, *History and Literature of Early Christianity* (Philadelphia: Fortress, 1982), 78: "The typical signs of a prophetic mission are missing from the preachings of Jesus. There is not a single tradition which reports Jesus' call; there are no visions, auditions, or stories of his receiving a commission. Jesus does not introduce his words with the formula, 'Thus says the Lord.'" Cf. Walter Kasper, *Jesus the Christ* (New York: Paulist, 1976), 102: "Jesus also speaks in a different way from a prophet. All the prophet does is transmit the word of God. . . . There is no trace of any such phrase in Jesus' teaching. He makes no distinction between his word and God's. He speaks from his own authority."

demonstrates concern for the poor and confronts the politico-religious authorities in the Jerusalem of his day. It is not difficult to see why "prophet" is such a common model for understanding Jesus today.[138] It seems self-evident.[139] Yet if we take the Gospels at face value, Jesus also seems to be a "prophet" who predicted an end time that never came. That is, if Jesus expected an "imminent ... cosmic act of destruction," then Jesus was wrong.[140] His hopes "were not fulfilled." His expectations were not realized. Jesus seems "proved wrong by the course of events."[141] Several sayings in the Gospels would seem to confirm this conclusion (Mark 9:1; 13:30; 14:62). If Jesus believed that "this generation" would not "pass away before all these things take place," he was evidently *wrong*: wrong about his imminent return as the Son of Man and wrong about a final judgment on "*this generation.*"[142] *This* apocalyptic Jesus "did in fact *erroneously* hail the end as near."[143] In short, either the historical Jesus was tragically mistaken or *we* have seriously misunderstood Jesus' eschatological timetable and/or self-understanding. Was Jesus a misguided messiah broken on the wheel of history?[144] Or is Jesus' apparent failure to accurately predict an era of end-time violence better understood as the failure of the Jesus tradition to "remember" Jesus accurately as well as *our* failure to understand the historical Jesus' "apocalypticism?" Again, it is the Dead Sea Scrolls that shed new light on this perennial problem.

The Dead Sea Scrolls show that wisdom, eschatology, and apocalypticism were not incompatible in Second Temple Judaism.[145] Many works of apocalyptic

---

[138] Dale C. Allison, *Jesus of Nazareth: Millenarian Prophet* (Minneapolis: Fortress, 1998); Bart D. Ehrman, *Jesus: Apocalyptic Prophet of the New Millennium* (New York: Oxford University Press, 1999); E. P. Sanders, *Jesus and Judaism* (Philadelphia: Fortress, 1985); Albert Schweitzer, *The Quest of the Historical Jesus: A Critical Study of Its Progress from Reimarus to Wrede*, trans. W. Montgomery (New York: Macmillan, 1910); John P. Meier, "The Present State of the 'Third Quest' for the Historical Jesus: Loss and Gain," *Biblica* 80 (1999): 459–87, 483. Craig A. Evans ("Prophet, Sage, Healer, Messiah, and Martyr: Types and Identities of Jesus," in *Handbook for the Study of the Historical Jesus*, ed. T. Holmén and S. Porter, 4 vols. [Leiden: Brill, 2011], 2: 1217–43, 1219) suggests that "the evidence that Jesus saw himself as a prophet is compelling," citing Jesus' proclamation of the "rule of God," call for repentance, and warning of judgment (Mark 1:15; Luke 4:43; 11:20). On Jesus as prophet, see also Morna D. Hooker, *The Signs of a Prophet: The Prophetic Actions of Jesus* (Harrisburg, Pa.: Trinity International, 1997).

[139] Collins, *Scepter and the Star*, 232.

[140] Ehrman, *Jesus*, 160.

[141] James D. G. Dunn, *Jesus Remembered* (Grand Rapids: Eerdmans, 2003), 479.

[142] Philip Vielhauer, "Gottesreich und Menschensohn in der Verkündigung Jesu," in *Festschrift für Günther Dehn, zum 75. Geburtstag am 18. April 1957* (Neukirchen: Kreis Moers, Verlag der Buchhandlung Erziehungsvereins, 1957), 51–79.

[143] Allison, *Jesus of Nazareth*, 166 (emphasis added).

[144] Schweitzer, *Quest of the Historical Jesus*, 370–71.

[145] Seth Schwartz, *Imperialism and Jewish Society, 200 B.C.E. to 640 C.E.* (Princeton: Princeton University Press, 2001), 76: "In its literary expression, at least, [apocalyptic] is in fact

literature incorporate wisdom traditions.¹⁴⁶ Wisdom and apocalypticism were not dichotomous categories, genres, or worldviews in early Judaism.¹⁴⁷ Literary genres and intellectual currents overlapped to a significant extent in Second Temple Jewish literature.¹⁴⁸ Insofar as biblical scholarship tends to construct (and reify) "hermetically sealed" categories,¹⁴⁹ the interpretive problem is not necessarily "in the texts" but rather in the "categories and methods" that we use to "describe and interpret" them.¹⁵⁰

The word "eschatology" (from the Greek τὸ ἔσχατον) refers to the "last things," but it can also refer to the expectation of a divine renewal without envisioning a catastrophic end of the space-time continuum.¹⁵¹ Similarly, the word "apocalypse" refers to a divine "revelation" (ἀποκάλυψις), but it does not necessarily envision a catastrophic end of the space-time continuum.¹⁵² Unfortunately, the

---

an elite or subelite phenomenon, for the most part socially coextensive with wisdom literature." Cf. P. R. Davies, "The Social World of Apocalyptic Writings," in *The World of Ancient Israel: Social, Anthropological, and Political Perspectives*, ed. R. E. Clements (Cambridge: Cambridge University Press, 1989), 251–71, esp. 263. Matthew J. Goff (*The Worldly and Heavenly Wisdom of 4QInstruction*, STDJ 50 [Leiden: Brill, 2003], 216, 218) identifies 4QInstruction as "a sapiential text that attests a transformation of wisdom," a "stream of the sapiential tradition ... characterized by the combination of traditional wisdom with an apocalyptic worldview."

¹⁴⁶ John J. Collins, "Wisdom, Apocalypticism, and Generic Compatibility," in *In Search of Wisdom: Essays in Memory of John G. Gammie*, ed. L. G. Perdue, B. B. Scott, and W. J. Wiseman (Louisville, Ky.: Westminster John Knox, 1993), 165–85.

¹⁴⁷ Richard A. Horsley ("Questions about Redactional Strata and the Social Relations Reflected in Q,"*SBLSP 28* [Atlanta: Society of Biblical Literature, 1989], 186–203, 192) questions "the conceptual apparatus of our field" and the "approach by categorization."

¹⁴⁸ John P. Meier, "Basic Methodology in the Quest for the Historical Jesus," in *How to Study the Historical Jesus*, ed. T. Holmén and S. E. Porter, vol. 1 of *Handbook for the Study of the Historical Jesus* (Leiden: Brill, 2011), 291–331, here 321–22.

¹⁴⁹ George Nickelsburg, "Wisdom and Apocalypticism in Early Judaism: Some Points for Discussion," in *Conflicted Boundaries in Wisdom and Apocalytpicsim*, ed. B. G. Wright III and L. M. Wills, SBLSS 35 (Atlanta: Society of Biblical Literature, 2005), 17–37, esp. 36.

¹⁵⁰ Nickelsburg, "Wisdom and Apocalypticism," 37.

¹⁵¹ Marcus J. Borg, *Jesus in Contemporary Scholarship* (Valley Forge, Pa.: Trinity International, 1994), 8–9, 70–71; John S. Kloppenborg, "Sources, Methods and Discursive Locations in the Quest of the Historical Jesus," in *How to Study the Historical Jesus*, ed. T. Holmén and S. E. Porter, vol. 1 of *Handbook for the Study of the Historical Jesus* (Leiden: Brill, 2011), 278–79; N. T. Wright, *Jesus and the Victory of God*, vol. 2, *Christian Origins and the Question of God* (London: SPCK, 1996), 73.

¹⁵² Christopher Rowland, "Apocalypticism: The Disclosure of Heavenly Knowledge," in *The Mystery of God: Early Jewish Mysticism and the New Testament*, ed. C. Rowland and C. R. A. Morray-Jones, CEINT 12 (Leiden: Brill, 2009), 13–31; cf. Richard A. Horsley, *The Prophet Jesus and the Renewal of Israel: Moving Beyond a Diversionary Debate* (Grand Rapids: Eerdmans, 2012), 38–52; Wright, *Jesus and the Victory of God*, 202–14; Dale C. Allison, "Jesus and the Victory of Apocalyptic," in *Jesus and the Restoration of Israel: A Critical Assessment of N. T.*

word "apocalyptic" has become a simplistic kind of scholarly shorthand for the idea of a supernatural catastrophe,[153] a cosmic conflict between the forces of good and evil where God will put an end to this conflict by punishing the wicked and rewarding the faithful, typically via an "apocalyptic" battle.[154]

The idea that *all* "apocalypticists" believed that "a period of great tribulation and unmatched woe" would soon "descend upon the world" conflates far too many texts and traditions into a kind of pan-apocalypticism, which then tends to shoehorn "the apocalyptic Jesus" into a predetermined role and purpose. The problem is that the Jesus of the Gospels does not predict the annihilation of the nations or announce the in-gathering of the twelve tribes of Israel.[155] Moreover, Jesus does not seem to be interested in delineating the periodization of history, nor does he seem preoccupied by astronomy, the calendar, or "cosmic cartography."[156] These "apocalyptic" literary motifs are conspicuous in their absence in the career of "the apocalyptic Jesus." On the other hand, the Jesus tradition repeatedly portrays the Jesus of history as vigorously engaged in halakhic controversies and debates with his contemporaries over how best to understand and implement the Torah–that is, the Law, Instruction, and will—of God.

Wright's *"Jesus and the Victory of God,"* ed. C. C. Newman (Carlisle, UK: Paternoster, 1999), 126–41, 129.

[153] Ehrman, *Jesus*, x.

[154] Dale C. Allison, "Apocalyptic, Polemic, Apologetics," in *Resurrecting Jesus: The Earliest Christian Tradition and Its Interpreters* (New York: T&T Clark, 2005), 111–48, esp. 112n1. See also John J. Collins, *The Apocalyptic Imagination: An Introduction to Jewish Apocalyptic Literature*, 2nd ed. (Grand Rapids: Eerdmans, 1998).

[155] Cf. Crispin Fletcher-Louis, "Jesus and Apocalypticism," in *The Historical Jesus*, ed. T. Holmén and S. E. Porter, vol. 3 of *Handbook for the Study of the Historical Jesus* (Leiden: Brill, 2011), 2884–2885. Fletcher-Louis recognizes the motif of the "eschatological banquet," but *Zion* is "never explicitly stated."

[156] Fletcher-Louis, "Jesus and Apocalypticism," 2885.

CHAPTER 4

THE ESCHATOLOGICAL TEACHER

The relationship between the historical Jesus and the Mosaic Law is one of the most contested topics in New Testament scholarship, reflecting the field's increasing sensitivity to Jesus' Jewish context.[1] The central importance of the Law at Qumran has also increasingly been recognized in recent years. Since the publication of 4QMMT, there has been a growing awareness that legal disagreements played a major role in the *Yahad*'s worldview and social identity. A similar discursive shift has occurred in Jesus Research. Today "the historical Jesus is the halakic Jesus."[2] The word *halakhah* (הלכה)—derived from the Hebrew הלך, or "the way one walks"—is a somewhat anachronistic term for analyzing prerabbinical interpretation of Torah, as it was not commonly used until the post-70 CE era.[3] We must also acknowledge significant differences between pre-70 and post-70 CE halakhic interpretation.[4] Halakhah is still a useful term, however, in signifying

---

[1] Tom Holmén (*Jesus and Jewish Covenant Thinking*, BI 55 [Leiden: Brill, 2001], 339) suggests that Jesus "usually kept the Sabbath according to the common demands ... participated in the religious feasts in the Temple and even otherwise in general lived as a law-abiding Jew" (342) but defied the Sabbath commandment, devalued tithing, implied that the Torah was inadequate, and proclaimed that the Temple cult was "futile."

[2] John P. Meier, *A Marginal Jew: Rethinking the Historical Jesus*, vol. 4, *Law and Love* (New Haven: Yale University Press, 2009).

[3] L. H. Schiffman, "The Dead Sea Scrolls and Rabbinic *Halakhah*," in *The Dead Sea Scrolls as Background to Postbiblical Judaism and Early Christianity: Papers from an International Conference at St. Andrews in 2001*, ed. J. R. Davila, STDJ 46 (Leiden: Brill, 2003), 3–24.

[4] Paul Heger (*The Pluralistic Halakhah: Legal Innovations in the Late Second Commonwealth and Rabbinic Periods*, SJ FWJ 22 [Berlin: de Gruyter, 2003], 2) notes that in the pre-70

that Jesus *interpreted* the Torah. Nonetheless, Jesus' halakhah continues to be an "enigma" due to the "fragmentary nature of our knowledge" and because "a fair amount of Jesus' hălākôt have been lost to history."[5] Yet if the key to understanding the historical Jesus is understanding his eschatological halakhah,[6] then locating Jesus' own "motives and principles" within Second Temple "halakic reasoning" is imperative.[7]

The Eschatological *Halakhah* of the Historical Jesus

The historical Jesus does not seem to have belonged to any particular "school" of halakhic interpretation.[8] He does not seem to be particularly interested or concerned with maintaining a state of ritual purity.[9] Yet Jesus' apparent indifference to ritual purity should be understood in the context of his enacted inauguration of the kingdom of God, the central theme of Jesus' ministry. Jesus' exorcisms, for example, can be understood as "a power struggle" between the power of the kingdom and the "demonic" forces of impurity.[10] Sometimes, Jesus' halakhic responses seem to suggest an ad hoc, spontaneous, and/or occasional approach to such matters. Yet there are also passages in which Jesus either suspends or reformulates the Law with an assumed Mosaic-like or "prophet-like-Moses"-like authority (Matt 5:17-18; 12:9-14).[11]

---

period, "religious rules were determined by tradition, and by the *ad hoc* decisions pronounced by various erudite men who enjoyed respect and obeisance in their respective communities," and that "contradictory halakhic decisions by different Sages were of no concern to the functioning of public institutions" and were not "archived" or "considered final and binding."

[5] Meier, *Marginal Jew*, 4:652.

[6] Simon J. Joseph, *Jesus and the Temple: The Crucifixion in Its Jewish Context*, SNTSMS 165 (New York: Cambridge University Press, 2016); Holmén, *Jesus and Jewish Covenant Thinking*; Thomas Kazen, *Scripture, Interpretation, or Authority? Motives and Arguments in Jesus' Halakic Conflicts*, WUNT 320 (Tübingen: Mohr Siebeck, 2013).

[7] Kazen, *Scripture, Interpretation, or Authority*, 30–31.

[8] Philip Sigal (*The Halakhah of Jesus of Nazareth according to the Gospel of Matthew*, SBL 18 [Atlanta: Society of Biblical Literature, 2007], 192) describes (the Matthean) Jesus as "a proto-rabbi" who was "neither a Sadducee nor a Pharisee, neither a Hillelite nor a Shammamite. He employed freedom of interpretation and authority in conformity with the fashion of proto-rabbinic Judaism" (12).

[9] Thomas Kazen, *Jesus and Purity Halakhah: Was Jesus Indifferent to Impurity?* ConBNT 38 (Winona Lake, Ind.: Eisenbrauns, 2010 [2002]), 344: "Jesus' behavior ... may be understood as indifferent, and there are signs that it was interpreted as such by his adversaries."

[10] Kazen, *Jesus and Purity Halakhah*, 346.

[11] Bernard S. Jackson, *Essays on Halakhah in the New Testament*, JCP 16 (Leiden: Brill, 2008), 29: "There existed both eschatological and non-eschatological models of the 'prophet-like-Moses' in the Second Commonwealth. ... The non-eschatological prophet ... could authorise individual actions which suspended the law, teach his sect his own interpretation of the law,

The historical Jesus does not seem to have developed a systematic approach to halakhic disputes with his contemporaries, but he does seem to have had one overriding priority in his interpretation: discerning and following the will of God.[12] In many cases of halakhic debate, Jesus "seems to appeal to divine intent, viewing revelation as based on a plain reading and a realist understanding of Scripture."[13] At the same time, Jesus also assumes the authority to *correct* Mosaic Law.[14] That is, Jesus does not oppose the Law but rather reinterprets certain aspects of the Law as inadequate in the eschatological era.[15] Jesus claimed the ability to perceive the will of God and to reinterpret, even reprioritize, the Law of Moses. In a number of sayings, for example, Jesus appeals to the authoritative "order of creation" as described in the book of Genesis.[16] For many Jews (and non-Jews), the first chapters of Genesis were enigmatic and even impenetrable mysteries of the will of God establishing the divine template of humankind:

בראשית ברא אלהים את השמים ואת הארץ
ויברא אלהים את האדם בצלמו בצלם אלהים
ברא אתו זכר ונקבה ברא אתם

In the beginning when God created the heavens and the earth . . .
And God created humankind in his image, in the image of God
he created them, male and female, he created them. (Gen 1:1, 26-27)

Genesis 1 established the parameters within which the original instructions of God's will could be known. For a religious visionary like Jesus,[17] the story of

---

and judge individual cases against the Law." It is the eschatological prophet, however, who possesses "the power to abrogate law—a model denied by the rabbis but anticipated in the Qumran Community Rule" (30) (cf. 1QS 9.11).

[12] Cf. Stephen Westerholm, *Jesus and Scribal Authority*, ConBNT 10 (Lund: CWK: Gleerup, 1978), 59, 91, 103, 112, 123.

[13] Kazen, *Scripture, Interpretation, or Authority*, 290.

[14] Chris Keith, *Jesus against the Scribal Elite: The Origins of the Conflict* (Grand Rapids: Baker Academic, 2014), 145–46.

[15] E. P. Sanders, *Jesus and Judaism* (Philadelphia: Fortress, 1985), 269, 272, 275; adding that the Mosaic Law was "not final" (252, 269) or eschatologically adequate (255, 260; cf. 250, 267–69).

[16] Kazen, *Scripture, Interpretation, or Authority*, 6. Cf. Andrea J. Mayer-Haas, "Geschenk aus Gottes Schatzkammer" (bShab 10b): Jesus und der Sabbat im Spiegel der neutestamentlichen Schriften, NTAbh NS 43 (Münster: Aschendorff, 2003).

[17] Geza Vermes (*Jesus the Jew: A Historian's Reading of the Gospels* [Philadelphia: Fortress, 1981 (1973)]) regards Jesus as a charismatic "holy man" or a "man of deed" (איש מעשה). Alan F. Segal ("Jesus and First-Century Judaism," in *Jesus at 2000*, ed. M. J. Borg [Boulder, Colo.: Westview, 1997], 68) proposes that Jesus was a mystic "who experienced religiously altered states of consciousness." Cf. Marcus J. Borg, *Conflict, Holiness and Politics in the Teachings of Jesus*, SBEC 5 (New York: Edwin Mellen, 1984), 230–47.

creation inscribed in Genesis would have been understood as the revealed will of God—the *Urzeit* to be reenacted in the *Endzeit*. Consequently, a halakhah derived from an inspired interpretation of Genesis could have led Jesus to reprioritize certain Mosaic ordinances in light of a perceived renewal of creation. This seems to have been the distinctive hermeneutic informing Jesus' approach to the Torah, allowing him to both intensify the demands of marital law and relax the halakhic restrictions of Sabbath law.[18] This is an eschatological hermeneutic that Jesus shared with a number of his contemporaries, *including the Essenes*, who looked forward to the renewal of creation. The authors of Ben Sira, Jubilees, and the *Animal Apocalypse* all envision the story of Israel as beginning at creation and being fulfilled by restoring God's plan from creation. Jesus' halakhah is thus best understood in light of "an *Urzeit-Endzeit* schema."[19] It is within this spectrum of interpretation, then, that we can identify Jesus as an early Jewish representative of an ancient theology of creation.[20]

It is not to be assumed here, however, that Jesus and/or the Essenes never changed their minds on legal matters or that we have a complete record of their complex halakhic thought. On the contrary, it is highly likely that they represent social formations that changed over time. Nonetheless, their ethnic, social, cultural, and geographical proximity in first-century Palestinian Judea inevitably lent itself to their mutual interaction and influence. The direction of influence may have been more likely to proceed from the Essene movement—that is, the earlier, older, larger, more dispersed, and diverse movement—to the Jesus movement, but the Jesus movement's influence on the Essenes cannot be ruled out either. The most fruitful approach, then, is to proceed chronologically: from the earlier pre-Christian Essenic halakhic context to the possibility of Essenic influence on Jesus while acknowledging the existence of both agreement and disagreement—that is, similarity and difference—along a continuum of relationship.

---

[18] Ari Mermelstein, *Creation, Covenant, and the Beginnings of Judaism: Reconceiving Historical Time in the Second Temple Period*, JSJSup 168 (Leiden: Brill, 2014), 181.

[19] Kazen, *Scripture, Interpretation, or Authority*, 300; Lutz Doering, "Urzeit-Endzeit Correlation in the Dead Sea Scrolls and Pseudepigrapha," in *Eschatologie: Eschatology*, ed. J. Eckstein, C. Landmesser, and H. Lichtenberger, WUNT 272 (Tübingen: Mohr Siebeck, 2011), 19–58.

[20] Bernard Och, "Creation and Redemption: Toward a Theology of Creation," in *Cult and Cosmos: Tilting toward a Temple-Centered Theology*, ed. L. M. Morales, BTS 18 (Leuven: Peeters, 2014), 331–50; B. W. Anderson, ed., *Creation in the Old Testament* (Philadelphia: Fortress, 1984). Gerhard von Rad, "The Theological Problem of the Old Testament Doctrines of Creation," in *The Problem of the Hexateuch and Other Essays* (Edinburgh: Oliver & Boyd, 1966), 131–43. On rabbinical interpretation of the creation narrative, see Jacob Neusner, *Judaism's Story of Creation: Scripture, Halakhah, Aggadah*, BRLAJ 3 (Leiden: Brill, 2000).

"From the Beginning of Creation": Jesus and Divorce

According to the Mosaic Law, a man may divorce his wife by issuing a certificate of divorce if she becomes "displeasing" to him (Deut 24:1-4). The divorcee is then free to remarry. The Mosaic Law also presupposes the validity of polygamy (Deut 21:15-17; Exod 21:10). In contrast, the *Damascus Document* (CD) and the *Temple Scroll* (11QT) contain sectarian rules regarding marriage as well as prohibitions of polygamy and remarriage after divorce. According to 11QT 57.17–18, the king is forbidden from taking a second wife.[21] 11QT refers specifically to the king in its prohibition of polygamy.[22] It is still debated whether CD refers explicitly to divorce or just prohibits polygamy.[23] CD 4.19–21 through 5.1–2 certainly proscribes polygamy.[24] Yet the exact meaning of the CD passage—and whether it refers to polygamy, divorce, and/or remarriage after divorce—remains unclear.[25] Interpretations range from a total prohibition of divorce,[26] to divorce being regarded as legitimate, and remarriage following divorce being prohibited.[27]

---

[21] Cf. J. R. Mueller, "The Temple Scroll and the Gospel Divorce Texts," *RQ* 10 (1980): 253–54.

[22] Cf. Joseph A. Fitzmyer, "The Matthean Divorce Texts and Some New Palestinian Evidence," *TS* 37 (1976): 216.

[23] See G. Brin, "Divorce at Qumran," in *Legal Texts and Legal Issues: Proceedings of the Second Meeting of the International Organization for Qumran Studies Cambridge 1995*, ed. M. Bernstein et al. (Leiden: Brill, 1997), 231–49.

[24] Cf. George J. Brooke, *The Dead Sea Scrolls and the New Testament* (Minneapolis: Fortress, 2005), 71. Dale C. Allison, *Jesus of Nazareth: Millenarian Prophet* (Minneapolis: Fortress, 1998), 64–65.

[25] Cf. F. García Martínez, "Man and Woman: Halakhah Based upon Eden in the Dead Sea Scrolls," in *Paradise Interpreted: Representations of Biblical Paradise in Judaism and Christianity*, ed. G. P. Luttikuizen, TBN 2 (Leiden: Brill, 1999), 104; J. Murphy-O'Connor, "An Essene Missionary Document? CD II, 4-VI, 1," *RB* 77 (1970): 220; Philip R. Davies, *Behind the Essenes: History and Ideology in the Dead Sea Scrolls*, BJS 84 (Atlanta: Scholars, 1987), 73–85; L. H. Schiffman, "Laws Pertaining to Women in the Temple Scroll," in *The Dead Sea Scrolls: Forty Years of Research*, ed. D. Dimant and U. Rappaport, STDJ 10 (Leiden: Brill, 1992), 217; Fitzmyer, "Divorce Texts," 96; Joseph M. Baumgarten, "The Qumran-Essene Restraints on Marriage," in *Archaeology and History in the Dead Sea Scrolls: The New York University Conference in Memory of Yigael Yadin*, ed. L. H. Schiffman (Sheffield: Sheffield Academic, 1990), 15; Geza Vermes, "Sectarian Matrimonial Halakhah in the Damascus Rule," *JJS* 25 (1974): 197–202; D. Instone-Brewer, "Nomological Exegesis in Qumran 'Divorce' Texts," *RdQ* 18 (1998): 561–79.

[26] See Mueller, "Temple Scroll," 253–54.

[27] Schiffman, "Laws Pertaining to Women," 217–18; A. Shemesh, "4Q271.3: A Key to Sectarian Matrimonial Law," *JJS* 49 (1998): 244–63, here 245–46; Baumgarten, "Qumran-Essene Restraints," 15.

It is perhaps best to view CD as referring to polygamy,[28] but not necessarily to divorce. Divorce is allowed in Deuteronomy and mentioned in CD 13.17, 4Q266 9 iii 1–5, and 11QT 54.4. It seems reasonable to conclude, therefore, that CD refers to polygamy.[29] Divorce seems to have been recognized as a legitimate practice at Qumran.[30] The *Yahad* may have only objected to divorce under certain conditions.[31] So while the Torah allows for both polygamy and divorce, the authors of CD and 11QT seem to have assumed the scribal and exegetical freedom to *revise* Torah. We find a similar exegetical freedom, based on similar exegetical principles, in the Jesus tradition.[32]

The divorce saying is widely regarded as authentic.[33] In contrast to the legally recognized norms of the day (cf. Deut 24:1-4), Matthew 5:32 // Luke 16:18 proscribes divorce.[34] This ruling on divorce is so contrary to both popular sentiment and Mosaic Law that it is generally regarded as belonging to the earliest Jesus tradition. Matthew 5:32 // Luke 16:18 is even arguably earlier than Paul's (1 Cor 7:10-11), which Paul cites as from "the Lord" (ὁ κύριος). As in Matthew 5:17, here also Matthew 5:32's exception clause παρεκτὸς λόγου πορνείας maintains the validity of the Mosaic Law's allowance for divorce and corrects possibly antinomian interpretations suggested by Matthew 5:32 // Luke 16:18, where the prohibition is given without further qualification.

The Jesus of Q seems to forbid divorce within an eschatological context: he neither contradicts the Law nor is entirely satisfied with it.[35] In contrast

---

[28] M. Kister, "Divorce, Reproof, and Other Sayings in the Synoptic Gospels: Jesus Traditions in the Context of 'Qumranic' and Other Texts," in *Text, Thought, and Practice in Qumran and Early Christianity: Proceedings of the Ninth International Symposium of the Orion Center for the Study of the Dead Sea Scrolls and Associated Literature, Jointly Sponsored by the Hebrew University Center for the Study of Christianity, 11–12 January, 2004*, ed. R. A. Clements and D. R. Schwartz (Leiden: Brill, 2009), 195–229, here 201.

[29] Fitzmyer, "Divorce Texts," 220.

[30] Brin, "Divorce," 231. See CD 13.16–17; 11QT 54.5.

[31] Brin, "Divorce," 237.

[32] Cf. M. Fander, *Die Stellung der Frau im Markusevangelium: Unter besonderer Berücksichtigung kultur- und religionsgeschichtlicher Hintergründe*, Münster theologische Abhandlungen 8 (Altenberge: Telos, 1990), 200–257.

[33] D. Kosch, *Die eschatologische Tora des Menschensohnes: Untersuchungen zur Rezeption der Stellung Jesu zur Tora in Q*, NTOA 12 (Göttingen: Vandenhoeck & Ruprecht, 1989), 443: "16,16 und 16,18 sind authentische Jesusworte." Cf. also E. P. Sanders, *The Historical Figure of Jesus* (London: Penguin, 1993), 198–204; John P. Meier, "The Historical Jesus and the Historical Law: Some Problems within the Problem," *CBQ* 65 (2003): 69n38.

[34] For the divorce sayings, see Fitzmyer, "Divorce Texts"; Amy-Jill Levine, "Jesus, Divorce, and Sexuality: A Jewish Critique," in *The Historical Jesus through Catholic and Jewish Eyes*, ed. B. F. le Beau (Harrisburg, Pa.: T&T Clark, 2000), 113–29.

[35] Sanders, *Jesus and Judaism*, 256–60. See also David R. Catchpole, "The Synoptic Divorce Material as a Traditio-historical Problem," *BJRL* 57 (1975): 125.

to the book of Deuteronomy, which presupposes the validity of both divorce and polygamy, Matthew 5:32 // Luke 16:18 forbids what is sanctioned in the Torah.[36] Matthew 5:32 // Luke 16:18's hard-line approach can be contrasted both with Matthew's version and later rabbinical traditions, which allowed for divorce.[37] Matthew 5:32 // Luke 16:18 is not rejecting or implying an abolition of the Law. If anything, this saying appears to be more rigorous, not more lenient, than the Torah.[38] Here Matthew 5:32 // Luke 16:18 shares with the *Yahad* a tendency to rewrite scripture and reinterpret Torah. Their similar use of scriptural references, as well as their high regard for their founding teachers, suggests a shared cultural tradition.[39]

In Mark 10:2 Jesus states, "Moses allowed a man to write a certificate of dismissal and to divorce her," but this was because of Israel's "hardness of heart." Jesus justifies his position by arguing that the allowance for divorce was due to an inability to uphold the original intention of creation.[40] Mark's Jesus corrects a Mosaic concession and restores the original design of creation.[41] He appeals to Genesis 1:27 (ἀπὸ δὲ ἀρχῆς κτίσεως ἄρσεν καὶ θῆλυ ἐποίησεν αὐτούς; Mark 10:6) and Genesis 2:24. "Jesus' appeal to the Genesis creation narrative ... is more than citing one scripture against another. It is an appeal to origins and reflects a theology and ideology: God's original purpose has priority."[42] The use of Genesis here suggests that Matthew 5:32 // Luke 16:18 should also be understood in an eschatological context. Remarkably, the author of the *Damascus Document* used this passage to justify his own view on remarriage.[43] Both Mark 10 and CD

---

[36] Meier, *Marginal Jew*, 4:113–14.

[37] Deut 24:1 does not clarify the grounds for divorce. Targum Onqelos and the Palestinian Targum interpreted it to mean any sinful matter. The Hillelite R.'Akiba allowed for divorce for any reason (*m.Git.* 9.10). Shammai limited divorce to cases of sexual immorality (*y.Git.* 50d; *y.Sot.* 16b). The Mishnah recognizes the validity of polygamy (*m.Yeb.* 1.1; *m.Ket.* 10.1).

[38] John S. Kloppenborg, "Nomos and Ethos in Q," in *Gospel Origins and Christian Beginnings: In Honor of James M. Robinson*, ed. J. E. Goehring, J. T. Sanders, and C. W. Hedrick (Sonoma, Calif.: Polebridge, 1990), 45.

[39] Cf. George J. Brooke, "Shared Intertextual Interpretations in the Dead Sea Scrolls and the New Testament," in *Biblical Perspectives: Early Use and Interpretation of the Bible in Light of the Dead Sea Scrolls*, ed. M. E. Stone and E. G. Chazon, STDJ 28 (Leiden: Brill, 1998), 35–57.

[40] Meier, *Marginal Jew*, 4:123–24.

[41] Cf. Levine, "Jesus," 121; Lutz Doering, "Marriage and Creation in Mark 10 and CD 4–5," in *Echoes from the Caves: Qumran and the New Testament*, ed. F. García Martínez, STDJ 85 (Leiden: Brill, 2009), 133–63, here 160–63; H. Stegemann, "Der lehrende Jesus: Der sogenannte biblische Christus und die geschichtliche Botschaft Jesu von der Gottesherrschaft," *NZSTh* 24 (1982): 3–20.

[42] William R. G. Loader, *Jesus' Attitude towards the Law: A Study of the Gospels* (Grand Rapids: Eerdmans, 2002), 89.

[43] J. De Waard, *A Comparative Study of the Old Testament Text in the Dead Sea Scrolls and in the New Testament*, STDJ 4 (Leiden: Brill, 1965), 31.

4–5 appeal to Genesis 1:27: Mark to denounce divorce; CD to ban polygamy.[44] This common appeal to Genesis "shows most clearly a common interpretative horizon, in which issues pertaining to marriage law are addressed by reference to texts from Gen 1–2 ... and by appeal to creation."[45] In Mark, Jesus explains that Moses allowed for divorce as a concession to human weakness.[46] Lifelong marriage was God's intention in creation ("from the beginning") and cannot be terminated. The Mosaic Law was a temporary concession[47] and eschatologically inadequate.[48] Mark's text is a "model of restoration of paradisiacal conditions."[49] The Mosaic Torah is being replaced by a *Schöpfungstora*; the Mosaic concession with God's original intention for marriage. Jesus is thus in accord with Malachi 2:14-16, where the prophet declares that God "hates divorce," and refers back to the original creation (2:10).

Mark 10:6-8 combines two passages from the creation account, Genesis 1:27 and Genesis 2:24.[50] Mark's argument is that God created the first humans ἄρσεν καὶ θῆλυ, "male and female." The force of the preposition ἀπό ("*from* the beginning of creation") indicates that the hermeneutical principle of creation is still valid.[51] Mark 10:9 shows that this is by divine command: "What God has joined together, let man not separate." Jesus restores God's original intention at creation.[52] This represents a certain degree of tension between Jesus and Torah: the Law requires a new interpretation.[53] Matthew 5:32 // Luke 16:18, like 11QT,

---

[44] Cf. Doering, "Marriage," 133–63. Sanders, *Jesus and Judaism*, 257; Geza Vermes, *The Authentic Gospel of Jesus* (London: Allen Lane, 2003), 56; E. B. Powery, *Jesus Reads Scripture: The Function of Jesus' Use of Scripture in the Synoptic Gospels* (Leiden: Brill, 2003), 52.

[45] Doering, "Marriage," 163.

[46] Cf. M. Hooker, *The Gospel according to St. Mark*, BNTC 2 (Peabody, Mass.: Hendrickson, 1991), 236.

[47] Doering, "Marriage," 145.

[48] Sanders, *Jesus and Judaism*, 260.

[49] Doering, "Marriage," 158. See also Sanders, *Jesus and Judaism*, 116, 230. D. Dungan, *The Sayings of Jesus in the Churches of Paul: The Use of the Synoptic Tradition in the Regulation of Early Church Life* (Philadelphia: Fortress, 1971), 117.

[50] See William Loader, *The Septuagint, Sexuality, and the New Testament: Case Studies on the Impact of the LXX in Philo and the New Testament* (Grand Rapids: Eerdmans, 2004), 80.

[51] Doering, "Marriage," 142; cf. Markus Tiwald, "Hat Gott sein Haus verlassen (vgl. Q 13,35)? Das Verhältnis der Logienquelle zum Frühjüdentum," in *Kein Jota wird vergehen: Das Gesetzesverstandnis der Logienquelle vor dem Hintergrund frühjüdischer Theologie*, BWANT 10 (Stuttgart: Kohlhammer, 2013), 63–89.

[52] Joachim Jeremias, *New Testament Theology: The Proclamations of Jesus*, trans. J. Bowden (London: SCM Press, 1971), 225. Cf. R. Le Déaut, "Le Targumic Literature and New Testament Interpretation," *BTB* 4 (1974): 251.

[53] Dale C. Allison, *Resurrecting Jesus: The Earliest Christian Tradition and Its Interpreters* (New York: T&T Clark, 2005), 166.

alters Mosaic Law and creates *new* Torah.[54] Matthew 5–7 // Luke 6:27-45 modifies and adds to the Mosaic Law.[55] Matthew 10:37 // Luke 14:26 inverts the commandment to "honor your father and mother."[56] Like Mark, Matthew 5:32 // Luke 16:18 also seems to affirm an Edenic eschatology, a "prelapsarian standard that revokes a temporary concession in the Torah."[57] Jesus' sayings revise Mosaic Law.[58] Matthew enhances this Mosaic motif by locating his Sermon on a "Mount" as a series of antitheses intended to correct, intensify, and "fulfill" Mosaic Law.[59] The seeds of an eschatological *redefinition* of the Law—which would result in various forms of Jewish-Christian sectarianism—were thus originally planted by the historical Jesus.

Like the Essenes, Jesus assumed the authority to correct the Law of Moses. He was not "abolishing" the Law; he was restoring the original Law of creation.[60] This bold claim and perceived offense to traditional sources of scriptural authority and practice would inevitably result in Jesus' death. He was directly challenging the authority and eschatological validity of the Mosaic Law. Like the Essenes at Qumran—and unlike the traditional first-century Jewish norms of the Mosaic Torah—Jesus challenged the adequacy of the Mosaic Torah in the new age, appealing to the exact same scriptural texts to justify his position as the Essenes.

---

[54] Allison, *Jesus of Nazareth*, 212.

[55] Cf. Allison, *Jesus of Nazareth*, 33.

[56] Allison, *Jesus of Nazareth*, 62–64. Levine, "Jesus," 121.

[57] Allison, *Resurrecting Jesus*, 186. Cf. George W. E. Nickelsburg, *Ancient Judaism and Christian Origins: Diversity, Continuity, and Transformation* (Minneapolis: Fortress, 2003), 194.

[58] Dale C. Allison, "Q's New Exodus and the Historical Jesus," in *The Sayings Source Q and the Historical Jesus*, ed. A. Lindemann, BETL 158 (Leuven: Peeters, 2001), 423; David R. Catchpole, *The Quest for Q* (Edinburgh: T&T Clark, 1993), 101–34; Christopher M. Tuckett, "Scripture and Q," in *The Scriptures in the Gospels*, ed. C. M. Tuckett, BETL 131 (Leuven: Leuven University Press, 1997), 25.

[59] Michael Tait ("The End of the Law: The Messianic Torah in the Pseudepigrapha," in *The Torah in the New Testament: Papers Delivered at the Manchester-Lausanne Seminar of June 2008*, ed. M. Tait and P. Oakes, LNTS 401 [London: T&T Clark, 2009], 198) affirms the divorce saying as an "eschatological provision" based on "an appeal to the Creation" but points out that (the narrative account of) creation is itself "part of the Torah" (206). On the "Messianic Torah," see Peter Schäfer, "Die Torah der Messianischen Zeit," *ZNW* 65 (1974): 27–42.

[60] Per Bilde, *The Originality of Jesus: A Critical Discussion and a Comparative Attempt*, SANT 1 (Göttingen: Vandenhoeck & Ruprecht, 2013), 145: "The most important feature of Jesus' relationship to the Mosaic Law is that Jesus tightened, strengthened and intensified the Law of Moses partly by referring to the more original, authentic and stricter 'law of the creation,' which he apparently regarded as superior to the Law of Moses." See also J. Roloff, "Jesus von Nazareth," *RGG* 4 (2001): 467; C. Breengaard, *Paradis-sekten: Frelseshistorie og kristen identitet* (Copenhagen: Museum Tusculanum Press, 2007), 51–69.

"Let Anyone Accept This Who Can": Jesus and Celibacy

Josephus, Philo, and Pliny report that the Essenes were celibate, (mostly) unmarried, and even shunned women. Celibacy is thus a distinctive element in classical descriptions of the Essenes.[61] Philo claims that the Essenes observe "celibacy" (ἐγκράτειαν) and "eschew marriage" and that "no Essene takes a wife" (*Hypoth.* 11.14). Pliny tells us that the Essenes "have no women and have renounced all sexual desire" (*Nat.* 5.73). Josephus tells us that they "disdain" marriage, although there is another "order" (τάγμα) of Essenes who do marry (albeit only to propagate the race; *B.J.* 2.120; 2.160–161). Josephus' report of two kinds of Essenes is supported by references to two kinds of groups in 1QS and CD, but these texts do not seem to support the emphasis Josephus places on *why* Essenes renounced marriage. Nonetheless, these accounts provide "sufficient evidence for us to conclude that some Essenes did not marry."[62]

On the other hand, several Qumran texts presuppose the existence of women and children (cf. *B.J.* 2.120; *Hypoth.* 14–17; *Nat.* 5.73).[63] 1QSa 1.4, for example, presupposes women and children. Similarly, CD 4.19, 5.2, and 5.7 contain rules on marriage, whereas CD 5.6 discusses rules about sex with menstruating women, while 7.6–7 contains rules about marriage and children. Consequently, there is some ongoing uncertainty about the requirement of celibacy in the movement as a whole since many texts presuppose the existence of families. The fact that Josephus refers to a "marrying" group of Essenes, however, suggests that there may have been a more ascetically inclined "priestly" group(s) within the *Yahad*.[64]

---

[61] Eyal Regev ("Cherchez les femmes: Were the *yahad* Celibates?" *DSD* 15 [2008]: 253–84, 253) describes this as "the Essenes' most distinctive characteristic."

[62] William Loader, *The Dead Sea Scrolls on Sexuality: Attitudes towards Sexuality in Sectarian and Related Literature at Qumran* (Grand Rapids: Eerdmans, 2009), 372.

[63] For the Essene position on marriage, see Baumgarten, "Qumran-Essene Restraints," 13–24; Joseph Coppens, "Le célibat essénien," in *Qumrân: Sa piété, sa théologie et son milieu*, ed. M. Delcor, BETL 46 (Paris: Duculot, 1978), 295–304; Yigael Yadin, "L'attitude essénienne envers la polygamie et le divorce," *RB* 79 (1972): 98–99; Antoine Guillaumont, "A propos du célibat des Esséniens," in *Hommages à A. Dupont-Sommer*, ed. A. Caquot and M. Philonenko (Paris: Adrien-Maisonneuve, 1971), 395–404; Alfred Marx, "Les racines du célibat essénien," *RevQ* 7 (1971): 323–42; Hans Hübner, "Zölibat in Qumran?" *NTS* 17 (1971): 153–67; Horst R. Moehring, "Josephus on the Marriage Customs of the Essenes," in *Early Christian Origins*, ed. A. P. Wikgren (Chicago: Quadrangle, 1961), 120–27.

[64] Alison Schofield, "Between Center and Periphery: The *Yahad* in Context," *DSD* 16, no. 3 (2009): 347: "Among the rule material as a whole, the *yahad* is mentioned and S-related material appears in texts where marrying and family life are assumed. The fragments of 4Q265 (cf. also 4Q504) address the *yahad* at least four times (1 ii 3, 6; 7 ii 7, 8) . . . 4Q265 legislates for a diverse community of men, women and children." Joan E. Taylor ("Women, Children, and Celibate Men in the *Serekh* Texts," *HTR* 104, no. 2 [2011]: 171–90, 174) identifies "elements in the *Serekh* texts that indicate the presence of women and children within the world of the

In any case, we need not accept Josephus' misogynistic views or opinions on sexual desire, as none of this is in the Qumran materials. Essene celibacy should not be confused with modern notions of lifelong celibacy. The Essenes may have been "made up of adult males, who . . . decided to join a group with special laws," and the movement may have been composed of "men of ripe years, already inclining to old age."[65] Essene members could have been married and had children *before* joining the group and then renounced marriage. Josephus seems to confirm this conclusion (*B.J.* 2.120). Yet there is no unambiguous evidence that the Qumran group and/or the *Yahad* were celibate.[66] The general identification of the Qumran community as "Essenic" certainly assumes that the *Yahad* was predominantly celibate,[67] but given the distinction between the Qumran group and the (greater) *Yahad*, it seems more likely that whereas the Qumran group *may* have been comprised primarily of celibate male members, the *Yahad* included men, women, and children.

Some scholars see CD 7.3–10 as a reference to a celibate community,[68] concluding that CD represents the rule for *all* the Essenes whereas 1QS legislates only for the Qumran group.[69] Yet the archaeological evidence is ambiguous: a large cemetery near Qumran contains the graves of 1,100 individuals, among which were women.[70] The question whether women were present in the Qumran

---

text," with the more strictly defined male-oriented עצה representing an inner "council" and community within the *Yahad* (cf. 1QS 6:2–3; 5:6–7).

[65] Gabriele Boccaccini, *Beyond the Essene Hypothesis: The Parting of the Ways between Qumran and Enochic Judaism* (Grand Rapids: Eerdmans, 1998), 39; citing *Hypoth.* 2–3.

[66] Lawrence H. Schiffman, *Reclaiming the Dead Sea Scrolls: The History of Judaism, the Background of Christianity, the Lost Library of Qumran* (Philadelphia: Jewish Publication Society, 1994), 143.

[67] Elisha Qimron, "Celibacy in the Dead Sea Scrolls and the Two Kinds of Sectarians," in *The Madrid Qumran Congress*, ed. J. Trebolle Barrera and L. Vegas Montaner, 2 vols., STDJ 11 (Leiden: Brill, 1992), 1:289.

[68] Baumgarten, "Qumran-Essene Restraints," 18–19, 23; Qimron, "Celibacy in the Dead Sea Scrolls"; Philip R. Davies, "Reflections on DJD XVIII," in *The Dead Sea Scrolls at Fifty: Proceedings of the 1997 Society of Biblical Literature Qumran Section Meetings*, ed. R. A. Kugler and E. M. Schuller (Atlanta: Scholars, 1999), 161; John J. Collins, "Family Life," in *The Encyclopedia of the Dead Sea Scrolls*, ed. L. H. Schiffman and J. C. VanderKam, 2 vols. (New York: Oxford University Press, 2000), 1:287; Sidnie White Crawford, "Not according to Rule: Women, the Dead Sea Scrolls and Qumran," in *Emanuel: Studies in Hebrew Bible, Septuagint and Dead Sea Scrolls in Honor of Emanuel Tov*, ed. S. M. Paul et al., VTSup 94 (Leiden: Brill, 2003), 149; Charlotte Hempel, "The Earthly Essene Nucleus of 1QSa," *DSD* 3, no. 3 (1996): 253–69.

[69] Crawford, "Not according to Rule," 149.

[70] Rachel Hachlili, "Burial Practices at Qumran," *RevQ* 62 (1994): 247–64; Nicu Haas and N. Nathan, "Anthropological Survey on the Human Skeletal Remains from Qumran," *RevQ* 6 (1968): 345–52; S. H. Steckoll, "Preliminary Excavation Report on the Qumran Cemetery," *RevQ* 6 (1968): 323–36.

group is therefore still open.⁷¹ Moreover, there are no family burials at the Qumran site, which appears to be unprecedented in ancient Jewish burial practice.⁷² The absence of anything indicating family housing or family life at Qumran is consistent with a predominantly male community who did not live in camps, marry, or have children. Yet a number of Qumran texts assume both marriage and divorce. And while sexuality was seen as a source of ritual impurity, it was not a source of moral impurity but, like marriage, was assumed to be "a natural part of human life."⁷³ The Qumran evidence, therefore, is ambiguous, although it is certain that the Essene movement included men, women, and children. For some Essenes, celibacy may have been temporary (CD 4.21; 1QS 1.6–11; 1QM 7.4–6). For others, it may have been lifelong. Clearly, not all Essenes were celibate, and, apart from temporary vows designed to ensure and maintain ritual purity, this may have been a matter of individual choice and voluntary decision.⁷⁴ Here again, then, we find a close *Essenic* correspondence in both theme (sexual renunciation) and variation ("let anyone accept this who can") with the Jesus tradition.

Ascetic practices and reservations toward sexual intercourse were part of the Judaism of Jesus' day.⁷⁵ It is not difficult to detect an underlying distrust of sexuality in the early Jesus tradition. Jesus' enigmatic statement about celibacy (Matt 19:12), in particular, is consistent with the ideal of lifelong celibacy "for the sake of

---

⁷¹ Linda Bennett Elder, "The Women Question and Female Ascetics among Essenes," *BA* 57, no. 4 (1994): 220–34.

⁷² Hachlili, "Burial Practices at Qumran."

⁷³ Loader (*Dead Sea Scrolls on Sexuality*, 389) notes that the *Temple Scroll*, 4QInstruction, CD, and 4QMMT all assume divorce.

⁷⁴ Marx, "Les racines du célibat essénien," 323–42; Hübner, "Zölibat in Qumran," 153–67; Anton Steiner, "Warum lebten die Essener asketisch?" *BZ* 15 (1971): 1–28. John J. Collins (*Beyond the Qumran Community: The Sectarian Movement of the Dead Sea Scrolls* [Grand Rapids: Eerdmans, 2010], 150–51) notes "several considerations" indicating that the *Yahad* was celibate.

⁷⁵ Matthew Black, "The Tradition of the Hasideaean-Essene Asceticism: Its Origin and Influence," in *Aspects du Judéo-Christianisme: Colloque de Strasbourg 23–25 avril 1964* (Paris: Presses Universitaires de France, 1965), 19–32; Baumgarten, "Qumran-Essene Restraints," 13–24; Allison, *Jesus of Nazareth*, 198; Steven Fraade, "The Nazirite in Ancient Judaism," in *Ascetic Behavior in Greco-Roman Antiquity*, SAC, ed. V. L. Wimbush (Minneapolis: Fortress, 1990), 213–23; idem, "Ascetical Aspects of Ancient Judaism," in *Jewish Spirituality: From the Bible through the Middle Ages*, ed. A. Green (New York: Crossroad, 1986), 261; Simon J. Joseph, "The Ascetic Jesus," *JSHJ* 8 (2010): 146–81. On Essene celibacy, see Pierre Benoit, "Qumran and the New Testament," in *Paul and Qumran: Studies in New Testament Exegesis*, ed. J. Murphy-O'Connor (Chicago: Priory, 1968), 9: "The eunuchs by choice (Mt 19:12) are probably the Essenes, as the religious ideal of celibacy is not attested anywhere else in Palestine at that period."

the kingdom of heaven."[76] Jesus says, "Let anyone accept this who can," endorsing this choice but not forcing it on anyone. Jesus was not recommending voluntary self-inflicted castration, as Origen believed, but the renunciation of sexual desire. Paul also advises celibacy for those who are able and sexual restraint for those who marry (1 Cor 7:25-32). Jesus' endorsement of celibacy seems to have been related to his understanding of life "in the resurrection," where people "neither marry nor are given to marriage, but are like angels in heaven" (Matt 22:30; Mark 12:18-27). Jesus seems to envision an idealized form of human nature apart from sexuality or marriage. In Luke, there is even the possibility that this life is possible *in the present* (Luke 20:27-40). In Matthew, Jesus teaches his disciples not to commit adultery or even look at a woman with lust (Matt 5:27-28). In Matthew's Sermon on the Mount, sexual desire is a dangerous temptation to be controlled.

Jesus' renunciation of sexual desire seems to have been part of his general eschatological conviction. He may have understood celibacy as part of the restoration of paradise in Eden. The early Christian tradition certainly contains many examples of asceticism marked by sexual renunciation as attempts to embody the divine ideal of Eden and the immortality of angelic life. The idea that sexual intercourse was not part of the primeval state of humanity, but only came as a result of the fall, is related to Jewish traditions that conceived of the original Adam/human as an androgynous being (Philo, *Opif.* 151–152; *Mek.* On Exod. 12:40; *b.Ber.* 61a; *b.Meg.* 9a; *b.ʿErub.* 18a; *Gen. Rab.* On 1:26), or of Adam and Eve not engaging in sexual intercourse before their disobedience as angelic beings (2 En. 30:11; Apoc. Adam 5:64.15–20, 76.4–6; *Conflict with Adam and Eve* 1:10). Jesus may have not only endorsed, but *embodied*, a way of life that rejected both marriage and children in favor of a life of voluntary celibacy.[77]

The early Jesus tradition contains numerous elements that point toward this renunciation of sexual desire. Like Jesus, John the Baptist is also portrayed in the Jesus tradition as unmarried and even more ascetic than Jesus. Philo, the

---

[76] Anthony J. Saldarini, "Asceticism and the Gospel of Matthew," in *Asceticism and the New Testament*, ed. V. L. Wimbush and L. E. Vaage (New York: Routledge, 1999), 22; W. D. Davies and Dale C. Allison Jr., *A Critical and Exegetical Commentary on the Gospel according to Saint Matthew*, ICC (Edinburgh: T&T Clark, 1988–1997); T. W. Manson, *The Sayings of Jesus* (London: SCM Press, 1949), 215–16.

[77] Anthony Le Donne (*The Wife of Jesus: Ancient Texts and Modern Scandals* [London: Oneworld, 2013], 145), suggests that the tradition of Jesus' celibacy emerged from his "teachings about civic masculinity" and that Jesus "might have been married in his young adulthood," but was probably not the "marrying type." That is, Jesus was "a sexual nonconformist" (118). Le Donne rightly notes that "the vast majority of Jewish men ... were married" and that there were "very few examples of celibate Jewish men" at that time (2), concluding that "it is highly unlikely that Jesus was married to Mary Magdalene or to any of his followers" because he seems too "anti-family" (128).

first-century Jewish historian, tells us that Moses renounced sexual intercourse in order "to hold himself always in readiness to receive oracular messages" (*Mos.* 2.68–69). It has been suggested that Jesus was celibate because he had transformed his sexuality into a higher form of spirituality, or perhaps became celibate in order to gain access to transcendent knowledge. Paul explicitly *recommended* celibacy, but he, too, did not *require* it (1 Cor 7:26, 29, 31). The fact that Paul does not appeal to Jesus for any "word of the Lord" on celibacy (1 Cor 7:25) is *not* evidence that Jesus was married. It simply indicates that Jesus did not make celibacy a requirement for everyone following him.

Jesus gave his life to God, and that life included his sexuality. Jesus was "married" to God. It is difficult to think that Jesus would have approved of a life of celibacy for anyone else if he could not live up to it himself. At the same time, Jesus did not advocate celibacy for everyone, especially since marriage was a sacred part of the original design of creation. Jesus *commended* those willing to practice celibacy, but he did not recommend this difficult path for everyone nor *command* it as a new "law" replacing the Mosaic Law blessing procreation.

Jesus' ascetic attitude toward sexuality is reminiscent of first-century reports about the Essenes. Despite Jesus' frequent interactions with women, his sexuality, marital status, family life, and extended family relations are all reminiscent of the heightened end-time convictions of the Essene movement. It is significant, therefore, to note that the passage commonly regarded as Jesus' positive endorsement of celibacy seems to refer to *Essene* celibates (Matt 19:12).

"Who among You . . . ?": Jesus and the Sabbath

Josephus tells us that the Essenes had a high regard for the Sabbath (*B.J.* 2.147). Philo tells us that they were stricter than other Jews in not working on the Sabbath (*Prob.* 12.81). The *Damascus Document* describes God's "holy Sabbath" as the first area in which "Israel of old had strayed" and how the community "must observe the Sabbath according to its exact rules" (CD 3.14; 6.18). CD lists numerous "rules on violations of the Sabbath" (CD 12.3–6) that are stricter than those of the Pharisees (CD 10.14–11.18), prohibiting a number of activities in particular, although *healing* is not listed among the Sabbath prohibitions (10.14–11.8). CD 11.16–17, however, is concerned with making sure that forbidden implements are not used:

> And any human (נפש אדם) who falls into a place of water
> or into a place of (. . .), / let no man bring him up with a ladder,
> a rope, or an implement (ובלי).[78]

---

[78] Joseph M. Baumgarten, *Qumran Cave 4.XIII: The Damascus Document (4Q266–273)*, DJD 18 (Oxford: Clarendon, 1996), 48.

4Q265 fr. 6 6–7 allows a garment to be thrown into a pit, but not implements:

> And if it is a human being (נפש אדם) that falls into the water / [on] the Sabbath [day],
> let him cast his garment (את בגדו) to him to raise him up therewith,
> but an implement (כלי) he may not carry.[79]

4Q265 fr. 7 1.6b–7a:

> Let no one draw up an animal that has fallen into water on the day of the Sabbath.

CD 11.13–14 forbids rescuing an animal from a pit or ditch on the Sabbath:

> Do not let a man deliver an animal (בהמה) on the Sabbath day (ביום השבת).
> And if it falls into a pit or a ditch (בור), he shall not lift it out on the Sabbath.

The author(s) of CD would not allow an animal (בהמה) to be rescued on the Sabbath. Yet in a remarkable parallel saying in the early Jesus tradition, Matthew and Luke take up Mark's Sabbath/Pharisee controversy stories and extend them even further, portraying Jesus as presupposing the validity of behavior explicitly *prohibited* in the *Damascus Document* (CD).[80] Whereas Matthew portrays Jesus as an "expositor of Torah without imposing heavy burdens" and Luke has Jesus arguing, "healing on the Sabbath should be justified on the same basis as rescuing an animal from a ditch,"[81] both disagree with CD 11.13–14:

> But he said to them, what man among you, having only one sheep,
> will not take hold of it and raise it up if it falls into a pit on the Sabbath?
> (Matt 12:11)

---

[79] Joseph M. Baumgarten, et al., eds., *Qumran Cave 4 XXV: Halakhic Texts*, DJD 35 (Oxford: Clarendon, 1999), 68.

[80] James H. Charlesworth, "The Dead Sea Scrolls and the Historical Jesus," in *Jesus and the Dead Sea Scrolls*, ed. J. H. Charlesworth (New York: Doubleday, 1992), 34. See also Heinz-Wolfgang Kuhn ("Qumran Texts and the Historical Jesus: Parallels in Contrast," in *The Dead Sea Scrolls: Fifty Years after Their Discovery: Proceedings of the Jerusalem Congress, July 20–25, 1997*, ed. L. H. Schiffman, E. Tov, and J. C. VanderKam [Jerusalem: Israel Exploration Society, 2000], 574), who calls this a "stunning," "impressive and astounding" example of contrast between Jesus and the Essenes. Cf. Heinz-Wolfgang Kuhn, "Jesus im Licht der Qumrangemeinde," in *Handbook for the Study of the Historical Jesus*, ed. T. Holmén and S. Porter, 4 vols. (Leiden: Brill, 2011), 1266: "Diese Vorschrift wäre für Jesus so absurd, dass er in einem Wort in Q 14:5 ganz selbstverständlich von dem Gegenteil ausgeht." Meier (*Marginal Jew*, 4:244) describes this as "the clearest parallel to a saying attributed to Jesus," a prohibition that is "strikingly contradicted by a saying of Jesus." For Meier, "Jesus was a Jew who pointedly stood over against the rigor" and "stringent casuistry of the Essenes" (4:267, 263).

[81] William R. G. Loader, "Jesus and the Law," in *Handbook for the Study of the Historical Jesus*, ed. T. Holmén and S. Porter (Leiden: Brill, 2011), 2750–51.

And he said to them, who of you [having] a son or an ox will not immediately lift him out if he/it will fall into a well on the day of the Sabbath? (Luke 14:5)

It would seem, then, that Jesus explicitly contradicted a Qumranic halakhic ruling. The problem is that Luke 14:5 // Matthew 12:11 is a notoriously difficult saying, especially among Q specialists. There is no consensus on the origin of this saying.[82] Did it originate and circulate as "ein isolierter Spruch" that Matthew and Luke utilized in similar ways?[83] Authorities weigh in on all sides.[84] Many scholars have identified this as a Q saying.[85] Others do not think that the "grounds for

---

[82] Luke 14:5 // Matt 12:11 is not included in *The Critical Edition of Q*. This omission indicates that two-thirds of the editing team voted against its inclusion.

[83] Rudolf Bultmann, *Die Geschichte der synoptischen Tradition*, 4th ed., FRLANT 29 (Göttingen: Vandenhoeck & Ruprecht, 1958 [1931]), 10. Meier (*Marginal Jew*, 4:260 [cf. 307n40]) suggests "two versions of a stray oral tradition (originally in Aramaic) that came independently to Matthew and Luke in somewhat different forms." Lutz Doering (*Schabbat: Sabbathalacha und -praxis im antiken Judentum und Urchristentum*, TSAJ 78 [Tübingen: Mohr Siebeck, 1999], 458–59) sees an Aramaic original in a Galilean setting (459–60), with the reference to "son" as secondary.

[84] Ky-Chun So, "The Sabbath Saying (Q 14:5)," International Q Project, 11 v 98.

[85] B. H. Streeter, "The Original Extent of Q," in *Oxford Studies in the Synoptic Problem* (Oxford: Clarendon, 1911), 193; W. Bussmann, *Synoptische Studien* (Halle: Buchhandlung des Waisenhauses, 1929); Heinz Schürmann, *Traditionsgeschichtliche Untersuchungen zu den synoptischen Evangelien* (Düsseldorf: Patmos, 1968), 213, 218; B. Weiß, *Die Evangelien des Markus und Lukas* (Göttingen: Vandenhoeck & Ruprecht, 1901), 518; idem, *Die Quellen der Synoptischen Überlieferung* (Leipzig: J. C. Hingischs'sche Buchhandlung, 1908), 74–75; I. H. Marshall, *The Gospel of Luke: A Commentary on the Greek New Testament*, NIGTC (Grand Rapids: Paternoster, 1978), 578; R. H. Gundry, *Matthew: A Commentary on His Literary and Theological Art* (Grand Rapids: Eerdmans, 1982), 225–28; Frans Neirynck, "Luke 14, 1-6. Lukan Composition and Q Saying," in *Der Treue Gottes Trauen: Festschrift für Gerhard Schneider*, ed. C. Bussmann and W. Radl (Freiburg: Herder, 1991), 259; Christopher Tuckett, *The Revival of the Griesbach Hypothesis* (Cambridge: Cambridge University Press, 1983), 98; idem, "Q, the Law and Judaism," in *Law and Religion*, ed. B. Lindars (Cambridge: James Clarke, 1988), 96; idem, *Q and the History of Early Christianity: Studies on Q* (Edinburgh: T&T Clark, 1996), 414–16; G. D. Kilpatrick, *The Origins of the Gospel according to St. Matthew* (Oxford: Clarendon, 1946), 27; A. Polag, *Fragmenta Q: Textheft zur Logienquelle* (Neukirchen-Vluyn: Neukirchener, 1979), 72; Loader, *Jesus' Attitude towards the Law*, 423; M. Trautmann, *Zeichenhafte Handlungen Jesu: Ein Beitrag zur Frage nach dem geschichtlichen Jesus*, FB 37 (Würzburg: Echter, 1980), 282–317; P. Rolland, *Les Premiers Évangiles*, LD 116 (Paris: Les Éditions du Cerf, 1984), 159; H. Weiss, "The Sabbath in the Synoptic Gospels," *JSNT* 38 (1990): 19; François Bovon, *Das Evangelium nach Lukas Lk 9,51–14,35*, EKKNT 3/2 (Zürich: Benziger, 1996), 2:421–22; Kosch, *Die eschatologische Tora*, 200–206; Ivan Havener, *Q: The Sayings of Jesus* (Wilmington: Michael Glazier, 1987), 142; Martin Hengel, *The Charismatic Leader and His Followers*, trans. J. Greig (New York: Crossroad, 1981), 18–24; Philip Francis Esler, *Community and Gospel in Luke-Acts: The Social and Political Motivations of Lucan Theology* (New York: Cambridge University Press, 1987), 117; Ky-chun So, "The Sabbath Controversy of Jesus:

inclusion" in Q are "substantial enough."[86] The International Q Project initially included Luke 14:5 in Q, giving it a grade of "C" for "doubtful,"[87] but retracted this decision in *The Critical Edition of Q*. Some scholars think the saying belongs to Matthean and Lukan *Sondergut*. Others think that it is a variant of Mark 3:1-6.[88] Many have concluded that Luke 14:5 was simply not in Q.[89] If Luke 14:5 // Matthew 12:11 *was* a Q saying, however, it would have been the only saying in Q that mentions the Sabbath.[90]

There are in fact a number of significant verbal agreements between the two versions.[91] Structurally, Matthew's and Luke's versions both begin with an interrogative pronoun, both refer to an animal falling into a pit, and both ask whether the owner would not draw it out on the Sabbath. This confluence of

---

Between Jewish Law and the Gentile Mission," Ph.D. diss., Claremont Graduate University, 1999.

[86] John S. Kloppenborg, "The Sayings Gospel Q and the Quest of the Historical Jesus," *HTR* 89 (1996): 332n106.

[87] James M. Robinson, "The International Q Project Work Session 16 November 1991," *JBL* 111 (1992): 506. See also James M. Robinson, Paul Hoffmann, and John S. Kloppenborg, eds., *The Critical Edition of Q: A Synopsis including the Gospels of Matthew and Luke, Mark and Thomas with English, German, and French Translations of Q and Thomas* (Minneapolis: Fortress, 2000).

[88] Bultmann, *Die Geschichte*, 10; Klaus Berger, *Die Gesetzesauslegung Jesu: Ihr historischer Hintergrund im Judentum und im Alten Testament* (Neukirchen-Vluyn: Neukirchener, 1972), 583; Paul-Gerhard Klumbies, "Die Sabbatheilungen Jesu nach Markus und Lukas," in *Jesu Rede von Gott und ihre Nachgeschichte im frühen Christentum: Beiträge zur Verkṇdigung Jesu und zum Kerygma der Kirche*, ed. D.-A. Koch, G. Sellin, and A. Lindemann (Gütersloher: Gerd Mohn, 1989), 173–74, 176–78; Yong-Eui Yang, *Jesus and the Sabbath in Matthew's Gospel*, JSNTSup 139 (Sheffield: Sheffield Academic, 1997), 258, 264n83.

[89] John S. Kloppenborg, *Q Parallels* (Sonoma, Calif.: Polebridge, 1988), 160; Neirynck, "Luke 14,1–6." See also Harry T. Fleddermann, *Q: A Reconstruction and Commentary*, BTS 1 (Leuven: Peeters, 2005), 708: "The saying makes sense without the frame." Schulz, *Q*, 41; B. Weiß (*Die Quellen des Lukasevangelium* [Stuttgart & Berlin: J.G. Cotta'sche Buchhandlung Nachfolger, 1907], 206) argued that Luke 14:1-6 comes from *Sondergut*. G. H. Müller (*Zur Synopse: Untersuchung über die Arbeitsweise des Lk und Mt und ihr Quellen*, FRLANT 11 [Göttingen: Vandenhoeck & Ruprecht, 1908], 54) considers Luke 14:1-6 as "Sonderüberlieferung." Rudolf Bultmann, *Die Geschichte*, 10; idem, *The History of the Synoptic Tradition* (Oxford: Blackwell, 1968), 12; Helmut Koester, *Ancient Christian Gospels: Their History and Development* (Philadelphia: Trinity International, 1992), 147n3; George DeWitt Castor, *Matthew's Saying of Jesus: The Non-Marcan Common Source of Matthew and Luke* (Chicago: University of Chicago Press, 1912), 173; Joseph A. Fitzmyer, *The Gospel according to Luke*, AB 28/28A (Garden City, N.Y.: Doubleday, 1985), 2:1039; Rudolf Laufen, *Die Doppelüberlieferung der Logienquelle und des Markusevangeliums*, BBB 54 (Königstein and Bonn: Hanstein, 1980), 81–82; J. D. Crossan, *In Fragments: The Aphorisms of Jesus* (San Francisco: Harper & Row, 1983), 340.

[90] Kloppenborg, "Sayings Gospel Q and the Quest of the Historical Jesus," 332.

[91] The verbal agreements are: εἶπεν αὐτοῖς τίς; ὑμῶν; ἐμπὲσῃ; σάββασιν εἰς; οὐχὶ; αὐτὸ (Matt 12:11); αὐτοὺς εἶπεν τίνος ὑμῶν; εἰς φρέαρ πεσεῖται; οὐχ; αὐτον; σαββάτου (Luke 14:5).

distinctive themes, presupposing a Sabbath controversy with Pharisees, is remarkable.[92] Finally, the diction, style, and rhetorical form of Luke 14:5 // Matthew 12:11 are reminiscent of Q. In particular, Luke 14:5 // Matthew 12:11 uses τίς ὑμῶν (a typical Q construction)[93] and the verb ἐγείρω ("to raise") (cf. Matt 3:7-9 // Luke 3:8 [ἐγεῖραι]; Matt 11:5 // Luke 7:22 [ἐγείρονται]; Matt 12:41 // Luke 11:31 [ἐγερθήσεται]),[94] and Matthew 15:14 // Luke 6:39 even refers to the blind falling "into a pit" (εἰς βόθυνον). On the other hand, the verbal agreements are not necessarily decisive. It is possible that isolated sayings circulated freely in the Jesus movement, although the verbal agreements between Matthew 12:11 and Luke 14:5, in conjunction with the near-identical placement of the saying in a Sabbath controversy context involving healing and Pharisees, suggest either Luke's use of Matthew or a Q saying.

Luke's version of the saying is text-critically problematic. Luke 14:5 refers to υἱὸς ἢ βοῦς ("a son *or* an ox"),[95] but many manuscript witnesses attest that it was regarded as "incongruous."[96] The Lukan witnesses vary, but the oldest and most difficult reading is υἱὸς ἢ βοῦς.[97] This consensus is supported by "son" being the

---

[92] Eduard von Lohse, "Jesu Wurte über den Sabbat," in *Judentum, Urchristentum, Kirche: Festschrift für Joachim Jeremias*, ed. W. Eltester (Berlin: Alfred Töpelmann, 1960), 81.

[93] Cf. Q 11:11, τίς ἐστιν ἐξ ὑμῶν; 12:25, τίς δὲ ἐξ ὑμῶν; 15:4, τίς ἄνθρωπος ἐξ ὑμῶν. See J. Jeremias, *The Parables of Jesus* (New York: Scribner's Sons, 1963), 145.

[94] Neirynck, "Luke 14,1–6," 253.

[95] Tuckett, *Q and the History of Early Christianity*, 414.

[96] Some scholars favor "ox and ass (ὄνος)." See J. M. Creed, *The Gospel according to St. Luke: The Greek Text with Introduction, Notes and Indices* (London: Macmillan, 1965), 189 (emphasis added): "υἱὸς ἢ βοῦς: this difficult reading is *doubtless prior to the variants*, but it can scarcely be right." C. F. Evans (*Saint Luke* [Philadelphia: Trinity International, 1990], 570) prefers "ass or ox" based on Deut 22:4. T. W. Manson (*Sayings of Jesus*, 227) favors the reading "ass," because "ox" and "ass" appear together in the OT. E. Haenchen, *Der Weg Jesu: Eine Erklärung des Markus-Evangeliums und der kanonischen Parallelen* (Berlin: de Gruyter, 1966), 126. There are manuscript witnesses for this (e.g., ℵ; K L X Π Ψ $f^1 f^{13}$ 33 892 1071 1079 1230 1241 1253 1546 1646), but this variant is better ascribed to copyists and/or assimilation to Luke 13:15 ("ox or [his] donkey"). Robert Banks, *Jesus and the Law in the Synoptic Tradition* (Cambridge: Cambridge University Press, 1975), 128n1: "The more dificult reading is to be accepted."

[97] Neirynck, "Luke 14,1-6," 254–55: "There is now almost a consensus on reading υἱὸς ἢ βοῦς in Lk 14,5." Bruce M. Metzger, *A Textual Commentary on the Greek New Testament*, 3rd ed. (New York: United Bible Societies, 1975), 164: "The oldest reading preserved in the manuscripts seems to be υἱὸς ἢ βοῦς." Fitzmyer, *Gospel according to Luke*, 1042: "The best texts (P^{45}, p^{75}, ℵ*, B and the Koine text-tradition) as well as the Ol and the OS versions read 'a child or an ox.'" Davies and Allison, *Commentary on Matthew*, 2:320: "Lk 14,5 has υἱὸς ἢ βοῦς ... is probably original." Neirynck, "Luke 14,1–6," 254–55: "The variant readings in Greek manuscripts and in ancient versions and the modern theories on Greek text and its Aramaic Vorlage have their origin in a common dissatisfaction with the incongruous combination of 'a son' with 'an ox.'" See also B. F. Westcott and F. J. A. Hort, "Appendix: I. Notes on Select

more difficult and better-attested reading.⁹⁸ Some scholars have thus concluded that the original form of the saying referred to a "son" who had fallen into a pit or well on the Sabbath.⁹⁹ This reading has the advantage of providing us with a far more halakhically persuasive version of the saying than that found in Matthew 12:11,¹⁰⁰ since the Pharisees would have regarded rescuing a human being whose life was in danger "a legitimate breach" of the Sabbath.¹⁰¹ *If* the original saying also referred to someone's "son" in a "well," this would increase the risk of mortal danger (by drowning). In short, Luke has intensified the halakhic dilemma, perhaps recognizing that Matthew's argument was halakhically problematic or even untenable and consequently raising the stakes by *adding* the "son" reference. Those who favor Luke's version, therefore, suggest that *Matthew* changed Q's "son" reference to "sheep,"¹⁰² perhaps because Matthew's reference to a "sheep" (πρόβατον) is characteristic of Matthew's editorial or theological interests (cf. 18:12-14). Alternatively, if Luke used Matthew, this would be Luke's redaction of Matthew. In the former case, Matthew's *a minore ad maius* argument would be a "secondary adaptation."¹⁰³ It has also been suggested that Matthew's reference to a "sheep" can be explained as a (mis)translation of an originally Aramaic (Q)

Readings," in *The New Testament in the Original Greek* (New York: Harper & Brothers, 1881), 62: "The obvious temptation to change υἱός to the easier word, supported by parallelism, and the difficulty of accounting for the converse change constitute strong transcriptional evidence, which agrees with the specially high excellence of the group attesting υἱός." M. J. Lagrange, *Évangile selon Saint Luc* (Paris: Librairie Lecoffre, 1941), 399. Adolf Schlatter, *Das Evangelium des Lukas* (Stuttgart: Calver, 1960), 340; W. Grundmann, *Das Evangelium nach Lukas* (Berlin: Evangelische Verlagsanstalt, 1961), 292; Marshall, *Gospel of Luke*, 579. See also P. Vouga, *Jésus et la Loi: Selon la Tradition Synoptique* (Genèva: Labor et Fides, 1988), 60; Bovon, *Das Evangelium nach Lukas*, 2: 422–23.

⁹⁸ P⁴⁵, P⁷⁵, ℵ*, B W Δ 28 209 565 700 1009 1010 1195 1216 1242 1365 2148.

⁹⁹ Tuckett, *Q and the History*, 414; idem, *Revival*, 99; G. Strecker, *Der Weg der Gerechtigkeit* (Göttingen: Vandenhoeck & Ruprecht, 1971), 19n3; U. Busse, *Die Wunder des Propheten Jesus*, Forschung zur Bibel 24 (Stuttgart: Katholiesches Bibelwerk, 1979), 310; W. Schenk, *Synopse zur Redenquelle der Evangelien: Q-Synopse und Rekonstruktion in deuscher Übersetzung mit kurzen Erläuterungen* (Düsseldorf: Patmos, 1981), 105; Kosch, *Die eschatologische Tora*, 206.

¹⁰⁰ Fleddermann (*Q*, 709–10) argues that Luke had βοῦς but added υἱός. Davies and Allison (*Commentary on Matthew*, 2:320) argue that Luke 14:5 is "probably original ... Matthew's text is explained by two considerations. First, the evangelist wished to make the argument *a fortiori* (cf. 12.12), and this excluded the use of 'son.' Secondly, in composing 12.9–14 he was probably reminded of the parable of the lost sheep (18.12–14; cf. Lk 15.4–7)."

¹⁰¹ Tuckett, *Q and the History*, 415 (emphasis added).

¹⁰² Tuckett, *Q and the History*, 414; idem, *Revival*, 98.

¹⁰³ Neirynck, "Luke 14,1–6," 255.

saying.¹⁰⁴ Alternatively, it has been argued that Luke's "son" (ברא) was mistakenly translated from "ox/beast" (בעירא).¹⁰⁵

What, then, are we to make of this enigmatic saying? Luke and Matthew both introduce the saying into a Markan narrative framework, presumably because the saying suggested a Sabbath healing controversy. After all, both narratives introduce the sick person in a formulaic way, and both have the Pharisees ask this question: "Is it permitted to heal on the Sabbath?" The saying thus presupposes a social location in which an *animal* fallen into a pit on the Sabbath *could* be presupposed as halakhically unproblematic, and that does not appear to have been an originally Pharisaic one. Therefore, it is not a warranted presupposition. Matthew and Luke both use the saying to stir up Jesus' controversy with the Pharisees, but Luke's version blunts the force of the rhetorical argument against the Pharisees by adding "son," thereby raising the stakes and making the situation more serious.¹⁰⁶ Whether or not the additional "son" could be explained by an Aramaic original, Luke seems to have thought that this textual addition even further exposed the Pharisees' hypocrisy: How could they object to an act of healing on the Sabbath when they were prepared to rescue their children from danger? Yet Luke does not portray the scene as a life-threatening situation. Nevertheless, Luke's reference to a "son" renders the argument less halakhically problematic, despite the fact that he also includes "ox/beast."

In contrast, Matthew's version resembles a rabbinic-like *qal wa-homer* argument, in which the sheep is compared with the man, which would seem to justify Jesus' healing. Yet Jesus' presupposition—that rescuing an animal on the Sabbath would be acceptable—would *not* have been acceptable to Pharisees.¹⁰⁷ The Jesus

---

¹⁰⁴ Sven-Olav Back ("Jesus and the Sabbath," in *Handbook for the Study of the Historical Jesus*, ed. T. Holmén and S. R. Porter [Leiden: Brill, 2011], 3:2627–2629) suggests that Matt 12:11 // Luke 14:5 referred to a "son" (ברא) in the original Aramaic with additional wordplays with בעירא ("ox") and בירא ("well"), but since this could not be considered an a fortiori argument—suggesting that help given to an animal should all the more be given to a human—it should rather be understood as a τίς ἐξ ὑμῶν–saying that makes an a fortiori argument from humans to God.

¹⁰⁵ Matthew Black suggests that the Aramaic word for "ox/beast" (בעירא) was mistaken for "son." This led to the introduction of "well" (בירא) instead of "pit" (בור). See Black, "The Aramaic Spoken by Christ and Luke 14,5," *JTS* 1 (1950): 61: "υἱός has arisen through a misunderstanding of the original." Cf. Fitzmyer, *Gospel according to Luke*, 1042: "It is highly unlikely that any play on underlying Aramaic words is involved in this pair."

¹⁰⁶ David B. Sloan ("The τίς ἐξ ὑμῶν Similitudes and the Extent of Q," *JSNT* 36, no. 3 [2016]: 345) concludes that this is a Q saying, that πρόβατον is Matthean, and that Luke added the word υἱός.

¹⁰⁷ Marshall (*Gospel of Luke*, 579) notes that *t.Shab.* 128b gives "both a mild ruling, allowing helping an animal out of a pit, and a harsh ruling, allowing only the provision of fodder to it in the pit." One school allowed for food to be lowered to the animal, while another allowed

of Matthew 12:11 seems to assume that a sheep could be lifted out of a pit on the Sabbath without further qualification. Yet there is no evidence that raising an animal out of a pit on the Sabbath was acceptable to Pharisees.[108] The saying could thus *not* have been intended for Pharisees.[109] As we have seen, CD forbids lifting an animal out of a pit (CD 11.13–14), and rabbinic discussions agree (*Tosefta*, *t.Shab.* 14.3; *m.Yoma* 8.6). This halakhic agreement between the Essenes and the rabbis against Jesus suggests that many sectarian Jews would have objected to lifting the animal out of the pit on the Sabbath. In Matthew's narrative setting, it is the Pharisees who question Jesus' regard for the Mosaic Law, yet there is no evidence that what Jesus presupposes as halakhically permissible was indeed regarded as permissible by them.[110] In fact, the opposite seems to be the case.[111]

Later rabbinical authorities held that an animal could be removed if it was in pain or its life was in danger.[112] The Babylonian Amoraim apparently thought that if an animal could stay comfortably in place, and be fed, it could stay in place; however, if this would cause pain, then it could be removed (*b.Shab.* 128b). This would correlate to Exodus 23:5, which requires assistance be given to suffering animals. An animal in pain should be assisted, even on the Sabbath.[113] This tradition would be an interesting parallel to Matthew 12:11 *if* the sheep was described as being in *pain*, or if its life were in danger, but that is not the case. The rabbinical tradition affirms the greater authority of preserving life over the Sabbath (*m.Yoma* 8.6), but we should not read this *into* the text. Jesus' presupposition—that his Pharisaic opponents *would* break the Sabbath in order to rescue a single sheep—is

---

for articles to be lowered into the pit to enable the animal to escape by itself. Neither school allowed the animal to be lifted up out of the pit on the Sabbath.

[108] Tuckett, *Revival*, 99.

[109] David Flusser with R. Steven Notley, *The Sage from Galilee: Rediscovering Jesus' Genius* (Grand Rapids: Eerdmans, 2007 [1968]), 40: "It is probable that those who stood by watching were not in fact Pharisees. Their description as such is the product of the hand of a later redactor."

[110] Tuckett, *Revival*, 98; idem, *Q and the History*, 11.

[111] Hyam Maccoby, *Early Rabbinic Writings* (Cambridge: Cambridge University Press, 1988), 171. The rabbis may have allowed for food to be thrown down for the day or for things to be dropped into the pit to enable the animal to climb out (*m.Besa* 3.4).

[112] Herbert W. Basser, "The Gospels and Rabbinic Literature," in *The Missing Jesus: Rabbinic Judaism and the New Testament*, ed. B. Chilton, C. A. Evans, and J. Neusner (Boston: Brill, 2002), 77–99, 97.

[113] While it was permissible to preserve life on a Sabbath (*m.Yoma* 8.6–7), *m.Betz* 3.4 preserves a ruling that solves the problem of not being able to bring up an animal out of a pit on the Sabbath by envisioning the animal in the pit as a firstborn with a blemish taken to slaughter. This source seems to "assume a ruling which allowed a person but not an animal to be brought up from a pit on a Sabbath or High Festival Day." See David Instone-Brewer, *Traditions of the Rabbis from the Era of the New Testament*, vol. 2A, *Feasts and Sabbaths: Passover and Atonement* (Grand Rapids: Eerdmans, 2011), 76–81.

difficult to sustain.¹¹⁴ We cannot extrapolate from the saying that the animal in question was suffering or in mortal danger.

If neither Pharisees, later rabbis, nor the Essenes endorsed Jesus' presupposition that it was halakhically acceptable to rescue an animal fallen into a pit on the Sabbath, it would seem to follow that the originally intended audience for this saying was *not* Pharisaic but a group of rural Judean or Galilean Jews. It seems more likely that Matthew has inherited a saying that was addressed *not* to Pharisees but to the halakhically lax rural inhabitants of Judea and/or Galilee,¹¹⁵ for whom rescuing an animal on the Sabbath could have been either acceptable or a nonissue altogether.¹¹⁶ Jesus is addressing "ordinary Palestinian Jews."¹¹⁷ Since Jesus seems to presuppose "a common view of sabbath observance that he and his audience share," this may be "a rare instance of Jesus fighting a battle-at-a-distance with the Essene movement . . . for the loyalty of ordinary Jews." In short, "Jesus is rejecting the strict practice of both the Essenes and the Pharisees . . with the commonsense approach of ordinary Jewish peasants."¹¹⁸

Since the saying presupposes an audience that would not object to its argument, it does provide a contrast between the implied audience and CD. That is, Jesus presupposes the permissibility of what CD prohibits, providing us with an opportunity to explore the nature of this apparent *difference* between Jesus and the Essenes. This difference, however, is between the contingent, provisional legal ruling of a second-century BCE community anticipating an imminent eschatological transformation (cf. 1QS 9.11) and an enigmatic, obscure saying of the historical Jesus reflecting the realized eschatology of the early Jesus movement.

What was Jesus' attitude toward the Sabbath? As is well known, the Synoptic Gospels contain numerous Sabbath controversies.¹¹⁹ Jesus heals on the Sabbath, picks grain on the Sabbath, and declares the Son of Man to be "Lord of the Sabbath." The Sabbath is "made for humankind, not humankind for the Sabbath" (Mark 2:27). The Sabbath plays a defining role in how conflicts between Jesus and his contemporaries are portrayed. The Synoptic Gospels portray Jesus as

---

¹¹⁴ Tuckett, *Q and the History*, 415: Matthew's presupposition fails "to satisfy Jewish sensibilities, since no Jew apparently accepted that one could rescue a sheep from a pit on the Sabbath."

¹¹⁵ Von Lohse, "Jesu Wurte über den Sabbat," 79–89.

¹¹⁶ Kuhn, "Qumran Texts and the Historical Jesus," 574: Jesus was "arguing from a Galilean or even a Gaulanitis point of view." Cf. M. Eugene Boring, *The Gospel of Matthew*, NIB (Nashville: Abingdon, 1995), 8:279.

¹¹⁷ Meier, *Marginal Jew*, 4:263.

¹¹⁸ Meier, *Marginal Jew*, 4:264.

¹¹⁹ See Doering, *Schabbat*; Donald A. Hagner, "Jesus and the Synoptic Sabbath Controversies," in *Key Events in the Life of the Historical Jesus*, ed. R. L. Webb and D. L. Bock (Tübingen: Mohr Siebeck, 2009), 251–92.

performing miracles of healing on the Sabbath (Mark 3:1-5; Matt 12:1-8; Luke 13:10-17). One passage has Jesus' disciples plucking (τίλλοντες) grain in a field on the Sabbath, and some Pharisees accuse him of violating the Sabbath (Mark 2:23-28; Matt 12:1-14; Luke 6:1-5), presumably because their actions could be interpreted as *working* on the Sabbath (Matt 12:2; cf. Num 15:32-36). Jesus, however, is not violating Sabbath law; he is *interpreting* Sabbath law.[120] There is no biblical law prohibiting the plucking of grain on the Sabbath.[121] The question, therefore, is not whether Jesus is violating Sabbath law but whether healing on the Sabbath is "work."[122] Yet there is no explicit prohibition of healing on the Sabbath in the Mosaic Torah. *Work* was forbidden (Exod 20:8-11). Harvesting and cooking were forbidden (Exod 34:21; 35:1-3), but healing or helping those in need and suffering was (arguably) *not* "work." Jesus may have offended *Pharisaic* customs, traditions, and sentiments, but he does not violate Mosaic Law.[123] As we have seen, Mark roots Jesus' halakhah in an argument from creation (Mark 2). As with divorce, Jesus appeals to an eschatological hermeneutic of creation. Jesus' attitude toward the Sabbath is best understood in light of Jesus' creation-Torah.[124] When Jesus says that "the Sabbath was made for humankind, not humankind for the Sabbath; so the Son of Man is Lord even of the Sabbath" (Mark 2:27), we are reminded of the creation narrative: Jesus' Sabbath healings are portrayed as divinely authorized acts of eschatological restoration. Jesus argues from creation,[125] affirming the Sabbath as what God originally intended for humanity.

---

[120] Loader, "Jesus and the Law," 2749: "One law overrules another.... Sabbath is not disparaged.... The lordship of the Son of Man is therefore not to reject the Sabbath, but to interpret it." See also Markus Bockmuehl, *Jewish Law in Gentile Churches: Halakhah and the Beginning of Christian Public Ethics* (Grand Rapids: Baker, 2000), 6.

[121] James G. Crossley, *Jesus and the Chaos of History: Redirecting the Life of the Historical Jesus*, Biblical Refigurations (New York: Oxford University Press, 2015), 42, 30. See also John P. Meier, "The Historical Jesus and the Plucking of the Grain on the Sabbath," *CBQ* 66 (2004): 561–81. CD forbids eating food lost in the field on the Sabbath (10.22–23). Similarly, *m Pes.* 4.8 forbids picking up fruit on the Sabbath.

[122] Loader, "Jesus and the Law," 2750.

[123] It is not until the Gospel of John that Jesus seems to set Sabbath law aside (5:16-20). Jesus violates the biblical Law by endorsing a man's carrying a "burden" on the Sabbath (John 5:1-18; cf. 9:14-16).

[124] Hagner, "Jesus and the Synoptic Sabbath Controversies," 287–88: "In good Jewish form, Jesus penetrates to the essence of the Sabbath, by going back to its foundation in Genesis" (283). Yang (*Jesus and the Sabbath in Matthew's Gospel*, 225) describes Jesus as "the recoverer and fulfiller of God's original and ultimate will for the Sabbath."

[125] Meier, *Marginal Jew*, 4:296, notes: "his vision of the end time as restoring the whole and wholesome goodness of creation that God willed in the beginning. By approaching the sabbath from this eschatological vantage point, Jesus seeks to instill a proper sense of priorities. The roots of the sabbath lie in creation itself, but a creation that is meant to serve the good of a humanity created by God in the beginning and now restored by him in the last days."

"Love Your Enemies": Jesus and (Non)Violence

The topic of violence in the Dead Sea Scrolls and its role in the ideological formation of the *Yahad* has not received sustained critical study.[126] Nonetheless, it seems that the *Yahad*'s conflicted relationship with other Jews led to the literary production of various apocalyptic fantasies and "narrative[s] of violence."[127] The *Yahad* was not necessarily able to *act* on or literally resolve these conflicts, so their internalized suppression of violence was literarily expressed in elaborate eschatological dramas of divine violence, vengeance, and vindication. The *Yahad*'s "violence" was imagined, sublimated, suppressed, postponed, and indefinitely deferred and thus "never actually becomes real violence."[128] In the *Rule of the Community* (1QS), for example, the Teacher(s) of the community are instructed "to hate all the Sons of Darkness" (1.10), to "conceal the teaching of the Law from men of injustice" (9.17), and to pledge an

> eternal hatred against the Men of the Pit in the spirit of concealment...
> as a slave does to the one who rules over him,
> and one oppressed before the one who dominates over him. (9.22–23)

This text advocates a kind of secret hatred toward the community's enemies—that is, those whom God also hates. It is this secret hatred that will ensure their terrible fate in the end-time judgment, when God will punish them:

> To no man will I return evil for evil, with good I will pursue humankind.
> For with God (is) the judgment of every living being, and he shall pay man his reward... but my anger I will not turn away from the Men of Deceit,
> I will not feel satisfied until he has accomplished judgment.
> I will not hold anger towards those who turn away from transgression;
> but I will not have compassion from all those who deviate from the Way. (10.17–21)

The *Yahad*, in other words, affirmed the ideal of not exacting vengeance on the enemy *for now* (1QS 10.17–18). Similarly, the *War Scroll* (1QM) describes an end-time battle between the "Sons of Light and Darkness." The text lists military equipment, army formations, battle plans, and rules about trumpets, standards, shields, cavalry, and soldiers. The angelic host is depicted as fully participating, even leading the battle. These details have led many to conclude that the Essenes were bent on political and military revolution, yet the

---

[126] See Alex P. Jassen, "The Dead Sea Scrolls and Violence: Sectarian Formation and Eschatological Imagination," *BibInt* 17 (2009): 12–44; R. Sollamo, "War and Violence in the Ideology of the Qumran Community," in *Verbum et Calamus*, ed. H. Juusola, J. Laulainen, and H. Palva (Helsinki: Finnish Oriental Society, 2004), 341–52.

[127] Jassen, "Dead Sea Scrolls and Violence," 15.

[128] Jassen, "Dead Sea Scrolls and Violence," 19.

apocalyptic battle envisioned in the *War Scroll* is a conflict of cosmic proportions and the outcome is known in advance. This is not a war that is going to be won by military force alone. The *War Scroll* is not a pragmatic training manual for "holy war"; it is an allegorical literary description of a cosmological conflict between the forces of good and evil. The Qumran group has sometimes been described as militant and hateful,[129] with appeals to the *War Scroll* as evidence of militancy.[130] Yet 1QM is an idealized depiction of an eschatological war,[131] not a military manual for soldiers.[132]

Josephus does name "John the Essene" (Ἰωάννης ὁ Ἐσσαῖος, *B.J.* 2.567; 3.11.19) as a leader in the Revolt, yet this hardly justifies characterizing the Essenes as having "participated" in the Revolt *en masse*,[133] especially if this particular reference to "Essene" refers to someone coming from the town of "Essa" (*B.J.* 2.567).[134] Yet even if "John the Essene" *was* an Essene, he may have already left the movement prior to joining the Revolt.[135] We simply don't know very much about this figure. The singular reference is anomalous, as if the mention of *one* Essene were an exception.[136] Josephus does tell us that the Essenes were tortured

---

[129] Christopher Rowland, *The Open Heaven: A Study in Apocalyptic in Judaism and Early Christianity* (New York: Crossroad, 1992), 38; cf. Loren L. Johns, "Identity and Resistance: The Varieties of Competing Models in Early Judaism," in *Qumran Studies: New Approaches, New Questions*, ed. M. T. Davis and B. A. Strawn (Grand Rapids: Eerdmans, 2007), 254–77; Sollamo, "War and Violence in the Ideology of the Qumran Community," 341–52.

[130] Jean Duhaime ("War Scroll," in *Damascus Document, War Scroll, and Related Documents*, ed. J. H. Charlesworth, vol. 2 of *The Dead Sea Scrolls: Hebrew, Aramaic, and Greek Texts with English Translations*, PTSDSSP 2 [Tübingen: Mohr Siebeck, 1995], 84) calls 1QM a "tactical treatise." Lester Grabbe ("Warfare," in *Encyclopedia of the Dead Sea Scrolls*, ed. L. H. Schiffman and J. C. VanderKam [New York: Oxford University Press, 2000], 2:965) claims that it contains data of a military manual. See also Hans Bardtke, "Die Kriegsrolle v. Qumran übersetzt," *TLZ* 80 (1955): 401–20; Leonard Rost, "Zum Buch der Kriege der Söhne des Lichtes gegen die Söhne der Finsternis," *TLZ* 80 (1955): 205–8. Geza Vermes (*The Complete Dead Sea Scrolls* [New York: Penguin, 1997], 163) argues, "it should not be mistaken for a manual of military warfare."

[131] John J. Collins, *Apocalypticism in the Dead Sea Scrolls* (New York: Routledge, 1997), 127.

[132] H. Ringgren, *The Faith of Qumran: Theology of the Dead Sea Scrolls*, trans E. T. Sander (New York: Crossroad, 1995), 18–19: "An actual war is completely out of the question."

[133] Norman Golb, *Who Wrote the Dead Sea Scrolls: The Search for the Secret of Qumran* (New York: Scribner, 1995), 136.

[134] Steve Mason (*Josephus, Judea, and Christian Origins: Methods and Categories* [Peabody, Mass: Hendrickson, 2009], 428) points out that Ἐσσαῖος may be an *ethnikon* designating John as someone from Essa. Josephus mentions a place called Essa in the Transjordan (*A.J.* 13.393). So also Abraham Schalit, *Namenwörterbuch zu Flavius Josephus* (Leiden: Brill, 1968), 46.

[135] Golb, *Who Wrote the Dead Sea Scrolls*, 141.

[136] Cecil Roth ("Why the Qumran Sect Cannot Have Been Essenes," *RevQ* 3 (1959): 417–22) argues that the idea that the Essenes joined the Revolt "has no foundation" in Josephus.

during the Revolt, but he does not tell us that they fought back (*B.J.* 2.152–153). On the contrary, the Essenes are described as passively resisting the Romans, while Roman soldiers are described as torturing them in order to make them "blaspheme against the Lawgiver" or "eat forbidden food."

There is no unambiguous evidence that the Essenes participated in the Revolt.[137] On the contrary, there are contemporary reports of their pacifism, their passive resistance to violence, their submission to foreign rule as willed by God, and their belief that God alone would settle their affairs.[138] Josephus describes the Essenes as "upright managers of anger" and "servants of peace" (εἰρήνης ὑπουργοί) (*B.J.* 2.135). They lived by moral principles and swore

> to practice piety towards the Deity; then to observe justice towards men
> and to do no wrong to any man, neither of his own accord
> nor at another's command; to hate the wicked always,
> and to fight together with the just. He swears constant loyalty to all,
> but above all to those in power; for authority never falls to a man
> without the will of God. (*B.J.* 2.139–140)[139]

Like Josephus, Philo praises the Essenes for their "love for God," their "unceasing purity," their "love of virtue," and their "continence and endurance," but above all for their "love of men" (*Prob.* 84). So while Josephus reports that the Essenes take an oath never to commit violence and to obey the rulers who have their power conferred on them by God (*B.J.* 2.139–140), Philo denies that they were violent at all. On the contrary, he asserts:

> In vain would one look among them for makers of arrows, or javelins, or swords,
> or helmets, or armour, or shields; in short, for makers of arms, or military machines,
> or any instrument of war. (*Prob.* 78)[140]

---

[137] Hippolytus describes the Essenes as "Zealots," whom Josephus describes following his description of the Essenes in *B.J.* 2.161. Alternatively, Hippolytus may have derived his information on the Essenes from the same source used by Josephus. For the latter possibility, see Morton Smith, "The Description of the Essenes in Josephus and the Philosophumena," *HUCA* 29 (1958): 273–313; Matthew Black, *The Scrolls and Christian Origins: Studies in the Jewish Background of the New Testament* (New York: Charles Scribner's Sons, 1961), 187–91.

[138] See Gordon Mark Zerbe, *Non-retaliation in Early Jewish and New Testament Texts: Ethical Themes in Social Contexts*, JSPSup13 (Sheffield: JSOT, 1993), 106–35.

[139] Cf. David Flusser (*The Spiritual History of the Dead Sea Sect*, trans. C. Glucker [Tel Aviv: MOD Books, 1989], 78) cites this passage as an example of how "hatred can turn into real non-violence, and an unconditional non-resistance to evil into all-embracing love."

[140] Joan E. Taylor (*The Essenes, the Scrolls, and the Dead Sea* [New York: Oxford University Press, 2012], 32) objects to the idea that Philo's Essenes are "pacifists," stating that "Philo is in full rhetorical mode here [*Prob.* 78], in stating that the Essenes have nothing to do with making

Essenic nonviolence presupposed that God would turn the tide in their favor. While they may have looked *forward* to the end time, their behavior seems to have been characterized by a temporary strategic nonviolence while they cooperated with the powers that be. The evidence is fragmentary and ambiguous, but the Essenes did not necessarily join the Revolt. Nonetheless, their strategic nonviolence does seem to have produced a covert *literary* hatred for the "enemy" and elaborate *textual* fantasies of divine judgment. The *Yaḥad* may have looked forward to the restoration of the "glory of Adam" and the arrival of an eschatological Jubilee, the "day of [peace]" (יום ה[שלום]),[141] but the *Yaḥad*'s sectarian orientation within early Judaism retained a certain hostile exclusivity and rivalry toward other Jewish groups.

In recent years, a number of publications have drawn attention to the complex relationship between Jesus and violence.[142] These publications are part of a wider disciplinary discussion on the topic of violence in the study of religion. Yet any discussion of religion, violence, and/or the historical Jesus depends on how we define and deploy our terms. For example, violence, militancy, revolution, revolt, rebellion, insurrection, resistance, and sedition are all politically loaded words that carry weight and wield considerable rhetorical power. The semantic range of *violence*, which can be defined as the intentional use of force in order to hurt, damage, or kill another person or group, involves different kinds of violence: physical, mental, and/or emotional. Similarly, *violent force* can take multiple forms: personal, physical, sexual, psychological, emotional, interpersonal, socio-political, military, systemic, and structural. Physical violence itself can refer to property, animals, and/or people. Justifications of violence can also depend on the agent(s), the context(s) in which violence occurs, and the end to which violence occurs.

---

instruments of war." Since Philo "makes war and peace counter-balance each other in dualistic imagery that is actually designed to emphasize the fact that the Essenes are not commercial businessmen ... Read with an awareness of Philo's rhetoric, evidence for Essene pacifism in this passage evaporates" (33).

[141] For bibliography, see Adam S. van der Woude, "Melchisedek als himmlische Erlösergestalt in den neugefundenen eschatologischen Midraschim aus Qumran Höhle XI," *Oudtestamentische Studien* 14 (1965): 354–73; James A. Sanders, "The Old Testament in 11QMelchizedek," *Janes* 5 (1973): 373–82.

[142] On Jesus as a revolutionary who advocated violence, see Dale B. Martin, "Jesus in Jerusalem: Armed and Not Dangerous," *JSNT* 37, no. 1 (2014): 3–24; Fernando Bermejo Rubio, "Jesus and the Anti-Roman Resistance: A Reassessment of the Arguments," *JSHJ* 12, no. 1/2 (2014): 1–105. On violence in early Christianity, see T. Nicholas Schonhoffer, "The Failure of Nerve to Recognize Violence in Early Christianity: The Case of the Parable of the Assassin," in *Failure and Nerve in the Academic Study of Religion: Essays in Honor of Donald Wiebe*, ed. W. E. Arnal, W. Braun, and R. T. McCutcheon (Sheffield: Equinox, 2012), 192–217.

Let us take, for example, Jesus' infamous Temple tantrum. While all four Gospels portray Jesus as disturbing commercial operations in the Temple, the Gospel of John alone describes Jesus making a "whip of cords" (φραγέλλιον ἐκ σχοινίων) in order to drive "all of them" out of the Temple.[143] Yet the fact that this reference to a "whip of cords" is found *only* in the Johannine narrative should urge caution.[144] John does not tell us that Jesus used this so-called "whip of cords" to actually *strike* anyone: Jesus "expels" the sheep and cattle out of the Temple. Yet a "whip of cords" could be used just as much to make a striking sound as to inflict bodily blows. So while Jesus is reported to have overturned the tables of the money-changers—presumably using *violent force* to do so—Jesus' use of physical force would not require it to have been an act of physical violence against animals or people, but could rather be read as an attempt to move animals by "shooing" them away without ever striking them.[145] Consequently, those who read John's account as evidence that Jesus used a "whip" to actually beat people up are reading this *into* the text. John's Gospel is a highly *symbolic* literary representation constructed in order to make the theological point that Jesus abolished animal sacrifice and replaced the Temple.

Jesus' act in the Temple could perhaps be described as "violent" toward the tables and chairs,[146] yet using the word "violent" to describe Jesus here is simultaneously problematic insofar as John does not depict Jesus actually striking anyone. The rhetorical appeal to *violence* confuses more than it clarifies. At the same time, it is difficult to deny that "Jesus'" apocalyptic rhetoric includes

---

[143] John 2:13. For discussion, see N. Clayton Croy, "The Messianic Whippersnapper: Did Jesus Use a Whip on People in the Temple (John 2:13)?" *JBL* 128 (2009): 555–68; Andy Alexis-Baker, "Violence, Nonviolence and the Temple Incident in John 2:13-15," *BibInt* 20 (2012): 73–96. Hector Avalos, *The Bad Jesus: The Ethics of New Testament Ethics* (Sheffield: Sheffield Phoenix, 2015), 110–26, argues that Jesus' actions in the Johannine Temple Incident scene should be interpreted as "violent" since Jesus is portrayed as using "violence" against people.

[144] David W. Chapman (review of Simon J. Joseph, *Jesus and the Temple: The Crucifixion in Its Jewish Context*, *JTS* 68, no. 2 [2017], https://doi-org.ezproxy.callutheran.edu/10.1093/jts/flx138) challenges my contention that there is "no good evidence Jesus ever used violence" and characterizes the Temple incident as an "angry assault on others," suggesting that Jesus' eschatology may point to his "accepting aspects of divine violence." Chapman also claims that I argue that "Jesus' Temple cleansing drove away sacrificial animals" (131), but neglects to mention that he is citing my discussion of the Johannine Gospel's *literary representation* of Jesus, which I read as *symbolic* of Jesus' relationship to the Temple and abolition of animal sacrifice.

[145] Thomas R. Yoder Neufeld, *Killing Enmity: Violence and the New Testament* (Grand Rapids: Baker Academic, 2011), 15.

[146] John 2:14-15; Matt 21:12-13; Mark 11:15-17; Luke 19:45-46. See Mark R. Bredin, "John's Account of Jesus' Demonstration in the Temple: Violent or Nonviolent?" *BTB* 33 (2003): 44–50.

eschatological scenarios of divine violence.¹⁴⁷ The problem is that we cannot conflate the historical Jesus with everything ascribed to "Jesus" without reinscribing contradictory expressions of violence in the tradition and losing sight of the particular apocalyptic and halakhic vision(s) that informed, inspired, and motivated the Jesus of history. Our composite "Jesus" would become the symbolic repository of everything ever said or recorded about Jesus between 30 and 100 CE, identifying him with the very kinds of violent insurrection he may have rejected. In short, we would lose sight of the possibility that Jesus' imperative to "love your enemies" participated in an ancient discourse on violence and represents an historically accurate representation—or "memory"—of Jesus' teachings.

Jesus' biographers clearly "remembered" Jesus as a Teacher who eschewed violence. The Matthean Jesus, for example, calls his disciples to be "peacemakers" (εἰρηνοποιοί) (Matt 5:9; cf. Matt 5:38-48 // Luke 6:27-32). This may have been, in part, a learned strategic response to the overwhelming military might of the Romans, but it rapidly became a "Christian" ideal.¹⁴⁸ This reading not only explains the presence of both "violent" and "nonviolent" sayings in the tradition without collapsing them into an undifferentiated body of material; it can also explain and account for why the "nonviolent" sayings could not be omitted in the developing tradition: they were dominical. Jesus' followers may not have *maintained* this vision, but they did *preserve* it. Nonetheless, Jesus' followers were also armed with centuries of apocalyptic Jewish tradition, empowered by their faith in Jesus' divine vindication, and frustrated by their contemporaries' continuing "unbelief." It is not difficult to understand why they picked up the vocabulary of apocalyptic violence and came to "remember" Jesus as the once-rejected-but-now-vindicated Son of Man who submitted to a violent but divine death but would soon return to complete his now-violent mission. The Jesus tradition came to "remember" Jesus as a prophet of apocalyptic violence, but also seems to have transformed a critic of violence into a perpetrator of violence.

The historical Jesus does not seem to have been inclined to acts of physical violence. Jesus may or may not have envisioned eschatological restoration as

---

¹⁴⁷ Schonhoffer, "Failure of Nerve to Recognize Violence," 192–217. See also Simon J. Joseph, "A Social Identity Approach to the Rhetoric of Apocalyptic Violence in the Sayings Gospel Q," *HR* 57, no. 1 (2017): 28–49.

¹⁴⁸ Dieter Lührmann, "Liebet eure Feinde (Lk 6,27-36/Mt 5,39-48)," *ZTK* 69 (1972): 412–38. Cf. Catherine Hezser, "Seduced by the Enemy or Wise Strategy? The Presentation of Non-Violence and Accommodation with Foreign Powers in Ancient Jewish Literary Sources," in *Between Cooperation and Hostility: Multiple Identities in Ancient Judaism and the Interaction with Foreign Powers*, ed. R. Albertz and J. Wöhrle (Göttingen: Vandenhoeck & Ruprecht, 2013), 221–50, 248: "By blessing peace-making and non-violence early Christians seem to have turned a necessity into an ideal."

inaugurating or culminating in divine violence,[149] but the idea that Jesus was a faithful Jew devoutly committed to God is neither controversial nor sensational. The idea that Jesus participated in early Jewish apocalypticism is, likewise, the dominant consensus of scholarship. To posit that Jesus had a *distinctive* vision of God—that is, a *theology*—is, likewise, a major presupposition of Jesus Research. It follows, therefore, that a major strand in the Jesus tradition affirms the Jesus of history as a nonviolent apocalypticist, a self-proclaimed recipient of divine revelation.[150] That is, Jesus seems to have adopted and foregrounded nonviolence—not as a temporary "strategy" or "interim ethic" to be replaced by "swords," an angelic cavalry, and supernatural warfare—but as the divine will of God.

It has been suggested that Jesus' distinctive teaching to "love your enemies" was a creative adaptation of the Essenes' "strategic nonviolence," but that he took their views one step further by advocating *love*, not *hatred*, of enemies.[151] It seems more likely, however, that Jesus rooted his innovative instruction in the nature of God—that is, in a *theological* revelation of divine impartiality. Divine peace may have been fundamental to the *Urzeit/Endzeit* paradigm of the eschatological tradition within early Judaism, but Jesus seems to have openly advocated and enacted a distinctive practice of nonviolence and nonretaliation.[152]

The term *nonviolence* refers to religious, philosophical, and theological ethical systems of abstention from violence as well as pragmatic strategies of political resistance oriented toward social change. The early Jesus tradition contains a number of sayings on nonjudgment, mercy, impartial love, forgiveness, and inclusivity.[153] The imperative to "love enemies," in particular, is punctuated by imperatives to pray for enemies, turn the other cheek (Matt 5:39b // Luke 6:29), walk the extra mile (Matt 5:41 // Luke 6:29-30), and not judge (Matt 7:1-2 // Luke 6:37-38). Jesus' instruction to "love enemies" is explicitly based on *God's* unconditional love. The instruction to be merciful is warranted because *God* is merciful. Jesus described God as a loving Father who loves *everyone* (Matt

---

[149] Martin, "Jesus in Jerusalem: Armed and Not Dangerous," 3-24.

[150] Cf. Christopher Rowland, "Apocalypticism: The Disclosure of Heavenly Knowledge," in *The Mystery of God: Early Jewish Mysticism and the New Testament*, ed. C. Rowland and C. R. A. Morray-Jones, CEINT 12 (Leiden: Brill, 2009), 13-31.

[151] Flusser with Notley, *Sage from Galilee*, 71.

[152] N. T. Wright, *Jesus and the Victory of God*, vol. 2, *Christian Origins and the Question of God* (Minneapolis: Fortress, 1996), 159, 290–91, 296, 420–21, 447–50, 462–65, 506–7, 549, 595. Richard Hays, "Victory over Violence: The Significance of N. T. Wright's Jesus for New Testament Ethics," in *Jesus & The Restoration of Israel: A Critical Assessment of N. T. Wright's "Jesus and the Victory of God,"* ed. C. C. Newman (Downers Grove, Ill.: InterVarsity, 1999), 142–58.

[153] Q 6:20; 6:27, 28, 35c-d; Q 6:31; Q 6:32-34; Q 6:36; Q 6:37-39; Q 7:22; Q 14:16-18, 21, 23; Q 15:4-5a, 7; Q 15:8-10; Q 17:3-4.

5:44-45 // Luke 6:27-28, 35c-d).[154] That is, Jesus seems to have based his vision of nonviolence on his understanding of the nature of God.[155]

Jesus' core insight seems to have been virtually unprecedented within early Judaism. There are, of course, examples of first-century Jewish nonviolent resistance to systemic violence (*B.J.* 2.174; 2.197), and Philo refers to *helping* the enemy (*QE* 2.11), but no one had ever said "*love* your enemies." While some scholars have suggested that Proverbs 25:21 may anticipate Jesus' command, a close reading of Proverbs 25:21-22 illustrates that the *motivation* for practicing kindness to one's enemies is completely different from Jesus' motivation:[156]

---

[154] Cf. 1 Thess 5:15; Rom 12:17; 1 Pet 3:9. For studies, see John Piper, *"Love Your Enemies": Jesus' Love Command in the Synoptic Gospels and in the Early Paraenesis: A History of the Tradition and Interpretation of Its Uses*, SNTSMS 38 (Cambridge: Cambridge University Press, 1979); William Klassen, "'Love Your Enemies': Some Reflections on the Current Status of Research," in *The Love of Enemy and Nonretaliation*, ed. W. M. Swartley (Louisville, Ky.: Westminster John Knox, 1992); R. Conrad Douglas, "'Love Your Enemies': Rhetoric, Tradents, and Ethos," in *Conflict and Invention: Literary, Rhetorical and Social Studies on the Sayings Gospel Q*, ed. J. S. Kloppenborg (Valley Forge, Pa.: Trinity International, 2004), 116–31; Ronald A. Piper, "The Language of Violence and the Aphoristic Sayings in Q," in *Conflict and Invention: Literary, Rhetorical, and Social Studies on the Sayings Gospel Q*, ed. J. S. Kloppenborg (Valley Forge, Pa.: Trinity International, 1995), 53–72. As authentic, see Jürgen Becker, "Feindesliebe-Nächstenliebe-Bruderliebe: Exegetische Beobachtungen als Anfrage an ein ethisches Problemfeld," *ZEE* 25 (1981): 5–18; Heinz-Wolfgang Kuhn, "Das Liebesgebot Jesus als Tora und als Evangelium: Zur Feindesliebe und zur christlichen und jüdischen Auslegung der Bergpredigt," in *Vom Urchristentum zu Jesus*, ed. H. Frankemölle and K. Kertelge, FS Joachim Gnilka (Freiburg: Herder, 1989), 194–230. Cf. Kuhn, "Jesus im Licht der Qumrangemeinde," 1268: "Die ausdrückliche Feindesliebe in dieser überfordernden, von der Gegenwart des Eschaton her ... zu verstehenden Formulierung, wie sie bei Jesus begegnet, hat in der jüdischen Literatur der Antike keine Parallele und ist zweifellos auf Jesus selbst zurückzuführen, der offenbar wieder von der Schöpfung her argumentiert, zumal selbst die frühen Christen ihre Schwierigkeiten mit dem Gebot der Feindesliebe hatten."

[155] Sarah E. Rollens (review of Simon J. Joseph, *The Nonviolent Messiah: Jesus, Q, and the Enochic Tradition*, *RBL*, June 2015, http://www.bookreviews.org/pdf/9811_10841.pdf [accessed January 3, 2016]) insinuates that my study has "a certain endgame ... to reveal a nonviolent historical Jesus" but does not deny that Q 6:20-49 is "characterized by nonviolence" nor that Q 6:20-49 represents early evidence of the historical Jesus' teachings. Rollens thus confuses constructing a historical hypothesis with advancing a (theological?) "endgame" without engaging or contesting the evidentiary basis of that historical hypothesis. On Q 6:20-49 as "characterized by nonviolence," see John S. Kloppenborg, "The Function of Apocalyptic Language in Q," in *SBL 1986 Seminar Papers* (Atlanta: Scholars, 1986), 235.

[156] Crispin Fletcher-Louis ("Jesus and Apocalypticism," in *The Historical Jesus*, ed. T. Holmén and S. E. Porter, vol. 3 of *Handbook for the Study of the Historical Jesus* [Leiden: Brill, 2011], 2900) notes that Jesus' "pacifism" is sometimes interpreted as strategic in light of the coming judgment, but "this is not the explanation given in the sources: they rather ground this ethic in a particular understanding of the imitation of God."

> If your enemy is hungry, give him food; if he is thirsty, give him a drink of water, for so you will heap live coals on his head, and the Lord will reward you.
> (Prov 25:21-22)[157]

This is simply another way of saying, "'Vengeance is mine,' sayeth the LORD," not an ethical imperative based on a theological vision of God's forgiveness. Jesus' commandment to "love your enemies" does not appear to be simply a "reformulation of earlier Jewish ideas"[158] but rather appears to be a "radicalization" of the imperative to love one's neighbor.[159] Here Jesus seems to eschew any hint or suspicion that he will fulfill the politico-military role of a Davidic messiah. Jesus may have been executed as a royal claimant by the Roman prefect.[160] He may even have "evoked recognition" as a royal messiah during his ministry,[161] but he does not seem to have aspired to the Davidic role.[162] He does not raise an army and does not support militant revolt (Matt 5:39).[163] He may have been a descendant of the Davidic line, but he appears to have rejected the generally accepted expectations of the Davidic messiah's role: military conquest. Jesus' nonviolent "revelation" is thus precisely what made Jesus different *and* dangerous to his contemporaries: different, because it was unprecedented, and dangerous, because it challenged assumptions about how God was going to act—here and now—to save his people.

---

[157] Cf. Rom 12:20.

[158] Bilde, *Originality of Jesus*, 104. Bilde admits that the Gospels present this imperative as "close to unique" and concedes that Jesus' "originality" is "found in parts of his ethical teachings" (107). On Jesus' enemy-love as something new or original, see E. P. Sanders, "The Question of the Uniqueness in the Teaching of Jesus," The Ethel M. Wood Lecture, February, 15 1990 (University of London, 1990), 13–14. On the absence of (early Jewish) parallels, see David Flusser, *Jesus in Selbstzeugnissen und Bilddokumenten* (Hamburg: Rowohlt, 1975), 68–69; C. H. Dodd, *The Founder of Christianity* (London: Macmillan, 1970), 67; Piper, "Love Your Enemies," 19–65, 64.

[159] A. Nissen, *Gott und der Nächste im antiken Judentum: Untersuchungen zum Doppelgebot der Liebe*, WUNT 15 (Tübingen: Mohr Siebeck, 1974), 304–39; Piper, "Love Your Enemies," 19–65.

[160] John J. Collins, *The Scepter and the Star: Messianism in Light of the Dead Sea Scrolls*, 2nd ed. (Grand Rapids: Eerdmans, 2010), 232n88; cf. Nils A. Dahl (*Jesus the Christ: The Historical Origins of Christological Doctrine*, ed. D. H. Juel [Minneapolis: Fortress, 1991], 27–47) suggests that the crucifixion charge was based on a claim to royal ("messianic") kingship.

[161] Adela Yarbro Collins, "The Worship of Jesus and the Imperial Cult, in *The Jewish Roots of Christological Monotheism: Papers from the St. Andrews Conference on the Historical Origins of the Worship of Jesus*, ed. C. C. Newman, J. R. Davila, and G. S. Lewis, JSJSup 63 (Leiden: Brill, 1999; repr. Waco, Tex.: Baylor University Press, 2017), 234–57, here 257.

[162] Collins, *Scepter and the Star*, 19.

[163] Cf. Mark 14:47; Matt 26:52; Luke 22:50; John 18:10-11; Walter Wink, "Neither Passivity nor Violence: Jesus' Third Way (Matt. 5:38-42 parr.)," in *The Love of Enemy and Nonretaliation in the New Testament*, ed. W. M. Swartley (Louisville, Ky.: Westminster John Knox, 1992), 102–5.

"Mercy, Not Sacrifice": Jesus and Sacrifice

There is an ongoing debate about whether the Essenes—as described by Josephus, Philo, and Pliny—participated in the Temple cult.[164] There are also ongoing discussions about whether the *Yahad*—as represented by the sectarian Scrolls—continued participating in the Temple cult.[165] On one hand, it has been suggested that the Essenes performed animal sacrifices outside of the Temple.[166] Josephus seems to suggest as much in his *Antiquities* where he states that the Essenes sacrificed "by themselves." The Qumran corpus also contains many texts that seem to presuppose the legitimacy of sacrifice. Since animal sacrifice was virtually ubiquitous in antiquity and a core tenet of the Torah, some scholars have concluded that the Essenes must have continued practicing animal sacrifice until 70 CE, that is, up until the time when the Temple was destroyed, and they could do so no longer.[167] On the other hand, our *earliest* evidence about the Essenes—Philo of Alexandria—denies that the Essenes practiced animal sacrifice:

---

[164] Martin Goodman ("Religious Variety and the Temple in the Late Second Temple Period and Its Aftermath," in *Sects and Sectarianism in Jewish History*, ed. S. Stern, IJS SJ 12 [Leiden: Brill, 2011], 21–38, 21) questions whether "any of the groups attested from pre-70 Judaism really separated themselves from the Temple." Goodman concedes that Philo and Josephus can be read as illustrating Essenic nonparticipation in the cult (this is "patently possible") (26) yet insists that this reading is not "inevitable" and should be "the last resort." Goodman suggests that Philo's report does not *"necessarily* [mean] that Essenes disapproved of animal sacrifices" (27, emphasis added) but *could* mean that they sanctified their minds in addition to offering animal sacrifices.

[165] Goodman ("Religious Variety and the Temple," 27) proposes that "nothing prevented sectarians from combining the continued practice of sacrifices with the notion that their own community could also be like a Temple" (29), although pre-70 CE discursive references to the "Temple" and "sacrifice" could also function as sites of symbolic *discourse* as well as contested sacred physical-ritual space.

[166] Joshua Ezra Burns ("Essene Sectarianism and Social Differentiation in Judaea After 70 C.E.," *HTR* 99, no. 3 [2006]: 247–74, 262n31) refers to "the preponderance of evidence indicating that the Essenes practiced sacrificial rituals outside of the Temple," asserting that Josephus unambiguously claims that they "continued to perform ritual sacrifices," but admits that Philo's divergence from this "preponderance of evidence" is "particularly troubling." Burns suggests, "Philo was motivated to make this claim in the service of his typological depiction of the sect as the paradigm of Jewish piety. Accordingly, it would have been against his interest to depict the Essenes as violating the scriptural laws against sacrificing outside of the Temple." On the "apparent discrepancy" between Josephus and Philo on the Essenes' "alleged rejection of sacrifice," Douglas Finkbeiner ("The Essenes according to Josephus: Exploring the Contribution of Josephus' Portrait of the Essenes to His Larger Literary Agenda," Ph.D. diss., University of Pennsylvania, 2010, 235n381 [emphasis added]) suggests that Philo is *"merely* subordinating the sacrificial ritual to internal piety and devotion."

[167] Taylor (*Essenes, the Scrolls, and the Dead Sea*, 28 [emphasis added]), questions the idea that the Essenes as "an entire group spurned animal sacrifices" and suggests that this reading

ἐπειδὴ κἄν τοῖς μάλιστα θεραπευταὶ θεοῦ γεγόνασιν, οὐ ζῷα καταθύντες,
ἀλλ᾽ ἱεροπρεπεῖς τὰς ἑαυτῶν διανοίας κατασκευάζειν ἀξιοῦντες.

Since they are men utterly dedicated to the service of God; they do *not*
offer animal sacrifice, judging it more fitting to render their minds truly holy.
(*Prob.* 75)[168]

Philo's report on the Essenes suggests that voluntary nonparticipation in the Temple cult was not unprecedented in the Second Temple period.[169] We could dismiss Philo's Εσσαῖοι as an invention of the Hellenized philosopher[170] and his criticism of animal sacrifice as kin to that of the Neoplatonic and Pythagorean Porphyry,[171] but Philo himself does seem to have preferred *bloodless* sacrifices.[172] Philo saw sacrifice as stemming from and meeting "a basic human desire, an aspiration to relationship with the Divine."[173] The slaughtered animal consequently represented symbolic aspects of the one sacrificing, the sacrificed animal thus representing "*self*-sacrifice."[174] Philo also describes the idealized and Essene-like Therapeutae of Alexandria as philosophical vegetarians, emphasizing their "table kept pure from the animal food" (τράπεζα καθαρὰ τῶν ἐναίμων, *Contempl.*

"simply *cannot* be right" because it represents the Essenes as "standing apart from *normative* modes of Judaism." Taylor adds that any "reading that would have Philo indicating that the Essenes spurned animal sacrifices in the Temple is simply wrong" (30–31).

[168] Geza Vermes and Martin Goodman, eds., *The Essenes according to the Classical Sources* OCT 1 (Sheffield: JSOT, 1989), 21. For Philo's critique of symbolic as opposed to literal observance, see *On the Migration of Abraham* 89–93.

[169] Taylor (*Essenes, the Scrolls, and the Dead Sea*, 29) suggests that Philo could *not* have thought that "Jews as a whole gave such a very complimentary name . . . to a group of people who rejected the Temple." Consequently, Philo must be contrasting "two types of service offered by ministers of God": whereas the Temple's priests offer animal sacrifices, the Essenes render their minds "holy," with this latter practice not entailing a rejection of the temple or sacrifice. Taylor's attempt to correct misconceptions about the Essenes as an anomalous marginal quasi-Jewish sect has led to a certain *over*-corrective emphasis on the Essenes' conformity to "normative Judaism" to such an extent that Philo himself must be "corrected" to say the opposite of what he in fact says.

[170] Albert I. Baumgarten, "Josephus on Essene Sacrifice," *JJS* 45 (1994): 169–83; Todd S. Beall, *Josephus' Description of the Essenes Illustrated by the Dead Sea Scrolls* (Cambridge: Cambridge University Press, 1988), 118.

[171] *On Abstinence from Killing Animals.*

[172] Jutta Leonhardt, *Jewish Worship in Philo of Alexandria*, TSAJ 84 (Tübingen: Mohr Siebeck, 2001), 276. See *Spec. Laws* 1.275.

[173] William K. Gilders, "Jewish Sacrifice: Its Nature and Function (According to Philo)," in *Ancient Mediterranean Sacrifice*, ed. J. W. Knust and Z. Várhelyi (New York: Oxford University Press, 2011), 94–105, here 97. See Philo, *Spec. Laws* 1.66–67; 1.195.

[174] Gilders, "Jewish Sacrifice," 98.

73–74).[175] It is not a question, therefore, of Philo's Essenes rejecting animal sacrifice on principle. Nonparticipation in the Temple cult is not to be understood as a rejection of the sanctity of the Temple. Nor would ethical objections to its administration make a first-century Jew be seen as any less righteous or devout. Philo's account does not represent a *rejection* of sacrificial *praxis*, but it does refer to nonparticipation.

Josephus' account of the Essenes' sacrificial practice is notoriously ambiguous. Josephus has been interpreted to mean both that the Essenes declined to take part in Temple sacrifices *and* that they offered their own (animal) sacrifices apart (or separate) from other Jews:[176]

εἰς δὲ τὸ ἱερὸν ἀναθήματα στέλλοντες θυσίας [οὐκ] ἐπιτελοῦσιν διαφορότητι
ἁγνειῶν ἃ νομίζοιεν καὶ δι' αὐτὸ εἰργόμενοι τοῦ κοινοῦ τεμενίσματος
ἐφ' αὑτῶν τὰς θυσίας ἐπιτελοῦσιν

They send votive offerings (ἀναθήματα) to the Temple,
but they [do not] offer sacrifices, using different rites of purification.
Because of this they [were] excluded [themselves] (εἰργόμενοι)
from the common court (τοῦ κοινοῦ τεμενίσματος),[177]
and offer their sacrifices by themselves. (A.J. 18.1.5)

Josephus' account could theoretically mean that the Essenes both sent votive offerings and performed (animal) sacrifices. It is also possible to read στέλλοντες as meaning that it is *through* sending votive offerings that they sacrifice because their sacrifices were different. It has also been suggested that Josephus' Essenes were given the right to perform animal sacrifices in their own private area of the Temple even though there is *no* evidence—outside of Josephus—supporting the idea that Essenes were ever given such special access to or from the Temple.

Since Josephus describes several Essenes *teaching* in the Temple courts—presumably because they revered the Temple and regarded it as holy ground (B.J. 1.3.5 §78; A.J. 15.10.5 §373; B.J. 2.20.4 §§562–567)—Essenic nonparticipation

---

[175] On the Therapeutae, see Joan E. Taylor, *Jewish Women Philosophers of First-Century Alexandria: Philo's "Therapeutae" Reconsidered* (New York: Oxford University Press, 2003).

[176] L. H. Schiffman, *Texts and Traditions* (Hoboken: Ktav, 1998), 275–76. See Baumgarten, "Josephus on Essene Sacrifice," 169–83.

[177] Translating εἰργόμενοι as a middle participle results in the Essenes separating themselves, whereas a passive signifies that the Essenes were excluded from the temple. On Josephus' Essenes corresponding to Philo's Essenes offering "spiritual" sacrifices as in the Qumran texts (CD 11.18–21; 1QS 9.3–5; 4QFlorilegium), see Jamal-Dominique Hopkins, "The Dead Sea Scrolls and the Greco-Roman World: Examining the Essenes' View of Sacrifice in Relation to the Scrolls," in *The Dead Sea Scrolls in Context: Integrating the Dead Sea Scrolls in the Study of Ancient Texts, Languages, and Cultures*, ed. A. Lange, E. Tov, M. Weigold, and B. Reynolds III, 2 vols., VTSup 140 (Leiden: Brill, 2011), 1:367–83.

in the Temple cult does not entail a categorical rejection of the Temple per se. That is a necessary corrective. But it is *over*-correcting to insist that Josephus, like Philo, could not possibly mean to say what he seems to say: that the Essenes affirmed the religious *need* for sacrifice but reenvisioned *what* was sacrificed, as well as where and how. Josephus reports that the Essenes send "offerings" (ἀναθήματα) to the Temple, but these "offerings" could simply be referring to the obligatory Temple tax.[178] The Josephan manuscript witnesses also contain a crucial variant. The earliest manuscript witness of *A.J.* 18.19, the Latin (Versio Latina, the Latin version of Cassiodorus), followed by E (The Epitome Antiquitatum), contains the negative οὐκ, meaning that the Essenes do *not* offer (animal) sacrifices. The Greek manuscript witnesses do not have the negative οὐκ.[179] This textual variant affects the meaning of the entire passage. Yet this reading is to be preferred on text-critical and historiographical grounds as the oldest manuscript witness.[180]

Second, εἰργόμενοι can be rendered either as a passive or middle participle. If it is read as a middle participle with οὐκ, then the passage can be translated as "they separated themselves" (from the Temple). This voluntary withdrawal of the Essenes from the Temple would then be reminiscent of Qumran Scroll passages which attest to the sect's withdrawal from the corrupt and illegitimate Temple. On the other hand, if εἰργόμενοι is translated as a passive participle, then the meaning of the passage changes to "they were excluded" (from the Temple).[181] The problem with this reading is that there is no evidence that the Essenes were

---

[178] Baumgarten, "Josephus on Essene Sacrifice," 169–83, 174–75.

[179] A (Codex bibliothecae Ambrosianae F 128), M (Codex Medicaeus bibliothecae Laurentianae plut. 69, codex 10), W (Codex Vaticanus Gr. No. 984), and Zon. (The Chronicon of Zonaras).

[180] Hopkins, "Dead Sea Scrolls," 371. Cf. idem, "Sacrifice in the Dead Sea Scrolls: Khirbet Qumran, The Essenes, and Cultic Spiritualization," Ph.D. diss., University of Manchester, 2005, 88. See also David Wallace, "The Essenes and Temple Sacrifice," *TZ* 13 (1957): 335–38. Cf. J. Thomas, *Le mouvement baptiste en Palestine et Syrie* (Gembloux, Belgium: Duclot, 1935), 12n3. John Nolland ("A Misleading Statement of the Essene Attitude to the Temple [Josephus, *Antiquities*, XVIII, 1, 5, 19]," *RevQ* 9, no. 4 [1978]: 555–62, 558) follows the Epitome reading "since the old Latin is at least five centuries older than the existing Greek manuscripts ... and it is generally agreed that the textual evidence is sufficiently indecisive." Nolland rightly points out that Josephus' use of ἄλλως ("*otherwise* they are of the highest character") indicates a contrast with what precedes and the Essenes sending "offerings" does not justify criticism (560 [emphasis in original]).

[181] Nolland ("Misleading Statement of the Essene Attitude to the Temple," 557) reads εἰργόμενοι as passive, suggesting that the Temple authorities excluded them because of their more stringent purification rites; there was "a dispute over the right purifications to be used," and the Temple authorities refused to allow them to sacrifice in the Temple. Josephus gives a "misleading" portrayal of the Essenes because he was "embarrassed" by Essenic nonparticipation (and their being "excluded" from the Temple), which is why he describes the Essenes as sending ἀναθήματα to the Temple (557), and also why they have to sacrifice elsewhere "by themselves."

ever "excluded" from the Temple and there is (arguably) positive evidence (that is, the Scrolls) that the Essenes voluntarily withdrew or "separated" themselves from the Temple.[182]

Third, Josephus' last phrase (ἐφ' αὑτῶν τὰς θυσίας ἐπιτελοῦσιν) seems to suggest that the Essenes "sacrificed by themselves," but Josephus does not specify *what, how,* or *where* the Essenes sacrifice. Josephus simply does not indicate the *nature* of the sacrifice/offering, whether animal, vegetable, communal meals, Torah study, or substitutionary prayer. There is no compelling reason, therefore, to conclude that the Essenes offered *animal* sacrifices in the Temple or outside of Jerusalem "by themselves."[183] Josephus—knowing that the Essenes did *not* offer sacrifices in the Temple—did not actually know *how* the Essenes conceptualized their sacrificial practice. He only knows that it was different and private.[184] A compelling argument for this interpretation is Josephus' report that the Essenes *send* "offerings" (ἀναθήματα) to the Temple, meaning, in other words, that they do not *go* there themselves.[185] After all, the Essenes would not need to "send"

---

[182] Baumgarten ("Josephus on Essene Sacrifice," 171) suggests, "Essene exclusion from the Temple was a *punishment* imposed on them by those in charge." Yet there is no unambiguous evidence that the Essenes were excluded; conversely, there is positive evidence that the Yahad voluntarily withdrew from the Temple because of their interpretations of the Law, a datum Baumgarten a priori disregards because he does not accept the Qumran/Essene hypothesis. For Baumgarten, "Josephus intended these remarks concerning Essene participation in sacrifice as criticism" (170); their only being allowed to send ἀναθήματα was also "a punishment of sorts" (175n25). Baumgarten notes that these "offerings" indicate "an acceptance of the Temple's legitimacy" (175), but recognizes that this conclusion results in "a paradoxical situation ... the Essenes acknowledged the legitimacy of the same Temple from which they were prohibited." A less "paradoxical" interpretation is that the Essenes acknowledged the sanctity of the Temple but voluntarily excluded themselves from sacrificing in it.

[183] Baumgarten ("Josephus on Essene Sacrifice," 177n34) speculates that the Essenes practiced "an alternative Red Heifer sacrifice" that the Temple authorities rejected, but admits, "what was wrong with the practice of the Temple authorities, and how the Essenes performed this ritual, are beyond our knowledge." For Baumgarten, the Essenes sacrificed "their own Red Heifers elsewhere ... somewhere other than at the Temple, by themselves" (172). Taylor (*Essenes, the Scrolls, and the Dead Sea*, 97) dismisses the Latin and Epitome witnesses as stating "slightly nonsensically that Essenes 'do not sacrifice.'" Taylor adds that it would be "absolutely perverse" to presume that Josephus' positive account of the Essenes "would contain any suggestion that they either rejected the Temple or refused to sacrifice" (98), but does not consider the idea that the motivations underlying Essenic nonparticipation were simply unknown to Josephus.

[184] On the animal bones as remnants of sacred meals (but not animal sacrifice), see Jodi Magness, "Communal Meals and Sacred Space at Qumran," in *Shaping Community: The Art and Archaeology of Monasticism: Papers from a Symposium Held at the Frederick R. Weisman Museum, University of Minnesota, March 10-12, 2000*, ed. S. McNally, BARIS 941 (Oxford: Archaeopress, 2001), 15–28, 19.

[185] Wallace, "Essenes and Temple Sacrifice," 335.

(στέλλοντες) anything to the Temple if they were in the habit and practice of offering their own (animal) sacrifices there in person.

There is no evidence or precedent for the Temple's administration giving a sectarian group of Jews special permission to perform animal sacrifices in any place other than the altar area designated for that practice, let alone specific evidence for the Essenes being granted this privilege of performing animal sacrifice outside of the Temple or in another part of the Temple. At the same time, there is no reason to doubt the Essenes' high regard for the sanctity of the Temple and their affirmation of sacrifice in principle, which is why they sent offerings to the Temple. While εἰργόμενοι can be read as a passive participle, with Essenic nonparticipation being interpreted *by Josephus* as punitive exclusion by the Temple administration (cf. *A.J.* 8.3.9 §95; 18.2.2 §30), it can also be read as a middle participle, suggesting an Essenic voluntary withdrawal from the Temple cult. Moreover, Josephus' explanation—that it was "because of this/for this reason" (καὶ δι᾽) that they withdrew (or were excluded)—further indicates an alternative sacrificial ideology, illustrating that the reason for their nonparticipation (and the likely cause of Josephus' apparent disapproval) is because they use different "purifications" (ἁγνειῶν) which prevented them from offering sacrifices in the Temple, but not from sending "offerings." Josephus' remark that the Essenes are "otherwise" (ἄλλως) virtuous implies his disapproval of their not offering sacrifices in the Temple. Josephus simply does not want to admit to his readers (or, perhaps more likely, was ignorant of) the real reason the Essenes had criticized and withdrawn from participating in the Temple cult. In short, it does not seem likely that the Temple administration would have excluded the Essenes simply because they purified themselves in a different way while at the same time also providing them an alternative area within the Temple's precincts for their own sacrificial *praxis*. It is more likely that Josephus interpreted Essenic nonparticipation in the Temple cult by supposing that the reason behind it was either peculiar "purificatory" rites and/or *exclusion* when in fact their nonparticipation was motivated by other factors. Josephus could not imagine (or endorse) virtuous Judeans/Jews not sacrificing at all, so he simply presumed that they sacrificed elsewhere "by themselves."

Fourth, Josephus' *later* account of the Essenes in *A.J.* 18.18–22 contains details (only) found in Philo's *earlier* description (*Quod omnis probus liber sit* 75–91), most conspicuously the number four thousand, the rejection of animal sacrifice, and slavery. This suggests that Josephus was familiar with this account and utilized it (or its source) to develop his portrayal of the Essenes,[186] and further supports Philo's report that the Essenes did not actually offer animal sacrifices (as

---

[186] Josephus' earlier description of the Essenes (*B.J.*) says nothing about their relationship to the Temple or sacrificial practices. On Josephus' possible use of Philo in writing *Antiquities* (ca. 93 CE), see Tessa Rajak, "Ciò che Flavio Giuseppe Vide: Josephus and the Essenes," in

Philo states), preferring instead to render their minds holy. If Josephus knew what, where, why, or how the Essenes sacrificed, he does not say. Josephus apparently only knew *that* the Essenes did not offer sacrifices in the Temple, not where, why, or how they fulfilled their sacrificial obligations. There is a likely explanation for Josephus' confusing passage: it is based on Philo's earlier account.[187] So whether or not Philo and Josephus both used a common source, or Josephus used Philo, it is reasonable to suppose that Josephus' confusing passage is his attempt to rehabilitate the Essenes' character by reinterpreting Philo's matter-of-fact account that the Essenes did *not* offer animal sacrifice but preferred to render their minds "holy."[188] In any case, both Philo and Josephus suggest that the Essenes retained the *principle* of sacrifice even while their sacrificial *practices* diverged from their contemporaries. The Essenes, in other words, reinterpreted and reinvented "sacrifice" for their particular time, place, and circumstances.

The question, therefore, of whether the Essenes actually practiced animal sacrifice requires a *negative* answer, based on both Philo and Josephus.[189] The slightly more difficult question of whether they themselves ritually sacrificed anything at all in the Jerusalem Temple is also to be answered in the negative. The historical evidence does not support a separate Essene entrance to the Temple or a separate enclosure for Essene practice. It does not seem very likely that the Temple administration allowed an "excluded" group from performing sacrifice with a special, separate entrance and official access. Philo flatly states that the Essenes prefer "to render their minds truly holy." Josephus seems to have reinterpreted Philo's account so as to ameliorate the offense of (Philo's) Essenes' nonparticipation in animal sacrifice.

As a result, Philo and Josephus both misinterpret the Essenes' motivation for withdrawal from the Temple: Philo "philosophizing" the Essenes into a kind of principled quasi-rejection of animal sacrifice; Josephus construing Philo's passage

Josephus and the History of the Greco-Roman Period: Essays in Memory of Morton Smith, ed. F. Parente and J. Sievers (Leiden: Brill, 1994), 141–60.

[187] Taylor (*Essenes, the Scrolls, and the Dead Sea*, 96) suggests that this passage (A.J. 18.18–22) could be borrowing from Philo's *Hypothetica* and *De Vita Contemplativa*, with Josephus "quarrying" Philo.

[188] Collins (*Beyond the Qumran Community*, 132–33) explains their different views on sacrifice by appealing to a common source. While Philo says that they do *not* offer sacrifices, Josephus (using the *present* tense in 90 CE!) says that they "send offerings to the Temple, but perform their sacrifices using different customary purifications" and are thereby forbidden to enter the common enclosure, "but only sacrifice among themselves."

[189] Baumgarten ("Josephus on Essene Sacrifice," 169n1) asserts that Philo's (earlier) comments about the Essenes are "not relevant to our discussion" and "imply only that sacrifice was not the focal point of Essene worship," yet that is not quite what Philo says. Philo, in fact, denies that the Essenes practiced animal sacrifice altogether. Baumgarten's dismissal of Philo precludes exploring the possibility of a Josephan (mis)representation of Philo.

into a fictional alternative sacrificial system in the Temple. In neither case should the Essenes be regarded as objecting to "sacrifice" per se or on principle. Essenic nonparticipation in the Temple's sacrificial system is an historical datum requiring explanation. While the Qumran texts elaborate that halakhic, calendrical, and ideological disagreements with the Jerusalem priesthood lay behind the withdrawal, Philo and Josephus are not privy to this information nor to the *Yahad*'s conceptualization of prayer and Torah study as effective (substitutionary) sacrificial "offerings" to the deity, with the *Yahad* itself being "offered" in atonement for the land (1QS 8.6, 10).

— ♦ —

The Dead Sea Scrolls represent a movement that originally participated in the sacrificial cult yet had subsequently withdrawn because the Temple had been defiled. As a result, the movement developed substitutes for Temple sacrifices while simultaneously hoping for the restoration of proper sacrifice in the future.[190] Many texts within the corpus display strong dissatisfaction(s) with the administration of the Temple cult, with sharp criticisms of its ritual and moral impurity.[191] The presectarian Enochic *Animal Apocalypse* (1 En. 85–90), for example, suggests that the Temple and its sacrificial cult have been polluted, alleging that the pre-Herodian Second Temple ("tower") was *never* properly administered:

All the bread on it was polluted and not pure. (1 En. 89:72-73b)[192]

---

[190] Joseph M. Baumgarten ("Sacrifice and Worship among the Jewish Sectarians of the Dead Sea [Qumrân] Scrolls," *HTR* 46, no. 3 [1953]," 146) sees the sacrificial legislation of CD as "survivals from a period when the sectarians were still participating in the worship of the Temple." Cf. Nolland, "A Misleading Statement," 556: "There was probably a time in the early history of the movement when the Jerusalem Temple was still used by the Covenanters and certain cultic regulations still survive in the Qumran literature as relics from this period. There was no disillusionment with sacrifice as such but rather sacrifice ceased when an irreparable rift with the Jerusalem leaders led to a situation where what the Covenanters considered the only proper place for sacrifice came to be thought of as defiled and unfit for use. Thus deprived of sacrifice in the present, the Covenanters looked forward intensely to the time when they would 'liberate' Jerusalem and restore a pure cult, and on the other hand they consoled themselves by developing for the interim a spiritualized understanding of sacrifice and Temple."

[191] Lawrence H. Schiffman, "Community without Temple: The Qumran Community's Withdrawal from the Jerusalem Temple," in *Gemeinde ohne Tempel—Community without Temple: Zur Substituierung und Transformation des Jerusalemer Tempels und seines Kultes im Alten Testament, antiken Judentum und frühen Christentum*, ed. B. Ego et al., WUNT 118 (Tübingen: Mohr Siebeck, 1999), 267–84; Baumgarten, "Sacrifice and Worship," 141–59; idem, "The Essenes and the Temple: A Reappraisal," in *Studies in Qumran Law* (Leiden: Brill, 1977), 59–62.

[192] George W. E. Nickelsburg, *1 Enoch 1: A Commentary on the Book of 1 Enoch*, Hermeneia (Minneapolis: Fortress, 2001), 387–88; cf. 394: "The author asserts that from its inception the cult of the Second Temple did not follow correct laws of ritual purity."

Here the Second Temple ("tower") has become the site of halakhic conflict, presumably centered on the calendar. The vision culminates in the replacement of the old house with a new one and the appearance of a "white bull" who represents the eschatological renewal of creation (1 En. 90:19-42). Similarly, the *Book of Jubilees* refers to the moral impurity of the Temple and the defilement of the "holy of holies" (Jub. 23:21; cf. 30:15), looking forward to a future age when God will build a new Temple "among them and live with them" in the new creation (Jub. 1:17; cf. 1:27, 29; 4:26), illustrating that the author was familiar with the Enochic tradition, especially the *Book of the Watchers*. The *Temple Scroll* also envisions plans for a future Temple anticipated at the Eschaton (29:9-10), when God promises to sanctify his Temple.

4QMMT (4Q394–4Q399), or *4Q Miqṣat Ma'aśe Ha-Torah*, is similarly focused.[193] The manuscripts are paleographically dated to circa 75 BCE to 50 CE and are variously known as a single letter, treatise, or epistle. The disagreement is both between this group and the Temple administration in Jerusalem as well as with another individual or group (or groups) within the same movement.[194] Yet the halakhic arguments presupposed in the letter are not simply theoretical.[195] 4QMMT indicates a voluntary withdrawal from the Temple cult, albeit with rhetorical efforts to resolve the halakhic conflict (with allies or those in power) that nonetheless seem to have failed, leading to a more substantial separation. The relationship(s) between the Enochic texts, the *Book of Jubilees*, the *Temple Scroll*, and 4QMMT represent a continuum of halakhic and ethical complaints registered against the current administration of the Temple cult.

The *Damascus Document* (CD) is part of this tradition. Although this work has generally been regarded as representing the wider Essenic movement out of which the Qumran group emerged—and thus presupposing diversity *within* the Essene movement—the text has been redacted to reflect the later views of the *Yahad* and so contains material presupposing participation in the Temple cult alongside severe criticism of its current administration.[196] CD 4.13–5.13a

---

[193] For the critical edition, see Elisha Qimron and John Strugnell, *Qumran Cave 4.V: Miqṣat Ma'aśe Ha-Torah*, DJD 10 (Oxford: Clarendon, 1994).

[194] 4QMMT C 6–7 (4Q397 14–21 i 6–7); 4QMMT C 26–32 (4Q398 14–17 ii 2–8).

[195] Eyal Regev, *Sectarianism in Qumran: A Cross-Cultural Perspective*. RS 45 (New York: de Gruyter, 2007), 98: "The debate was not with the theoretical concepts underlying the cultic laws, but with actual contemporary Temple practices."

[196] Texts refer both to the Sabbath sacrifice (CD 11.17b–18a) and the freewill offering (4Q266 5 ii 1–16). Hopkins, "Sacrifice in the Dead Sea Scrolls," 174: "As the Qumran-related community developed, they viewed D in two ways . . . both before and during their occupation at Qumran, the community viewed D, especially its original core which focused on sacrificial regulations, in an ideological and eschatological way. Later, most notably at Qumran, the community read and practised most of these same sacrificial regulations in a predominantly

describes three ways in which Israel has erred: fornication or improper sexual relations (polygamy), wealth, and the defilement of the Temple. According to CD 5.7–8:

> They also defile (מטמאים) the Temple (המקדש)
> because they do not separate in accordance with the Torah (כתורה).

As a result, it would seem that those belonging to "The New Covenant" (הברית החדשה) were *not* to offer sacrifices in the Jerusalem Temple:

> All those who have been brought into the Covenant
> shall not enter the Temple (המקדש) to kindle his altar in vain. (CD 6.11–7.3b
> [4Q266 s ii 17–24])[197]

Moreover, CD 11.18b–21a presupposes that righteous prayer is an acceptable substitute for sacrifice (when the sacrificial cult has been defiled). Here the prayer of the just is a more agreeable offering than impure sacrifice (cf. Prov 15:8). CD 11.20–21 ("The sacrifice of the wicked ones is an abomination, but the prayer of the righteous ones is like a pleasant offering") also seems to echo the substitutionary emphasis on sacrifice present in 1QS.[198]

The *Temple Scroll*, the *Book of Jubilees*, 4QMMT, and the *Damascus Document* all presuppose the legitimacy of sacrificial offerings in principle, but criticize how sacrifice is actually currently conducted in Jerusalem. At the same time, these texts represent reflection on the proper sacrificial legislation and anticipation that it will be restored in the future. According to the *Temple Scroll*, bribery seems to have been a major concern:

> For the bribe twists judgement, overturns the works of justice,
> blinds the eyes of the wise, produces great guilt, and profanes the house by the
>   iniquity of sin. (11QT 51.11–15)[199]

In the *Damascus Document*, priestly sexual impropriety was also a problem:

spiritualised way." Cf. Kenneth A. Matthews, "John, Jesus and the Essenes: Trouble at the Temple," *CTR* 3 (1988): 114: "The Covenant Community represented in CD was critical of the ritual appropriateness of temple sacrifices; however, this did not preclude them from participating whenever proper conditions were met. The tendency on the part of the Essenes at Qumran to substitute spiritual sacrifices also did not necessarily prevent them from offering temple sacrifices."

[197] Cf. Mal 1:10.

[198] Kapfer ("The Relationship Between the Damascus Document and the Community Rule: Attitudes toward the Temple as a Test Case," *DSD* 14, no. 2 [2007]: 172) suggests, "at this stage in the development of the sect, the notion of the community as a temporary substitute for the profaned temple had not yet coalesced."

[199] Vermes, *Complete Dead Sea Scrolls*, 209.

they profane the Temple because they do not observe the distinction
(between clean and unclean) in accordance with the Law. (CD 5.6–9)[200]

The *Pesher Habakkuk* reflects on how the Wicked Priest became arrogant, stole the wealth of the poor, and defiled the Temple through sin, theft, and greed:

> When he ruled over Israel his heart became proud, and he forsook God
> and betrayed the precepts for the sake of riches. He robbed and amassed
> the riches of the men of violence who rebelled against God, and he took
> the wealth of the peoples, heaping sinful iniquity upon himself.
> And he lived in the ways of abominations admist every unclean defilement.
>   (1QpHab 8.10)
>
> *The city* is Jerusalem where the Wicked Priest committed
> abominable acts and defiled the Temple of God. (1QpHab 12.8–10)[201]

The *Yahad* viewed the Temple as ethically corrupt and ritually deficient.[202] 11QT provides detailed instructions for how the new Temple is to be operated (45.7–51.10), implying that the ritually impure were currently allowed to enter its precincts, and legislates purity laws even stricter than the Torah (cf. 45.7–10; Lev 15:16; Deut 23:10-11). The current Temple administration was not following proper ritual protocol and procedure.[203] The high priest was illegitimate and the correct calendar was not being used. Purification procedures were inadequate, especially the red heifer rite (Num 19), and ritual impurity was being contracted due to proximity that was too close to the Temple.[204] Given that these texts presuppose the propriety of participating in the Temple cult under ideal

---

[200] Vermes, *Complete Dead Sea Scrolls*, 131.

[201] Vermes, *Complete Dead Sea Scrolls*, 482, 484.

[202] On its ritual inadequacy, see the prohibition of leaving cereal offerings overnight (4QMMT B 9–13; 11QT 20.12–13), and the requirement that fourth-year produce and tithes be given to the priests (4QMMT B 62–64). Other issues involve the "solar" calendar followed by 4QMMT, 11QT, and the Songs of the Sabbath Sacrifice. On its structural inadequacy, the *New Jerusalem* texts anticipate a new temple (1Q32; 2Q24; 4Q554–555; 5Q15; 11Q18)—a city with a golden wall (11Q18, fr. 10); jeweled buildings (4Q554, fr. 2, 2.15); streets paved in white stone, alabaster, and onyx (5Q15 fr. 1, 1.6–7); and a radiant temple (2Q24 fr. 3; fr. 8). The *Temple Scroll* also envisions a new expanded temple that will last until God constructs his own sanctuary (29.9–10).

[203] Menahem Kister, "Studies in 4Miqsat Ma'aseh ha-Torah and Related Texts: Law, Theology, Language and Calendar," *Tarbiz* 68, no. 3 (1999): 317–72; Eyal Regev, "Abominated Temple and a Holy Community: The Formation of the Notions of Purity and Impurity in Qumran," *DSD* 10, no. 2 (2003): 245–49. Regarding the Red Heifer, 4QMMT B13–17 and 4Q277 1 emphasize that those involved with its preparation are ritually impure until evening (cf. *m.Parah* 3.7).

[204] 11QT 45.11–12 bans men defiled by semen from the *city*, not just the temple; in CD 12.1–2, sexual relations must not take place in the city.

conditions—which currently do not exist—it would seem that these texts reflect historical tensions which ultimately resulted in separation from the Temple cult and the innovative development of the idea of substitutionary prayer.[205]

The *Rule of the Community* (סרך היחד, 1/4QS), preserved in twelve manuscripts from three caves (1QS, 4Q255–264; 5Q11; cf. 5Q13, 11Q29), has been dated between 125 BCE and circa 50 CE, with 1QS dated around 100–75 BCE. According to 1QS, the *Yaḥad* does not participate in the Temple cult because the *Yaḥad* itself is a substitute "Temple" and prayer seems to have been substituted for animal "sacrifice."[206] The *Yaḥad* abandoned the ethically and ritually impure Temple and regarded the community itself as a substitute, transforming the idea of Temple worship so that the community *substituted* for the sacrificial cult (1QS 5.6; 8.3; 9.4). The Law could be fulfilled in one's purified heart and mind.[207] Prayers, righteous deeds, and inspired exegesis would now be the true "sacred offerings" atoning for Israel:

> The Council of the Community shall be established in truth.
> It shall be an Everlasting Plantation, a House of Holiness for Israel
> (בית קודש לישראל),
> an Assembly of Supreme Holiness for Aaron . . . who shall atone for the Land . . .
> It shall be a Most Holy Dwelling for Aaron, with everlasting knowledge
> of the Covenant of justice, and shall offer up sweet fragrance.
> It shall be a House of Perfection and Truth . . .
> And they shall be an agreeable offering, atoning for the Land. (1QS 8.5–12)[208]

The *Rule of the Community* explicitly states that there will be *no* animal sacrifices:

> They shall establish the spirit of holiness (רוח קודש) according to everlasting truth.
> They shall atone for guilty rebellion and for sins of unfaithfulness,
> that they may obtain loving-kindness for the Land *without the flesh of holocausts and the fat of sacrifice*. And prayer rightly offered shall be as an acceptable fragrance of righteousness, and perfection of way as an acceptable free-will offering. (1QS 9.1–5)[209]

1QS 9.3–6 states that "offerings of the lips" (תרומת שפתים) and the "perfection of way" (תמים דרך) are kin to a "fragrance of righteousness" (ניחוח צדק) and "an

---

[205] Robert Kugler, "Rewriting Rubrics: Sacrifice and the Religion of Quman," in *Religion in the Dead Sea Scrolls*, ed. J. J. Collins and R. A. Kugler, SDSSRL (Grand Rapids: Eerdmans, 2000), 90–112, 90–94.

[206] Hopkins, "Sacrifice in the Dead Sea Scrolls," 240.

[207] See Schiffman, *Reclaiming the Dead Sea Scrolls*, 299.

[208] Vermes, *Complete Dead Sea Scrolls*, 109 (emphasis in original).

[209] Vermes, *Complete Dead Sea Scrolls*, 110.

acceptable freewill offering" (מנחת רצון) in place of the flesh of burnt-offerings and the fat of sacrifice.[210]

Similarly, 4QFlorilegium 1–2 i 6–7 envisions a "Temple of Adam" in which the "smoke of incense" (מקטירים) and the "works of thanksgiving" (מעשי תודה) are sent up instead of sacrifices.[211] The *Yahad* is a Temple that atones for the land without animal sacrifice: the "offering of the lips" (תרומת שפתים) is a "fragrance of righteousness" (ניחוח צדק) and "an acceptable freewill offering" (מנחת רצון).[212] The *Yahad*'s "perfection of way" is an acceptable "offering" (1QS 9.4; cf. 8.10). The combination of Edenic "plant" and "Temple" imagery is present in 1QS,[213] which employs architectural Temple-imagery to portray the *Yahad* as "an eternal planting" (למטעת עולם) and "a house of holiness" (בית קודש) (1QS 8.5). The *Yahad* will be "a *foundation* of truth" (מוסד אמת) and a "house of truth" (בית האמת) (1QS 5.5), the "*foundation* of the holy spirit" (יסוד רוח קודש, 1QS 9.3), a "*house* of perfection" (בית תמים, 8.9), and "a most holy *dwelling* for Aaron" (מעון קודש קודשים לאהרון, 1QS 8.8–9).

The *Yahad*-as-Temple is also envisioned as the Garden of Eden in 1QH[a] 16.5–41, which refers to "the eternal planting" (למטעת עולם, 16.7) and explicitly to "Eden" (16.21). According to 4Q175, or 4QFlorilegium, the *Yahad* is an eschatological Temple of Adam (מקדש אדם), a restored Eden.[214] 4QFlorilegium refers to the time when God "commanded that a Temple of Adam be built for himself, that there they may send up, like smoke of incense, the works of the Law" (4QFlor 1–2 i 6–7). Here the author alludes to the *Book of Jubilees*, which also describes the Garden of Eden as a Temple

---

[210] Michael A. Knibb, *The Qumran Community* (New York: Cambridge University Press, 1987), 138–39.

[211] On מעשי תורה ("acts of Torah"), see J. Milgrom, *Pesharim, Other Commentaries, and Related Documents*, PTSDSSP 6B (Louisville, Ky.: Westminster John Knox, 2002), 248.

[212] Cf. 1QS 9.4b (4Q258 7.5); 9.26b; 10.6a, 8b, 14b.

[213] Paul Swarup, *The Self-Understanding of the Dead Sea Scrolls Community: An Eternal Planting, A House of Holiness*, LSTS 59 (New York: T&T Clark, 2006), 2: "The nexus of ideas in the eternal planting, the echoes of Eden, the glory of Adam and the establishing of the temple point to a nostalgia for the restoration of the land and her people." Cecilia Wassen ("Do You Have to Be Pure in a Metaphorical Temple? Sanctuary Metaphors and Construction of Sacred Space in the Dead Sea Scrolls and Paul's Letters," in *Purity, Holiness, and Identity in Judaism and Christianity: Essays in Memory of Susan Haber*, ed. C. S. Ehrlich, A. Runesson, and E. Schuller, WUNT 305 [Tübingen: Mohr Siebeck, 2013], 55–86, 55) also identifies the garden "planting" metaphors in relationship to the Temple, claiming this to be "rarely noted."

[214] George J. Brooke, "Miqdash Adam, Eden and the Qumran Community," in *Gemeinde ohne Tempel—Community without Temple: Zur Substituierung und Transformation des Jerusalemer Tempels und seines Kultes im Alten Testament, antiken Judentum und fruhen Christentum*, ed. B. Ego, et al., WUNT 118 (Tübingen: Mohr Siebeck, 1999), 297.

(Jub. 8:19), with Adam serving as a "priest" offering incense (מקטירים) in the original (Edenic) Temple (3:27).²¹⁵

The Temple of Adam is a sanctuary of "smoke offerings as works of thanksgiving" (מקטירים לפניו מעשי תודה, 4QFlor 1 i 21 2:6). A number of sectarian texts allude to the *Yaḥad* offering incense.²¹⁶ It would seem, then, that the *Book of Jubilees'* commemoration of Adam's offering of *incense* as the very *first* sacrifice ever performed supported the *Yaḥad's* innovative conceptualization of a Temple-without-animal sacrifice.²¹⁷ This indicates an increasing emphasis on substitutionary conceptualizations of sacrifice, with the paradoxical result that the restoration of Eden could theoretically abolish the need for animal sacrifice altogether: there *was* no animal sacrifice in Eden.²¹⁸ The successful realization of the Edenic sanctuary thus stands in tension with the common prevalent assumption that animal sacrifices would be "restored" in the *Endzeit*.²¹⁹

The Essene movement may have originally withdrawn from the Temple because it was convinced that the Temple administration was corrupt and defiled, but they also seem to have envisioned a future when God would restore ideal conditions. As the *Yaḥad* began to envision itself as a structural substitute for the Temple cult, however, life without animal sacrifice became the status quo. Alternative "sacrificial" rituals—including prayer, Torah study, sacred meals, and liturgical worship—temporarily sufficed, yet the most idealized version of the *Yaḥad's* dream came to be the restoration of creation, a dream they came to realize and enact in the conceptualization of the community-as-Temple, and the Temple-as-new-Eden.

---

²¹⁵ James C. VanderKam, "Adam's Incense Offering (Jubilees 3:27)," in *Meghillot: Studies in the Dead Sea Scrolls* V–VI (Jerusalem: Bialik Institute, 2007), 141–56. Cf. J. Milgrom, "The Burning of Incense in the Time of the Second Temple" (Hebrew), in *Studies in Bible and the History of Israel: Festschrift for Ben-Zion Luria* (Jerusalem: Kiryat-Sepher, 1979), 330–34. Adam "sacrifices" by burning frankincense, galbanum, stacte, and aromatic spices (cf. Jub. 16:24). Interestingly, an incense altar *was* discovered at Qumran.

²¹⁶ 1QM 2.5; 1QS 3.11; 8.9; 9.5; 4Q259 2.15; 4Q265 7 ii 9; 4Q266 11.4; 4Q270 7 i 18.

²¹⁷ Martha Himmelfarb, "Earthly Sacrifice and Heavenly Incense: The Law of the Priesthood in Aramaic Levi and Jubilees," in *Heavenly Realms and Earthly Realities in Late Antique Religions*, ed. R. S. Boustan and A. Y. Reed (Cambridge: Cambridge University Press, 2004), 103–22, 120. For Himmelfarb, *Jubilees* represents "an effort to make the cult on earth more like the cult in heaven through its stress on aroma and incense" (122).

²¹⁸ Hopkins, "Sacrifice in the Dead Sea Scrolls," 126, interprets *Jubilees'* influence on Qumran: "In the Eden sanctuary, Adam served as humanity's first priest where his duties served as a type of offering unto the Lord. This view of Adam (as priest who performed spiritualised sacrifice) served as an impetus to the Qumran-related community."

²¹⁹ This tension may have come to the surface among the (later) Essenes, with different factions both participating and not participating in the Temple cult.

Whether or not the *Yahad* ultimately saw its alternative means of atonement as a temporary or permanent replacement for an ethically and ritually corrupt Temple,[220] it does seem to have effectively replaced animal sacrifice with prayer and "perfection of way." There is an ongoing debate whether the Qumran group built its own altar and performed animal sacrifice,[221] but while animal bones were found at Qumran, and several texts seem to presuppose sacrifice,[222] there is no compelling evidence that the Qumran group ever practiced animal sacrifice.[223] The incense altar is too small for communal worship, and the bone burials are not evidence of any known form of sacrificial practice. The Qumran corpus undoubtedly represents different stages in the *Yahad*'s development, but its nonparticipation in Temple worship began in the mid-second century BCE and included "rewriting" the Torah to suit its sectarian needs, redefining Temple practice through their own ethical and ritual activities, and reimagining itself as the "place" where atonement was now being offered "for Israel."[224]

According to the *Yahad*, the Temple was ritually and morally impure, and the sacrifices being offered there were invalid. This would result in destruction, exile, and the departure of the divine presence. *Jubilees* 23:22 asserts that the generation that defiles the Temple will be oppressed, exiled, and destroyed. *T.Levi* 14.5–15.1 asserts that the wages of sin will be the desolation of the Temple. The *Yahad* thus seems to have abandoned the (physical) Temple in expectation of its divine judgment, yet continued to worship God through prayer, common meals, and purification, transforming the ideal of Temple worship through alternative services in which the community itself was the Temple. The community became a "Temple of Adam" (מקדש אדם).[225] There are ongoing debates whether

---

[220] Jonathan Klawans (*Purity, Sacrifice, and the Temple: Symbolism and Supersessionism in the Study of Ancient Judaism* [New York: Oxford University Press, 2005], 163) favors the former.

[221] Frank Moore Cross, *The Ancient Library of Qumran*, 3d ed. (Minneapolis: Fortress, 1995), 85–86; Jean-Baptiste Humbert, "L'espace sacré á Qumrân: Propositions pour l'archéologie (Planches I–III)," *Revue Biblique* 101 (1994): 184–91, 199–201. But see Jodi Magness, *The Archaeology of Qumran and the Dead Sea Scrolls* (Grand Rapids: Eerdmans, 2002), 105–32.

[222] 11QTemple and 1/4QM describe burnt offerings; CD 4.2 presupposes sacrifice. It is possible that the Qumran community envisioned a future temple with burnt offerings. See 1QM 2.4–6; 4Q171 3.10–11; 11QT 29.10; 11Q18 fr. 13 4; 16–17 II/1.1–5). The *War Scroll* imagines future priests administering burnt offerings and other sacrifices in the temple (1QM 2.4–6; 7.10–11). The *Temple Scroll* speaks of a future temple (29.10) and the *New Jerusalem* texts imagine a future rebuilt temple (11Q18 fr. 13 4; fr. 16–17 II/1.1–5).

[223] Klawans, *Purity, Sacrifice, and the Temple*, 162.

[224] Kapfer, "The Relationship Between the Damascus Document and the Community Rule," 152–77.

[225] Bertil Gärtner, *The Temple and the Community in Qumran and the New Testament: A Comparative Study in the Temple Symbolism of the Qumran Texts and the New Testament*

מקדש אדם refers to a sanctuary "among the people," an "Adamic sanctuary of Eden restored,"[226] or a new "holy place that will signify the fulfillment of God's original creation,"[227] but the *Yahad* undoubtedly saw itself as inheriting the eschatological "glory of Adam" (כבוד אדם, 1QS 4.22–23; CD 3.20; and 1QH 4.15).

By 30 CE the *Yahad* would not have participated in Temple worship for over a century. Its members would have come to see their movement as a substitute for the Temple in Jerusalem, fulfilling the priestly function of atonement through *alternative* forms and expressions. This would have resulted in tension between the members of the *Yahad* and other Jews, especially the Sadducees and high-priestly families. It is within this conflicted political atmosphere that both the *Yahad* and Jesus reimagined the eschatological Temple and its role in Israel.[228] By the early first century CE, it would seem that the Essenes did not offer animal sacrifice in Jerusalem. Philo gives this distinct impression and the *Rule of the Community* (1QS) affirms prayer and Torah study as acceptable substitutes for animal sacrifice. While different Essenes at different times undoubtedly held different views about the Temple, their willful, voluntary withdrawal from the central public rites of the Temple—especially when accompanied by a secretive alternative system of sacrifice and atonement—would have stood out as subversive to the status quo. John the Baptist, Jesus, and their followers would have encountered a form of Essenism that presented itself as a devout Judean community providing an alternative system of atonement. While the *Yahad* withdrew from participating in the Temple cult and developed an alternative sacrificial system, there is no criticism of the implicit *logic* of sacrifice. The Qumran corpus represents an

---

(Cambridge: Cambridge University Press, 1965), 30–42; Knibb, *Qumran Community*, 258–62; Michael Wise, "4QFlorilegium and the Temple of Adam," *RevQ* 15 (1991): 103–32. 4Q500 and Jub. 3:9-12 associates Eden with the Holy of Holies. See also George J. Brooke, *Dead Sea Scrolls and the New Testament*, 242–43; idem, *Exegesis at Qumran: 4QFlorilegium in its Jewish Context*, JSOTSup 29 (Sheffield: JSOT, 1985), 184–93; D. Dimant, "4QFlorilegium and the Idea of Community as Temple," in *Hellenica et Judaica: Hommage à Valentin Nikiprowetzky*, ed. A. Caquot et al. (Leuven: Peeters, 1986), 165–89.

[226] Brooke, *Dead Sea Scrolls and the New Testament*, 245; idem, "Miqdash Adam, Eden and the Qumran Community," 285–330. On the cult and Eden, see Jub. 3:26-27; 8:19; Martha Himmelfarb, "The Temple and the Garden of Eden in Ezekiel, the Book of Watchers, and the Wisdom of Ben Sira," in *Sacred Places and Profane Spaces: Essays in the Geographies of Judaism, Christianity and Islam*, ed. J. S. Scott and P. Simpson-Housely (Westport, Conn.: Greenwood, 1991), 63–78; Sandra R. Shimoff, "Gardens: From Eden to Jerusalem," *JSJ* 26 (1995): 145–55; Lawrence E. Stager, "Jerusalem and the Garden of Eden," *Eretz-Israel* 26 (1999): 183–94.

[227] Klawans, *Purity, Sacrifice, and the Temple*, 163.

[228] On Temple imagery, see Georg Klinzing, *Die Umdeutung des Kultus in der Qumrangemeinde und im Neuen Testament*, SUNT 7 (Göttingen: Vandenhoeck & Ruprecht, 1971); Elisabeth Schüssler Fiorenza, "Cultic Language in Qumran and in the NT," *CBQ* 38 (1976): 159–77.

alternative, innovative reenvisioning of the logic and efficacy of sacrifice. Similar innovations can be registered within contemporaneous Second Temple literature. The rise of the Maccabean martyr literature, for example, illustrates the ideal of "self-offering" on behalf of the nation.

The Jewish martyrological tradition was shaped by the persecutions under Antiochus IV Epiphanes (ca. 175–164 BCE).[229] 4 Maccabees, in particular, portrays the Maccabean martyr or "witness" (μάρτυς) as an atoning sacrifice offered to God "for" the *nation* (4 Macc 6:28-29; cf. 2 Macc 7:32-38).[230] In 2 Maccabees it is the martyrdom of the mother and her seven sons that seem to be represented as atoning sacrifices (7:32-38). Although the seventh son states that "we suffer because of our own sins" (7:32),[231] his prayer is that God "will be reconciled" (καταλλαγήσεται, 7:33). The son prays to God "to be merciful quickly to the nation" (ἵλεως ταχὺ τῷ ἔθνει γενέσθαι, 7:37-38) and "to end the wrath of the Almighty in [through] me and my brothers" (ἐν ἐμοὶ δὲ καὶ τοῖς ἀδελφοῖς μου στῆσαι τὴν τοῦ παντοκράτορος ὀργὴν, 7:38). In 4 Maccabees, Eleazar asks God to forgive Israel through his death (6:28-29), that is, "for" them, or "on their behalf" (ὑπὲρ αὐτῶν, 6:28). He also asks God to accept his *blood* for the "purification" of the nation (καθάρσιον αὐτῶν ποίησον τὸ ἐμὸν αἷμα). Since Eleazar is a "priest" (a "scribe" in 2 Macc 6:18) unable to perform rites in the Temple, he prays that his death will serve as a "substitute" to purify the sin of his people,[232] a "ransom" (ἀντίψυχον) for the nation (6:29; 17:21).[233]

Although there is no compelling evidence of direct literary dependence between 2 or 4 Maccabees and any of the writings of the New Testament, these texts do represent a contemporary Jewish-Hellenistic intertestamental attestation

---

[229] Jonathan Klawans (*Josephus and the Theologies of Ancient Judaism* [New York: Oxford University Press, 2013], 122) describes the martyr's death as "the self-chosen premature violent (but nonbattlefield) deaths of the heroes whose reverence for God and divine law is placed far above their love of life."

[230] 2 Maccabees is a pre-Christian Jewish text dated to the first century BCE. There is no consensus on the date of 4 Macc. Dates range from the first century BCE to the second century CE. Regarding 4 Macc, Klawans (*Josephus and the Theologies of Ancient Judaism*, 123) notes, "the martyr's deaths serve quasi-sacrificial functions, expiating for the people's sins."

[231] In 2 Maccabees the martyrs are said to suffer for their "own sins" (7:18, 32). In 4 Maccabees the martyrs are innocent, suggesting that the sons die "on behalf of" or "for" the sins of the nation.

[232] Jarvis J. Williams, *Maccabean Martyr Traditions in Paul's Theology of Atonement: Did Martyr Theology Shape Paul's Conception of Jesus's Death?* (Eugene, Ore.: Wipf & Stock, 2010), 47.

[233] Stanley K. Stowers (*A Rereading of Romans: Justice, Jews, and Gentiles* [New Haven: Yale University Press, 1994], 212) suggests that the martyrs of 4 Macc 6:28-29 and 17:21-22 represent faithful "endurance" and have "nothing to do with sacrifice or the temple cult." Here Stowers presupposes a rather narrow semantic range of what constitutes "sacrifice."

of the death of one (or a few) being "offered/sacrificed" on behalf of many. Since the voluntary and vicarious self-sacrifice on behalf of others was well known in Greco-Roman literature,[234] and Isaiah 53 envisions the Servant-Israel as suffering (53:3, 7-8) and bearing the sins of others (53:4),[235] the idea of vicarious atonement does seem to have appeared in some circles within pre-Christian early Judaism,[236] even if there is no evidence of a pre-Christian suffering, dying, and atoning Messiah tradition.

— ♦ —

Our earliest "Christian" sources focus on Jesus' death as a sacrifice, complicating our historical-critical decisions about the Temple incident, the Last Supper accounts, and Jesus' relationship to the Temple. Jesus undoubtedly shared a last meal with his disciples, knew he was in imminent danger, predicted his death, and asked his followers to remember him, but our sources are ambiguous, inconsistent, and even somewhat contradictory on Jesus' attitude toward the Temple, its cultic worship, current administration, and role in the future of Israel.[237] Indeed, this is one of the most intractable problems in Jesus Research, especially since this question is inextricably linked with the soteriological imagery of Jesus' death envisioned as a "sacrifice" that *replaces* the sacrificial system. Yet if Jesus' relationship to the Torah can be understood in terms of his eschatological halakhah, then it is reasonable to suppose that his relationship to the Temple cult could also be so illuminated. Let us recall Jesus' position on divorce: Here, Jesus challenges Mosaic Law by calling for Torah observance that is actually more stringent than the Law requires.[238] Since the Mosaic Law does not command divorce, but only permits it, forbidding divorce institutes a more strict position that can be interpreted as

---

[234] Cf. Euripides, *Iphigeneia among the Tauri* 21-24; *Alcestis* 14; Plato, *Menexenus* 237a, 243a, 246b; Livy, *History of Rome* 8.9.

[235] The Hebrew Isaiah (MT) does not unambiguously refer to the Servant's vicarious suffering and death in Isa 53:5-8 ("*because of* our transgressions/iniquities" [MT]) (cf. "*for* our transgressions/iniquities" [LXX]).

[236] This conclusion stands in some tension with both Torah and prophetic passages proscribing the transfer of sin (cf. Exod 32:30-35; Deut 24:16; Ezek 18:4, 20; Jer 31:29-30). These passages illustrate the position that *individuals* are responsible for their own sins.

[237] Chapman (review of *Jesus and the Temple*) suggests that I "dismiss[es] the Lord's Supper traditions, asserting they derive from Paul" whereas "variant wording in Mark and Matthew testifies to independence from Paul." On the contrary, I do not "dismiss" these traditions nor do I assert that they "derive" entirely from Paul. I affirm that there was a "last supper" or commemorative meal. I simply do not affirm that the historical Jesus intended it to represent a replacement of the Temple cult enacted in his blood. Moreover, "Mark" was a creative literary author fully capable of adopting and adapting Pauline ideas and Matthew was, in turn, directly influenced by Mark.

[238] Sanders, *Jesus and Judaism*, 256–60.

criticism of the Mosaic Law's eschatological adequacy. If Jesus was inspired by the ideal of the eschatological restoration of creation anticipated by the prophet Isaiah, and this ideal informed his eschatological halakhah, then Jesus' interpretation of Torah was going to collide and conflict with his contemporaries.[239]

A casual, harmonizing reading of the New Testament Gospels could lead one to conclude that Jesus participated in the Temple's sacrificial system, celebrated Passover with a Passover lamb, regularly taught in its precincts, legislated for proper sacrificial protocol, and endorsed the legitimacy of the priests *while* criticizing the Temple's administration, predicting its destruction, and claiming that he was the Temple as well as a sacrificial "ransom" for "many."[240] The reader could be forgiven for being confused about Jesus' relationship to the Temple.

The Gospels suggest that Jesus threatened or predicted the Temple's destruction and/or sought to replace the Temple with himself and/or his new community of disciples and apostles. But did Jesus' message and promise of divine repentance require or presuppose animal sacrifice and participation in the Temple—or not?[241] It is often assumed that Jesus "accepted the Jerusalem temple *as part of the present order of things*"[242] and so "used the present temple even as he prophesied the temple's destruction."[243] Nonetheless, according to this common assumption, the writing was already on the wall, and Jesus' last week "unleashe[d] the imminent end of the present temple." As a result, "the full coming of the kingdom of God in power would do away with the temple Jesus and his contemporaries used."[244]

There are substantial interpretive problems with this common assumption. First of all, the Gospels portray Jesus' last week as setting the stage for the inauguration of a "new covenant" during Passover, but while the Synoptic Gospels suggest that the meal was a Passover *seder*, associating Jesus with the sacrificial lambs slaughtered for the festival, John's Gospel does not, since it occurs on the day before the Passover meal (John 19:14, 31, 42). According to John, Jesus has *a*

---

[239] Chapman (review of *Jesus and the Temple*) claims that I seek "a single cause" for Jesus' death and "downplay[s]" Jesus' economic critique of the Temple's administration. Cf. Joseph, *Jesus and the Temple*, 149: "Commercialism, economic exploitation, corruption, impurity, and priestly illegitimacy were valid concerns and common criticisms in Second Temple Judaism (and probably bothered Jesus, too)." Seeking a *primary* cause is not the same thing as reductionistically seeking a "single" cause.

[240] John P. Meier, *A Marginal Jew: Rethinking the Historical Jesus*, vol. 3, *Companions and Competitors* (New York: Doubleday, 2001), 3:499: "In all the Gospels, the fact that Jesus goes up to the temple, teaches in the temple, and—in the Synoptics—celebrates the Passover with a lamb slain in the temple according to the temple's ritual is taken for granted as an obvious datum that needs no explanation and generates no dispute."

[241] Wright, *Jesus and the Victory of God*, 257, 417.

[242] Meier, *Marginal Jew*, 4:500.

[243] Meier, *Marginal Jew*, 4:634.

[244] Meier, *Marginal Jew*, 4:502.

last meal, not a *Passover* meal (John 13). Second, some scholars do not regard the Last Supper as a historical event at all.[245] Others suggest that Jesus' death occurred "*around* Passover," but that is about all we know.[246] It is certainly possible that Jesus celebrated a "traditional" Passover meal,[247] including the sacrificial lamb, before his death, but there are good reasons to doubt this. First, the texts do not explicitly refer to a sacrificial "lamb" being present at the "Last Supper," whether slaughtered at the Temple or eaten during the meal. Second, the word *Pascha* "had at least four different meanings" and could refer to the Passover *lamb*; the Passover *meal*; the Passover *peace offering*; and the Passover *week*.[248] Consequently, narrative references to the *Pascha* are not necessarily references to a Passover *lamb*. Third, it is not at all apparent that Jesus participated "regularly in the Jewish Temple cult" (Luke 2:41; Mark 1:40-45; Matt 4:23-26).[249] The New Testament Gospels never depict Jesus performing an act of sacrifice. Fourth, there were early Jewish communities, like the Essenes, that celebrated Passover without a Passover lamb.[250] Fifth, the Passover meal-as-Passover-lamb is implicitly connected to a larger theological exegetical argument in which Jesus presented himself as a "new Moses" inaugurating a new "exodus" and a new "Passover" by shedding his blood for the "new covenant."

The problem, of course, is that the historical Jesus did not intend to create a new "religion" or "Church" that excluded Jewish observance or membership. It is also difficult to envision Jesus advocating the drinking of human blood.[251] Leviticus 17:11 states that blood should not be consumed because the "life" is in the blood. It is impossible to avoid the halakhic problem: consuming sacrificial blood is never allowed in the Torah. In fact, the Torah explicitly forbids eating

---

[245] Dennis E. Smith, *From Symposium to Eucharist: The Banquet in the Early Christian World* (Minneapolis: Fortress, 2003); R. Cameron and M. P. Miller, eds., *Redescribing Christian Origins*, SBLSymS 28 (Atlanta: Society of Biblical Literature, 2004); John W. Riggs, "The Sacred Food of Didache 9–10 and Second-Century Ecclesiologies," in *The Didache in Context: Essays on Its Text, History, and Transmission*, ed. C. N. Jefford, NovTSup 77 (Leiden: Brill, 1995), 256–83.

[246] Helen K. Bond, "Dating the Death of Jesus: Memory and the Religious Imagination," *NTS* 59, no. 4 (2013): 461–75.

[247] Brant Pitre (*Jesus and the Last Supper* [Grand Rapids: Eerdmans, 2015], 290–92) suggests that *Pascha* was the "customary way of referring to the Passover lamb."

[248] Pitre, *Jesus and the Last Supper*, 331.

[249] Contra Pitre, *Jesus and the Last Supper*, 401.

[250] Contra Pitre, *Jesus and the Last Supper*, 306–7, where he claims there is no evidence of a "lambless Passover" meal in early Judaism.

[251] Pitre (*Jesus and the Last Supper*, 108 [emphasis added]) suggests that Jesus' "command to drink wine that he identifies as his blood does not actually break any positive command of the Jewish Torah." Since the Torah does not prohibit "the consumption of *human* [as opposed to animal] blood," Jesus was not breaking any law.

human flesh and drinking blood. Scholars have sought to explain this tradition by appealing to sacrificial symbolism, substitutionary martyrdom, scriptural exegesis, and Greco-Roman/Mystery cultic traditions of fellowship meals, but the fact remains: ancient Jews, even when they sacrificed animals, never drank sacrificial blood (Gen 9:3-4; Lev 17:10-12; Deut 12:16). When Moses offered sacrificial blood at Sinai, the people did not *drink* it (Exod 24). The Last Supper accounts are theologically laden with symbolic meaning: Jesus celebrates the Passover because he is the Passover lamb to be sacrificed, which is precisely why the evangelists fail to mention Jesus *eating* a Passover lamb—*Jesus* is the "lamb" to be eaten.

Paul's letters describe Jesus' death in sacrificial terms: "Jesus died *for our sins*" (1 Cor 15:3), a *"sacrifice of atonement in his blood"* (Rom 3:24-25), a holy sacrifice (2 Cor 5:21). According to Mark, Jesus is an obedient, suffering, and sacrificial figure. He comes to call sinners (Mark 2:17) and predicts the suffering and death of the Son of Man (8:31), giving his life as "a *ransom* for many" (10:45). The *wine* of the Last Supper is "the *blood* of the covenant ... poured out for many" (14:22-24; cf. Exod 24:1-11). Matthew echoes Mark's pattern of Jesus' prediction of suffering and death (Matt 16:21; 17:12, 22; 20:18-19; 26:2), repeats the Markan saying that the Son of Man came to give his life as "a ransom for many" (Matt 20:28), and adds "for the forgiveness of sins" (Matt 26:28), associating the Eucharist with Jesus' atoning sacrifice, with echoes of Isaiah's Servant bearing "the sins of many" (Isa 53:12).[252] John portrays Jesus being handed over to death at the moment the Passover lambs are slaughtered (John 19:14-16), the "Lamb of God who takes away the sins of the world" (John 1:29).

The disciples' traumatic experience of Jesus' death required a theological explanation. Paul's letters attest to this early meaning-making process. An interpretive trajectory, centered on Jesus' death as a "saving" event, and supported by sacrificial terms and concepts, provided new frameworks within which to make sense of Jesus' death. That is why Paul could claim that just as "we have been justified by his *blood*, we will be saved through him from the wrath [of God]" (Rom 5:9-11) and that "reconciliation" (καταλλαγὴν) comes "through" Jesus' death (Rom 5:10-11; cf. 2 Cor 5:15-17). Paul announced, "Jesus *gave himself* (δόντος ἑαυτὸν) for our sins, so that he would rescue us from this present evil age" (Gal 1:4; cf. 3:10-14). Jesus and his followers could now be represented as "sacrifices" and the "Temple" of God. The early sacrificial *kerygma* took the

---

[252] Chapman (review of *Jesus and the Temple* [emphasis added]) claims that my discussion of Isa 53 is "limited" and suffers from "neglecting how the Servant Songs *progressively* become *individualized* to a *single* representative who restores Israel and atones for their sins (Isa. 49:6-8; 53:4-6)." Yet such a "progressive" trajectory of individualization is not unambiguously apparent in the text. Cf. Joseph, *Jesus and the Temple*, 224n108.

historical datum of Jesus' death interpreted in light of a soteriological system and provided the narrative framework for the Gospels (Mark 10:45), captivating the attention of non-Judeans and facilitating the movement's "parting ways" with its Judean networks.

Jesus' final days could now be understood as a faithful witness in the face of hostility and opposition.[253] That is, Jesus "sacrificed" himself, "offering" his life to God. Adapting the historical memory that Jesus "offered" his life *to* God into a theology of Jesus being "handed over" *by* God, Paul does not advocate offering animal sacrifices but he does use sacrificial terminology, both reconfiguring sacrificial ideology and reaffirming the ancient logic of sacrifice. Paul calls for community members to regard themselves as a "living sacrifice":

> I urge you, brothers, by the mercies of God, to present your bodies
> as a living sacrifice (θυσίαν ζῶσαν), holy (ἁγίαν) and pleasing to God …
> be transformed by the renewal of your mind (τῇ ἀνακαινώσει τοῦ νοὸς)
> so that you may discern what is the will of God. (Rom 12:1-2)

Paul is not calling for "martyrdom" per se, but rather for the transformation of the mind and body as "offerings" to God. Paul advocates taking on "the mind (νοῦν) of Christ" (1 Cor 2:16): just as Jesus "offered" himself up as a "sacrifice," so should his follower. Paul even describes himself being "poured out as a libation" on behalf of his community members' "sacrifice":

> Do all things without murmuring and arguing so that you may
> become blameless and pure, children of God
> without blemish in the midst of a crooked and twisted generation …
> but even if I am poured out as a libation (σπένδομαι)
> upon the sacrifice (θυσίᾳ) and priestly service (λειτουργίᾳ)
> of your faith (πίστεως), I rejoice. (Phil 2:14-18)

Here Paul sees his own ministry in sacrificial terms, describing himself as being "poured out as a libation (σπένδομαι)." Similarly, he calls his community members to become "a living sacrifice" (θυσίαν ζῶσαν) to God. Since Paul envisions Jesus' death in sacrificial terms, it seems fairly clear that Paul is participating in a philosophical discourse on sacrifice, the central question being: What is the *best* "offering" to the divine? Without rejecting the logic of sacrifice, Paul internalizes the "offering" as one's self—mind, heart, and body—as the highest form of sacrifice. The fact that this language is amenable to martyrological readings does not mean that the deity is envisioned as "desiring" or "needing" (blood) sacrifice. Paul, after all, does not base his soteriological-sacrificial interpretation of Jesus'

---

[253] On "self-mastery" in Greco-Roman society, see Stowers, *A Rereading of Romans*, 42–82.

death on a literal reading of "sin offerings" in the book of Leviticus.[254] Rather, Paul is mixing metaphors informed by sacrificial ideology, including a "messianic" exegesis of Isaiah 53,[255] Greco-Roman "noble death" traditions, and Hellenistic Jewish martyr traditions.[256] That is why Paul can say that Christ, "our Passover (lamb), has been sacrificed" (τὸ πάσχα ἡμῶν ἐτύθη, 1 Cor 5:7) even though the Passover lamb was not associated with the forgiveness of sins. For Paul, Jesus' death redeems Gentiles because that is the nature of the "mystery" revealed by God. The meaning of Jesus' death thus has less to do with precise terminological equivalents to biblical descriptions of the Temple cult and more with mixing metaphors for Gentile audiences relatively unfamiliar with Judean cultic practices. It is this transference of sacrificial metaphor from Palestinian Judea to the Gentiles and Judean diaspora that transformed the movement beyond its Judean ethnic and geographical borders.

Within the *Yahad*, self-sacrifice was internalized and enacted by its members. The community produced new interpretations of Torah, new forms of messianism, and new collective conceptualizations of atonement. The *Yahad* did not envision anyone dying in atonement for the sins of Israel nor were they waiting for the messiah to die for the sins of Israel. It was the *community* that was to generate and/or to be acceptable sacrifice(s).[257] The members were to "offer" themselves, individually and collectively, to God. There was no need for the sacrificial system in Jerusalem, as direct prayer and communion with God (and his angels) were now possible. Holiness and purity were available outside the Temple's cultic context and collective atonement was possible through prayer and Torah study. But what we do not see at Qumran is the idea that the suffering or death of an individual person will atone for the sins of Israel.

As with the Maccabean martyrs, it is Jesus' "faithfulness" to the *Torah*—understood as the eschatologically revealed will of God—that led to identifying

---

[254] Aaron Glaim ("Reciprocity, Sacrifice, and Salvation in Judean Religion at the Turn of the Era," Ph.D. diss., Brown University, 2014, 161) challenges the idea that Paul portrays Jesus' death as a "sin offering" or "sin sacrifice" (חטאת) "in broad accordance with biblical instructions for offering such sacrifices in the Septuagint versions of Leviticus and Numbers." Glaim translates ἱλαστήριον (Rom 3:25) as "conciliaton," "an adjectival/substantive" derivative of the verb *hilaskomai* ("conciliate," "placate") (183). For Glaim, Paul envisions Christ's death as "for sin," but not "as a sin-sacrifice."

[255] Cf. Simon Gathercole, *Defending Substitution: An Essay on Atonement in Paul*, Acadia Studies in Bible and Theology (Grand Rapids: Baker Academic, 2015).

[256] Williams, *Maccabean Martyr Traditions*.

[257] Regev (*Sectarianism in Qumran*, 122), citing 1QS 9.3–5, refers to "righteous behavior as a substitute for sacrificial offerings... Here, 'the perfect of the way' (*temim derekh*) performed by the *yahad* serves as an offering which pleases God." Regev recognizes that the idea that "moral behavior" replaces sacrifice as a means of atonement was "a revolutionary concept" (123).

his death as "atoning,"[258] even if Jesus' interpretation of the Torah was different from theirs. Nonetheless, the central presupposition behind Jewish martyrological tradition is the idea that loyalty or "faithfulness" toward the Law is worth living and dying for.[259] Jesus may have anticipated (but not necessarily sought or welcomed) a martyr's death, but that does not mean that he believed it would have atoning significance for the nation or that it would appease the eschatological "wrath" of God. Methodologically, we must differentiate between Jesus' acceptance of his death and the theological-soteriological significance it came to have for his followers. The Maccabean martyrs are portrayed as dying in defending the Law. Their deaths are said (esp. 4 Macc) to atone for the nation's sin. According to Josephus, the Essenes were also known for dying for the Law, in faithfulness to "the Lawgiver" (ὁ νομοθέτης), but their deaths did not have atoning power. The Essenes are nonetheless "remembered" and commemorated as martyrs dying for the Law:

> The war against the Romans fully revealed their souls.
> During it their limbs were twisted and broken, burned
> and shattered; they were subjected to every instrument
> of torture to compel them either to blaspheme
> against the Lawgiver (νομοθέτην) or to eat forbidden food.
> But they refused to do either, or even to flatter their butchers
> or weep. Smiling amidst pain, and mocking
> those who tortured them, they gave up their souls cheerfully,
> convinced that they would recover them again. (*B.J.* 152–153)[260]

Despite the rhetorical exaggeration which identifies the heroism of the Essenes as characteristic of *all* Judeans,[261] Josephus' representation of the Essenes illustrates the martyrological framework within which they were remembered: as heroically

---

[258] Cf. Jan Willem van Henten, *The Maccabean Martyrs as Saviours of the Jewish People: A Study of 2 and 4 Maccabees*, JSJSup 57 (Leiden: Brill, 1997), where the martyrs are described as dying in perfect loyalty to God and the Law as examples of "faithfulness."

[259] 2 Macc 6:28, 7:9, 37; cf. 4 Macc 5:16, 9:1-8, 16:17-22. Cf. Josephus on the Essenes. For the discursive exploration of this theme in Late Antiquity, see Daniel Boyarin, *Dying for God: Martyrdom and the Making of Christianity and Judaism* (Palo Alto: Stanford University Press, 1999).

[260] Vermes and Goodman, *Essenes according to the Classical Sources*, 45, 47.

[261] Steve Mason ("Josephus' Pharisees: The Philosophy," in *In Quest of the Historical Pharisees*, ed. J. Neusner and B. D. Chilton [Waco, Tex.: Baylor University Press, 2007], 41–66, 54) notes that in this passage the Essenes "display the same virtues of courage and toughness in the face of torture that characterizes Judeans throughout the work ... but most clearly in a comparison with the *Apion*. There, what Josephus has said about the Essenes in *War* 2 is applied to all Judeans: *the whole nation* observes the laws with the strictest discipline and solemnity, lives in utmost simplicity, values virtue above all else, holds death in contempt" (emphasis in original).

defying Roman persecution while convinced of their postmortem vindication.[262] It is not difficult to draw parallels and comparisons between Josephus' description of the Essenes and early Christian commemoration of Jesus.

The Jesus of the Gospels is never portrayed as offering animal sacrifice,[263] yet Jesus certainly seems to have visited the Temple, taught in the Temple, honored the Temple, and criticized its administration. Jesus never criticizes the pilgrims and worshipers in the Temple for participating in the cultic system, which suggests that Jesus sought neither to *destroy* the Temple nor to *replace* it with himself.[264] Yet if Jesus' eschatological halakhah is our interpretive key, then Jesus' attitude toward the Temple cult may have been informed by eschatological convictions that God's forgiveness did not *require* animal sacrifice. Jesus' public nonparticipation and popular following—in conjunction with his declaration that God forgave sins without sacrifice and his implied criticism of the Temple's administration—would have made him an offensive, disruptive, and potentially dangerous presence. While our sources are ambiguous, they suggest that Jesus did not participate in the Temple cult. Jesus' nonparticipation has its closest known parallel to the Essenes and the *Yahad*, the only other known *Palestinian* Jewish group that willfully withdrew from Temple cultic ritual at the time of Jesus.

— ✦ —

Have the Dead Sea Scrolls shed any new light on the relationship between Jesus and the Temple? Yes, but only to a limited extent. The classical sources and the Qumran corpus both indicate that voluntary nonparticipation in the Temple cult could be combined with ancestral reverence for the Temple and affirmation of the ongoing need for sacrificial practices, even if in an alternative form. It is highly likely that the Essene movement underwent a series of internal developments during different historical periods under different historical circumstances. Those details are perhaps forever lost to us, but a movement that was once active within the Temple (CD) came to criticize its current administration (4QMMT), imagine its grand new eschatological architecture (11QT), and ultimately withdraw from its cultic system (1QS).

---

[262] Klawans (*Josephus and the Theologies of Ancient Judaism*, 116) points out that "the account is strange, if for no other reason than the fact that Josephus does not elsewhere indicate that the Romans forced Jews to commit blasphemy or eat forbidden foods." Josephus seems to be conflating Essenic heroism with that of Judeans in general as well as adopting motifs from the Maccabean martyrological tradition.

[263] Robert Daly, *Christian Sacrifice: The Judaeo-Christian Background Before Origen*, Studies in Christian Antiquity 18 (Washington, D.C.: Catholic University of America, 1978), 214.

[264] Cf. J. H. Charlesworth, "Jesus and the Temple," in *Jesus and Temple: Textual and Archaeological Explorations*, ed. J. H. Charlesworth (Minneapolis: Fortress, 2014), 145–83.

The Dead Sea Scrolls provide us with the closest known "parallels" to how the earliest Palestinian Jesus movement seems to have understood the Temple. While the historical Jesus seems to have regarded the Temple as the house of God, there is no compelling evidence that he himself participated in the sacrificial cult. The Gospels portray Jesus as critical of the Temple's administration and instituting a new cultic system within a community setting during the Last Supper. Paul and the evangelists extend this symbolism by portraying Jesus as the Passover "lamb" sacrificed "for our sins." While the evidence from Acts is ambiguous and suggests that Jesus' followers continued *teaching* in the Temple precincts, there is no compelling evidence to suggest that early Jewish Christians actually participated in the sacrificial cult.[265]

The *Yahad* withdrew from participating in the sacrificial cult while criticizing the Temple's administration and instituting a new cultic system of atonement within a group setting. Like the *Yahad*, the Jesus movement developed the idea that the community itself substituted for the Temple. But whereas the *Yahad* substituted the "offerings of the lips" (תרומת שפתים) and the "perfection of way" (תמים דרך) (1QS 9.3–6) as acceptable substitutes for animal sacrifice, the Jesus movement envisioned Jesus' *death* as the substitute for animal sacrifice, introducing what would become a fundamental difference between the Essenes and early Christians, an idea unprecedented in pre-Christian Judaism: the suffering messiah as an atoning sacrifice.

Since the discovery of the Dead Sea Scrolls, biblical scholars have searched the Qumran corpus for any evidence of a pre-Christian Jewish suffering-and-dying "messianic" figure. One popular theory focuses on the "Teacher of Righteousness" as a precursor for Jesus.[266] The problem with this claim, however,[267] is that the Teacher of Righteousness is never identified as "messianic,"[268] let alone as a suffering, dying, atoning, and resurrected figure. In fact, the most exegetically innovative components of "Christianity" are not "paralleled" in the Scrolls at

---

[265] Cf. Simon J. Joseph, "'I Have Come to Abolish Sacrifices' (Epiphanius, *Pan.* 30.16.5): Reexamining a Jewish-Christian Text and Tradition," NTS 63 no. 1 (2017): 92–110.

[266] André Dupont-Sommer (*The Dead Sea Scrolls: A Preliminary Survey*, trans. E. M. Rowley [Oxford: Blackwell, 1952], 99) suggests that Jesus appeared to be "an astonishing reincarnation" of the Teacher, a messianic figure who was "the object of the hostility of the priests," "condemned and put to death," and expected to return as "the supreme judge."

[267] Louis Ginzberg, *An Unknown Jewish Sect* (New York: Jewish Theological Seminary of America, 1976), 221; André Dupont-Sommer, *Aperçus préliminaires sur les manuscrits de la Mer Morte* (Paris: Maisonneuve, 1950), 73–78; John M. Allegro, "Further Messianic References in Qumran Literature," *JBL* 75 (1956): 176–77; Krister Stendahl, ed., *The Scrolls and the New Testament* (New York: Harper & Brothers, 1957), 12; W. D. Davies, *Torah in the Messianic Age and/or the Age to Come*, SBLMS 7 (Philadelphia: Society of Biblical Literature, 1952), 46–47.

[268] John J. Collins, *The Dead Sea Scrolls: A Biography*, Lives of Great Religious Books (Princeton: Princeton University Press, 2012), 147–48.

all. Consequently, any attempt to find such "parallels" undermines what is most distinctive about the tradition: the *unprecedented* combination(s) of Jesus' historical agency and particular fate.

Since the publication of the Cave 1 texts, there has been some discussion of possible "messianic" readings in the Isaiah Scroll (1QIsa^a).[269] The Qumran text of Isaiah 52:14, for example, has a variant that describes the Servant's appearance not as "marred," as in the MT (משחת), but as "anointed" (משחתי).[270]

MT 52:14: כן משחת מאיש מראהו ותארו מבני אדם
DSS 52:14: כן משחתי מאיש מראהו ותוארו מבני האדם

Similarly, the Isaiah Scroll also has a different reading of Isaiah 53:11 ("out of his travail of his soul he will see light [אור]"), from the MT ("he will see of the travail of his soul and will be satisfied"):

MT 53:11: מעמל נפשו יראה ישבע בדעתו
DSS 53:11: מעמל נפשוה יראה אור וישבע ובדעתו

Not much can be made of these variant readings, however. If 1QIsa^a 52:14 does describe the Servant as "anointed," there is still no direct identification of the Servant with the Davidic messiah. Another theory suggests that the Teacher of Righteousness—as the so-called first messiah—was a Jewish priest named Judah who lived in the early first century BCE and served as the prototype for Jesus.[271] Judah came into conflict with the Pharisees and then fled with his followers to the "land of Damascus," where he wrote the Thanksgiving Hymns (1QH), identifying himself with the Servant of Isaiah 53, and thus became the model for Jesus as the suffering-and-dying Servant Messiah.[272]

While the similarities between Jesus and the Teacher are striking, the historical problems are legion. First, "Judah" is never identified by name in the Scrolls.[273] Second, there is no evidence that the Teacher ever claimed to be a "messiah." The Teacher was more likely *awaiting* the messianic age. Third, there is no way to prove that the Thanksgiving Hymns were written by the Teacher. Fourth, there is no way to identify the Teacher with a particular historical figure. Fifth, there is no

---

[269] J. V. Chamberlain, "The Functions of God as Messianic Titles in the Complete Qumran Isaiah Scroll," *VT* 5 (1955): 366–72; W. H. Brownlee, "The Servant of the Lord in the Qumran Scrolls," *BASOR* 132 (1950): 546–49.

[270] A. Guillaume, "Some Readings in the Dead Sea Scroll of Isaiah," *JBL* 76, no. 1 (1957): 40–43.

[271] Michael O. Wise, *The First Messiah: Investigating the Saviour Before Christ* (San Francisco: HarperOne, 1999).

[272] Wise, *First Messiah*, 91, 253–77.

[273] Wise suggests the name "the Teacher" based on a loose association with the "House of Judah."

compelling evidence that the Teacher's death was interpreted as soteriological or atoning "for sins."[274] The Teacher may have been a (Zadokite) "priest" (1QpHab 2.8), an inspired interpreter of the Law (1QpHab 7.1–14) who came into conflict with a figure identified as the "Wicked Priest." Another theory suggests that the author of the "Self-Glorification Hymn" (4Q491) from Cave 4 was a "messianic" leader of the Qumran community who saw himself as the "Servant" of Isaiah 53.[275] The problem is that while this fragmentary hymn does use "Servant" imagery from Isaiah 53, we do not know whom the text refers to, who wrote it, what role the authors played in the community, or whether the leader regarded himself as "messianic." In short, we have no reason to believe that a *messianic* interpretation of Isaiah 53 is a pre-Christian Jewish tradition, especially because the Servant of Isaiah 53 is a collective personification of Israel, not a "messianic" figure.

Another recent attempt to find evidence for a pre-Christian suffering messiah focuses on "Gabriel's Revelation," or *Hazon Gabriel* ("Gabriel's Vision"), an ancient stone tablet discovered in Jordan, presumably in the vicinity of the Dead Sea. With eighty-seven lines of Hebrew text, this so-called Dead Sea Scroll in Stone has caused quite a stir, mostly because it contains a reference to the archangel Gabriel and allegedly contains a reference to a messianic figure dying and rising again after three days. The tablet is indeed a first-century Jewish apocalyptic text that refers to "three days" and a "prince of princes," but there is no direct correlation between the "three days," a messiah, and resurrection. This must be read *into* the text. Serious interpretive problems also beset "Gabriel's Revelation." The text is fragmentary, and there is no justification for correlating the "three days" (*shloshet yamim*) with an archangelic prediction of a *messiah*'s resurrection. Nor is there any particular reason to identify this text with a particular historical individual, let alone an *Essene* "messiah."

Another theory holds that the idea of the suffering messiah was "part and parcel of Jewish tradition from antiquity to modernity," claiming that "many Jewish authorities, maybe even most, until nearly the modern period have read Isaiah 53 as being about the Messiah." Unfortunately, the sources supporting this theory are either from the Talmud, a *sixth-century CE* work (*Sukkah* 5:2 55b; *Sanh.* 98), or *later* (*Pesiqta Rabbati*). In other words, the messianic identification of the "Servant" is a *late* development within *rabbinical* Judaism, not ancient apocalyptic

---

[274] Bilde, *Originality of Jesus*, 187.

[275] Maurice Baillet, *Qumrân Grotte 4.III (4Q482–4Q520)*, DJD 7 (Oxford: Clarendon, 1982), 26–30; Morton Smith, "Ascent to the Heavens and Deification in 4QM^a," in *Archaeology and History in the Dead Sea Scrolls: The New York University Conference in Memory of Yigael Yadin*, ed. L. H. Schiffman, JSPSup 8 (Sheffield: JSOT, 1990), 181–88.

Judaism. The idea of a suffering and dying messiah was not common among the rabbis; it was "re-appropriated" by the rabbis.²⁷⁶

The Qumran corpus, in short, has not yielded any compelling evidence that the *Yahad* (or any other known Jewish author or group) identified Isaiah 53 as a prophecy foretelling the sacrificial atoning death of the royal Davidic messiah. The most intriguing possibility of such an identification—the *Levi Apocryphon* (4Q541)—only refers to the probably cultic atonement of an eschatological high priest. 4Q541, an Aramaic nonsectarian text closely related to the *Testament of Levi* (c. 100 BCE), is represented by twenty-four fragments from Cave 4, and it describes a person who will be opposed by the people of "his generation":

> And he will atone for all the children of his generation (ויכפר על כול בני דרה).
> (4Q541 9 i 2)
>
> His word is like the word of the heavens, and his teaching,
> according to the will of God (מאמרה כמאמר שמין ואלפונה ברעות). (9 i 3)
>
> They will utter many words against him, and an abundance of [false]ness.
> And they will fabricate fables against him,
> and utter every kind of disparagement against him. (9 i 5–6)²⁷⁷

Based on the fact that 4Q541 refers to this figure's atoning function (יכפר), it is reasonable to think that the text refers to a high priest. It is certain that this figure will be opposed by "his generation." The author also makes several literary allusions to the Suffering Servant Songs of Isaiah 52:13–53:12.²⁷⁸ It has been suggested that "we may have in this composition the earliest *individualistic* interpretation of the Isaianic Servant Songs in a particularly cultic direction"²⁷⁹—that is, "a Jewish text whose author used the Servant passages of Isaiah to support the idea that there was to be an eschatological priest who would suffer, possibly even that the suffering involved death, death that would lead to joyous benefits

---

²⁷⁶ Peter Schäfer, "The Jew Who Would Be God," review of Daniel Boyarin, *The Jewish Gospels: The Story of the Jewish Christ*, New Republic, May 18, 2012, https://newrepublic.com/article/103373/jewish-gospels-christ-boyarin (accessed April 22, 2016).

²⁷⁷ Florentino García Martínez, *The Dead Sea Scrolls Translated: The Qumran Texts in English*, 2nd ed. (Grand Rapids: Eerdmans, 1996), 270.

²⁷⁸ George J. Brooke, "4QTestament of Levi and the Messianic Servant High Priest," in *From Jesus to John: Essays on Jesus and New Testament Christology in Honour of Marinus de Jonge*, ed. M. C. DeBoer, JSNTSup 84 (Sheffield: JSOT, 1993), 83–96. The text does *not* refer to the "crucifixion" of the figure, as suggested by Émile Puech, "Fragments d'un apocryphe de Lévi et le personnage eschatologie, 4Q Test-Lévi (c–d[?]) et 4QAJa," in *The Madrid Qumran Congress: Proceedings of the International Congress on the Dead Sea Scrolls, Madrid, 18–21 March, 1991*, 2 vols., ed. J. Trebolle Barrera and L. Vegas Montaner (Leiden: Brill, 1992), 475–78.

²⁷⁹ Brooke, *Dead Sea Scrolls and the New Testament*, 151 (emphasis added).

for others."²⁸⁰ While it is true that the figure in question is said to provide "atonement" for "his generation," the text does not say that this "atonement" will be the "joyous" result of the figure's suffering. Moreover, the figure is nowhere described as "anointed" or "messiah" and is most certainly not portrayed as a royal Davidic messiah.²⁸¹ The figure is said to be slandered, but the text does not say he will be put to death, let alone *crucified*. There is also no hint of the idea that the atonement made by the priestly figure will replace the Temple cult or serve as the cornerstone of a "new covenant."²⁸²

Despite Herculean efforts to discover suffering-and-dying messiah proof-texts in the Qumran corpus—including the *Levi Apocryphon* (4Q541), the so-called "Pierced Messiah" text (4Q285), the *Hodayot*, and "Gabriel's Revelation"—none of these texts have provided evidence of such a figure. Nonetheless, what the Qumran texts do suggest is that this scriptural interpretation of Jesus' death probably occurred initially *within* such an apocalyptic Jewish exegetical matrix.

The idea that Jesus' death was an atoning sacrifice may not have been the earliest interpretation among Jesus' Aramaic-speaking followers in Jerusalem.²⁸³ Nonetheless, Paul's claim that he had "received" this tradition—that "Christ died for our sins according to the scriptures" (1 Cor 15:3)—suggests that the suffering-and-dying messiah tradition was very quickly developed in light of Jesus' actual suffering, death, and resurrection.²⁸⁴ The identification of Jesus' death as atoning originated within circles familiar with Jewish martyrological traditions

---

²⁸⁰ Brooke, *Dead Sea Scrolls and the New Testament*, 153.

²⁸¹ Collins, *Scepter and the Star*, 93–94.

²⁸² N. T. Wright (*Simply Jesus: A New Vision of Who He Was, What He Did, and Why He Matters* [New York: HarperOne, 2011], 175) suggests that Jesus understood himself to be the Servant Messiah whose death had atoning, redemptive significance.

²⁸³ James D. G. Dunn ("When Did the Understanding of Jesus' Death as an Atoning Sacrifice First Emerge?" in *Israel's God and Rebecca's Children: Christology and Community in Early Judaism and Christianity: Essays in Honor of Larry W. Hurtado and Alan F. Segal*, ed. D. B. Capes, A. D. DeConick, H. K. Bond, and T. Miller [Waco, Tex.: Baylor University Press, 2007], 169–82) suggests this identification emerged among Greek-speaking "Hellenists" driven from Jerusalem who instructed Paul. He proposes that "the thought of Jesus' death as an atoning sacrifice could have emerged as part of or even the reason for the hostility to the temple" in Luke's account of the Hellenists (181), adding that the idea "that Jesus was the first to understand his death in terms of atoning sacrifice cannot be demonstrated with any confidence" (176), and concluding: "The understanding of Jesus' death in soteriological terms does not seem to have been grasped or articulated within the earliest Jerusalem community." Dunn even suggests that this understanding of "the gospel" began "to create the tensions" between Paul and the Jerusalem church (182).

²⁸⁴ On the catalytic function of the resurrection, see Simon J. Joseph, "Redescribing the Resurrection: Beyond the Methodological Impasse?" *BTB* 45, no. 3 (2015): 155–73.

who interpreted Jesus' life in light of the Servant of Isaiah.²⁸⁵ The Scriptures began to make sense out of Jesus' suffering and death. The book of Isaiah, in particular, with its description of a personified Servant "rejected" by men, came to serve as the scriptural prototype of what happened to Jesus. Yet the messianic reading of Isaiah 53 was unprecedented because it required the catalytic death of Jesus to create it.²⁸⁶ At the same time, the proclamation of the death, resurrection, and *re*-appearance (παρουσία) of Jesus, now associated with the coming of *Yahweh* (1 Thess 4:15; 5:1-11; Phil 2:6-11),²⁸⁷ transformed the Jewish Jesus movement into an empire-wide Gentile religion, precipitated by the Gospels' representation of Jesus as the "Son of Man."

Once Jesus was identified as both "Son of Man" and the "Servant" of Isaiah, the Danielic tradition of the *corporate* suffering of the "people of the holy ones," once only indirectly connected to the "one like a son of man,"²⁸⁸ could now be attributed to the *individualized* Son of Man/Servant.²⁸⁹ And just as the Isaianic Servant was originally a collective symbol now individualized *as Jesus*, so too was the Son of Man, once a collective symbol of "Israel," now personified and individualized *as Jesus*. These interpretive innovations—transforming corporate symbols into individualized human agents and corporate experiences into divine representatives—document a Jewish exegetical tradition witnessed in the Enochic writings, Qumran, and nascent Gospel tradition.²⁹⁰ The identification of Jesus as

---

²⁸⁵ 2 Macc 6:30; 7:9, 11, 14, 16-17, 22-23, 29, 30-38; 4 Macc 6:27-29; 17:20-22. Cf. Sam K. Williams, *Jesus' Death as Saving Event: The Background and Origin of a Concept*, HDR 2 (Missoula, Mont.: Scholars, 1975); Marinus de Jonge, "Jesus' Death for Others and the Death of the Maccabean Martyrs," in *Text and Testimony: Essays on the New Testament and Apocryphal Literature in Honour of A. F. J. Klijn*, ed. T. Baarda (Kampen: Kok, 1988), 146–47.

²⁸⁶ Collins, *Dead Sea Scrolls*, 127.

²⁸⁷ Cf. Larry W. Hurtado, "YHWH's Return to Zion: A New Catalyst for Earliest High Christology?" in *God and the Faithfulness of Paul*, ed. C. Heilig, J. T. Hewitt, and M. F. Bird (Tübingen: Mohr Siebeck, 2016), 417–38.

²⁸⁸ J. R. Daniel Kirk (*A Man Attested by God: The Human Jesus of the Synoptic Gospels* [Grand Rapids: Eerdmans, 2016], 147) interprets the "one like a son of man" as representative of the plural earthly-suffering "people of the holy ones"—that is, a "vindicated sufferer" (149).

²⁸⁹ Thomas A. Kazen ("Son of Man as Kingdom Imagery: Jesus between Corporate Symbol and Individual Redeemer Figure," in *Jesus from Judaism to Christianity: Continuum Approaches to the Historical Jesus*, ed. T. Holmén, LNTS 352 [London: T&T Clark, 2007], 87–108) suggests that the Daniel's "son of man" is a corporate-collective representation of the "kingdom" of *Israel*.

²⁹⁰ Loren T. Stuckenbruck and Gabriele Boccaccini ("1 Enoch and the Synoptic Gospels: The Method and Benefits of a Conversation," in *Enoch and the Synoptic Gospels: Reminiscences, Allusions, Intertextuality*, ed. L. T. Stuckenbruck and G. Boccaccini, EJL 44 [Atlanta: Society of Biblical Literature, 2016], 6) state that a "connection" between the Gospel of Matthew and the Parables is "certain." Cf. Johannes Theisohn, *Der auserwählte Richter: Untersuchungen zum traditionsgeschichtlichen Ort der Menschensohngestalt der Bilderreden des Äthiopischen Henoch*

Χριστός, Κύριος, Son of God, Son of Man, and "the last Adam" reflects a major development in early Jewish messianism. Early Christians adopted and adapted this very high Christology as early as the 30s CE in light of their "visions" and experiences of the risen Jesus.[291] The public proclamation of Jesus' death and resurrection served as a catalytic force, effectively transforming the early Jesus movement far beyond its originally Palestinian Judean/Jewish ethnic boundaries and cultural matrices.[292]

(Göttingen: Vandenhoeck & Ruprecht, 1975), 153, 182; Leslie W. Walck, *The Son of Man in the Parables of Enoch and in Matthew*, JCT 9 (Edinburgh: T&T Clark, 2011), 224. Cf. Matt 25:31; 19:28; cf. 1 En. 62–63).

[291] Larry W. Hurtado, *Lord Jesus Christ: Devotion to Jesus in Earliest Christianity* (Grand Rapids: Eerdmans, 2003); idem, *One God, One Lord: Early Christian Devotion and Ancient Jewish Monotheism* (New York: T&T Clark, 1988).

[292] Larry W. Hurtado, "Resurrection-Faith and the 'Historical' Jesus," *JSHJ* 11 (2013): 35–52.

CHAPTER 5

BEYOND THE ESSENES

The relationship between Jesus and the Essenes has fascinated biblical scholars and the general public for over three hundred years, yet there is no compelling evidence that the Essenes even *knew* about Jesus, let alone supported or followed him. There is also no compelling evidence that Jesus was ever a member of the *Qumran* group or ever visited Qumran. On the other hand, Jesus' halakhah on divorce and the Sabbath is both reminiscent and subversive of the halakhah recorded in the *Damascus Document*, widely regarded as originating among the Essene movement. Moreover, Jesus' emphasis on "loving enemies" also seems to correct, and so presuppose, *Essenic* principles of "hating" enemies. Like the Essenes, Jesus challenges the eschatological adequacy of the Mosaic Torah (Mark 10; Matt 5:32 // Luke 16:18; cf. Deut 24:1-4) and claims authority over the Temple and its administration. Jesus reinterprets Mosaic Law in light of an halakhic principle of creation, engages in legal conflicts with Pharisees and Sadducees, and interprets his ministry in light of the prophecies of Isaiah. These identity markers place Jesus in ideological proximity to the Essenes. Historical explanations of the relationship(s) between Jesus and the Essenes thus require positing similarities and differences along a spectrum or continuum of ideological compatibilities within Second Temple Judaism.

The historical Jesus was a creative agent, reacting and responding to thought currents within his world that he regarded as both ideal and inadequate, sometimes agreeing, sometimes disagreeing with his contemporaries.[1] It is this constellation

---

[1] On Jesus as "unclassifiable," see Daniel Marguerat, "Historical Jesus and Christ of Faith: A Relevant Dichotomy?" in *Jesus—Gestalt und Gestaltungen: Rezeption des Galiläers in*

of data that sheds new light on Jesus' cultural context within Judaism. If we presuppose points of both similarity and difference with the Essenes, the historical Jesus can be understood as the leader of a movement that rejected some of their halakhic conclusions while engaging others. The "parallels" between Jesus and the Essenes—in such close sociocultural, geographical, and chronological proximity—require explanations more compelling than coincidence, "common tradition," and "parallel development." While no single parallel may persuade us of relationship, their cumulative effect and combined evidentiary weight suggests that the similarities and the differences add up to a more complex but coherent narrative of Christianity's emergence within early Judaism. This does *not* mean that everything in the early Jesus tradition is "paralleled" or precedented in the Scrolls. What it does mean is that future discussions of the historical Jesus can now acknowledge the Essenes as a major part of the cultural matrix of the early Jewish Jesus movement.

Was the historical Jesus influenced by the Essenes? Yes. Was the Jesus movement influenced by the Essenes? Yes. Did the early Jesus movement develop in ideological proximity and relationship to the Essenes? Yes. Is the Jesus movement to be *identified* as "Essenic?" No. Conceptually, the two movements were subject to different historical factors and events that affected their development along different trajectories. Nonetheless, given their proximity in time and space, their similarities and differences must be studied diachronically, as movements along a continuum that (always) presupposes *relationship*, with the geographical and ideological proximities between some of Jesus' first Jewish followers and some Essenes giving rise to some of the literary and theological features of the earliest Jesus tradition.[2]

This hypothesis is supported by the terminological and organizational parallels between the Qumran texts and the early Jesus movement. The term "holy spirit," for example, seems to have been common to both.[3] Similarly, both groups used "the Way" as self-designations.[4] In the book of Acts, "the Way" refers to "the

---

Wissenschaft, Kirche und Gesellschaft. FS Gerd Theißen, ed. P. von Gemünden, D. G. Horrell, and M. Küchler, NTOASUNT 100 (Göttingen: Vandenhoeck & Ruprecht, 2013), 429–47, 445.

[2] Simon J. Joseph, "The Quest for the 'Community' of Q: Mapping Q Within the Social, Scribal, Textual, and Theological Landscape(s) of Second Temple Judaism," *HTR* 111, no. 1 (2018):90–114.

[3] James H. Charlesworth, "The Dead Sea Scrolls and the Historical Jesus," in *Jesus and the Dead Sea Scrolls*, ed. J. H. Charlesworth (New York: Doubleday, 1992), 22: "One of our unexpected discoveries is that Jesus was apparently influenced by the Essenes' concept of 'the Holy Spirit.'" See also F. F. Bruce, "Holy Spirit in the Qumran Texts," *The Annual of Leeds University Oriental Society* 6 (1969): 49–55.

[4] Magen Broshi, "What Jesus Learned from the Essenes: The Blessing of Poverty, the Bane of Divorce," *BAR* 30, no. 1 (2004): 32–37, 64 (64).

sect of the Nazoreans" that Paul is accused of belonging to (Acts 24:5; 22:4; 9:2; 19:9; 24:14, 22).[5] Similarly, the *Yaḥad* is described as "those who have chosen the Way" (1QS 9.17–18), while those who leave the community are "they who turn aside from the Way" (CD 1.13). The *Rule of the Community* contains "the regulations of the Way for the master" (1QS 9.21). The *Yaḥad* was "the perfect Way" and taught the "perfection of Way" (1QS 8.18, 21; 9.5, 6, 8, 9). Both groups also seem to have developed Isaiah 40:3, with its explicit reference to "the Way of the Lord," in their self-representations.

Many scholars have noted that the strongest parallels between the *Yaḥad* and the early Jesus movement seem to be located in the organizational frameworks of the two groups. These "parallels" may be relatively late Essene influences and could be explained by Essenes joining the Jesus movement,[6] but the mere accumulation of textual parallels between the early Jesus movement and the Essenes does not amount to an *equation* of the two movements. On the contrary, Jesus' ministry, death, and resurrection represent specific historical "events" that fundamentally shaped the Jesus movement's social identity. The Jesus movement may have identified itself as the true Israel living at the end of days, with an organizational framework similar to the *Yaḥad* in containing an assembly of "the Many" (Acts 4:32; 6:2; 6:5; 1QS 6.1; 7.16; 8.19) as well as a select group of twelve men who composed an inner council of the community, with both groups of twelve probably representing the eschatological twelve tribes of Israel (1QS 8.1; Acts 6:2; 1:15; 2:14), but the correspondence is neither exact nor functionally identical. Both groups may have had "overseers" (Acts 1:17-25; 20:28; Phil 1:1; 1QS 6.11; 6.14; CD 13:7–9) who acted as "shepherds," and may have cast "the lot" to decide the ranking of members within the community (Acts 1:17; 1:25; 2:24; 1QS 1.10; 6.16; 6.22; 2.23; 9.7; CD 13.22; 20.4), but the communities themselves are very different. The Jerusalem community and the *Yaḥad* may have shared communal meals with eschatological significance (Acts 2:46; 1QS 6.4–5; 1QSa 2.11–22),[7]

---

[5] Joseph A. Fitzmyer, *The Semitic Background of the New Testament* (Grand Rapids: Eerdmans, 1997), 282–83: "the same absolute use of 'the Way' occurs in the Qumran writings to designate the mode of life of the Essenes ... the close similarity of usage suggests in this case Essene influence." Cf. S. V. McCasland, "The Way," *JBL* 77 (1958): 222–30.

[6] Fitzmyer, *Semitic Background of the New Testament*, 296: "There were undoubtedly some Essenes among the priests converted to Christianity (Acts 6:7) ... they were most likely the bridge of contact between the two communities." Cf. Otto Betz and Rainer Riesner, *Jesus, Qumran and the Vatican: Clarifications*, trans. J. Bowden (London: SCM Press, 1994), 155: "A whole group of Essenes were converted.... These converted Essenes formed a body of theologians who were highly qualified for their time."

[7] Matthew Black, *The Scrolls and Christian Origins: Studies in the Jewish Background of the New Testament* (New York: Charles Scribner's Sons, 1961), 102–15; K. G. Kuhn, "The Lord's Supper and the Communal Meal at Qumran," in *The Scrolls and the New Testament*, ed. K.

but the central meal of the Pauline community was the Eucharist commemorating Jesus' last supper and atoning death, whereas the *Yahad* envisioned a "messianic banquet" to be overseen by the Messiah of Israel in triumphant celebration of the "new covenant."

According to the book of Acts, the early Jerusalem community shared "all things in common" (Acts 2:42, 46; 4:32-35; 6:1), a communality of goods paralleled within the *Yahad* (1QS 1.11–13; 6.19; CD 13.11), but the historicity of Acts' portrait of "the early church" is notoriously difficult to assess. The Jerusalem community and the *Yahad* may have conceived of themselves as eschatological Temples,[8] with James, Peter, and John the "pillars" (Gal 2:9), Peter the "rock" (Matt 16:18), the apostles the "foundation" (Eph 2:20), Christ's followers "a living sacrifice, holy and acceptable" (Rom 12:1), and Jesus being the "cornerstone" (1 Pet 2:4; Eph 2:20), but the historical trajectories of these two alternative Temple movements ultimately travelled in two very different directions.

The categorical complexities involved in identifying the differences between early Christianity and Essene Judaism, especially during their most creatively generative periods, do not allow simplistic questions and answers. We simply do not know the full extent of Jesus' formative influences, family alliances, and social networks. It is virtually certain that Jesus, John, and their first followers were aware of the Essenes and developed in relationship to the older order,[9] but we have no compelling evidence of Essene support or opposition to Jesus in the last forty years of the movement's historical existence (30–70 CE), the very period that is *least* well represented in the literary output of the Qumran corpus. It is certainly possible that *some* Essenes were convinced that these new movements were fulfillments of their own eschatological convictions. It is perhaps more likely that many, if not most, Essenes *disagreed*, leading to a disintegrative split within the *Yahad*. This could explain, in part, the disappearance of the Essenes. Some

---

Stendahl (New York: Harper, 1957), 65–93; J. van der Ploeg, "The Meals of the Essenes," *JSS* 2 (1957): 163–75; E. F. Sutcliffe, "Sacred Meals at Qumran?" *Heythrop Journal* 1 (1960): 48–65.

[8] Richard Bauckham, "For What Offence Was Jesus Put to Death?" in *James the Just and Christian Origins*, ed. B. Chilton and C. A. Evans (Leiden: Brill, 1999), 207: "Like the Qumran community, which also understood itself as a Temple, the first Christians could describe themselves and their leaders as various parts of the structure of the Temple building." Cf. Geza Vermes, *The Dead Sea Scrolls: Qumran in Perspective* (Philadelphia: Fortress, 1977), 218: "The parallelism between Paul's theology and that of Qumran is too pronounced to be no more than a coincidence. It is very probable that he was acquainted with Qumran Temple symbolism and adapted it in shaping his own teaching on spiritual worship."

[9] Gabriele Boccaccini ("Forgiveness of Sins: An Enochic Problem, a Synoptic Solution," in *Enoch and the Synoptic Gospels: Reminiscences, Allusions, Intertextuality*, ed. L. T. Stuckenbruck and G. Boccaccini, EJL 44 [Atlanta: Society of Biblical Literature, 2016], 153) notes "a special connection between the Jesus and the Enoch movements," the latter being "the *kind* of Judaism from which the early followers of Jesus developed" (154–55 [emphasis added]).

Essene traditions could also have been integrated into and absorbed by "Jewish Christian" circles, where Jesus would be "remembered" as the "True Prophet" like Moses.¹⁰

Today the relationship between ancient "Judaism" and "Christianity" tends to be envisioned as two distinct religions "parting ways" at a number of different point(s) in time. A full assessment of the factors leading to the split(s) between Jewish and Christian followers of Jesus, which is variously conceived as involving Jesus' identification with/as God, his contested Davidic identity, and/or his messianic legitimacy, also needs to include (1) a sudden influx of Gentiles; (2) an increasing marginalization of Jewish followers of Jesus; (3) an increasing demonization of "the Jews" as opponents of Jesus; (4) the Gentile Christian abandonment of Torah *praxis*; (5) the redefinition(s) of Torah (as fulfilled in Christ), "the Messiah" (as dying "for our sins"), and Scripture (as predicting Christ); (6) the violent deaths of Peter and James; and (7) the disintegration and disappearance of the early Jerusalem community.

By the middle of the second century CE, the Jesus movement—and the Judean people—had experienced a series of violent revolts and internal conflicts that further disintegrated the sectarian world in which Jesus was raised. The historical events of the early first century were retrospectively reconfigured to serve the needs of different communities for whom "Jesus" was much more than a Jew within Judaism; he was now the Savior of the world, the Son of God, the Lord. The Essenes suffered a different fate, disappearing—first from the Judean landscape, then from the historical record. Josephus suggests that they were tortured and killed during the Revolt and writes about them in the present tense in his *Antiquities* (c. 93 CE), but he seems to be using the "literary present" and/or sources that referred to them in the present. We do not know much about sectarian literary activity during the last phase of the Qumran site's occupation (30–70 CE),¹¹ although there seems to have been a notable "decline in literary output" during this late period.¹² The archaeological evidence suggests a Roman destruction of the Qumran settlement around 68 CE, but it is not entirely clear

---

¹⁰ James M. Robinson (*The Sayings Gospel Q: Collected Essays*, ed. C. Heil and J. Verheyden, BETL 189 [Leuven: Leuven University Press, 2005], 184) proposes that the Palestinian Jewish "Q movement" subsequently "faded from history as the heresy of the Ebionites."

¹¹ Daniel Stökl Ben Ezra ("Old Caves and Young Caves: A Statistical Reevaluation of a Qumran Consensus," *DSD* 14 [2007]: 318) proposes that ninety-seven of the texts from Cave 4 have been dated to the first century CE. Cf. John J. Collins, *Beyond the Qumran Community: The Sectarian Movement of the Dead Sea Scrolls* (Grand Rapids: Eerdmans, 2010), 91: "Paleographic dating is at best relative. Even its proponents typically allow a margin of plus or minus 25 years."

¹² Collins, *Beyond the Qumran Community*, 210n3.

who was actually living there at the time and/or whether some Qumran sectarians fled to Masada and perished there circa 73 CE.

It is possible that at least some Essenes survived long after the destruction of the Temple, only to be identified by the rabbis as *minim* or "heretics."[13] Josephus does not say that *all* of the Essenes died during the Revolt.[14] That some Essenes coexisted with the early rabbis should indeed be given careful consideration.[15] It is true, after all, that the destruction of the Temple in 70 CE precipitated radical religious and "social reorganization."[16] While the rabbis *never* identify the Essenes by name, there are oblique references to unacceptable deviations from the emerging rabbinical consensus.[17] The absence of evidence on the fate of the Essenes is not evidence that they ceased to exist.[18] Nor does it mean that they continued existing in sectarian isolation. We simply do not know whether Essenes embraced or rejected the emergent Jesus movement nor do we know how they interpreted the destruction of the Temple.[19] Some Essenes may have developed strategic alliances with some of Jesus' followers and viewed the destruction of the Temple as divine confirmation of their sectarian views, not unlike how many early Christians viewed the catastrophe. What we do know is that neither the Essenes nor the Jewish Jesus movement was entirely welcome within the emergent rabbinical conceptualization of a "normative Jewish society."[20] Since the early rabbinic texts do not provide any unambiguous evidence of an ongoing Essene presence

---

[13] Joshua Ezra Burns, "Essene Sectarianism and Social Differentiation in Judaea After 70 C.E.," *HTR* 99, no. 3 (2006): 247–74. On their possible continued existence, see Martin Goodman, "Sadducees and Essenes after 70 CE," in *Crossing the Boundaries: Essays in Biblical Interpretation in Honor of Michael D. Goulder*, ed. S. E. Porter et al., BI 8 (Leiden: Brill, 1994), 347–55, 347–48. On the "Essenes" transforming into a Christian sect of "Iesseans" (*Pan.* 29.1.3–4, 29.4.9–5.7), see Simon C. Mimouni, "Qui sont les Jesséens dans la notice 29 du Panarion d'Epiphane de Salamine?" *NovT* 43 (2001): 264–99.

[14] Burns, "Essene Sectarianism," 250: "The idea that a group so large and so geographically diffuse could have been restricted to the modest confines of Qumran is patently absurd."

[15] Burns, "Essene Sectarianism," 251: "The continued occurrence of Essene sectarianism can be detected in the legal rhetoric of the ancient rabbis ... nothing happened to them at all ... the sect simply became irrelevant."

[16] Burns, "Essene Sectarianism," 251.

[17] Burns, "Essene Sectarianism," 260, admits that the late date of the Mishnah and the Tosefta preclude "any attempt to establish direct and absolute continuity between the Essenes and the *minim* in question."

[18] Burns, "Essene Sectarianism," 268.

[19] Cf. Burns, "Essene Sectarianism," 269: "The destruction of the Temple was simply not as acute to the constitutional integrity of Essenism."

[20] Burns, "Essene Sectarianism," 272: The rabbis "would have had every reason to exclude the belligerent Essenes from their plans for a normative Jewish society."

in post-70 CE Judaism,[21] we would do well not to reinscribe either rabbinical Jewish or orthodox Christian heresiological discourses of the "inevitability" of the disappearance of Essenism within "normative" Judaism.[22] It seems clear that sectarian Judaism(s) survived well into the fourth century CE even as the rabbis and the fathers began closing ranks on their memberships within Judaism and Christianity. The construction of "Judaism" and "Christianity"—and the simultaneous exclusion of "Jewish Christians"—ensured that those struggling to maintain allegiance to Jesus within a Jewish context were ultimately erased from history. Fortunately, the discovery of the Dead Sea Scrolls—and the rediscovery of the Essenes—sheds new light on this lost context within which the historical Jesus, the Jesus movement, and early Christianity arose.

The Essene movement, to all appearances, seems to have virtually disappeared after 70 CE. Like the Sadducees and the Jerusalem community, the Essenes did not survive the Revolt, although their library did, albeit in fragmentary form, in the dry desert caves of the Judean wilderness. Nonetheless, the influence of the Essenes can still be detected—albeit again in fragmentary form—in the pages of the New Testament, a lost people who survive now only in the imaginations of their modern interpreters, a missing link in the study of early Christian origins.

---

[21] Burns, "Essene Sectarianism," 273: "The early rabbinic texts ... are not unequivocal evidence that the rabbis of post-70 C.E. Judaea knew the Essenes as contemporaries."

[22] Jonathan Klawans, *Josephus and the Theologies of Ancient Judaism* (New York: Oxford University Press, 2013), 219: "we have no idea when the Essenes disappeared, let alone why." Cf. Geza Vermes, *The omplete Dead Sea Scrolls* (New York: Penguin, 1997), 25: "Essenism is dead. The brittle structure of its stiff and exclusive brotherhood was unable to withstand the national catastrophe." Klawans colorfully criticizes this as "blatant religious supersessionism, laced with a lethal dose of social Darwinism" (202).

BIBLIOGRAPHY

Abegg, M. G. "Messianic Hope and 4Q285: A Reassessment." *JBL* 113 (1994): 81–91.
Albani, M. "Horoscopes in the Qumran Scrolls." Pages 2:279–330 in *The Dead Sea Scrolls after Fifty Years: A Comprehensive Assessment*. Edited by P. W. Flint and J. C. VanderKam. 2 vols. Leiden: Brill, 1999.
Albright, William F., and C. S. Mann. "Qumran and the Essenes: Geography, Chronology, and Identification of the Sect." Pages 11–25 in *The Scrolls and Christianity: Historical and Theological Significance*. Edited by M. Black. London: SPCK, 1969.
Alexander, P. S. "Physiognomy, Initiation and Rank in the Qumran Community." Pages 385–94 in *Geschichte—Tradition—Reflexion 1, Festschrift Martin Hengel*. Edited by P. Schaeffer et al. Tübingen: Mohr Siebeck, 1996.
Alexis-Baker, Andy. "Violence, Nonviolence and the Temple Incident in John 2:13-15." *BibInt* 20 (2012): 73–96.
Allegro, John M. "Further Messianic References in Qumran Literature." *JBL* 75 (1956): 176–77.
Allison, Dale C. "Apocalyptic, Polemic, Apologetics." Pages 111–48 in Allison, *Resurrecting Jesus: The Earliest Christian Tradition and Its Interpreters*. New York: T&T Clark, 2005.
———. *Constructing Jesus: Memory, Imagination, and History*. Grand Rapids: Baker Academic, 2010.
———. "Elijah Must Come First." *JBL* 103 (1984): 256–58.
———. *The Intertextual Jesus: Scripture in Q*. Harrisburg, Pa.: Trinity International, 2000.
———. "Jesus and the Victory of Apocalyptic." Pages 126–41 in *Jesus and the Restoration of Israel: A Critical Assessment of N. T. Wright's "Jesus and the Victory of God."* Edited by C. C. Newman. Carlisle, UK: Paternoster, 1999.

———. *Jesus of Nazareth: Millenarian Prophet.* Minneapolis: Fortress, 1998.
———. "Q's New Exodus and the Historical Jesus." Pages 395–428 in *The Sayings Source Q and the Historical Jesus.* Edited by A. Lindemann. BETL 158. Leuven: Peeters, 2001.
———. *Resurrecting Jesus: The Earliest Christian Tradition and Its Interpreters.* New York: T&T Clark, 2005.
Anderson, B. W., ed. *Creation in the Old Testament.* Philadelphia: Fortress, 1984.
Argall, Randall A. "A Hellenistic Jewish Source on the Essenes." Pages 13–24 in *For a Later Generation: The Transformation of Tradition in Israel, Early Judaism, and Early Christianity.* Edited by R. A. Argall, B. A. Bow, and R. A. Werline. Harrisburg, Pa.: Trinity International, 2000.
Arnal, William E. "The Trouble with Q." *Forum: Foundations and Facets* 3 (2013): 7–79.
Atkinson, Kenneth and Jodi Magness. "Josephus's Essenes and the Qumran Community." *JBL* 129, no. 2 (2010): 317–42.
Attridge, Harold W. "The Gospel of John and the Dead Sea Scrolls." Pages 109–26 in *Text, Thought, and Practice in Qumran and Early Christianity: Proceedings of the Ninth International Symposium of the Orion Center for the Study of the Dead Sea Scrolls and Associated Literature, Jointly Sponsored by the Hebrew University Center for the Study of Christianity, 11–12 January, 2004.* Edited by R. A. Clements and D. R. Schwartz. STDJ 84. Leiden: Brill, 2009.
Avalos, Hector. *The Bad Jesus: The Ethics of New Testament Ethics.* Sheffield: Sheffield Phoenix, 2015.
Bach, Eugen. *Die Feindesliebe nach dem natürlichen Sittengesetz: Eine historisch-ethische Untersuchung.* Kempten: J. Kösel, 1914.
Back, Sven-Olav. "Jesus and the Sabbath." Pages 3:2597–2633 in *Handbook for the Study of the Historical Jesus.* Edited by T. Holmén and S. R. Porter. 4 vols. Leiden: Brill, 2011.
Badia, Leonard F. *The Qumran Baptism and John the Baptist's Baptism.* Lanham, Md.: University Press of America, 1980.
Bahrdt, Karl Friedrich. *Ausführung des Plans und Zwecks Jesu. In Briefen an Wahrheit suchende Leser.* 11 vols. Berlin: August Mylius, 1784–1792.
Baillet, Maurice. *Qumrân Grotte 4.III (4Q482–4Q520).* DJD 7. Oxford: Clarendon, 1982.
Baldensperger, Wilhelm. *Das Selbstbewusstein Jesu im Lichte der messianischen Hoffnungen seiner Zeit.* Strassburg: Heitz & Mündel, 1888.
Bammel, Ernst. "The Baptist in Early Christian Tradition." *NTS* 18 (1972): 95–128.
Bampfylde, Gillian. "The Similitudes of Enoch: Historical Allusions." *JSJ* 15 (1984): 9–31.
Banks, Robert. *Jesus and the Law in the Synoptic Tradition.* Cambridge: Cambridge University Press, 1975.
Bardtke, Hans. "Die Kriegsrolle v. Qumran übersetzt." *TLZ* 80 (1955): 401–20.
Bar-Nathan, Rachel. "Qumran and the Hasmonean and Herodian Winter Palaces of Jericho: The Implication of the Pottery Finds on the Interpretation of the

Settlement at Qumran." Pages 263–77 in *Qumran: The Site of the Dead Sea Scrolls: Archaeological Interpretations and Debates: Proceedings of a Conference Held at Brown University, November 17–19, 2002*. Edited by K. Galor, J.-B. Humbert, and J. K. Zangenberg. Leiden: Brill, 2006.

Barrett, Charles K. *The Holy Spirit and the Gospel Tradition*. London: SPCK, 1947.

Basser, Herbert W. "The Gospels and Rabbinic Literature." Pages 77–99 in *The Missing Jesus: Rabbinic Judaism and the New Testament*. Edited by B. Chilton, C. A. Evans, and J. Neusner. Boston: Brill, 2002.

Bauckham, Richard. "The Early Jerusalem Church, Qumran and the Essenes." Pages 63–89 in *The Dead Sea Scrolls as Background to Postbiblical Judaism and Early Christianity: Papers from an International Conference at St. Andrews in 2001*. Edited by J. R. Davila. STDJ 46. Leiden: Brill, 2003.

———. "For What Offence Was Jesus Put to Death?" Pages 199–232 in *James the Just and Christian Origins*. Edited by B. Chilton and C. A. Evans. Leiden: Brill, 1999.

———. *God Crucified: Monotheism and Christology in the New Testament*. Carlisle, UK: Paternoster, 1998.

———. *Jesus and the God of Israel: God Crucified and Other Studies on the New Testament's Christology of Divine Identity*. Grand Rapids: Eerdmans, 2008.

———. "Qumran and the Fourth Gospel: Is There a Connection?" Pages 267–79 in *The Scrolls and the Scriptures: Qumran Fifty Years After*. Edited by S. E. Porter and C. A. Evans. JSPSup 26. Sheffield: Sheffield University Press, 1997.

———. "The Son of Man: 'A Man in My Position' or 'Someone'?" *JSNT* 23 (1985): 23–33.

Baumgarten, Albert I. "He Knew that He Knew that He Knew that He Was an Essene." *JJS* 48 (1997): 53–61.

———. "Josephus on Essene Sacrifice." *JJS* 45 (1994): 169–83.

———. "He Knew that He Knew that He Knew that He Was an Essene." *JJS* 48 (1997): 53–61.

———. "Seekers after Smooth Things." Pages 2:857–58 in *The Encyclopedia of the Dead Sea Scrolls*. Edited by L. H. Schiffman and J. C. VanderKam. New York: Oxford University Press, 2000.

Baumgarten, Joseph M. "The Essenes and the Temple: A Reappraisal." Pages 59–62 in *Studies in Qumran Law*. Leiden: Brill, 1977.

———. "The Heavenly Tribunal and the Personification of *Sedeq* in Jewish Apocalyptic." Pages 233–36 in *ANRW* 2.19. Berlin: de Gruyter, 1979.

———. "The Purification Liturgies." Pages 202–12 in *The Dead Sea Scrolls after Fifty Years: A Comprehensive Assessment*. Edited by P. W. Flint and J. C. VanderKam. Leiden: Brill, 1999.

———. *Qumran Cave 4.XIII: The Damascus Document (4Q266–273)*. DJD 18. Oxford: Clarendon, 1996.

———. "The Qumran-Essene Restraints on Marriage." Pages 13–24 in *Archaeology and History in the Dead Sea Scrolls: The New York University Conference in Memory of Yigael Yadin*. Edited by L. H. Schiffman. Sheffield: Sheffield Academic, 1990.

———. "Sacrifice and Worship among the Jewish Sectarians of the Dead (Qumrân) Scrolls." *HTR* 46, no. 3 (1953): 141–59.

———. "The Unwritten Law in the Pre-rabbinic Period." Pages 13–35 in *Studies in Qumran Law*. SJLA 24. Leiden: Brill, 1977 [1972].

Baumgarten, Joseph M., et al., eds. *Qumran Cave 4.XXV: Halakhic Texts*. DJD 35. Oxford: Clarendon, 1999.

Bazzana, Giovanni. *Kingdom of Bureaucracy: The Political Theology of Village Scribes in the Sayings Gospel Q*. BETL 274. Leuven: Peeters, 2015.

Beall, Todd S. *Josephus' Description of the Essenes Illustrated by the Dead Sea Scrolls*. Cambridge: Cambridge University Press, 1988.

Becker, Jürgen. "Feindesliebe-Nächstenliebe-Bruderliebe: Exegetische Beobachtungen als Anfrage an ein ethisches Problemfeld." *ZEE* 25 (1981): 5–18.

———. *Jesus von Nazaret*. Berlin: de Gruyter, 1996.

———. *Johannes der Täufer und Jesus von Nazareth*. Neukirchen-Vluyn: Neukirchener, 1972.

Becker, Michael. "4Q521 und die Gesalbten." *RevQ* 18 (1997): 73–96.

———. "Die 'messianische Apokalypse' 4Q521 und der Interpretationsrahmen der Taten Jesu." Pages 237–303 in *Apokalyptik und Qumran*. Edited by J. Frey and M. Becker. Paderborn: Bonifatius, 2007.

Benoit, Pierre. "Qumran and the New Testament." Pages 1–30 in *Paul and Qumran: Studies in New Testament Exegesis*. Edited by J. Murphy-O'Connor. Chicago: Priory, 1968.

Berger, Klaus. *Die Gesetzesauslegung Jesu: Ihr historischer Hintergrund im Judentum und im Alten Testament*. Neukirchen-Vluyn: Neukirchener, 1972.

Bergmeier, Roland. "Beobachtungen zu 4Q521 f2, II, 1–13." *ZDMG* 145 (1995): 44–45.

———. "Die drei jüdischen Schulrichtungen nach Josephus und Hippolyt von Rom: Zu den Paralleltexten Josephus, B.J.2, 119–6 und Hippolyt, Haer. IX 18, 2–29,4." *JSJ* 34, no. 4 (2003): 443–70.

———. *Die Essener-Berichte des Flavius Josephus: Quellenstudien zu den Essenertexten im Werk des Jüdischen Historiographen*. Kampen: Kok Pharos, 1993.

———. "Zum historischen Wert der Essenerberichte von Philo und Josephus." Pages 11–22 in *Qumran kontrovers: Beiträge zu den Textfunden vom Toten Meer*. Edited by J. Frey and H. Stegemann. Bonifatius: Paderborn, 2003.

Bergsma, John Sietze. *The Jubilee from Leviticus to Qumran: A History of Interpretation*. VTSup 115. Leiden: Brill, 2007.

Bermejo Rubio, Fernando. "Jesus and the Anti-Roman Resistance: A Reassessment of the Arguments." *JSHJ* 12, no. 1/2 (2014): 1–105.

Besant, Annie. *Esoteric Christianity: Or the Lesser Mysteries*. 5th ed. Adyar, Madras: Theosophical Publishing House, 1950 [1901].

Beskow, Per. *Strange Tales about Jesus: A Survey of Unfamiliar Gospels*. Philadelphia: Fortress, 1983.

Betz, Hans Dieter. *Galatians: A Commentary on Paul's Letters to the Churches in Galatia*. Hermeneia. Philadelphia: Fortress, 1979.

Betz, Otto. "Das Jerusalem Essenviertel und die Urgemeinde: Josephus, Bellum Judaicum V 145; 11QMiqdash 46, 13–16; Apostelgeschichte 1–6 und die Archäologie." Pages 1775–1922 in *ANRW* 2.26.2. Edited by Wolfgang Haase. New York: de Gruyter, 1995.

———. "Essener und Therapeuten." *TRE* 10 (1982): 386–91.

———. "Was John the Baptist an Essene?" *BR* 18 (1990): 18–25.

Betz, Otto, and Rainer Riesner. *Jesus, Qumran and the Vatican: Clarifications.* Translated by J. Bowden. London: SCM Press, 1994.

———. *Jesus, Qumran und der Vatikan: Klarstellungen.* Giessen: Brunnen, 1993.

Bieringer, R., and D. Pollefeyt, eds. *Paul and Judaism: Crosscurrents in Pauline Exegesis and the Study of Jewish-Christian Relations.* London: T&T Clark, 2012.

Bilde, Per. "The Essenes in Philo and Josephus." Pages 32–68 in *Qumran between the Old and New Testaments.* Edited by F. H. Cryer and T. L. Thompson. JSOTSup 290. Sheffield: Sheffield Academic, 1998.

———. *The Originality of Jesus: A Critical Discussion and a Comparative Attempt.* SANT 1. Göttingen: Vandenhoeck & Ruprecht, 2013.

Bird, Michael F. *Are You the One Who Is to Come? The Historical Jesus and the Messianic Question.* Grand Rapids: Baker Academic, 2009.

Bird, Michael F., Craig A. Evans, Simon J. Gathercole, Charles E. Hill, and Chris Tilling. *How God Became Jesus: The Real Origins of Belief in Jesus' Divine Nature.* Grand Rapids: Zondervan, 2014.

Black, Matthew. "The Aramaic Spoken by Christ and Luke 14,5." *JTS* 1 (1950): 60–62.

———. *The Book of Enoch, or, 1 Enoch: A New English Edition with Commentary and Textual Notes.* SVTP 7. Leiden: Brill, 1985.

———. "The Dead Sea Scrolls and Christian Origins." Pages 97–106 in *The Scrolls and Christianity: Historical and Theological Significance.* Edited by M. Black. London: SPCK, 1969.

———. *The Scrolls and Christian Origins: Studies in the Jewish Background of the New Testament.* New York: Charles Scribner's Sons, 1961.

———. "The Tradition of the Hasideaean-Essene Asceticism: Its Origin and Influence." Pages 19–32 in *Aspects du Judéo-Christianisme: Colloque de Strasbourg 23–25 avril 1964.* Paris: Presses Universitaires de France, 1965.

Blavatsky, Helena P. *Isis Unveiled: A Mastery-Key to the Mysteries of Ancient and Modern Science and Theology.* 2 vols. Pasadena: Theosophical University Press, 1976 [1877].

———. *The Secret Doctrine: The Synthesis of Science, Religion, and Philosophy.* Pasadena: Theosophical University Press, 1963 [1888].

Blenkinsopp, Joseph. *Isaiah 56–66.* AB 19B. Garden City, N.Y.: Doubleday, 2003.

Bloom, Harold. *The Anxiety of Influence.* New York: Oxford University Press, 1973.

Blosser, Donald W. "Jesus and the Jubilee (Luke 4:16-30): The Year of Jubilee and Its Significance in the Gospel of Luke." Ph.D. diss., St. Andrew's University, 1979.

Boccaccini, Gabriele. *Beyond the Essene Hypothesis: The Parting of the Ways between Qumran and Enochic Judaism.* Grand Rapids: Eerdmans, 1998.

―――, ed. *Enoch and the Messiah Son of Man: Revisiting the Book of Parables.* Grand Rapids: Eerdmans, 2007.

―――. "Enochians, Urban Essenes, Qumranites: Three Social Groups, One Intellectual Movement." Pages 301–26 in *The Early Enoch Literature.* Edited by G. Boccaccini and J. J. Collins. JSJSup 121. Leiden: Brill, 2007.

―――. "Forgiveness of Sins: An Enochic Problem, a Synoptic Solution." Pages 153–67 in *Enoch and the Synoptic Gospels: Reminiscences, Allusions, Intertextuality.* Edited by L. T. Stuckenbruck and G. Boccaccini. EJL 44. Atlanta: Society of Biblical Literature, 2016.

Bockmuehl, Markus. *Jewish Law in Gentile Churches: Halakhah and the Beginning of Christian Public Ethics.* Grand Rapids: Baker, 2000.

―――. "A 'Slain Messiah' in 4Q Serek Milhamah (4Q285)?" *TynBul* 43 (1992): 155–69.

Boda, Mark J., Daniel K. Falk, and Rodney A. Werline, eds. *Seeking the Favor of God.* Vol. 1, *The Origins of Penitential Prayer in Second Temple Judaism.* EJL. Atlanta: Society of Biblical Literature, 2006.

Bond, Helen K. "Dating the Death of Jesus: Memory and the Religious Imagination." *NTS* 59, no. 4 (2013): 461–75.

Borg, Marcus J. *Conflict, Holiness, and Politics in the Teachings of Jesus.* SBEC 5. New York: Edwin Mellen, 1984.

―――. *Jesus in Contemporary Scholarship.* Valley Forge, Pa.: Trinity International, 1994.

Boring, M. Eugene. *The Gospel of Matthew.* Vol. 8. NIB. Nashville: Abingdon, 1995.

Bovon, François. *Das Evangelium nach Lukas Lk 9,51–14,35.* 2 vols. EKKNT 3/2. Zürich: Benziger, 1996.

Boyarin, Daniel. *Border Lines: The Partition of Judaeo-Christianity.* Divinations. Philadelphia: University of Pennsylvania Press, 2004.

―――. *Dying for God: Martyrdom and the Making of Christianity and Judaism.* Palo Alto: Stanford University Press, 1999.

―――. "How Enoch Can Teach Us about Jesus." *EC* 2 (2011): 51–76.

―――. *The Jewish Gospels: The Story of the Jewish Christ.* New York: New Press, 2012.

Brandt, W. *Die jüdischen Baptismen oder das Religiose Waschen und Baden im Judentum mit Einschluss des Judenchristentums.* Giessen: Topelmann, 1910.

Braun, Herbert. *Qumran und das Neue Testament* I–II. Tübingen: Mohr, 1966.

―――. "The Significance of Qumran for the Problem of the Historical Jesus." Pages 69–78 in *The Historical Jesus and the Kerygmatic Christ: Essays on the New Quest of the Historical Jesus.* Edited by C. E. Braaten and R. A. Harrisville. Nashville: Abingdon, 1964.

Braun, Willi. "Were New Testament Herodians Essenes? A Critique of an Hypothesis." *RQ* 14 (1989): 75–88.

Bredin, Mark R. "John's Account of Jesus' Demonstration in the Temple: Violent or Nonviolent?" *BTB* 33 (2003): 44–50.

Breengaard, C. *Paradis-sekten: Frelseshistorie og kristen identitet.* Copenhagen: Museum Tusculanum Press, 2007.

Brin, G. "Divorce at Qumran." Pages 231–49 in *Legal Texts and Legal Issues: Proceedings of the Second Meeting of the International Organization for Qumran Studies Cambridge 1995.* Edited by M. Bernstein et al. Leiden: Brill, 1997.

Brodie, Thomas L. *The Birthing of the New Testament: The Intertextual Development of the New Testament Writings.* Sheffield: Sheffield University Press, 2004.

Brooke, George J. "4QTestament of Levi and the Messianic Servant High Priest." Pages 83–96 in *From Jesus to John: Essays on Jesus and New Testament Christology in Honour of Marinus de Jonge.* Edited by M. C. DeBoer. JSNTSup 84. Sheffield: JSOT, 1993.

———. "Aspects of the Theological Significance of Prayer and Worship in the Qumran Scrolls." Pages 35–54 in *Prayer and Poetry in the Dead Sea Scrolls and Related Literature: Essays in Honor of Eileen Schuller on the Occasion of Her 65th Birthday.* Edited by J. Penner, K. M. Penner, and C. Wassen. Leiden: Brill, 2012.

———. *The Dead Sea Scrolls and the New Testament.* Minneapolis: Fortress, 2005.

———. *Exegesis at Qumran: 4QFlorilegium in its Jewish Context.* JSOTSup 29. Sheffield: JSOT, 1985.

———. "Jesus, the Dead Sea Scrolls, and Scrolls Scholarship." Pages 19–26 in *The Dead Sea Scrolls and the New Testament.* Minneapolis: Fortress, 2005.

———. "Kingship and Messianism in the Dead Sea Scrolls." Pages 447–54 in *King and Messiah in Israel and the Ancient Near East: Proceedings of the Oxford Old Testament Seminar.* Edited by J. Day. Sheffield: Sheffield Academic, 1998.

———. "Miqdash Adam, Eden and the Qumran Community." Pages 285–330 in *Gemeinde ohne Tempel—Community without Temple: Zur Substituierung und Transformation des Jerusalemer Tempels und seines Kultes im Alten Testament, antiken Judentum und fruhen Christentum.* Edited by B. Ego et al. WUNT 118. Tübingen: Mohr Siebeck, 1999.

———. "The Pre-Sectarian Jesus." Pages 33–48 in *Echoes from the Caves: Qumran and the New Testament.* Edited by F. García Martínez. STDJ 85. Leiden: Brill, 2009.

———. "Prophecy and Prophets in the Dead Sea Scrolls: Looking Backwards and Forwards." Pages 151–65 in *Prophets, Prophecy, and Prophetic Texts in Second Temple Judaism.* Edited by M. H. Floyd and R. D. Haak. LHB/OTS 427. New York: T&T Clark, 2006.

———. *Qumran and the Jewish Jesus: Reading the New Testament in the Light of the Scrolls.* Cambridge: Grove Books, 2005.

———. "Qumran: The Cradle of the Christ?" Pages 23–34 in *The Birth of Jesus: Biblical and Theological Reflections.* Edited by G. J. Brooke. Edinburgh: T&T Clark, 2000.

———. "Shared Intertextual Interpretations in the Dead Sea Scrolls and the New Testament." Pages 35–57 in *Biblical Perspectives: Early Use and Interpretation of the Bible in Light of the Dead Sea Scrolls.* Edited by M. E. Stone and E. G. Chazon. STDJ 28. Leiden: Brill, 1998.

Broshi, Magen. "Essenes at Qumran? A Rejoinder to Albert Baumgarten." *DSD* 14 (2007): 25–33.

———. "What Jesus Learned from the Essenes: The Blessing of Poverty, the Bane of Divorce." *BAR* 30, no. 1 (2004): 32–37, 64.

Broshi, Magen, and Hanan Eshel. "How and Where Did the Qumranites Live?" Pages 267–73 in *The Provo International Conference on the Dead Sea Scrolls: Technological Innovations, New Texts, and Reformulated Issues*. Edited by D. W. Parry and E. Ulrich. Leiden: Brill, 1999.

Brown, Raymond E. "The Dead Sea Scrolls and the New Testament." Pages 1–8 in *John and the Dead Sea Scrolls*. Edited by J. H. Charlesworth. New York: Crossroad, 1990.

———. "The Qumran Scrolls and the Johannine Gospels and Epistles." *CBQ* 17 (1955): 403–19, 559–74.

———. "Second Thoughts, the Dead Sea Scrolls and the New Testament." *ExpTim* 10 (1966): 19–23.

Brownlee, William H. "Biblical Interpretation among the Sectaries of the Dead Sea Scrolls." *BA* 14 (1951): 54–76.

———. "Jesus and Qumran." Pages 52–81 in *Jesus and the Historian*. Edited by F. T. Trotter. Philadelphia: Westminster, 1968.

———. "John the Baptist in the New Light of Ancient Scrolls." Pages 33–53 in *The Scrolls and the New Testament*. Edited by K. Stendahl. New York: Harper, 1957.

———. *The Midrash Pesher of Habakkuk*. Missoula, Mont.: Scholars, 1979.

———. "The Servant of the Lord in the Qumran Scrolls." *BASOR* 132 (1950): 546–49.

Bruce, F. F. "Holy Spirit in the Qumran Texts." *The Annual of Leeds University Oriental Society* 6 (1969): 49–55.

———. "Qumran and Early Christianity." *NTS* 2 (1955–1956): 176–90.

———. "Qumran and the New Testament." *Faith and Thought* 90 (1958): 92–102.

———. *Second Thoughts on the Dead Sea Scrolls*. Grand Rapids: Eerdmans, 1956.

Bultmann, Rudolf. *Die Geschichte der synoptischen Tradition*. 4th ed. FRLANT 29. Göttingen: Vandenhoeck & Ruprecht, 1958 [1931].

———. *The History of the Synoptic Tradition*. Oxford: Blackwell, 1968.

Burchard, Christian. "Pline et les Esséniens: À propos d'un article récent." *RB* 69 (1962): 533–69.

Burkett, Delbert. *The Son of Man Debate: A History and Evaluation*. SNTSMS 107. Cambridge: Cambridge University Press, 1999.

Burns, Joshua Ezra. "Essene Sectarianism and Social Differentiation in Judaea After 70 C.E." *HTR* 99, no. 3 (2006): 247–74.

Burrows, Millar. *The Dead Sea Scrolls*. New York: Viking, 1955.

———. *More Light on the Dead Sea Scrolls*. New York: Viking, 1958.

Busse, U. *Die Wunder des Propheten Jesus*. Forschung zur Bibel 24. Stuttgart: Katholiesches Bibelwerk, 1979.

Bussmann, W. *Synoptische Studien*. Halle: Buchhandlung des Waisenhauses, 1929.

Cadbury, Henry J. "A Qumran Parallel to Paul." *HTR* 51 (1958): 1–2.

Caird, George B. *Jesus and the Jewish Nation*. Ethel M. Wood Lecture, March 9, 1965. London: Athlone, 1965.
———. *The Language and Imagery of the Bible*. Philadelphia: Westminster, 1980.
Callaway, Philip R. "Qumran Origins: From the *Doresh* to the *Moreh*." *RevQ* 14, no. 56 (1990): 637–50.
Cameron, R., and M. P. Miller, eds. *Redescribing Christian Origins*. SBLSymS 28. Atlanta: Society of Biblical Literature, 2004.
Campbell, Jonathan. *The Dead Sea Scrolls: The Complete Story*. Berkeley: Ulysses, 1998.
———. "Essene-Qumran Origins in the Exile: A Scriptural Basis?" *JJS* 46 (1995): 143–56.
Cansdale, Lena. *Qumran and the Essenes: A Re-evaluation of the Evidence*. TSAJ 60. Tübingen: Mohr Siebeck, 1997.
Capper, Brian J. "The New Covenant in Southern Palestine at the Arrest of Jesus." Pages 90–116 in *The Dead Sea Scrolls as Background to Postbiblical Judaism and Early Christianity: Papers from an International Conference at St. Andrews in 2001*. Edited by J. R. Davila. STDJ 46. Leiden: Brill, 2003.
Caragounis, Chrys C. *The Son of Man: Vision and Interpretation*. WUNT 38. Tübingen: Mohr Siebeck, 1986.
Cargill, Robert R. "The Qumran Digital Model: An Argument for Archaeological Reconstruction in Virtual Reality." *NEA* 72 (2009): 28–41, 44–47.
———. *Qumran through (Real) Time: A Virtual Reconstruction of Qumran and the Dead Sea Scrolls*. Bible in Technology 1. Piscataway: Gorgias, 2009.
Carmignac, Jean. "La Notion d'Eschatologie dans la Bible et à Qumran." *RevQ* 7 (1969): 17–31.
Carter, Jeffrey. "Comparison in the History of Religions: Reflections and Critiques." *MTSR* 16 (2004): 3–11.
Casey, P. Maurice. *An Aramaic Approach to Q: Sources for the Gospels of Matthew and Luke*. SNTSMS 122. Cambridge: Cambridge University Press, 2002.
———. *The Solution to the "Son of Man" Problem*. London: T&T Clark, 2007.
Castor, George DeWitt. *Matthew's Saying of Jesus: The Non-Marcan Common Source of Matthew and Luke*. Chicago: University of Chicago Press, 1912.
Catchpole, David R. "The Angelic Son of Man in Luke 12:8." *NovT* 24 (1982): 255–65.
———. "The Poor on Earth and the Son of Man in Heaven: A Re-appraisal of Matthew XXV. 31-46." *BJRL* 61 (1979): 355–97.
———. *The Quest for Q*. Edinburgh: T&T Clark, 1993.
———. "The Synoptic Divorce Material as a Traditio-historical Problem." *BJRL* 57 (1975): 92–127.
Chamberlain, J. V. "The Functions of God as Messianic Titles in the Complete Qumran Isaiah Scroll." *VT* 5 (1955): 366–72.
Chapman, David W. Review of Simon J. Joseph, *Jesus and the Temple: The Crucifixion in its Jewish Context*. *JTS* 68, no. 2 (2017). https://doi-org.ezproxy.callutheran.edu/10.1093/jts/flx138 (accessed June 6, 2016).

Charles, R. H. *The Book of Enoch: Translated from Dillmann's Ethiopic Text*. London: SPCK, 1917.

———. "Messianic Doctrine of the Book of Enoch, and Its Influence on the New Testament." *ET* 4 (1892–1893): 301–3.

———. "The Son of Man." *ET* 4 (1892–1893): 504–6.

Charlesworth, James H. "The Dead Sea Scrolls and the Historical Jesus." Pages 1–74 in *Jesus and the Dead Sea Scrolls*. Edited by J. H. Charlesworth. New York: Doubleday, 1992.

———. "From Jewish Messianology to Christian Christology: Some Caveats and Perspectives." Pages 225–64 in *Judaisms and Their Messiahs at the Turn of the Christian Era*. Edited by J. Neusner and W. Scott Green. New York: Cambridge University Press, 1987.

———. "Have the Dead Sea Scrolls Revolutionized Our Understanding of the New Testament?" Pages 116–32 in *The Dead Sea Scrolls Fifty Years after Their Discovery: Proceedings of the Jerusalem Congress, July 20–25, 1997*. Edited by L. H. Schiffman, E. Tov, and J. C. VanderKam. Jerusalem: Israel Exploration Society, 2000.

———. "Jesus and the Temple." Pages 145–82 in *Jesus and Temple: Textual and Archaeological Explorations*. Edited by J. H. Charlesworth. Minneapolis: Fortress, 2014.

———. *John and Qumran*. London: Chapman, 1972.

———. "Messianology in the Biblical Pseudepigrapha." Pages 21–52 in *Qumran Messianism: Studies on the Messianic Expectations in the Dead Sea Scrolls*. Edited by J. H. Charlesworth, H. Lichtenberger, and G. S. Oegema. Tübingen: Mohr Siebeck, 1998.

———. "The Portrayal of the Righteous as an Angel." Pages 131–51 in *Ideal Figures in Ancient Judaism: Profiles and Paradigms*. Edited by J. J. Collins and G. W. E. Nickelsburg. Chico, Calif.: Scholars, 1980.

———. "Qumran, John and the Odes of Solomon." Pages 107–36 in *John and the Dead Sea Scrolls*. Edited by J. H. Charlesworth. New York: Crossroad, 1990.

———. Review of David Stacey and Gregory L. Doudna, *Qumran Revisited: A Reassessment of the Archaeology of the Site and Its Texts*. *Review of Biblical Literature*, June 2015. https://www.bookreviews.org/pdf/9403_10380.pdf (accessed June 6, 2016).

Charlesworth, James H., and Darrell L. Bock, eds. *Parables of Enoch—A Paradigm Shift*. New York: T&T Clark, 2013.

Charlesworth, James H., et al., eds. *The Dead Sea Scrolls: Hebrew, Aramaic, and Greek Texts with English Translations*. Vol. 1, *The Rule of the Community and Related Documents*. Louisville, Ky.: Westminster John Knox, 1994.

Chazon, Esther G. "The Creation and Fall of Adam in the Dead Sea Scrolls." Pages 13–24 in *The Book of Genesis in Jewish and Oriental Christian Interpretation: A Collection of Essays*. Edited by J. Frishman and L. Van Rompay. TEG 5. Leuven: Peeters, 1997.

---. "On the Special Character of the Sabbath Prayer: New Data from Qumran." *JJML* 15 (1993): 1–21.

---. "Prayers from Qumran and Their Historical Implications." *DSD* 1, no. 3 (1994): 265–84.

Chester, Andrew. *Messiah and Exaltation: Jewish Messianic and Visionary Traditions and New Testament Christology*. WUNT 207. Tübingen: Mohr Siebeck, 2007.

Chilton, Bruce D. *The Isaiah Targum: Introduction, Translation, Apparatus, and Notes*. Wilmington: Michael Glazier, 1987.

---. "John the Purifier." Pages 1–37 in *Judaic Approaches to the Gospels*. USFISFCJ 21. Atlanta: Scholars, 1994.

Chilton, Bruce D., and Craig A. Evans. "Jesus and Israel's Scriptures." Pages 283–335 in *Studying the Historical Jesus: Evaluations of the State of Current Research*. Edited by B. Chilton and C. Evans. NTTS 19. Leiden: Brill, 1994.

Cohen, Shaye J. D. *The Beginnings of Jewishness: Boundaries, Varieties, Uncertainties*. HCS 31. Berkeley: University of California Press, 1999.

---. *From the Maccabees to the Mishnah*. Philadelphia: Westminster, 1987.

Collins, Adela Yarbro. "Apocalyptic Son of Man Sayings." Pages 220–28 in *The Future of Early Christianity*. Edited by Birger A. Pearson. Minneapolis: Fortress, 1991.

---. "The Origin of Christian Baptism." *Studia Liturgica* 19 (1989): 28–46.

---. "The Worship of Jesus and the Imperial Cult." Pages 234–57 in *The Jewish Roots of Christological Monotheism: Papers from the St. Andrews Conference on the Historical Origins of the Worship of Jesus*. Edited by C. C. Newman, J. R. Davila, and G. S. Lewis. JSJSup 63. Leiden: Brill, 1999; reprint Waco, Tex.: Baylor University Press, 2017.

Collins, John J. *The Apocalyptic Imagination: An Introduction to Jewish Apocalyptic Literature*. 2nd ed. Grand Rapids: Eerdmans, 1998.

---. *The Apocalyptic Imagination: An Introduction to Jewish Apocalyptic Literature*. 3rd ed. Grand Rapids: Eerdmans, 2016.

---. *The Apocalyptic Vision of the Book of Daniel*. HSM 16. Atlanta: Scholars, 1977.

---. *Apocalypticism in the Dead Sea Scrolls*. New York: Routledge, 1997.

---. *Beyond the Qumran Community: The Sectarian Movement of the Dead Sea Scrolls*. Grand Rapids: Eerdmans, 2010.

---. "Beyond the Qumran Community: Social Organization in the Dead Sea Scrolls." *DSD* 16, no. 3 (2009): 351–69.

---. *The Dead Sea Scrolls: A Biography*. Lives of Great Religious Books. Princeton: Princeton University Press, 2012.

---. "Enoch and the Son of Man: A Response to Sabino Chialà and Helge Kvanvig." Pages 216–27 in *Enoch and the Messiah Son of Man: Revisiting the Book of Parables*. Edited by G. Boccaccini. Grand Rapids: Eerdmans, 2007.

---. "Family Life." Pages 1:287–90 in *Encyclopedia of the Dead Sea Scrolls*. Edited by L. H. Schiffman and J. C. VanderKam. 2 vols. New York: Oxford University Press, 2000.

———. "Forms of Community in the Dead Sea Scrolls." Pages 97–111 in *Emanuel: Studies in Hebrew Bible, Septuagint and Dead Sea Scrolls in Honor of Emanuel Tov.* Edited by S. M. Paul, R. A. Kraft, L. H. Schiffman, and W. W. Fields. VTSup 94. Leiden: Brill, 2003.

———. "The Interpretation of Psalm 2." Pages 49–66 in *Echoes from the Caves: Qumran and the New Testament.* Edited by F. García Martínez. STDJ 85. Leiden: Brill, 2009.

———. "Jesus, Messianism and the Dead Sea Scrolls." Pages 100–120 in *Qumran Messianism: Studies in the Messianic Expectations in the Dead Sea Scrolls.* Edited by J. H. Charlesworth, H. Lichtenberger, and G. S. Oegema. Tübingen: Mohr Siebeck, 1998.

———. "Prayer and the Meaning of Ritual in the Dead Sea Scrolls." Pages 69–86 in *Prayer and Poetry in the Dead Sea Scrolls and Related Literature: Essays in Honor of Eileen Schuller on the Occasion of Her 65th Birthday.* Edited by J. Penner, K. M. Penner, and C. Wassen. STDJ 98. Leiden: Brill, 2011.

———. "Qumran, Apocalypticism, and the New Testament." Pages 133–38 in *The Dead Sea Scrolls Fifty Years after Their Discovery: Proceedings of the Jerusalem Congress, July 20–25, 1997.* Edited by L. H. Schiffman, E. Tov, and J. C. VanderKam. Jerusalem: Israel Exploration Society, 2000.

——— Review of Eyal Regev, *Sectarianism in Qumran. DSD* 16 (2009): 150–54.

———. *The Scepter and the Star: Messianism in Light of the Dead Sea Scrolls.* 2nd ed. Grand Rapids: Eerdmans, 2010.

———. "The Scrolls and Christianity in American Scholarship." Pages 197–215 in *The Dead Sea Scrolls in Scholarly Perspective: A History of Research.* Edited by D. Dimant. STDJ 99. Leiden: Brill, 2012.

———. "The Second Coming." *CS* 34 (1995): 262–74.

———. "The *Son of God* Text." Pages 65–82 in *From Jesus to John: Essays on Jesus and New Testament Christology.* Edited by M. C. De Boer. Sheffield: JSOT, 1993.

———. "The Son of Man in First-Century Judaism." *NTS* 38 (1992): 448–66.

———. "Wisdom, Apocalypticism, and Generic Compatibility." Pages 165–85 in *In Search of Wisdom: Essays in Memory of John G. Gammie.* Edited by L. G. Perdue, B. B. Scott, and W. J. Wiseman. Louisville, Ky.: Westminster John Knox, 1993.

———. "Wisdom Reconsidered, in Light of the Scrolls." *DSD* 4, no. 3 (1997): 265–81.

———. "The Works of the Messiah." *DSD* 1 (1994): 98–112.

———. "The Yahad and 'The Qumran Community.'" Pages 81–96 in *Biblical Traditions in Transmission: Essays in Honour of Michael A. Knibb.* Edited by C. Hempel and J. Lieu. Leiden: Brill, 2006.

Collins, John J., and Peter W. Flint, eds. *The Book of Daniel: Composition and Reception.* 2 vols. Leiden: Brill, 2002.

Collins, John J., and G. W. E. Nickelsburg, eds. *Ideal Figures in Ancient Judaism: Profiles and Paradigms.* SCS 12. Chico, Calif.: Scholars, 1980.

Collins, John J., Gregory E. Sterling, and Ruth A. Clements, eds. *Sapiential Perspectives: Wisdom Literature in Light of the Dead Sea Scrolls: Proceedings of the Sixth*

International Symposium of the Orion Center for the Study of the Dead Sea Scrolls and Associated Literature, 20–22 May, 2001. STDJ 51. Leiden: Brill, 2004.

Coloe, M. L., and T. Thatcher, eds. *John, Qumran, and the Dead Sea Scrolls: Sixty Years of Discovery and Debate*. EJL 32. Atlanta: Society of Biblical Literature, 2011.

Colpe, Carsten. "ὁ υἱὸς τοῦ ἀνθρώπου." *TDNT* 8 (1972): 400–477.

Conybeare, F. C. "Essenes." Pages 1:767–72 in *A Dictionary of the Bible*. Edited by James Hastings. 5 vols. New York: Scribner, 1902–1904.

Conzelmann, Hans. *Die Apostelgeschichte*. HNT. Tübingen: Mohr Siebeck, 1963.

Coppens, Joseph. "Le célibat essénien." Pages 295–304 in *Qumrân: Sa piété, sa théologie et son milieu*. Edited by M. Delcor. BETL 46. Paris: Duculot, 1978.

Crawford, Sidnie White. "Not according to Rule: Women, the Dead Sea Scrolls and Qumran." Pages 127–50 in *Emanuel: Studies in Hebrew Bible, Septuagint, and Dead Sea Scrolls in Honor of Emanuel Tov*. Edited by S. M. Paul, R. A. Kraft, L. H. Schiffman, and W. W. Fields. VTSup 94. Leiden: Brill, 2003.

———. "The Qumran Collection as a Scribal Library." Pages 109–31 in *The Dead Sea Scrolls at Qumran and the Concept of a Library*. Edited by S. W. Crawford and C. Wassen. STDJ 116. Leiden: Brill, 2015.

Creed, J. M. *The Gospel according to St. Luke: The Greek Text with Introduction, Notes and Indices*. London: Macmillan, 1965.

Cross, Frank M. *The Ancient Library of Qumran*. 3rd ed. Minneapolis: Fortress, 1995.

———. *Canaanite Myth and Hebrew Epic*. Cambridge, Mass.: Harvard University Press, 1973.

———. "The Early History of the Qumran Community." Pages 70–89 in *New Directions in Biblical Archaeology*. Edited by D. Freedman and J. Greenfield. Garden City, N.Y.: Doubleday, 1976.

Crossan, John Dominic. *The Birth of Christianity: Discovering What Happened in the Years Immediately after the Execution of Jesus*. San Francisco: HarperSanFrancisco, 1998.

———. *In Fragments: The Aphorisms of Jesus*. San Francisco: Harper & Row, 1983.

Crossley, James G. *Jesus and the Chaos of History: Redirecting the Life of the Historical Jesus*. Biblical Refigurations. New York: Oxford University Press, 2015.

Crown, Alan David, and Lena Cansdale. "Focus on Qumran: Was It an Essene Settlement?" *BAR* 20 (1994): 24–35, 73.

Croy, N. Clayton. "The Messianic Whippersnapper: Did Jesus Use a Whip on People in the Temple (John 2:13)?" *JBL* 128 (2009): 555–68.

The Crucifixion, By an Eye-Witness: A Letter Written Seven Years After the Crucifixion. Supplemental Harmonic Series, vol. 2. Repr. ed. Chicago: Indo-American Book, 1907.

Cullmann, Oscar. *The Christology of the New Testament*. London: SCM Press, 1963.

———. "The Significance of the Qumran Texts for Research into the Beginnings of Christianity." *JBL* 74 (1955): 213–26.

Dahl, Nils Alstrup. "Eschatology and History in the Light of the Dead Sea Scrolls." Pages 3–18 in *The Future of Our Religious Past: Essays in Honour of Rudolf*

Bultmann. Edited by J. M. Robinson. Translated by C. E. Carlston and R. P. Scharlemann. London: SCM Press, 1971.

———. *Jesus the Christ: The Historical Origins of Christological Doctrine.* Edited by D. H. Juel. Minneapolis: Fortress, 1991.

———. "Messianic Ideas and the Crucifixion of Jesus." Pages 382–403 in *The Messiah: Developments in Earliest Judaism and Christianity: The First Princeton Symposium on Judaism and Christian Origins.* Edited by J. H. Charlesworth. Minneapolis: Fortress, 1992.

Daly, Robert. *Christian Sacrifice: The Judaeo-Christian Background before Origen.* Studies in Christian Antiquity 18. Washington, D.C.: Catholic University of America Press, 1978.

Daniel, Constantin. "Nouveaux arguments in faveur de l'identification des Hérodiens et des Esséniens." *RevQ* 7 (1969–1971): 397–402.

Daniélou, Jean. *The Dead Sea Scrolls and Primitive Christianity.* Translated by Salvator Attanasio. New York: New American Library, 1958.

———. *The Work of John the Baptist.* Translated by J. Horn. Baltimore: Helicon, 1966.

Davidson, M. J. *Angels at Qumran: A Comparative Study of 1 Enoch 1–36, 72–108 and Sectarian Writings from Qumran.* Sheffield: Sheffield Academic, 1992.

Davies, A. Powell. *The Meaning of the Dead Sea Scrolls.* New York: Mentor, 1956.

Davies, Philip R. *Behind the Essenes: History and Ideology in the Dead Sea Scrolls.* BJS 84. Atlanta: Scholars, 1987.

———. "The Birthplace of the Essenes: Where Is 'Damascus?'" *RevQ* 14, no. 56 (1990): 503–19.

———. *Damascus Covenant: An Interpretation of the "Damascus Document."* Sheffield: Sheffield Academic, 1983.

———. "Halakhah at Qumran." Pages 37–50 in *A Tribute to Geza Vermes: Essays on Jewish and Christian Literature and History.* Edited by P. R. Davies and R. T. White. JSOTSup 100. Sheffield: JSOT, 1990.

———. "Hasidim in the Maccabean Period." *JJS* 28 (1977): 127–40.

———. "Reflections on DJD XVIII." Pages 151–65 in *The Dead Sea Scrolls at Fifty: Proceedings of the 1997 Society of Biblical Literature Qumran Section Meetings.* Edited by R. A. Kugler and E. M. Schuller. Atlanta: Scholars, 1999.

———. *Sects and Scrolls: Essays on Qumran and Related Topics.* Atlanta: Scholars, 1996.

———. "The Social World of Apocalyptic Writings." Pages 251–71 in *The World of Ancient Israel: Social, Anthropological, and Political Perspectives.* Edited by R. E. Clements. Cambridge: Cambridge University Press, 1989.

Davies, W. D. *Torah in the Messianic Age and/or the Age to Come.* SBLMS 7. Philadelphia: Society of Biblical Literature, 1952.

Davies, W. D., and Dale C. Allison Jr. *A Critical and Exegetical Commentary on the Gospel according to Saint Matthew.* 3 vols. ICC. Edinburgh: T&T Clark, 1988–1997.

Davis, Carl J. *The Name and Way of the Lord: Old Testament Themes, New Testament Christology*. JSNTSup 129. Sheffield: Sheffield Academic, 1996.

Deasley, Alex R. G. *The Shape of Qumran Theology*. Carlisle, UK: Paternoster, 2000.

De Jonge, Marinus. "Jesus' Death for Others and the Death of the Maccabean Martyrs." Pages 142–51 in *Text and Testimony: Essays on the New Testament and Apocryphal Literature in Honour of A. F. J. Klijn*. Edited by T. Baarda. Kampen: Kok, 1988.

———. "The Use of the Word 'Anointed' in the Time of Jesus." *NovT* 8 (1966): 132–48.

De Jonge, M., and A. S. van der Woude. "11QMelchizedek and the New Testament." *NTS* 12 (1965): 301–26.

Del Medico, Henri E. *Le Mythe des Esséniens: Des Origines a la Fin du Moyen Age*. Paris: Librarie Plon, 1958.

De Quincey, Thomas. "The Essenes." Pages 101–72 in *Historical Essays and Researches*. Edited by D. Masson. Vol. 7 of *The Collected Writings of Thomas De Quincey*. London: A&C Black, 1897.

De Vaux, Roland. *Archaeology and the Dead Sea Scrolls*. London: Oxford University Press, 1973.

De Waard, J. *A Comparative Study of the Old Testament Text in the Dead Sea Scrolls and in the New Testament*. STDJ 4. Leiden: Brill, 1965.

De Wit, Willem J. "Expectations and the Expected One: 4Q521 and the Light It Sheds on the New Testament." Doctoral thesis, Utrecht University, 2000.

Dibelius, Martin. *Die urchristliche Überlieferung von Johannes dem Täufer*. FRLANT 15. Göttingen: Vandenhoeck & Ruprecht, 1911.

Dillmann, August. *Das Buch Henoch übersetzt und erklärt*. Leipzig: Vogel, 1853.

Dimant, Devorah. "4QFlorilegium and the Idea of Community as Temple." Pages 165–89 in *Hellenica et Judaica: Hommage à Valentin Nikiprowetzky*. Edited by A. Caquot et al. Leuven: Peeters, 1986.

———. *History, Ideology and Bible Interpretation in the Dead Sea Scrolls: Collected Studies*. FAT 90. Tübingen: Mohr Siebeck, 2014.

———. "The Library of Qumran: Its Contents and Character." Pages 170–76 in *The Dead Sea Scrolls Fifty Years after Their Discovery: Proceedings of the Jerusalem Congress, July 20–25, 1997*. Edited by L. H. Schiffman, E. Tov, and J. C. VanderKam. Jerusalem: Israel Exploration Society, 2000.

———. "On Remembering and Forgetting Research." *Katharsis* 13 (2010): 22–53.

DiTommaso, Lorenzo. "Penitential Prayer and Apocalyptic Eschatology in Second Temple Judaism." Pages 115–33 in *Prayer and Poetry in the Dead Sea Scrolls and Related Literature: Essays in Honor of Eileen Schuller on the Occasion of Her 65th Birthday*. STDJ 98. Edited by J. Penner, K. M. Penner, and C. Wassen. Leiden: Brill, 2011.

Dodd, C. H. *The Founder of Christianity*. London: Macmillan, 1970.

———. "The Theology of Christian Pacifism." Pages 5–15 in *The Bases of Christian Pacifism*. Edited by C. Raven. London: Council of Christian Pacifist Groups, 1938.

Doering, Lutz. "Marriage and Creation in Mark 10 and CD 4–5." Pages 133–63 in *Echoes from the Caves: Qumran and the New Testament*. Edited by F. García Martínez. STDJ 85. Leiden: Brill, 2009.

———. "Parallels without 'Parallelomania': Methodological Reflections on Comparative Analysis of Halakhah in the Dead Sea Scrolls." Pages 87–112 in *Rabbinic Perspectives*. Edited by S. Fraade, A. Shemesh, and R. A. Clements. STDJ 62. Leiden: Brill, 2006.

———. *Schabbat: Sabbathalacha und –praxis im antiken Judentum und Urchristentum*. TSAJ 78. Tübingen: Mohr Siebeck, 1999.

———. "*Urzeit-Endzeit* Correlation in the Dead Sea Scrolls and Pseudepigrapha." Pages 19–58 in *Eschatologie: Eschatology*. Edited by J. Eckstein, C. Landmesser, and H. Lichtenberger. WUNT 272. Tübingen: Mohr Siebeck, 2011.

Donceel, Robert, and Pauline Donceel-Voûte. "The Archaeology of Khirbet Qumran." Pages 1–38 in *Methods of Investigation of the Dead Sea Scrolls and the Khirbet Qumran Site: Present Realities and Future Prospects*. Edited by M. O. Wise, N. Golb, J. J. Collins, and D. G. Pardee. ANYAS 722. New York: New York Academy of Sciences, 1994.

Doudna, Gregory. "The Sect of the Qumran Texts and Its Leading Role in the Temple in Jerusalem during Much of the First Century BCE: Toward a New Framework for Understanding." Pages 75–124 in *Qumran Revisited: A Reassessment of the Archaeology of the Site and Its Texts*. BARIS 2520. Oxford: Archaeopress, 2013.

Douglas, R. Conrad. "'Love Your Enemies': Rhetoric, Tradents, and Ethos." Pages 116–31 in *Conflict and Invention: Literary, Rhetorical and Social Studies on the Sayings Gospel Q*. Edited by J. S. Kloppenborg. Valley Forge, Pa.: Trinity International, 2004.

Dowling, Levi. *The Aquarian Gospel of Jesus the Christ*. Marina del Rey, Calif.: DeVorss, 1972 [1907].

Downing, F. Gerald. *Jesus and the Threat of Freedom*. London: SCM Press, 1987.

Driver, G. R. *The Judaean Scrolls: The Problem and a Solution*. Oxford: Blackwell, 1965.

Duhaime, Jean. "War Scroll." Pages 80–203 in *Damascus Document, War Scroll, and Related Documents*. Edited by J. H. Charlesworth. Vol. 2 of *The Dead Sea Scrolls: Hebrew, Aramaic, and Greek Texts with English Translations*. PTSDSSP 2. Tübingen: Mohr Siebeck, 1995.

Dungan, D. *The Sayings of Jesus in the Churches of Paul: The Use of the Synoptic Tradition in the Regulation of Early Church Life*. Philadelphia: Fortress, 1971.

Dunn, James D. G. *Baptism in the Holy Spirit*. London: SCM Press, 1970.

———. *Christology in the Making*. London: SCM Press, 1980.

———. *Jesus and the Spirit: A Study of the Religious and Charismatic Experience of Jesus and the First Christians as Reflected in the New Testament*. London: SCM Press, 1975.

———. *Jesus Remembered*. Grand Rapids: Eerdmans, 2003.

———. *The New Perspective on Paul*. Rev. ed. Grand Rapids: Eerdmans, 2008.

———. "Remembering Jesus: How the Quest of the Historical Jesus Lost Its Way." Pages 199–225 in *The Historical Jesus: Five Views*. Edited by J. K. Beilby and P. R. Eddy. Downers Grove, Ill.: InterVarsity, 2009.

———. "'Son of God' as 'Son of Man' in the Dead Sea Scrolls? A Response to John Collins on 4Q246." Pages 198–210 in *The Scrolls and the Scriptures: Qumran Fifty Years After*. Edited by S. E. Porter and C. A. Evans. Sheffield: Sheffield Academic, 1997.

———. *The Theology of Paul the Apostle*. Grand Rapids: Eerdmans, 1998.

———. "When Did the Understanding of Jesus' Death as an Atoning Sacrifice First Emerge?" Pages 169–82 in *Israel's God and Rebecca's Children: Christology and Community in Early Judaism and Christianity: Essays in Honor of Larry W. Hurtado and Alan F. Segal*. Edited by D. B. Capes, A. D. DeConick, H. K. Bond, and T. Miller. Waco, Tex.: Baylor University Press, 2007.

Dupont-Sommer, André. *Aperçus préliminaires sur les manuscrits de la Mer Morte*. Paris: Maisonneuve, 1950.

———. *The Dead Sea Scrolls: A Preliminary Survey*. Translated by E. M. Rowley. Oxford: Blackwell, 1952.

———. *The Essene Writings from Qumran*. Translated by Geza Vermes. Oxford: Blackwell, 1961.

———. *The Jewish Sect of Qumran and the Essenes: New Studies on the Dead Sea Scrolls*. Translated by R. D. Barnett. New York: Macmillan, 1955.

Ehrman, Bart D. *How Jesus Became God: The Exaltation of a Jewish Preacher from Galilee*. New York: HarperOne, 2014.

———. *Jesus: Apocalyptic Prophet of the New Millennium*. New York: Oxford University Press, 1999.

Eidevall, Göran. *Sacrificial Rhetoric in the Prophetic Literature of the Hebrew Bible*. Lewiston, N.Y.: Edwin Mellen, 2012.

Eisenman, Robert H. *James the Just in the Habakkuk Pesher*. Leiden: Brill, 1986.

———. *James the Just: The Key to Unlocking the Secrets of Early Christianity and the Dead Sea Scrolls*. New York: Viking, 1996.

———. "A Messianic Vision." *BAR* 17, no. 6 (1991): 65.

———. *The New Testament Code: The Cup of the Lord, the Damascus Document, and the Blood of Christ*. London: Watkins, 2006.

Eisenman, Robert, and Michael O. Wise. *The Dead Sea Scrolls Uncovered*. Shaftesbury: Element, 1992.

Elder, Linda Bennett. "The Women Question and Female Ascetics among Essenes." *BA* 57, no. 4 (1994): 220–34.

Elgvin, Torleif. "Admonition Texts from Qumran Cave 4." Pages 137–52 in *Methods of Investigation of the Dead Sea Scrolls and the Khirbet Qumran Site: Present Realities and Future Prospects*. Edited by M. O. Wise et al. New York: Academy of Arts and Sciences, 1993.

———. "The Mystery to Come: Early Essene Theology of Revelation." Pages 113–50 in *Qumran Between the Old and New Testaments*. Edited by F. H. Cryer and T. L. Thompson. Sheffield: Sheffield Academic, 1998.

———. "Wisdom and Apocalypticism in the Early Second Century BCE—The Evidence of 4QInstruction." Pages 226–47 in *The Dead Sea Scrolls Fifty Years after Their Discovery: Proceedings of the Jerusalem Congress, July 20–25, 1997*. Edited by L. H. Schiffman, E. Tov, and J. C. VanderKam. Jerusalem: Israel Exploration Society, 2000.

———. "Wisdom, Revelation, and Eschatology in an Early Essene Writing." Pages 440–63 in *Society of Biblical Literature 1995 Seminar Papers*. Edited by E. H. Lovering. Atlanta: Scholars, 1995.

———. "The *Yahad* Is More than Qumran." Pages 273–79 in *Enoch and Qumran Origins: New Light on a Forgotten Connection*. Edited by G. Boccaccini. Grand Rapids: Eerdmans, 2005.

Elior, Rachel. זיכרון ונשייה סודן של מגילות מדבר יהודה [*Memory and Oblivion: The Mystery of the Dead Sea Scrolls*]. Jerusalem: Hakibbutz Hameuchad–Van Leer Institute, 2009.

———. *The Three Temples: On the Emergence of Jewish Mysticism*. Translated by David Louvish. Portland, Ore.: Littman Library of Jewish Civilization, 2004.

Elliott, Mark A. "Sealing Some Cracks in the Groningen Foundation." Pages 263–72 in *Enoch and Qumran Origins*. Edited by G. Boccaccini. Grand Rapids: Eerdmans, 2005.

Elukin, Jonathan M. "A New Essenism: Heinrich Graetz and Mysticism." *JHI* 59, no. 1 (1998): 135–48.

Enslin, Morton S. "John and Jesus." *ZNW* 66 (1975): 1–18.

Eshel, Esther. "Prayer in Qumran and the Synagogue." Pages 323–34 in *Community Without Temple*. Edited by B. Ego, A. Lange, and P. Pilhofer. Tübingen: Mohr Siebeck, 1999.

Esler, Philip Francis. *Community and Gospel in Luke-Acts: The Social and Political Motivations of Lucan Theology*. New York: Cambridge University Press, 1987.

Evans, C. F. *Saint Luke*. Philadelphia: Trinity International, 1990.

Evans, Craig A. "Jesus and the Dead Sea Scrolls." Pages 573–98 in *The Dead Sea Scrolls after Fifty Years: A Comprehensive Assessment*. Edited by P. W. Flint and J. C. VanderKam. Leiden: Brill, 1999.

———. "Jesus and the Messianic Texts from Qumran: A Preliminary Assessment of the Recently Published Materials." Pages 83–154 in *Jesus and His Contemporaries: Comparative Studies*. Leiden: Brill, 1995.

———. "Prophet, Sage, Healer, Messiah, and Martyr: Types and Identities of Jesus." Pages 2:1217–243 in *Handbook for the Study of the Historical Jesus*. Edited by T. Holmén and S. Porter. 4 vols. Leiden: Brill, 2011.

———. "Qumran's Messiah: How Important Is He?" Pages 135–49 in *Religion in the Dead Sea Scrolls*. Edited by J. J. Collins and R. A. Kugler. SDSSRL. Grand Rapids: Eerdmans, 2000.

Faierstein, Morris M. "Why Do the Scribes Say that Elijah Must Come First?" *JBL* 100 (1981): 75–86.

Falk, Daniel K. "The Contribution of the Qumran Scrolls to the Study of Ancient Jewish Liturgy." Pages 617–51 in *The Oxford Handbook of the Dead Sea Scrolls*. Edited by T. H. Lim and J. J. Collins. New York: Oxford University Press, 2010.

———. *Daily, Sabbath, and Festival Prayers in the Dead Sea Scrolls*. STDJ 27. Leiden: Brill, 1998.

———. "Petition and Ideology in the Dead Sea Scrolls." Pages 135–59 in *Prayer and Poetry in the Dead Sea Scrolls and Related Literature: Essays in Honor of Eileen Schuller on the Occasion of Her 65th Birthday*. STDJ 98. Edited by J. Penner, K. M. Penner, and C. Wassen. Leiden: Brill, 2011.

———. "Qumran Prayer Texts and the Temple." Pages 106–26 in *Sapiential, Liturgical and Poetical Texts from Qumran*. Edited by D. K. Falk, F. García Martínez, and E. M. Schuller. STDJ 35. Leiden: Brill, 2000.

Fander, M. *Die Stellung der Frau im Markusevangelium: Unter besonderer Berücksichtigung kultur- und religionsgeschichtlicher Hintergründe*. Münster theologische Abhandlungen 8. Altenberge: Telos, 1990.

Finkbeiner, Douglas P. "The Essenes according to Josephus: Exploring the Contribution of Josephus' Portrait of the Essenes to His Larger Literary Agenda." Ph.D. diss., University of Pennsylvania, 2010.

Finnegan, Jack. *Light from the Ancient Past*. Princeton: Princeton University Press, 1959.

Fischel, Henry A. *The First Book of Maccabees*. New York: Schocken, 1948.

Fitzmyer, Joseph A. "The Contribution of Qumran Aramaic to the Study of the New Testament." NTS 20 (1974): 382–407.

———. *The Dead Sea Scrolls and Christian Origins*. Grand Rapids: Eerdmans, 2000.

———. "The Dead Sea Scrolls and Christian Origins: General Methodological Considerations." Pages 1–19 in *The Dead Sea Scrolls and Christian Faith: In Celebration of the Jubilee Year of the Discovery of Qumran Cave 1*. Edited by J. H. Charlesworth and W. P. Weaver. Harrisburg, Pa.: Trinity International, 1998.

———. "Further Light on Melchizedek from Qumran Cave 11." JBL 86 (1967): 25–41.

———. *The Gospel according to Luke*. 2 vols. AB 28/28A. Garden City, N.Y.: Doubleday, 1981, 1985.

———. "The Matthean Divorce Texts and Some New Palestinian Evidence." TS 37 (1976): 197–226.

———. "More About Elijah Coming First." JBL 104 (1985): 295–96.

———. "A Palestinian Collection of Beatitudes." Pages 1:509–15 in *The Four Gospels. 1992: Festschrift Frans Neirynck*. Edited by F. Van Segbroek. BETL 100. Leuven: Peeters, 1992.

———. *Responses to 101 Questions on the Dead Sea Scrolls*. New York: Paulist, 1992.

———. *The Semitic Background of the New Testament*. Grand Rapids: Eerdmans, 1997.

———. "The Use of Explicit Old Testament Quotations in Qumran Literature and in the New Testament." NTS 7 (1961): 297–333.

Fleddermann, Harry T. *Q: A Reconstruction and Commentary*. BTS 1. Leuven: Peeters, 2005.
Fletcher-Louis, Crispin. *All the Glory of Adam: Liturgical Anthropology in the Dead Sea Scrolls*. Leiden: Brill, 2002.
———. "Jesus and Apocalypticism." Pages 2877–2909 in *The Historical Jesus*. Edited by T. Holmén and S. E. Porter. Vol. 3 of *Handbook for the Study of the Historical Jesus*. 4 vols. Leiden: Brill, 2011.
———. *Luke-Acts: Angels, Christology and Soteriology*. WUNT 2/94. Tübingen: Mohr Siebeck, 1997.
———. "The Similitudes of Enoch (*1 Enoch* 37–71): The Son of Man, Apocalyptic Messianism, and Political Theology." Pages 58–79 in *The Open Mind: Essays in Honour of Christopher Rowland*. Edited by K. Sullivan and J. Knight. LNTS. New York: T&T Clark, 2015.
Flusser, David. "The Hubris of the Antichrist in a Fragment from Qumran." *Imm* 10 (1980): 31–37.
———. *Jesus in Selbstzeugnissen und Bilddokumenten*. Hamburg: Rowohlt, 1975.
———. *Judaism and the Origins of Christianity*. Jerusalem: Magnes, 1988.
———. "Melchizedek and the Son of Man." *Christian News from Israel* 17 (1966): 23–29.
———. *The Spiritual History of the Dead Sea Sect*. Translated by C. Glucker. Tel Aviv: MOD Books, 1989.
Flusser, David, with R. Steven Notley. *The Sage from Galilee: Rediscovering Jesus' Genius*. Grand Rapids: Eerdmans, 2007 [1968].
Fraade, Steven. "Ascetical Aspects of Ancient Judaism." Pages 253–88 in *Jewish Spirituality: From the Bible through the Middle Ages*. Edited by A. Green. New York: Crossroad, 1986.
———. "The Nazirite in Ancient Judaism." Pages 213–23 in *Ascetic Behavior in Greco-Roman Antiquity*. Edited by V. L. Wimbush. SAC. Minneapolis: Fortress, 1990.
———. "Rhetoric and Hermeneutics in Miqsat Ma'ase ha-Torah (4QMMT): The Case of the Blessings and Curses." *DSD* 10 (2003): 150–61.
Frankemölle, Hubert. "Jesus als deuterojesajanische Freudenbote? Zur Rezeption von Jes 52,7 und 61,1 im Neuen Testament, durch Jesus und in den Targumim." Pages 34–67 in *Vom Christentum zu Jesus. Festschrift für Joachim Gnilka*. Edited by H. Frankemölle. Freiberg: Herder, 1989.
Freedman, David N. "Early Christianity and the Scrolls: An Inquiry." Pages 97–102 in *Jesus in History and Myth*. Edited by R. J. Hoffmann and G. A. Larue. Buffalo, N.Y.: Prometheus, 1986.
Freidenreich, David M. "Comparisons Compared: A Methodological Survey of Comparisons of Religion from 'A Magic Dwells' to *A Magic Still Dwells*." *MTSR* 16 (2004): 80–101.
Frey, Jörg. "Critical Issues in the Investigation of the Scrolls and the New Testament." Pages 519–40 in *The Oxford Handbook of the Dead Sea Scrolls*. Edited by J. J. Collins and T. H. Lim. New York: Oxford University Press, 2010.

———. "Essenes." Pages 599–602 in *The Eerdmans Dictionary of Early Judaism.* Edited by J. J. Collins and D. C. Harlow. Grand Rapids: Eerdmans, 2010.

———. "The Impact of the Dead Sea Scrolls on New Testament Interpretation: Proposals, Problems, and Further Perspectives." Pages 407–61 in *The Scrolls and Christian Origins: The Second Princeton Symposium on Judaism and Christian Origins.* Edited by J. H. Charlesworth. Vol. 3 of *The Bible and the Dead Sea Scrolls.* Waco, Tex.: Baylor University Press, 2006.

———. "Zur historischen Auswertung der antiken Essenerberichte: Ein beitrag zum Gespräch mit Roland Bergmeier." Pages 23–57 in *Qumran Kontrovers: Beiträge zu den Textfunden vom Toten Meer.* Paderborn: Bonifatius, 2003.

Freyne, S. *Galilee and Gospel: Collected Essays.* WUNT 125. Tübingen: Mohr Siebeck, 2000.

———. *Galilee, Jesus and the Gospels: Literary Approaches and Historical Investigations.* Philadelphia: Fortress, 1988.

Fritsch, Charles. *The Qumran Community.* New York: Macmillan, 1956.

Fröhlich, Ida. "The Parables of Enoch and Qumran Literature." Pages 343–51 in *Enoch and the Messiah Son of Man: Revisiting the Book of Parables.* Edited by G. Boccaccini. Grand Rapids: Eerdmans, 2007.

Fuller, Reginald. "The Son of Man: A Reconsideration." Pages 207–17 in *The Living Text: Essays in Honor of Ernest W. Saunders.* Edited by D. E. Groh and R. Jewett. Lanham, Md.: University Press of America, 1985.

Funk, Robert W., and the Jesus Seminar. *The Acts of Jesus: The Search for the Authentic Deeds of Jesus.* San Francisco: HarperSanFrancisco, 1998.

Furst, Jeffrey, ed. *Edgar Cayce's Story of Jesus.* New York: Berkeley, 1968.

Gager, John G. *The Origins of Anti-Semitism: Attitudes toward Judaism in Pagan and Christian Antiquity.* New York: Oxford University Press, 1985.

García Martínez, Florentino. *The Dead Sea Scrolls Translated: The Qumran Texts in English.* 2nd ed. Grand Rapids: Eerdmans, 1996.

———. "The Eschatological Figure of 4Q246." Pages 162–79 in *Qumran and Apocalyptic: Studies on the Aramaic Texts from Qumran.* STDJ 9. Leiden: Brill, 1992.

———. "Man and Woman: Halakhah Based upon Eden in the Dead Sea Scrolls." Pages 95–115 in *Paradise Interpreted: Representations of Biblical Paradise in Judaism and Christianity.* Edited by G. P. Luttikuizen. TBN 2. Leiden: Brill, 1999.

———. "Messianic Hopes in the Qumran Writings." Pages 159–89 in *The People of the Dead Sea Scrolls.* Edited by F. García Martínez and J. Trebolle Barrera. Leiden: Brill, 1995.

———. "Messianische Erwartungen in den Qumranschriften." Pages 171–208 in *Der Messias.* Vol. 8 of *Jahrbuch für Biblische Theologie.* Neukirchen-Vluyn: Neukirchener, 1993.

———. "Qumran between the Old and the New Testament." Pages 1–6 in *Echoes from the Caves: Qumran and the New Testament.* Edited by F. García Martínez. STDJ 85. Leiden: Brill, 2009.

———. "Qumran Origins and Early History: A 'Groningen Hypothesis.'" *FO* 25 (1989): 113–36.

———. "Two Messianic Figures in the Qumran Texts." Pages 13–32 in *Qumranica Minora II: Thematic Studies on the Dead Sea Scrolls*. Edited by E. J. C. Tigchelaar. STDJ 64. Leiden: Brill, 2006.

García Martínez, Florentino, and J. T. Barrera. *The People of the Dead Sea Scrolls*. Translated by W. G. E. Watson. Leiden: Brill, 1995.

Gärtner, Bertil. *The Temple and the Community in Qumran and the New Testament: A Comparative Study in the Temple Symbolism of the Qumran Texts and the New Testament*. Cambridge: Cambridge University Press, 1965.

Gaster, Theodore H. *The Dead Sea Scriptures*. New York: Doubleday/Anchor, 1964.

Gathercole, Simon. *Defending Substitution: An Essay on Atonement in Paul*. Acadia Studies in Bible and Theology. Grand Rapids: Baker Academic, 2015.

Geyser, A. S. "The Youth of John the Baptist: A Deduction from the Break in the Parallel Account of the Lucan Infancy Story." *NovT* 1 (1956): 70–75.

Gibson, Shimon. *The Final Days of Jesus: The Archaeological Evidence*. New York: HarperOne, 2009.

———. "Suggested Identifications for 'Bethso' and the 'Gate of the Essenes' in the Light of Magen Broshi's Excavations on Mount Zion." Pages 25–33 in *New Studies in the Archaeology of Jerusalem and Its Region: Collected Papers*. Edited by J. Patrich and D. Amit. Jerusalem: Israel Antiquities Authority, 2007.

Gilders, William K. "Jewish Sacrifice: Its Nature and Function (According to Philo)." Pages 94–105 in *Ancient Mediterranean Sacrifice*. Edited by J. W. Knust and Z. Várhelyi. New York: Oxford University Press, 2011.

Ginsburg, Christian D. *The Essenes: Their History and Doctrines; The Kabbalah: Its Doctrines, Development and Literature*. London: Longman & Green, 1864; reprint New York: Samuel Weiser, 1974.

Ginzberg, Louis. *An Unknown Jewish Sect*. New York: Jewish Theological Seminary of America, 1976.

Glaim, Aaron. "Reciprocity, Sacrifice, and Salvation in Judean Religion at the Turn of the Era." Ph.D. diss., Brown University, 2014.

Goergen, Donald J. *The Mission and Ministry of Jesus*. Wilmington, Del.: Michael Glazier, 1986.

Goff, Matthew J. "Discerning Trajectories: 4QInstruction and the Sapiential Background of the Sayings Source Q." *JBL* 124, no. 4 (2005): 657–73.

———. "The Mystery of Creation in 4QInstruction." *DSD* 10, no. 2 (2003): 163–86.

———. *The Worldly and Heavenly Wisdom of 4QInstruction*. STDJ 50. Leiden: Brill, 2003.

Goguel, Maurice. *Au seuil de l'Évangile: Jean-Baptiste*. Paris: Payot, 1928.

Golb, Norman. *Who Wrote the Dead Sea Scrolls?: The Search for the Secret of Qumran*. New York: Scribner, 1995.

Goodacre, Mark S. *The Case against Q: Studies in Markan Priority and the Synoptic Problem*. Harrisburg, Pa.: Trinity International, 2002.

Goodenough, Erwin R. "The Perspective of Acts." Pages 51–59 in *Studies in Luke-Acts: Essays in Honour of Paul Schubert*. Edited by L. E. Keck and J. L. Martyn. Nashville: Abingdon, 1966.

Goodman, Martin. "Constructing Ancient Judaism from the Scrolls." Pages 81–89 in *The Oxford Handbook of the Dead Sea Scrolls*. Edited by T. H. Lim and J. J. Collins. New York: Oxford University Press, 2010.

———. "A Note on the Qumran Sectarians, the Essenes and Josephus." *JJS* 46 (1995): 161–66.

———. "Religious Variety and the Temple in the Late Second Temple Period and Its Aftermath." Pages 21–38 in *Sects and Sectarianism in Jewish History*. Edited by S. Stern. IJS Studies in Judaica 12. Leiden: Brill, 2011.

———. "Sadducees and Essenes after 70 CE." Pages 347–55 in *Crossing the Boundaries: Essays in Biblical Interpretation in Honor of Michael D. Goulder*. Edited by S. E. Porter et al. BI 8. Leiden: Brill, 1994.

Goranson, Stephen. "'Essenes': Etymology from עשה." *RevQ* 44 (1984): 483–98.

———. "Rereading Pliny on the Essenes." Orion Center for the Dead Sea Scrolls, 1998. http://orion.mscc.huji.ac.il/orion/programs/Goranson98.shtml (accessed December 21, 2016).

Gordis, Robert. "The 'Begotten' Messiah in the Qumran Scrolls." *VT* 7 (1957): 191–94.

Gottstein, M. H. "Anti-Essene Traits in the Dead Sea Scrolls." *VT* 4 (1954): 141–47.

Grabbe, Lester L. "Digging among the Roots of the Groningen Hypothesis." Pages 280–85 in *Enoch and Qumran Origins: New Light on a Forgotten Connection*. Edited by G. Boccaccini. Grand Rapids: Eerdmans, 2005.

———. *Judaism from Cyrus to Hadrian*. 2 vols. Minneapolis: Fortress, 1992.

———. "The Parables of Enoch in Second Temple Jewish Society." Pages 386–402 in *Enoch and the Messiah Son of Man*. Edited by G. Boccaccini. Grand Rapids: Eerdmans, 2007.

———. "Warfare." Pages 2:963–65 in *Encyclopedia of the Dead Sea Scrolls*. Edited by L. H. Schiffman and J. C. VanderKam. New York: Oxford University Press, 2000.

Graetz, Heinrich Hirsch. *History of the Jews*. Pennsylvania: Jewish Publication Society of America, 1893.

Green, Dennis. "Halakhah at Qumran? The Use of 'h.l.k' in the Dead Sea Scrolls." *RevQ* 22 (2005): 235–51.

Greenfield, J. C., M. E. Stone, and E. Eshel. *The Aramaic Levi Document: Edition, Translation, Commentary*. SVTP 19. Leiden: Brill, 2004.

Greenfield, Jonas C., and Michael E. Stone. "The Enochic Pentateuch and the Date of the Similitudes." *HTR* 70 (1977): 51–65.

Grelot, P. "La géographie mytique d'Hénoch et ses sources orientales." *RB* 65 (1958): 33–69.

———. "La légende d'Hénoch dans les apocryphes et dans la Bible: Origine et signification." *RSR* 46 (1958): 5–26, 181–220.

Grossman, Maxine L. *Reading for History in the Damascus Document: A Methodological Method*. STDJ 45. Leiden: Brill, 2002.

———. "Mystery or History: The Dead Sea Scrolls as Pop Phenomenon." *DSD* 12, no. 1 (2005): 68–86.

Gruenwald, I., S. Shaked, and G. G. Stroumsa, eds. *Messiah and Christos: Studies in the Jewish Origins of Christianity, Presented to David Flusser on the Occasion of His Seventy-Fifth Birthday.* Tübingen: Mohr Siebeck, 1992.

Grundmann, W. *Das Evangelium nach Lukas.* Berlin: Evangelische Verlagsanstalt, 1961.

Guelich, R. A. "The Antitheses of Matt 5:21-48: Traditional and/or Redactional?" *NTS* 22 (1976): 444–57.

Guillaume, A. "Some Readings in the Dead Sea Scroll of Isaiah." *JBL* 76, no. 1 (1957): 40–43.

Guillaumont, Antoine. "A propos du célibat des Esséniens." Pages 395–404 in *Hommages à A. Dupont-Sommer.* Edited by A. Caquot and M. Philonenko. Paris: Adrien-Maisonneuve, 1971.

Gundry, R. H. *Matthew: A Commentary on His Literary and Theological Art.* Grand Rapids: Eerdmans, 1982.

Gunnweg, Jan, and Marta Balla. "Neutron Activation Analysis: Scroll Jars and Common Ware." Pages 3–53 in *Khirbet Qumrân et 'Ain Feshkha II: Études d'anthropologie, de physique et de chimie.* Edited by J.-B. Humbert and J. Gunneweg. Fribourg: Academic Press, 2003.

Haas, Nicu, and N. Nathan. "Anthropological Survey on the Human Skeletal Remains from Qumran." *RevQ* 6 (1968): 345–52.

Haber, Susan, and Adele Reinhartz. *They Shall Purify Themselves: Essays on Purity in Early Judaism.* Atlanta: Society of Biblical Literature, 2008.

Hachlili, Rachel. "Burial Practices at Qumran." *RevQ* 62 (1994): 247–64.

Haenchen, Ernst. *The Acts of the Apostles: A Commentary.* Translated by B. Noble and G. Shinn. Philadelphia: Westminster, 1971.

———. *Der Weg Jesu: Eine Erklärung des Markus-Evangeliums und der kanonischen Parallelen.* 2nd ed. Berlin: de Gruyter, 1968.

Hagner, Donald A. "Jesus and the Synoptic Sabbath Controversies." Pages 251–92 in *Key Events in the Life of the Historical Jesus.* Edited by R. L. Webb and D. L. Bock. Tübingen: Mohr Siebeck, 2009.

———. *The Jewish Reclamation of Jesus: An Analysis and Critique of Modern Jewish Study of Jesus.* Grand Rapids: Academie Books, 1984.

Hampel, Volker. *Menschensohn und historischer Jesus.* Neukirchen-Vluyn: Neukirchener, 1990.

Han, Kyu Sam. *Jerusalem and the Early Jesus Movement: The Q Community's Attitude Toward the Temple.* JSNTSup 207. Sheffield: Sheffield Academic, 2002.

Hannah, Darrell. "The Elect Son of Man of the *Parables of Enoch.*" Pages 130–58 in *Who Is This Son of Man? The Latest Scholarship on a Puzzling Expression of the Historical Jesus.* Edited by L. W. Hurtado and P. L. Owen. LNTS 390. New York: T&T Clark, 2011.

Hanson, R. Kenneth. *The Dead Sea Scrolls.* New York: Harper & Row, 1961.

Harrington, Daniel J. "The *Raz Nihyeh* in a Qumran Wisdom Text (1Q26, 4Q415–418, 4Q243)." *RevQ* 17 (1996): 449–53.

---. "Wisdom at Qumran." Pages 137–52 in *The Community of the Renewed Covenant: The Notre Dame Symposium on the Dead Sea Scrolls*. Edited by E. Ulrich and J. VanderKam. Notre Dame, Ind.: University of Notre Dame Press, 1994.

---. *Wisdom Texts from Qumran*. London: Routledge, 1996.

Harrington, Daniel J., and John Strugnell. "Qumran Cave 4 Texts: A New Publication." *JBL* 112 (1993): 490–99.

Havener, Ivan. *Q: The Sayings of Jesus*. Wilmington: Michael Glazier, 1987.

Hayes, John H., and Sara R. Mandell. *The Jewish People in Classical Antiquity: From Alexander to Bar Kochba*. Louisville, Ky.: Westminster John Knox, 1998.

Hays, Richard. "Victory over Violence: The Significance of N. T. Wright's Jesus for New Testament Ethics." Pages 142–58 in *Jesus & The Restoration of Israel: A Critical Assessment of N. T. Wright's "Jesus and the Victory of God."* Edited by C. C. Newman. Downers Grove, Ill.: InterVarsity, 1999.

Heger, Paul. *The Pluralistic Halakhah: Legal Innovations in the Late Second Commonwealth and Rabbinic Periods*. SJ FWJ 22. Berlin: de Gruyter, 2003.

Hempel, Charlotte. "CD Manuscript B and the *Rule of the Community*—Reflections on a Literary Relationship." *DSD* 16, no. 3 (2009): 370–87.

---. "Community Origins in the *Damascus Document* in the Light of Recent Scholarship." Pages 316–29 in *The Provo International Conference on the Dead Sea Scrolls: Technological Innovations, New Texts, and Reformulated Issues*. Edited by D. W. Parry and E. Ulrich. STDJ 30. Leiden: Brill, 1999.

---. *The Damascus Texts*. CQS. Sheffield: Sheffield Academic, 2000.

---. "The Earthly Essene Nucleus of 1QSa." *DSD* 3, no. 3 (1996): 253–69.

---. "The Essenes." Pages 65–80 in *Religious Diversity in the Graeco-Roman World: A Survey of Recent Scholarship*. Edited by D. Cohn-Sherbok and J. M. Court. Sheffield: Sheffield Academic, 2001.

---. *The Laws of the Damascus Document: Sources, Traditions and Redaction*. STDJ 29. Leiden: Brill, 1998.

---. "Qumran Communities: Beyond the Fringes of Second Temple Society." Pages 43–53 in *The Scrolls and the Scriptures: Qumran Fifty Years After*. Edited by S. E. Porter and C. A. Evans. Sheffield: Sheffield Academic, 1997.

Hengel, Martin. "Abba, Maranatha, Hosanna und die Anfänge der Christologie." Pages 496–534 in *Studien zur Christologie, Kleine Schriften IV*. WUNT 201. Tübingen: Mohr Siebeck, 2006.

---. *The Charismatic Leader and His Followers*. Translated by J. Greig. New York: Crossroad, 1981.

---. *Judaism and Hellenism: Studies in Their Encounter in Palestine During the Early Hellenistic Period*. Philadelphia: Fortress, 1974.

---. *The Son of God*. Philadelphia: Fortress, 1976.

Heschel, Susannah. *Abraham Geiger and the Jewish Jesus*. CSHJ. Chicago: University of Chicago Press, 1998.

---. "The Image of Judaism in Nineteenth-Century Christian New Testament Scholarship in Germany." Pages 215–40 in *Jewish-Christian Encounters over the Centuries: Symbiosis, Prejudice, Holocaust, Dialogue*. Edited by M. Perry and F. M. Schweitzer. AUS 136. New York: Peter Lang, 1994.

Hezser, Catherine. "Seduced by the Enemy or Wise Strategy? The Presentation of Non-Violence and Accommodation with Foreign Powers in Ancient Jewish Literary Sources." Pages 221–50 in *Between Cooperation and Hostility: Multiple Identities in Ancient Judaism and the Interaction with Foreign Powers*. Edited by R. Albertz and J. Wöhrle. Göttingen: Vandenhoeck & Ruprecht, 2013.

Hiers, R. H. *The Kingdom of God in the Synoptic Tradition*. Gainesville: University of Florida Press, 1970.

Himmelfarb, Martha. *Ascent to Heaven in Jewish and Christian Apocalypses*. New York: Oxford University Press, 1993.

———. "Earthly Sacrifice and Heavenly Incense: The Law of the Priesthood in Aramaic Levi and Jubilees." Pages 103–22 in *Heavenly Realms and Earthly Realities in Late Antique Religions*. Edited by R. S. Boustan and A. Y. Reed. Cambridge: Cambridge University Press, 2004.

———. "The Temple and the Garden of Eden in Ezekiel, the Book of Watchers, and the Wisdom of Ben Sira." Pages 63–78 in *Sacred Places and Profane Spaces: Essays in the Geographies of Judaism, Christianity and Islam*. Edited by J. S. Scott and P. Simpson-Housely. Westport, Conn.: Greenwood, 1991.

Hirschfeld, Yizhar. "Early Roman Manor Houses in Judea and the Site of Khirbet Qumran." *JNES* 57 (1998): 161–89.

———. *Qumran in Context: Reassessing the Archaeological Evidence*. Peabody, Mass.: Hendrickson, 2004.

Hoffmann, Paul. *Studien zur Theologie der Logienquelle*. NTAbh n. F. 8. Münster: Aschendorff, 1972.

———. "Tradition und Situation: Zur 'Verbindlichkeit' des Gebots der Feindesliebe in der synoptischen Überlieferung und in der gegenwärtigen Friedendiskussion." Pages 50–118 in *Ethik im Neuen Testament*. Edited by K. Kertelge. QD 102. Freiburg im Breisgau: Herder, 1984.

Hogeterp, Albert I. A. *Expectations of the End: A Comparative Traditio-historical Study of Eschatological, Apocalyptic and Messianic Ideas in the Dead Sea Scrolls and the New Testament*. STDJ 83. Leiden: Brill, 2009.

Hollenbach, Paul W. "The Conversion of Jesus: From Jesus the Baptizer to Jesus the Healer." Pages 198–206 in *ANRW* 2.25.1. Berlin: de Gruyter, 1982.

———. "Social Aspects of John the Baptist's Preaching Mission in the Contexts of Palestinian Judaism." Pages 850–75 in *ANRW* 2.19.1. Berlin: de Gruyter, 1972.

Holmén, Tom. *Jesus and Jewish Covenant Thinking*. BI 55. Leiden: Brill, 2001.

Hooker, Morna D. *The Gospel according to St. Mark*. BNTC 2. Peabody, Mass.: Hendrickson, 1991.

———. *The Signs of a Prophet: The Prophetic Actions of Jesus*. Harrisburg, Pa.: Trinity International, 1997.

Hopkins, Jamal-Dominique. "The Dead Sea Scrolls and the Greco-Roman World: Examining the Essenes' View of Sacrifice in Relation to the Scrolls." Pages 1:367–83 in *The Dead Sea Scrolls in Context: Integrating the Dead Sea Scrolls in the Study of Ancient Texts, Languages, and Cultures*. Edited by A. Lange, E. Tov, M. Weigold, and B. Reynolds III. 2 vols. VTSup 140. Leiden: Brill, 2011.

———. "Sacrifice in the Dead Sea Scrolls: Khirbet Qumran, The Essenes, and Cultic Spiritualization." Ph.D. diss., University of Manchester, 2005.

Horbury, William. "'Gospel' in Herodian Judaea." Pages 7–30 in *The Written Gospel*. Edited by M. Bockmuehl and D. Hagner. Cambridge: Cambridge University Press, 2005.

Horsley, Richard A. "The Dead Sea Scrolls and the Historical Jesus." Pages 37–60 in *The Scrolls and Christian Origins: The Second Princeton Symposium on Judaism and Christian Origins*. Edited by J. H. Charlesworth. Vol. 3 of *The Bible and the Dead Sea Scrolls*. Waco, Tex.: Baylor University Press, 2006.

———. *The Prophet Jesus and the Renewal of Israel: Moving Beyond a Diversionary Debate*. Grand Rapids: Eerdmans, 2012.

———. "Questions about Redactional Strata and the Social Relations Reflected in Q." Pages 186–203 in *Society of Biblical Literature Seminar Papers 28*. Atlanta: Society of Biblical Literature, 1989.

Howlett, Duncan. *The Essenes and Christianity*. New York: Harper, 1957.

Hübner, Hans. "Zölibat in Qumran?" *NTS* 17 (1971): 153–67.

Hughes, John H. "John the Baptist: Forerunner of God." *NovT* 14 (1972): 190–218.

Hultgren, Stephen. "4Q521 and Luke's *Magnificat* and *Benedictus*." Pages 119–32 in *Echoes from the Caves: Qumran and the New Testament*. Edited by F. García Martínez. STDJ 85. Leiden: Brill, 2009.

———. "4Q521, the Second Benediction of the Tefilla, the Hasidim, and the Development of Royal Messianism." *RevQ* 23 (2008): 313–40.

———. *From the Damascus Covenant to the Covenant of the Community: Literary, Historical, and Theological Studies in the Dead Sea Scrolls*. STDJ 66. Leiden: Brill, 2007.

Humbert, Jean-Baptiste. "L'espace sacré á Qumrân: Propositions pour l'archéologie (Planches I–III)." *Revue Biblique* 101 (1994): 161–214.

Hurtado, Larry W. *Lord Jesus Christ: Devotion to Jesus in Earliest Christianity*. Grand Rapids: Eerdmans, 2003.

———. *One God, One Lord: Early Christian Devotion and Ancient Jewish Monotheism*. New York: T&T Clark, 1988.

———. "Resurrection-Faith and the 'Historical' Jesus." *JSHJ* 11 (2013): 35–52.

———. "Summary and Concluding Observations." Pages 160–77 in *Who Is This Son of Man? The Latest Scholarship on a Puzzling Expression of the Historical Jesus*. Edited by L. W. Hurtado and P. L. Owen. LNTS 390. New York: T&T Clark, 2011.

———. "YHWH's Return to Zion: A New Catalyst for Earliest High Christology?" Pages 417–38 in *God and the Faithfulness of Paul*. Edited by C. Heilig, J. T. Hewitt, and M. F. Bird. Tübingen: Mohr Siebeck, 2016.

Hutchesson, Ian. "The Essene Hypothesis after Fifty Years: An Assessment." *Qumran Chronicle* 9 (2000): 17–34.

Hutt, Curtis. "Qumran and the Ancient Sources." Pages 274–93 in *The Provo International Conference on the Dead Sea Scrolls: Technological Innovation, New Texts, and Reformulated Issues.* Edited by D. W. Parry and E. Ulrich. STDJ 30. Leiden: Brill, 1999.

Instone-Brewer, David. "Nomological Exegesis in Qumran 'Divorce' Texts." *RdQ* 18 (1998): 561–79.

———. *Traditions of the Rabbis from the Era of the New Testament.* Vol. 2A, *Feasts and Sabbaths: Passover and Atonement.* Grand Rapids: Eerdmans, 2011.

Jackson, Bernard S. *Essays on Halakhah in the New Testament.* JCP 16. Leiden: Brill, 2008.

Jassen, Alex P. "The Dead Sea Scrolls and Violence: Sectarian Formation and Eschatological Imagination." *BibInt* 17 (2009): 12–44.

———. *Mediating the Divine: Prophecy and Revelation in the Dead Sea Scrolls and Second Temple Judaism.* STDJ 68. Leiden: Brill, 2007.

Jaubert, Annie. "Le pays de Damas." *RB* 65 (1958): 214–48.

Jeremias, Joachim. *New Testament Theology: The Proclamations of Jesus.* Translated by J. Bowden. London: SCM Press, 1971.

———. *The Parables of Jesus.* New York: Scribner's Sons, 1963.

Johns, Loren L. "Identity and Resistance: The Varieties of Competing Models in Early Judaism." Pages 254–77 in *Qumran Studies: New Approaches, New Questions.* Edited by M. T. Davis and B. A. Strawn. Grand Rapids: Eerdmans, 2007.

Johnson, Sherman E. "The Dead Sea Manual of Discipline and the Jerusalem Church of Acts." Pages 129–42 in *The Scrolls and the New Testament.* Edited by K. Stendahl. New York: Harper & Brothers, 1958.

Jokiranta, Jutta. Review of John J. Collins, *Beyond the Qumran Community. DSD* 20 (2013): 314–17.

Jones, Allen H. *Essenes: The Elect of Israel and Priests of Artemis.* Lanham, Md.: University Press of America, 1985.

Joseph, Simon J. "The Ascetic Jesus." *JSHJ* 8 (2010): 146–81.

———. "'Blessed Is Whoever is Not Offended by Me': The Subversive Appropriation of (Royal) Messianic Ideology in Q 3–7." *NTS* 57, no. 3 (2011): 307–24.

———. "'I Have Come to Abolish Sacrifices' (Epiphanius, *Pan.* 30.16.5): Reexamining a Jewish-Christian Text and Tradition." *NTS* 63, no. 1 (2017): 92–110.

———. "The Quest for the 'Community' of Q: Mapping Q Within the Social, Scribal, Textual, and Theological Landscape(s) of Second Temple Judaism." *HTR* 111, no. 1 (2018): 90–114.

———. *Jesus and the Temple: The Crucifixion in its Jewish Context.* SNTSMS 165. New York: Cambridge University Press, 2016.

———. *Jesus, Q, and the Dead Sea Scrolls: A Judaic Approach to Q.* WUNT 2/333. Tübingen: Mohr Siebeck, 2012.

———. *The Nonviolent Messiah: Jesus, Q, and the Enochic Tradition.* Minneapolis: Fortress, 2014.

———. "Redescribing the Resurrection: Beyond the Methodological Impasse?" *BTB* 45, no. 3 (2015): 155–73.

———. "'Seventh from Adam' (Jude 1:14-15): Re-examining Enoch Traditions and the Christology of Jude." *JTS* (2013): 463–81.
———. "A Social Identity Approach to the Rhetoric of Apocalyptic Violence in the Sayings Gospel Q." *HR* 57, no. 1 (2017): 28–49.
———. "Was Daniel 7:13's 'Son of Man' Modeled After the 'New Adam' of the *Animal Apocalypse*?" *JSP* 22, no. 4 (2013): 269–94.
Josephus. *Jewish Antiquities*. Books 18–19. Translated by L. H. Feldman. Cambridge, Mass.: Harvard University Press, 1996.
Kampen, John. "A Reconsideration of the Name Essene." *HUCA* 57 (1986): 61–81.
Kapfer, Hilary Evans. "The Relationship Between the Damascus Document and the Community Rule: Attitudes toward the Temple as a Test Case." *DSD* 14, no. 2 (2007): 152–77.
Karrer, Martin. *Der Gesalbte: Die Grundlagen des Christustitels*. FRLANT 151. Göttingen: Vandenhoeck & Ruprecht, 1990.
Kasper, Walter. *Jesus the Christ*. New York: Paulist, 1976.
Kattenbusch, F. "Über die Feindesliebe im Sinne des Christentums." *TSK* 89 (1916): 1–70.
Kazen, Thomas A. *Jesus and Purity Halakhah: Was Jesus Indifferent to Impurity?* ConBNT 38. Winona Lake, Ind.: Eisenbrauns, 2010 [2002].
———. *Scripture, Interpretation, or Authority? Motives and Arguments in Jesus' Halakic Conflicts*. WUNT 320. Tübingen: Mohr Siebeck, 2013.
———. "Son of Man as Kingdom Imagery: Jesus Between Corporate Symbol and Individual Redeemer Figure." Pages 87–108 in *Jesus from Judaism to Christianity: Continuum Approaches to the Historical Jesus*. Edited by T. Holmén. LNTS 352. London: T&T Clark, 2007.
Kearns, Rollin. *Die Entchristologisierung des Menschensohnes: Die Übertragung des Traditionsgefüges um den Menschensohn auf Jesus*. Tübingen: Mohr Siebeck, 1988.
Kee, Howard Clark. "The Bearing of the Dead Sea Scrolls on Understanding Jesus." Pages 54–75 in *Jesus in History and Myth*. Edited by R. J. Hoffmann and G. A. Larue. Buffalo, N.Y.: Prometheus, 1986.
Keith, Chris. "The Indebtedness of the Criteria Approach to Form Criticism and Recent Attempts to Rehabilitate the Search for an Authentic Jesus." Pages 25–48 in *Jesus, Criteria, and the Demise of Authenticity*. Edited by C. Keith and A. Le Donne. New York: T&T Clark, 2012.
———. *Jesus against the Scribal Elite: The Origins of the Conflict*. Grand Rapids: Baker Academic, 2014.
Keith, Chris, and L. W. Hurtado, eds. *Jesus among Friends and Enemies: A Historical and Literary Introduction to Jesus in the Gospels*. Grand Rapids: Baker Academic, 2011.
Kilpatrick, G. D. *The Origins of the Gospel according to St. Matthew*. Oxford: Clarendon, 1946.
Kim, Seyoon. *The "Son of Man" as the Son of God*. WUNT 30. Tübingen: Mohr Siebeck, 1983.

King, Karen L. "Factions, Variety, Diversity, Multiplicity: Representing Early Christian Differences for the 21st Century." *MTSR* 23 (2011): 217–37.
Kirk, Alan. *Ancient Media, Memory, and Early Scribal Transmission of the Jesus Tradition.* LNTS 564. London: T&T Clark, 2016.
———. *The Composition of the Sayings Source: Genre, Synchrony, and Wisdom Redaction in Q.* NovTSup 91. Leiden: Brill, 1998.
Kirk, J. R. Daniel. *A Man Attested by God: The Human Jesus of the Synoptic Gospels.* Grand Rapids: Eerdmans, 2016.
Kister, Menahem. "Divorce, Reproof, and Other Sayings in the Synoptic Gospels: Jesus Traditions in the Context of 'Qumranic' and Other Texts." Pages 195–229 in *Text, Thought, and Practice in Qumran and Early Christianity: Proceedings of the Ninth International Symposium of the Orion Center for the Study of the Dead Sea Scrolls and Associated Literature, Jointly Sponsored by the Hebrew University Center for the Study of Christianity, 11–12 January, 2004.* Edited by R. A. Clements and D. R. Schwartz. Leiden: Brill, 2009.
———. "Studies in 4Miqsat Ma'aseh ha-Torah and Related Texts: Law, Theology, Language and Calendar." *Tarbiz* 68, no. 3 (1999): 317–72.
Klassen, William. "Coals of Fire: Sign of Repentance or Revenge?" *NTS* 9 (1963): 337–50.
———. *Love of Enemies: The Way to Peace.* Philadelphia: Fortress, 1984.
———. "'Love Your Enemies': Some Reflections on the Current Status of Research." Pages 1–31 in *The Love of Enemy and Nonretaliation.* Edited by W. M. Swartley. Louisville, Ky.: Westminster John Knox, 1992.
———. "Love Your Enemy: A Study of New Testament Teaching on Coping with an Enemy." *MQR* 37 (1963): 147–71.
Klausner, Joseph. *From Jesus to Paul.* New York: Macmillan, 1943.
Klawans, Jonathan. "The Essene Hypothesis: Insights from Religion 101." *DSD* 23 (2016): 51–78.
———. *Josephus and the Theologies of Ancient Judaism.* New York: Oxford University Press, 2013.
———. *Purity, Sacrifice, and the Temple: Symbolism and Supersessionism in the Study of Ancient Judaism.* New York: Oxford University Press, 2005.
Klijn, A. F. J. "From Creation to Noah in the Second Dream-Vision of the Ethiopic Enoch." Pages 1:147–59 in *Miscellanea Neotestamentica.* 2 vols. NovTSup 46–47. Leiden: Brill, 1977.
Klinghardt, M. *Gesetz und Volk Gottes: Das lukanische Verständnis des Gesetzes nach Herkunft, Funktion und seinem Ort in der Geschichte des Urchristentums.* WUNT 2/32. Tübingen: Mohr Siebeck, 1988.
Klinzing, Georg. *Die Umdeutung des Kultus in der Qumrangemeinde und im Neuen Testament.* SUNT 7. Göttingen: Vandenhoeck & Ruprecht, 1971.
Kloppenborg, John S. "Alms, Debt and Divorce: Jesus' Ethics in their Mediterranean Context." *TJT* 6 (1990): 182–200.
———. *The Earliest Gospel: An Introduction to the Original Stories and Sayings of Jesus.* Louisville, Ky.: Westminster John Knox, 2008.

———. *The Formation of Q: Trajectories in Ancient Christian Wisdom Collections.* Philadelphia: Fortress, 1987.
———. "The Function of Apocalyptic Language in Q." Pages 224–35 in *Society of Biblical Literature 1986 Seminar Papers.* Atlanta: Scholars, 1986.
———. "Nomos and Ethos in Q." Pages 35–48 in *Gospel Origins and Christian Beginnings: In Honor of James M. Robinson.* Edited by J. E. Goehring, J. T. Sanders, and C. W. Hedrick. Sonoma, Calif.: Polebridge, 1990.
———. *Q Parallels.* Sonoma, Calif.: Polebridge, 1988.
———. "The Sayings Gospel Q and the Quest of the Historical Jesus." *HTR* 89 (1996): 307–44.
———. "Sources, Methods and Discursive Locations in the Quest of the Historical Jesus." Pages 241–90 in *How to Study the Historical Jesus.* Edited by T. Holmén and S. E. Porter. Vol. 1 of *Handbook for the Study of the Historical Jesus.* Leiden: Brill, 2011.
Kloppenborg Verbin, John S. *Excavating Q: The History and Setting of the Sayings Gospel.* Edinburgh: T&T Clark, 2000.
Klumbies, Paul-Gerhard. "Die Sabbatheilungen Jesu nach Markus und Lukas." Pages 173–78 in *Jesu Rede von Gott und ihre Nachgeschichte im frühen Christentum: Beiträge zur Verk,ndigung Jesu und zum Kerygma der Kirche.* Edited by D.-A. Koch, G. Sellin, and A. Lindemann. Gütersloher: Gerd Mohn, 1989.
Knibb, Michael A. "The Community of the Dead Sea Scrolls: Introduction." *DSD* 16, no. 3 (2009): 297–308.
———. "The Date of the Parables of Enoch: A Critical Review." *NTS* 25 (1979): 345–59.
———. *Essays on the Book of Enoch and Other Early Jewish Texts and Traditions.* Leiden: Brill, 2009.
———. *The Ethiopic Book of Enoch: A New Edition in the Light of the Aramaic Dead Sea Fragments.* 2 vols. New York: Oxford University Press, 1978.
———. "Exile in the Damascus Document." *JSOT* 25 (1983): 99–117.
———. "The Place of the Damascus Document in Recent Scholarship." Pages 153–60 in *The Provo International Conference on Methods of Investigation of the Dead Sea Scrolls and the Khirbet Qumran Site: Present Realities and Future Prospects.* Edited by M. O. Wise, N. Golb, J. J. Collins, and D. G. Pardee. New York: New York Academy of Sciences, 1994.
———. *The Qumran Community.* New York: Cambridge University Press, 1987.
———. "The Structure and Composition of the Parables of Enoch." Pages 48–64 in *Enoch and the Messiah Son of Man: Revisiting the Book of Parables.* Edited by G. Boccaccini. Grand Rapids: Eerdmans, 2007.
Knox, John. *The Humanity and Divinity of Christ: A Study of Pattern in Christology.* Cambridge: Cambridge University Press, 1967.
Koester, Helmut. *Ancient Christian Gospels: Their History and Development.* Philadelphia: Trinity International, 1992.
———. *Introduction to the New Testament.* Vol. 2, *History and Literature of Early Christianity.* Philadelphia: Fortress, 1982.

Kohler, Kaufmann. *The Origins of the Synagogue and the Church*. New York: Macmillan, 1929.

Kosch, D. *Die eschatologische Tora des Menschensohnes: Untersuchungen zur Rezeption der Stellung Jesu zur Tora in Q*. NTOA 12. Göttingen: Vandenhoeck & Ruprecht, 1989.

Kranenborg, Reender. "The Presentation of the Essenes in Western Esotericism." JCR 13, no. 2 (1998): 245–56.

Kreplin, Matthias. "The Self-Understanding of Jesus." Pages 3:2473–2516 in *Handbook for the Study of the Historical Jesus*. Edited by T. Holmén and S. E. Porter. 4 vols. Leiden: Brill, 2011.

Kugler, Robert A. "Priesthood at Qumran." Pages 2:93–116 in *The Dead Sea Scrolls after Fifty Years: A Comprehensive Assessment*. Edited by P. W. Flint and J. C. VanderKam. 2 vols. Leiden: Brill, 1999.

———. "Rewriting Rubrics: Sacrifice and the Religion of Qumran." Pages 90–112 in *Religion in the Dead Sea Scrolls*. Edited by J. J. Collins and R. A. Kugler. SDSSRL. Grand Rapids: Eerdmans, 2000.

Kuhn, Heinz-Wolfgang. "Das Liebesgebot Jesus als Tora und als Evangelium: Zur Feindesliebe und zur christlichen und jüdischen Auslegung der Bergpredigt." Pages 194–230 in *Vom Urchristentum zu Jesus*. Edited by H. Frankemölle and K. Kertelge. FS Joachim Gnilka. Freiburg: Herder, 1989.

———. "Jesus im Licht der Qumrangemeinde." Pages 2:1245–85 in *Handbook for the Study of the Historical Jesus*. Edited by T. Holmén and S. Porter. 4 vols. Leiden: Brill, 2011.

———. "Qumran Texts and the Historical Jesus: Parallels in Contrast." Pages 573–79 in *The Dead Sea Scrolls: Fifty Years after Their Discovery: Proceedings of the Jerusalem Congress, July 20–25, 1997*. Edited by L. H. Schiffman, E. Tov, and J. C. VanderKam. Jerusalem: Israel Exploration Society, 2000.

Kuhn, Karl Georg. "Die in Palästina gefundenen hebräischen Texte und das neue Testament." ZTK 47 (1950): 192–211.

———. "The Lord's Supper and the Communal Meal at Qumran." Pages 65–93 in *The Scrolls and the New Testament*. Edited by K. Stendahl. New York: Harper, 1957.

Kümmel, Werner G. *Heilsgeschehen und Geschichte. Gesammelte Aufsätze, 1933–1964*. Edited by E. Grässer, O. Merk, and A. Fritz. MTS 3. Marburg: N. G. Elwert, 1965.

———. "Jesu Antwort an Johannes den Täufer: Ein Beispiel zum Methodenproblem in der Jesusforschung." Pages 2:177–200 in *Heilsgeschehen und Geschichte. Gesammelte Aufsätze, 1965–1977*. Edited by E. Grässer and O. Merk. 2 vols. MTS 16. Marburg: N. G. Elwert, 1965–1978.

———. *Promise and Fulfillment: The Eschatological Message of Jesus*. Translated by D. M. Barton. London: SCM Press, 1958.

Kvalbein, Hans. "Die Wunder der Endzeit: Beobachtungen zu 4Q521 und Matth 11,5f." NTS 43 (1997): 111–25.

———. "The Wonders of the End-Time: Metaphoric Language in 4Q521 and the Interpretation of Matt 11.5 par." *JSP* 18 (1998): 87–110.

Kvanvig, H. S. *Roots of Apocalyptic: The Mesopotamian Background of the Enoch Figure and of the Son of Man*. WMANT 61. Neukirchen-Vluyn: Neukirchener, 1988.

———. "The Son of Man in the Parables of Enoch." Pages 179–215 in *Enoch and the Messiah Son of Man: Revisiting the Book of Parables*. Edited by G. Boccaccini. Grand Rapids: Eerdmans, 2007.

Labahn, Michael. Review of Simon J. Joseph, *Jesus, Q, and the Dead Sea Scrolls: A Judaic Approach to Q*. *Review of Biblical Literature*, February 13, 2015. http://www.bookreviews.org/pdf/8811_9701.pdf (accessed September 28, 2015).

Lagrange, M. J. *Évangile selon Saint Luc*. Paris: Librairie Lecoffre, 1941.

Lange, Armin. "The Essene Position on Magic and Divination." Pages 377–433 in *Legal Texts and Legal Issues: Proceedings of the Second Meeting of the International Organization for Qumran Studies, Cambridge, 1995: Published in Honour of Joseph M. Baumgarten*. Edited by F. García Martínez, M. J. Bernstein, and J. Kampen. STDJ 23. Leiden: Brill, 1997.

Lasor, William S. *The Dead Sea Scrolls and the New Testament*. Grand Rapids: Eerdmans, 1972.

Laufen, Rudolf. *Die Doppelüberlieferung der Logienquelle und des Markusevangeliums*. BBB 54. Königstein and Bonn: Hanstein, 1980.

Lawlor, H. J. "Early Citations from the Book of Enoch." *Journal of Philology* 25 (1897): 164–225.

Leaney, Alfred C. *The Rule of Qumran and Its Meaning*. London: SCM Press, 1966.

Le Déaut, R. "Le Targumic Literature and New Testament Interpretation." *BTB* 4 (1974): 243–89.

Le Donne, Anthony. *The Wife of Jesus: Ancient Texts and Modern Scandals*. London: Oneworld, 2013.

Lefebvre, Jean-François. *Le jubilé biblique: Lv 25—exégèse et théologie*. OBO 194. Göttingen: Vandenhoeck & Ruprecht, 2003.

Legasse, Simon. *"Et qui est mon prochain?" Etude sur l'objet de l'agapè dans le Nouveau Testament*. LD 136. Paris: Editions du Cerf, 1989.

Lenzi, Alan. *Secrecy and the Gods: Secret Knowledge in Ancient Mesopotamia and Biblical Israel*. SAAS 19. Winona Lake, Ind.: Eisenbrauns, 2008.

Leonhardt, Jutta. *Jewish Worship in Philo of Alexandria*. TSAJ 84. Tübingen: Mohr Siebeck, 2001.

Levine, Amy-Jill. "The Earth Moved: Jesus, Sex, and Eschatology." Pages 83–97 in *Apocalypticism, Anti-Semitism and the Historical Jesus: Subtexts in Criticism*. Edited by J. S. Kloppenborg and J. Marshall. London: T&T Clark, 2005.

———. "Jesus, Divorce, and Sexuality: A Jewish Critique." Pages 113–29 in *The Historical Jesus through Catholic and Jewish Eyes*. Edited by B. F. le Beau. Harrisburg, Pa.: T&T Clark, 2000.

Levison, John R. *The Spirit in First-Century Judaism*. AGJU 29. Leiden: Brill, 1997.

Licht, Jacob. "Legs as Signs of Election." *Tarbiz* 35 (1965–1966): 18–26.

———. "Time and Eschatology in Apocalyptic Literature and in Qumran." *JJS* 16 (1965): 177–82.
Lichtenberger, Hermann. "The Dead Sea Scrolls and John the Baptist: Reflections on Josephus' Account of John the Baptist." Pages 340–46 in *The Dead Sea Scrolls: Forty Years of Research*. Edited by D. Dimant and U. Rappaport. STDJ 10. Leiden: Brill, 1992.
———. "Reflections on the History of John the Baptist's Communities." *Folia Orientalia* 25 (1988): 45–49.
Lightfoot, J. B. *Saint Paul's Epistles to the Colossians and to Philemon*. London: Macmillan, 1912.
Lim, Timothy. *The Dead Sea Scrolls: A Very Short Introduction*. New York: Oxford University Press, 2005.
Lindars, Barnabas. *Jesus Son of Man: A Fresh Examination of the Son of Man Sayings in the Gospels in the Light of Recent Research*. Grand Rapids: Eerdmans, 1984.
Liver, Jacob. "The Sons of Zadok the Priests' in the Dead Sea Sect." *RevQ* 6, no. 21 (1967): 3–32.
Loader, William R. G. *The Dead Sea Scrolls on Sexuality: Attitudes towards Sexuality in Sectarian and Related Literature at Qumran*. Grand Rapids: Eerdmans, 2009.
———. "Jesus and the Law." Pages 2745–2772 in *Handbook for the Study of the Historical Jesus*. Edited by T. Holmén and S. Porter. Leiden: Brill, 2011.
———. *Jesus' Attitude towards the Law*. Tübingen: Mohr Siebeck, 1997.
———. *Jesus' Attitude towards the Law: A Study of the Gospels*. Grand Rapids: Eerdmans, 2002.
———. *The Septuagint, Sexuality, and the New Testament: Case Studies on the Impact of the LXX in Philo and the New Testament*. Grand Rapids: Eerdmans, 2004.
Lohmeyer, Ernst. *Das Urchristentum I: Johannes der Täufer*. Göttingen: Vandenhoeck & Ruprecht, 1932.
Longenecker, Richard N. *The Christology of Early Jewish Christianity*. SBT 17. Naperville, Ill.: Allenson, 1970.
Lönnqvist, Minna, and Kenneth Lönnqvist. *Archaeology of the Hidden Qumran: The New Paradigm*. Helsinki: Helsinki University Press, 2002.
Lüdemann, Gerd. *Jesus after 2000 Years: What He Really Said and Did*. Amherst, N.Y.: Prometheus, 2001.
Lührmann, Dieter. "Liebet eure Feinde (Lk 6,27-36/Mt 5,39-48)." *ZTK* 69 (1972): 412–38.
Maccoby, Hyam. *Early Rabbinic Writings*. Cambridge: Cambridge University Press, 1988.
Magen, Yizhak, and Yuval Peleg. *The Qumran Excavations 1993–2004: Preliminary Report*. JSP 6. Jerusalem: Israel Antiquities Authority, 2007.
Magness, Jodi. *The Archaeology of Qumran and the Dead Sea Scrolls*. Grand Rapids: Eerdmans, 2002.
———. "Communal Meals and Sacred Space at Qumran." Pages 15–28 in *Shaping Community: The Art and Archaeology of Monasticism: Papers from a Symposium Held at the Frederick R. Weisman Museum, University of Minnesota, March 10-12,*

2000. Edited by S. McNally. British Archaeological Reports International Series 941. Oxford: Archaeopress, 2001.

———. "Digital Qumran: Virtual Reality or Virtual Fantasy?" Pages 275–84 in *A Teacher for All Generations: Essays in Honor of James C. VanderKam*. Edited by E. F. Mason et al. JSJSup 153. Leiden: Brill, 2012.

———. "The Essenes and the Qumran Settlement." Review of Joan Taylor, *The Essenes, the Scrolls, and the Dead Sea*. Marginalia, May 1, 2014. http://marginalia.lareviewofbooks.org/the-essenes-and-the-qumran-settlement-by-jodi-magness/ (accessed April 23, 2016).

———. "The Qumran Digital Model: A Response." *NEA* 72 (2009): 42–45.

———. "Qumran: Not a Country Villa." *BAR* 22, no. 6 (1996): 38, 40–47, 72–73.

———. "A Response to D. Stacey, 'Some Archaeological Observations on the Aqueducts of Qumran.'" *DSD* 14, no. 2 (2007): 244–53.

———. "'They Shall See the Glory of the Lord' (Isa 35:2): Eschatological Purity at Qumran and in Jesus' Movement." Pages 179–94 in *Q in Context II: Social Setting and Archeological Background of the Sayings Source*. Edited by M. Tiwald. BBB 173. Bonn: Bonn University Press, 2015.

———. "A Villa at Khirbet Qumran?" *RevQ* 16 (1994): 397–419.

Maier, Johann. "Die Mittel der Darstellung der Geschichte Israels in Texten aus Qumran und ähnlichen Schriften: Zwischen Protologie und Eschatologie." Pages 19–42 in *Q in Context I: The Separation between the Just and the Unjust in Early Judaism and in the Sayings Source*. Edited by M. Tiwald. BBB 172. Bonn: Bonn University Press, 2015.

Malina, Bruce. "What Is Prayer." *Bible Today* 18 (1980): 214–20.

Manson, T. W. *The Sayings of Jesus*. London: SCM Press, 1949.

Marcus, Joel. "John the Baptist and Jesus." Pages 179–97 in *When Judaism and Christianity Began: Essays in Memory of Anthony J. Saldarini*. Edited by A. J. Avery-Peck et al. JSJSup 85. Leiden: Brill, 2004.

Marcus, Ralph. "Pharisees, Essenes and Gnostics." *JBL* 63 (1954): 157–61.

Marguerat, Daniel. "Historical Jesus and Christ of Faith: A Relevant Dichotomy?" Pages 429–47 in *Jesus—Gestalt und Gestaltungen: Rezeption des Galiläers in Wissenschaft, Kirche und Gesellschaft. FS Gerd Theißen*. Edited by P. von Gemünden, D. G. Horrell, and M. Küchler. NTOASUNT 100. Göttingen: Vandenhoeck & Ruprecht, 2013.

Marshall, I. H. *The Gospel of Luke: A Commentary on the Greek New Testament*. NIGTC. Grand Rapids: Paternoster, 1978.

Martin, Dale B. "Jesus in Jerusalem: Armed and Not Dangerous." *JSNT* 37, no. 1 (2014): 3–24.

Marx, Alfred. "Les racines du célibat essénien." *RevQ* 7 (1971): 323–42.

Mason, Steve. "Essenes and Lurking Spartans in Josephus' Judean War: From Story to History." Pages 219–61 in *Making History: Josephus and Historical Method*. Edited by Z. Rodgers. JSJ 110. Leiden: Brill, 2007.

———. *Flavius Josephus on the Pharisees: A Composition-Critical Study*. Leiden: Brill, 1991.

———. "The Historical Problem of the Essenes." Pages 201–51 in *Celebrating the Dead Sea Scrolls: A Canadian Contribution*. Edited by P. W. Flint, J. Duhaime, and K. S. Baek. SBLEJL 30. Atlanta: Society of Biblical Literature, 2011.

———. *Josephus, Judea, and Christian Origins: Methods and Categories*. Peabody, Mass.: Hendrickson, 2009.

———. "Josephus' Pharisees: The Philosophy." Pages 41–66 in *In Quest of the Historical Pharisees*. Edited by J. Neusner and B. D. Chilton. Waco, Tex: Baylor University Press, 2007.

———. "Was Josephus a Pharisee? A Re-examination of *Life* 10–12." *JJS* 40 (1989): 31–45.

———. "What Josephus Says about the Essenes in His *Judean War*." Pages 434–67 in *Text and Artifact in the Religions of Mediterranean Antiquity: Essays in Honour of Peter Richardson*. Edited by S. G. Wilson and M. Desjardins. Waterloo: Wilfrid Laurier University Press, 2000.

Matthews, Kenneth A. "John, Jesus and the Essenes: Trouble at the Temple." *Criswell Theological Review* 3 (1988): 101–26.

Mayer-Haas, Andrea J. *"Geschenk aus Gottes Schatzkammer" (bShab 10b): Jesus und der Sabbat im Spiegel der neutestamentlichen Schriften*. NTAbh NS 43. Münster: Aschendorff, 2003.

McCartney, Dan. "*Ecce Homo*: The Coming of the Kingdom as the Restoration of Human Vicegerency." *WTJ* 56 (1994): 1–21.

McCasland, S. V. "The Way." *JBL* 77 (1958): 222–30.

McDonald, J. Ian H. "What Did You Go Out to See? John the Baptist, the Scrolls and Late Second Temple Judaism." Pages 53–64 in *The Dead Sea Scrolls in Their Historical Context*. Edited by T. H. Lim. Edinburgh: T&T Clark, 2000.

Meadors, Edward P. *Jesus the Messianic Herald of Salvation*. WUNT 72. Tübingen: Mohr Siebeck, 1995.

Mearns, Christopher L. "The Son of Man Trajectory and Eschatological Development." *ExpTim* 97 (1985/1986): 8–12.

Meeks, Wayne A. *The First Urban Christians: The Social World of the Apostle Paul*. New Haven: Yale University Press, 1983.

Meier, John P. "Basic Methodology in the Quest for the Historical Jesus." Pages 291–331 in *How to Study the Historical Jesus*. Edited by T. Holmén and S. E. Porter. Vol. 1 of *Handbook for the Study of the Historical Jesus*. Leiden: Brill, 2011.

———. "The Historical Jesus and the Historical Herodians." *JBL* 119 (2000): 740–46.

———. "The Historical Jesus and the Historical Law: Some Problems within the Problem." *CBQ* 65 (2003): 52–79.

———. "The Historical Jesus and the Plucking of the Grain on the Sabbath." *CBQ* 66 (2004): 561–81.

———. "Is There *Halaka* (the Noun) at Qumran?" *JBL* 122 (2003): 150–55.

———. *A Marginal Jew: Rethinking the Historical Jesus*. Vol. 2, *Mentor, Message, and Miracles*. ABRL. New York: Doubleday, 1994.

———. *A Marginal Jew: Rethinking the Historical Jesus*. Vol. 3, *Companions and Competitors*. ABRL. New York: Doubleday, 2001.
———. *A Marginal Jew: Rethinking the Historical Jesus*. Vol. 4, *Law and Love*. ABRL. New Haven: Yale University Press, 2009.
———. "The Present State of the 'Third Quest' for the Historical Jesus: Loss and Gain." *Biblica* 80 (1999): 459–87, 483.
Mendels, Doron. "Hellenistic Utopia and the Essenes." *HTR* 72, nos. 3–4 (1979): 207–22.
Mermelstein, Ari. *Creation, Covenant, and the Beginnings of Judaism: Reconceiving Historical Time in the Second Temple Period*. JSJSup 168. Leiden: Brill, 2014.
Metso, Sarianna. "Methodological Problems in Reconstructing History from Rule Texts Found at Qumran." *DSD* 11 (2004): 315–35.
———. *The Serekh Texts*. LSTS 62. CQS 9. London: T&T Clark, 2007.
———. *The Textual Development of the Community Rule*. Leiden: Brill, 1997.
———. "Whom Does the Term *Yahad* Identify?" Pages 213–35 in *Biblical Traditions in Transmission: Essays in Honour of Michael A. Knibb*. Edited by C. Hempel and J. M. Lieu. Leiden: Brill, 2006.
Metzger, Bruce M. *A Textual Commentary on the Greek New Testament*. 3rd ed. New York: United Bible Societies, 1975.
Meurois-Givaudan, Anne, and Daniel Meurois-Givaudan. *The Way of the Essenes: Christ's Hidden Life Remembered*. Rochester, Vt.: Destiny, 1993.
Meyer, Ben F. "Appointed Deeds, Appointed Doer: Jesus and the Scriptures." Pages 162–74 in *Authenticating the Activities of Jesus*. Edited by B. Chilton and C. A. Evans. NTTS 28, no. 2. Leiden: Brill, 1999.
———. "Jesus' Scenario of the Future." *Drev* 109 (1991): 1–15.
Milgrom, J. "The Burning of Incense in the Time of the Second Temple" (Hebrew). Pages 330–34 in *Studies in Bible and the History of Israel: Festschrift for Ben-Zion Luria*. Jerusalem: Kiryat-Sepher, 1979.
———. *Pesharim, Other Commentaries, and Related Documents*. PTSDSSP 6B. Louisville, Ky.: Westminster John Knox, 2002.
Milik, J. T. *The Books of Enoch: Aramaic Fragments of Qumrân Cave 4*. Oxford: Clarendon, 1976.
———. "Milkî-Sedeq et Milkî-Reš' dans les anciens écrits juifs et chrétiens." *JJS* 23 (1972): 95–112, 124–26.
———. *Ten Years of Discovery in the Wilderness of Judaea*. Translated by John Strugnell. 2nd ed. London: SCM Press, 1963.
Miller, Merrill P. "The Function of Isa 61:1-2 in 11QMelchizedek." *JBL* 88, no. 4 (1969): 467–69.
Mimouni, Simon C. "Qui sont les Jesséens dans la notice 29 du Panarion d'Epiphane de Salamine?" *NovT* 43 (2001): 264–99.
Miner, Daniel F. "A Suggested Reading for 11QMelchizedek 17." *JSJ* 2 (1971): 144–48.

Moehring, Horst R. "Josephus on the Marriage Customs of the Essenes." Pages 120–27 in *Early Christian Origins*. Edited by A. P. Wikgren. Chicago: Quadrangle, 1961.

Mowinckel, Sigmund. *He That Cometh*. Translated by G. W. Anderson. New York: Abingdon, 1954.

Mowry, Lucetta. *The Dead Sea Scrolls and the Early Church*. Chicago: University of Chicago Press, 1962.

Mroczek, Eva. *The Literary Imagination in Jewish Antiquity*. New York: Oxford University Press, 2016.

Mueller, J. R. "The Temple Scroll and the Gospel Divorce Texts." *RQ* 10 (1980): 247–56.

Müller, G. H. *Zur Synopse: Untersuchung über die Arbeitsweise des Lk und Mt und ihr Quellen*. FRLANT 11. Göttingen: Vandenhoeck & Ruprecht, 1908.

Müller, Ulrich. *Messias und Menschensohn in jüdischen Apokalypsen und in der Offenbarung des Johannes*. Gütersloh: Mohn, 1972.

Murphy, Catherine M. *Wealth in the Dead Sea Scrolls and the Qumran Community*. STDJ 40. Leiden: Brill, 2002.

Murphy-O'Connor, Jerome. "An Essene Missionary Document? CD II, 4-VI, 1." *RB* 77 (1970): 201–229.

———. "The Essenes and their History." *RB* 81 (1974): 219–23.

———. "John the Baptist and Jesus: History and Hypothesis." *NTS* 36 (1990): 359–74.

———, ed. *Paul and Qumran: Studies in New Testament Exegesis*. Chicago: Priory, 1968.

———. "Qumran and the New Testament." Pages 55–71 in *The New Testament and Its Modern Interpreters*. Edited by J. Epp and G. W. MacRae. Atlanta: Scholars, 1989.

Najman, Hindy. *Seconding Sinai: The Development of Mosaic Discourse in Second Temple Judaism*. JSJSup 77. Leiden: Brill, 2004.

Neirynck, Frans. "Luke 14,1-6. Lukan Composition and Q Saying." Pages 243–63 in *Der Treue Gottes Trauen: Festschrift für Gerhard Schneider*. Edited by C. Bussmann and W. Radl. Freiburg: Herder, 1991.

Neufeld, Thomas R. Yoder. *Killing Enmity: Violence and the New Testament*. Grand Rapids: Baker Academic, 2011.

Neusner, Jacob. *Judaism's Story of Creation: Scripture, Halakhah, Aggadah*. BRLAJ 3. Leiden: Brill, 2000.

———. *The Rabbinic Traditions about the Pharisees before 70*. Leiden: Brill, 1971.

Neusner, Jacob, and B. Chilton, eds. *In Quest of the Historical Pharisees*. Waco, Tex.: Baylor University Press, 2007.

Neusner, Jacob, and William Scott Green, eds. *Judaisms and Their Messiahs at the Turn of the Christian Era*. New York: Cambridge University Press, 1987.

Newman, Hillel. *Proximity to Power and Jewish Sectarian Groups of the Ancient Period: A Review of Lifestyle, Values, and Halacha in the Pharisees, Sadducees, Essenes, and Qumran*. BRLJ 25. Leiden: Brill, 2006.

Newman, Judith Hood. *Praying by the Book: The Scripturalization of Prayer in Second Temple Judaism*. Atlanta: Scholars, 1999.

Newsom, Carol A. *The Self as Symbolic Space: Constructing Identity and Community at Qumran*. STDJ 52. Leiden: Brill, 2004.

———. *Songs of the Sabbath Sacrifice: A Critical Edition*. Atlanta: Scholars, 1985.

Newton, Michael. *The Concept of Purity at Qumran and in the Letters of Paul*. SNTSMS 53. Cambridge: Cambridge University Press, 1985.

Nickelsburg, George W. E. *1 Enoch: A Commentary on the Book of 1 Enoch*. Hermeneia. Philadelphia: Fortress, 2001.

———. *Ancient Judaism and Christian Origins: Diversity, Continuity, and Transformation*. Minneapolis: Fortress, 2003.

———. "The Books of Enoch at Qumran: What We Know and What We Need to Think About." Pages 99–113 in *Antikes Judentum und Frühes Christentum: Festschrift für Hartmut Stegemann zum 65. Geburtstag*. Edited by B. Kollmann, W. Reinbold, and A. Steudel. BZNW 97. Berlin: de Gruyter, 1999.

———. *Jewish Literature between the Bible and the Mishnah: A Historical and Literary Introduction*. Philadelphia: Fortress, 1981.

———. "Son of Man." *ABD* 6 (1992): 138–49.

———. "Wisdom and Apocalypticism in Early Judaism: Some Points for Discussion." Pages 17–37 in *Conflicted Boundaries in Wisdom and Apocalypticism*. Edited by B. G. Wright III and L. M. Wills. SBLSS 35. Atlanta: Society of Biblical Literature, 2005.

Nickelsburg, George W. E. and James C. VanderKam. *1 Enoch: A New Translation*. Minneapolis: Fortress, 2004.

———. *1 Enoch 2: A Commentary on the Book of 1 Enoch, Chapters 37–82*. Minneapolis: Fortress, 2012.

Niebuhr, Karl Wilhelm. "4Q521, 2 II—Ein eschatologischer Psalm." Pages 151–68 in *Mogilany 1995: Papers on the Dead Sea Scrolls Offered in Memory of Aleksy Klawek*. Edited by Z. J. Kapera. Krakow: Enigma, 1996.

———. "Die Werke des eschatologischen Freudenboten (4Q521 und die Jesusüberlieferung)." Pages 637–46 in *The Scriptures in the Gospels*. Edited by C. M. Tuckett. BETL 131. Leuven: Leuven University Press, 1997.

Nissen, A. *Gott und der Nächste im antiken Judentum: Untersuchungen zum Doppelgebot der Liebe*. WUNT 15. Tübingen: Mohr Siebeck, 1974.

Nitzan, Bilhah. "Eschatological Motives in Qumran Literature: The Messianic Concept." Pages 132–51 in *Eschatology in the Bible and in Jewish and Christian Tradition*. Edited by H. G. Reventlow. Sheffield: Sheffield Academic, 1997.

———. *Qumran Prayer and Religious Poetry*. Leiden: Brill, 1994.

Nodet, Étienne. "*Asidaioi* and Essenes." Pages 63–88 in *Flores Florentino: Dead Sea Scrolls and Other Early Jewish Studies in Honour of Florentino García Martínez*. Edited by A. Hilhorst, É. Puech, and E. Tigchelaar. JSJSup 122. Leiden: Brill, 2007.

Nolland, John. "A Misleading Statement of the Essene Attitude to the Temple (Josephus, *Antiquities*, XVIII, 1, 5, 19)." *RevQ* 9, no. 4 (1978): 555–62.

North, Robert G. *Sociology of the Biblical Jubilee*. AnBib 4. Rome: Pontificio Instituto Biblico, 1954.
Novakovic, Lidija. "4Q521: The Works of the Messiah or the Signs of the Messianic Time?" Pages 208–31 in *Qumran Studies: New Approaches, New Questions*. Edited by M. T. Davis and B. A. Strawn. Grand Rapids: Eerdmans, 2007.
———. *Messiah, the Healer of the Sick: A Study of Jesus as the Son of David in the Gospel of Matthew*. WUNT 2/70. Tübingen: Mohr Siebeck, 2003.
Novenson, Matthew V. *Christ Among the Messiahs: Christ Language in Paul and Messiah Language in Ancient Judaism*. New York: Oxford University Press, 2012.
O'Callaghan, José. *Los papiros griegos de la cueva 7 de Qumrân*. BAC 353. Madrid: Editorial católica, 1974.
Och, Bernard. "Creation and Redemption: Toward a Theology of Creation." Pages 331–50 in *Cult and Cosmos: Tilting toward a Temple-Centered Theology*. Edited by L. M. Morales. BTS 18. Leuven: Peeters, 2014.
O'Collins, G., and D. Kendall. "On Reissuing Venturini." *Gregorianum* 75 (1994): 241–65.
Oegema, Gerbern S. *The Anointed and His People: Messianic Expectations from the Maccabees to Bar Kochba*. JSPSup 27. Sheffield: Sheffield Academic, 1998.
Oesterreicher, J. M. "The Community of Qumran." Pages 91–134 in *The Bridge*. New York: Pantheon Books, 1956.
Olson, Daniel C. *A New Reading of the Animal Apocalypse of 1 Enoch: "All Nations Shall Be Blessed": With a New Translation and Commentary*. Studia in Veteris Testamenti Pseudepigrapha 24. Leiden: Brill, 2013.
Ouseley, Gideon Jasper. *The Gospel of the Holy Twelve*. Repr. ed. London: Edson, 1923 [1901].
Pedersen, Johs. "Zur Erklärung der eschatologischen Visionen Henochs." *Islamica* 2 (1926): 416–29.
Penner, Jeremy. *Patterns of Daily Prayer in Second Temple Period Judaism*. STDJ 104. Leiden: Brill, 2012.
Petersen, D. *Late Israelite Prophecy*. SBLMS 23. Missoula, Mont.: Scholars, 1977.
Piper, John. *"Love Your Enemies": Jesus' Love Command in the Synoptic Gospels and in the Early Paraenesis: A History of the Tradition and Interpretation of Its Uses*. SNTSMS 38. Cambridge: Cambridge University Press, 1979.
Piper, Ronald A. "The Language of Violence and the Aphoristic Sayings in Q." Pages 53–72 in *Conflict and Invention: Literary, Rhetorical, and Social Studies on the Sayings Gospel Q*. Edited by J. S. Kloppenborg. Valley Forge, Pa.: Trinity International, 1995.
Pitre, Brant. *Jesus and the Last Supper*. Grand Rapids: Eerdmans, 2015.
Pixner, Bargil. "Archäologische Beobachtungen zum Jerusalemer Essener-Viertel und zur Urgemeinde." Pages 89–113 in *Christen und Christliches in Qumran?* Edited by B. Mayer. ES 32. Regensburg: F. Pustet, 1992.
———. "Das Essener-Quarter in Jerusalem." Pages 180–207 in *Wege des Messias und Stätten der Urkirche*. Edited by R. Riesner. Giessen: Brunnen, 1991.

———. "Das letzte Abendmahl Jesu." Pages 219–28 in *Wege des Messias und Stätten der Urkirche*. Edited by R. Riesner. Giessen: Brunnen, 1991.

———. "An Essene Quarter on Mount Zion?" Pages 245–86 in *Studi Archeologici*. Edited by G. C. Bittini. Vol. 1 of *Studia Hierosolymitana in onore dei P. Bellarmino Bagatti*. SBFCM 22. Jerusalem: Franciscan Printing, 1976.

———. "Essener-Viertel und Urgemeinde." Pages 327–34 in *Wege des Messias und Stätten der Urkirche*. Edited by R. Riesner. Giessen: Brunnen, 1991.

———. "Jerusalem's Essene Gateway: Where the Community Lived in Jesus' Time." *BAR* 23 (1997): 23–31.

Pixner, Bargil, Doron Chen, and Shlomo Margalit. "Mount Zion: The Gate of the Essenes Reexcavated." *Zeitschrift des deutschen Palästina Vereins* 105 (1989): 85–95.

Polag, A. *Die Christologie der Logienquelle*. WMANT 45. Neukirchen-Vluyn: Neukirchener, 1977.

———. *Fragmenta Q: Textheft zur Logienquelle*. Neukirchen-Vluyn: Neukirchener, 1979.

Pomykala, Kenneth E. *The Davidic Dynasty Tradition in Early Judaism: Its History and Significance for Messianism*. SBLEJL 7. Atlanta: Scholars, 1995.

Powery, E. B. *Jesus Reads Scripture: The Function of Jesus' Use of Scripture in the Synoptic Gospels*. Leiden: Brill, 2003.

Prideaux, Humphrey. *The Old and New Testaments Connected in the History of Jews & Neighboring Nations, from the Declensions of the Kingdoms of Israel and Judah to the Time of Christ*. 16th ed. 4 vols. London: W. Baynes, 1808 [1717].

Priest, John F. "The Messiah and the Meal in 1QSa." *JBL* 82 (1963): 95–100.

Puech, Émile. "246. 4QApocryphe de Daniel ar." Pages 165–84 in *Qumran Cave 4 XVII. Parabiblical Texts, Part 3*. Edited by G. Brooke et al. Oxford: Clarendon, 1996.

———. "4Q525 et les péricopes des béatitudes en Ben Sira et Matthieu." *RB* 98 (1991): 80–106.

———. "Fragments d'un apocryphe de Lévi et le personnage eschatologie, 4Q Test-Lévi (c–d[?]) et 4QAJa." Pages 2:449–501 in *The Madrid Qumran Congress: Proceedings of the International Congress on the Dead Sea Scrolls, Madrid, 18–21 March, 1991*. Edited by J. Trebolle Barrera and L. Vegas Montaner. 2 vols. Leiden: Brill, 1992.

———. "Messianism, Resurrection, and Eschatology at Qumran and in the New Testament." Pages 235–56 in *The Community of the Renewed Covenant: The Notre Dame Symposium on the Dead Sea Scrolls*. Edited by E. Ulrich and J. VanderKam. Notre Dame, Ind.: University of Notre Dame Press, 1994.

———. "Notes sur le manuscrit de XIMelkîsédeq." *RevQ* 12 (1987): 483–513.

———. "Some Remarks on 4Q246 and 4Q521 and Qumran Messianism." Pages 545–65 in *The Provo International Conference on the Dead Sea Scrolls: Technological Innovations, New Texts, and Reformulated Issues*. Edited by D. W. Parry and E. Ulrich. STDJ 30. Leiden: Brill, 1999.

———. "Une Apocalypse Messianique (4Q521)." *RevQ* 15 (1992): 475–519.
———. "Un Hymne essénien en partie retrouvé et les Béatitudes. 1QH V 12–VI 18 (=col. XIII–XIV 7) et 4QBéat." *RevQ* 13 (1988): 59–88.
Qimron, Elisha. "Celibacy in the Dead Sea Scrolls and the Two Kinds of Sectarians." Pages 1:287–94 in *The Madrid Qumran Congress*. Edited by J. Trebolle Barrera and L. Vegas Montaner. 2 vols. STDJ 11. Leiden: Brill, 1992.
Qimron, E., and J. Sturgnell, eds. *Qumran Cave 4, V, Miqsat Ma'aśe Ha-Torah*. DJD 10. Oxford: Clarendon, 1994.
Rabin, Ira, Oliver Hahn, Timo Wolff, and Admir Masic. "On the Origin of the Ink of the Thanksgiving Scroll (1QHodayota)." *DSD* 16, no. 1 (2009): 97–106.
Rabinowitz, Isaac. "A Reconsideration of Damascus." *JBL* 73 (1954): 11–35.
Rajak, Tessa. "Ciò che Flavio Giuseppe Vide: Josephus and the Essenes." Pages 141–60 in *Josephus and the History of the Greco-Roman Period: Essays in Memory of Morton Smith*. Edited by F. Parente and J. Sievers. Leiden: Brill, 1994.
Randlinger, Stephan. *Die Feindesliebe nach dem natürlichen und positiven Sittengesetz: Eine historisch-ethische Studie*. Paderborn: F. Schöningh, 1906.
Reed, Annette Yoshiko. *Fallen Angels and the History of Judaism and Christianity: The Reception of Enochic Literature*. New York: Cambridge University Press, 2005.
Reed, Jonathan L. *Archaeology and the Galilean Jesus: A Re-examination of the Evidence*. Harrisburg, Pa.: Trinity International, 2000.
Reeves, John C. "Complicating the Notion of an 'Enochic Judaism.'" Pages 373–83 in *Enoch and Qumran Origins: New Light on a Forgotten Connection*. Edited by G. Boccaccini. Grand Rapids: Eerdmans, 2005,
Regeffe, A. *La Secte des Esséniens: Essai critique sur son organization, sa doctrine, son origine*. Lyons: Emmanuel Vitte, 1898.
Regev, Eyal. "Abominated Temple and a Holy Community: The Formation of the Notions of Purity and Impurity in Qumran." *DSD* 10, no. 2 (2003): 245–49.
———. "Cherchez les femmes: Were the *yahad* Celibates?" *DSD* 15 (2008): 253–84.
———. *Sectarianism in Qumran: A Cross-Cultural Perspective*. RS 45. New York: de Gruyter, 2007.
———. "The 'Yahad' and the 'Damascus Covenant': Structure, Organization, and Relationship." *RevQ* 21 (2003): 233–62.
Reinach, Théodore. *Textes d'auteurs grecs et romains relatifs au Judäisme*. Paris: Ernest Laroux, 1895.
Reiser, Marius. *Jesus and Judgment*. Minneapolis: Fortress, 1997.
Renan, Ernest. *Histoire du Peuple d'Israël*. Paris: Calman-Lévy, 1893.
Reumann, John. "The Quest for the Historical Baptist." Pages 181–99 in *Understanding the Sacred Text: Essays in Honor of Morton S. Enslin on the Hebrew Bible and Christian Beginnings*. Edited by J. Reumann. Valley Forge, Pa.: Judson Press, 1972.
Reventlow, Henning Graf. "The Eschatologization of the Prophetic Books: A Comparative Study." Pages 169–88 in *Eschatology in the Bible and in Jewish and Christian Tradition*. Edited by H. G. Reventlow. Sheffield: Sheffield Academic, 1997.

Riaud, Jean. "Les Thérapeutes d'Alexandrie dans la tradition et dans la recherche critique jusqu'aux découvertes de Qumran." Pages 1189–1295 in *ANRW* 2.20.2. Berlin: de Gruyter, 1987.

Richardson, H. Neil. "Some Notes on 1QSa." *JBL* 76 (1957): 108–22.

Riesner, Rainer. "Das Jerusalemer Essenerviertel: Antwort auf einige Einwände." Pages 179–86 in *Intertestamental Essays in Honour of Jozef Tadeusz Milik*. Edited by Z. J. Kapera. QM6. Krakow: Enigma, 1992.

———. "Essene Gate." Pages 2:618–19 in *ABD*. Edited by D. N. Freedman, Gary A. Herion, David F. Graf, and John David Pleins. 3 vols. New York: Doubleday, 1992.

———. "Essener und Urkirche in Jerusalem." Pages 139–55 in *Christen und Christliches in Qumran?* Edited by B. Mayer. ESNF 32. Regensburg: Friedrich Pustet, 1992.

———. "Jesus, the Primitive Community, and the Essene Quarter of Jerusalem." Pages 198–234 in *Jesus and the Dead Sea Scrolls*. Edited by J. H. Charlesworth. New York: Doubleday, 1991.

———. "Josephus' Gate of the Essenes in Modern Discussion." *Zeitschrift des deutschen Palästina Vereins* 105 (1989): 105–9.

Riggs, John W. "The Sacred Food of Didache 9–10 and Second-Century Ecclesiologies." Pages 256–83 in *The Didache in Context: Essays on Its Text, History, and Transmission*. Edited by C. N. Jefford. NovTSup 77. Leiden: Brill, 1995.

Ringe, Sharon H. "The Jubilee Proclamation in the Ministry and Teachings of Jesus: A Tradition-Critical Study in the Synoptic Gospels and Acts." Ph.D. diss., Union Theological Seminary, 1981.

Ringgren, H. *The Faith of Qumran: Theology of the Dead Sea Scrolls*. Translated by E. T. Sander. New York: Crossroad, 1995.

Rivkin, E. "Defining the Pharisees: The Tannaitic Sources." *HUCA* 43 (1972): 205–40.

Roberts, Colin H. "On Some Presumed Papyrus Fragments of the New Testament from Qumran." *JTS* 23 (1972): 446–47.

Robinson, James M. "The International Q Project Work Session 16 November 1991." *JBL* 111 (1992): 506.

———. "The Sayings Gospel Q." Rel 484. Unpublished class notes. Claremont Graduate School, Fall 1992.

———. *The Sayings Gospel Q: Collected Essays*. Edited by C. Heil and J. Verheyden. BETL 189. Leuven: Leuven University Press, 2005.

Robinson, James M., Paul Hoffmann, and John S. Kloppenborg, eds. *The Critical Edition of Q: A Synopsis including the Gospels of Matthew and Luke, Mark and Thomas with English, German, and French Translations of Q and Thomas*. Minneapolis: Fortress, 2000.

Robinson, John A. "The Baptism of John and the Qumran Community." *HTS* 50 (1957): 175–91.

Rofé, Alexander. "Revealed Wisdom: From the Bible to Qumran." Pages 1–11 in *Sapiential Perspectives: Wisdom Literature in Light of the Dead Sea Scrolls: Proceedings* of the Sixth International Symposium of the Orion Center for the Study of the Dead Sea Scrolls and Associated Literature, 20–22 May, 2001. Edited by J. J. Collins, G. E. Sterling, and R. A. Clements. STDJ 51. Leiden: Brill, 2004.

Rolland, P. *Les Premiers Évangiles*. LD 116. Paris: Les Éditions du Cerf, 1984.

Rollens, Sarah E. Review of Simon J. Joseph, *The Nonviolent Messiah: Jesus, Q, and the Enochic Tradition*. RBL, June 2015. http://www.bookreviews.org/pdf/9811_10841.pdf (accessed January 3, 2016).

Roloff, J. "Jesus von Nazareth." *RGG* 4 (2001): 463–67.

Rost, Leonard. "Zum Buch der Kriege der Söhne des Lichtes gegen die Söhne der Finsternis." *TLZ* 80 (1955): 205–8.

Roth, Cecil. *The Historical Background of the Dead Sea Scrolls*. Oxford: Blackwell, 1958.

———. "Why the Qumran Sect Cannot Have Been Essenes." *RevQ* 3 (1959): 417–22.

Rothschild, Clare K. Review of Simon J. Joseph, *Jesus, Q, and the Dead Sea Scrolls*. *DSD* 22, no. 1 (2015): 129–31.

Rowland, Christopher. "Apocalypticism: The Disclosure of Heavenly Knowledge." Pages 13–31 in *The Mystery of God: Early Jewish Mysticism and the New Testament*. Edited by C. Rowland and C. R. A. Morray-Jones. Compendia Rerum Iudaicarum ad Novum Testamentum 12. Leiden: Brill, 2009.

———. *Christian Origins: From Messianic Movement to Christian Religion*. Minneapolis: Augsburg, 1985.

———. "Enoch in Jewish and Early Christian Tradition." Pages 33–61 in *The Mystery of God: Early Jewish Mysticism and the New Testament*. Edited by C. Rowland and C. R. A. Morray-Jones. Compendia Rerum Iudaicarum ad Novum Testamentum 12. Leiden: Brill, 2009.

———. *The Open Heaven: A Study in Apocalyptic in Judaism and Early Christianity*. New York: Crossroad, 1992.

Sacchi, Paolo. *Jewish Apocalyptic and Its History*. Translated by William J. Short. JSPSup 20. Sheffield: Sheffield Academic, 1990.

———. "Qumran e la datazione del Libro delle Parabole di Enoc." *Henoch* 25 (2003): 149–66.

Saldarini, Anthony J. "Asceticism and the Gospel of Matthew." Pages 11–27 in *Asceticism and the New Testament*. Edited by V. L. Wimbush and L. E. Vaage. New York: Routledge, 1999.

———. *Pharisees, Scribes and Sadducees in Palestinian Society: A Sociological Approach*. Wilmington: Michael Glazier, 1998.

Sanders, E. P. "The Dead Sea Sect and Other Jews: Commonalities, Overlaps and Differences." Pages 7–43 in *The Dead Sea Scrolls in Their Historical Context*. Edited by T. H. Lim, L. W. Hurtado, A. G. Auld, and A. J. Edinburgh: T&T Clark, 2001.

———. *The Historical Figure of Jesus*. London: Penguin, 1993.

———. *Jesus and Judaism*. Philadelphia: Fortress, 1985.

———. *Paul and Palestinian Judaism: A Comparison of Patterns of Religion*. Philadelphia: Fortress, 1977.

———. "The Question of the Uniqueness in the Teaching of Jesus." The Ethel M. Wood Lecture, February 15, 1990. University of London, 1990.

Sanders, James A. "From Isaiah 61 to Luke 4." Pages 1:75–106 in *Christianity, Judaism and Other Greco-Roman Cults: Studies for Morton Smith at Sixty*. Edited by J. Neusner. Leiden: Brill, 1975.

———. "Isaiah in Luke." Pages 75–85 in *Interpreting the Prophets*. Edited by J. L. Mays and P. J. Achtemeier. Philadelphia: Fortress, 1987.

———. "The Old Testament in 11QMelchizedek." *Janes* 5 (1973): 373–82.

———. "Sins, Debts, and Jubilee Release." Pages 84–92 in *Luke and Scripture: The Function of Sacred Tradition in Luke-Acts*. Edited by C. A. Evans and J. A. Sanders. Minneapolis: Fortress, 1993.

Sandmel, Samuel. *Judaism and Christian Beginnings*. New York: Oxford University Press, 1978.

———. "Parallelomania." *JBL* 81 (1962): 1–13.

Schäfer, Peter. "Die Torah der Messianischen Zeit." *ZNW* 65 (1974): 27–42.

———. "The Jew Who Would Be God." Review of Daniel Boyarin, *The Jewish Gospels: The Story of the Jewish Christ*. New Republic, May 18, 2012. https://newrepublic.com/article/103373/jewish-gospels-christ-boyarin (accessed April 22, 2016).

Schalit, Abraham. *Namenwörterbuch zu Flavius Josephus*. Leiden: Brill, 1968.

Schattner-Rieser, Ursula. "Das Aramäische zur Zeit Jesu, 'ABBA!,' und das Vaterunser: Reflexionen zur Muttersprache Jesu anhand der Texte von Qumran und der frühen Targumim." Pages 81–144 in *Jesus, Paulus und die Texte vom Toten Meer*. WUNT 2/390. Edited by J. Frey and E. E. Popkes. Tübingen: Mohr Siebeck, 2015.

Schenk, W. *Synopse zur Redenquelle der Evangelien: Q-Synopse und Rekonstruktion in deuscher Übersetzung mit kurzen Erläuterungen*. Düsseldorf: Patmos, 1981.

Schiffman, Lawrence H. "Community without Temple: The Qumran Community's Withdrawal from the Jerusalem Temple." Pages 267–84 in *Gemeinde ohne Tempel–Community without Temple: Zur Substituierung und Transformation des Jerusalemer Tempels und seines Kultes im Alten Testament, antiken Judentum und fruhen Christentum*. Edited by B. Ego et al. WUNT 118. Tübingen: Mohr Siebeck, 1999.

———. *The Courtyards of the House of the Lord: Studies on the Temple Scroll*. STDJ 75. Leiden: Brill, 2008.

———. "The Dead Sea Scrolls and Rabbinic *Halakhah*." Pages 3–24 in *The Dead Sea Scrolls as Background to Postbiblical Judaism and Early Christianity: Papers from an International Conference at St. Andrews in 2001*. Edited by J. R. Davila. STDJ 46. Leiden: Brill, 2003.

———. *The Eschatological Community of the Dead Sea Scrolls: A Study of the Rule of the Congregation*. SBLMS 38. Atlanta: Scholars, 1989.

———. "Halakhah and Sectarianism in the Dead Sea Scrolls." Pages 123–42 in *The Dead Sea Scrolls in their Historical Context*. Edited by T. H. Lim with L. W. Hurtado, A. Graeme Auld, and A. Jack. New York: T&T Clark, 2000.

———. *The Halakhah at Qumran.* SJLA 16. Leiden: Brill, 1975.

———. "Jewish Law at Qumran." Pages 85–88 in *The Judaism of Qumran: A Systemic Reading of the Dead Sea Scrolls.* Vol. 1, *Theory of Israel.* JLA 5/1. HOS 56. Leiden: Brill, 2001.

———. "Laws Pertaining to Women in the Temple Scroll." Pages 210–28 in *The Dead Sea Scrolls: Forty Years of Research.* Edited by D. Dimant and U. Rappaport. STDJ 10. Leiden: Brill, 1992.

———. "The Pharisees and Their Legal Traditions according to the Dead Sea Scrolls." *DSD* 8 (2001): 262–77.

———. "The Place of 4QMMT in the Corpus of Qumran Manuscripts." Pages 81–98 in *Reading 4QMMT, New Perspectives on Qumran Law and History.* Edited by J. Kampen and M. J. Bernstein. SBLSS 2. Atlanta: Scholars, 1996.

———. *Reclaiming the Dead Sea Scrolls: The History of Judaism, the Background of Christianity, the Lost Library of Qumran.* Philadelphia: Jewish Publication Society, 1994.

———. *Texts and Traditions.* Hoboken: Ktav, 1998.

Schlatter, Adolf. *Das Evangelium des Lukas.* Stuttgart: Calver, 1960.

Schmidt, F. "Astrologie juive ancienne: Essai d'interprétation de 4QCriptique (4Q186)." *RevQ* 18 (1997): 125–41.

Schofield, Alison. "Between Center and Periphery: The *Yahad* in Context." *DSD* 16, no. 3 (2009): 330–50.

———. *From Qumran to the Yahad: A New Paradigm of Textual Development for The Community Rule.* STDJ 77. Leiden: Brill, 2009.

Schonhoffer, T. Nicholas. "The Failure of Nerve to Recognize Violence in Early Christianity: The Case of the Parable of the Assassin." Pages 192–217 in *Failure and Nerve in the Academic Study of Religion: Essays in Honor of Donald Wiebe.* Edited by W. E. Arnal, W. Braun, and R. T. McCutcheon. Sheffield: Equinox, 2012.

Schreiber, Stefan. "Henoch als Menschensohn. Zur problematischen Schlußidentifikation in den Bilderreden des äthiopischen Henochbuches (äthHen 71,14)." *ZNW* 91 (2000): 1–17.

Schröter, Jens. *Jesus von Nazaret: Jude aus Galiläa—Retter der Welt.* 4th ed. BG 15. Leipzig: Evangelische Verlagsanstalt, 2006.

Schubert, Kurt. *The Dead Sea Community: Its Origins and Teachings.* Translated by J. W. Doberstein. Westport, Conn.: Greenwood, 1959.

———. *Die Qumran-Essener: Texte der Schriftrollen und Lebensbild der Gemeinde.* UTB 224. Munich: Basel, 1973.

———. "The Sermon on the Mount and the Qumran Texts." Pages 118–29 in *The Scrolls and the New Testament.* Edited by K. Stendahl. New York: Harper, 1957.

Schuller, Eileen. "A Hymn from a Cave Four Hodayot Manuscript: 4Q427 7 i + II." *JBL* 112 (1993): 605–28.

———. "Petitionary Prayer and the Religion of Qumran." Pages 29–45 in *Religion in the Dead Sea Scrolls.* Edited by J. J. Collins and R. A. Kugler. Grand Rapids: Eerdmans, 2000.

———. "Some Reflections on the Function and Use of Poetical Texts among the Dead Sea Scrolls." Pages 173–89 in *Liturgical Perspectives: Prayer and Poetry in Light of the Dead Sea Scrolls: Proceedings of the Fifth International Symposium of the Orion Center for the Study of the Dead Sea Scrolls and Associated Literature, 19–23 January, 2000*. Edited by E. G. Chazon. STDJ 48. Leiden: Brill, 2003.

Schulz, Siegfried. *Q: Spruchquelle der Evangelisten*. Zurich: Theologischer Verlag, 1972.

Schuré, Edouard. *Jesus: The Last Great Initiate*. Chicago: Yogi, 1917.

Schürer, Emil. *A History of the Jewish People in the Time of Jesus Christ*. Second Division. Vol. 2. Edinburgh, 1893.

Schürmann, Heinz. *Das Lukasevangelium*. Freiburg: Herder, 1969.

———. *Traditionsgeschichtliche Untersuchungen zu den synoptischen Evangelien*. Düsseldorf: Patmos, 1968.

Schüssler Fiorenza, Elisabeth. "Cultic Language in Qumran and in the NT." *CBQ* 38 (1976): 159–77.

Schütz, J. *Johannes der Täufer*. Zürich: Zwingli, 1967.

Schwartz, Daniel R. "Arguments *a minore ad majore (qal wahomer)*—Sadducean Realism." *Massekhet* 5 (2006): 145–56.

———. "Law and Truth: On Qumran-Sadducean and Rabbinic Views of the Law." Pages 229–40 in *The Dead Sea Scrolls: Forty Years of Research*. Edited by D. Dimant and U. Rappaport. STDJ 10. Leiden: Brill, 1992.

———. *Studies in the Jewish Background of Christianity*. WUNT 60. Tübingen: Mohr Siebeck, 1992.

Schwartz, Seth. *Imperialism and Jewish Society, 200 B.C.E. to 640 C.E*. Princeton: Princeton University Press, 2001.

Schweitzer, Albert. *The Quest of the Historical Jesus: A Critical Study of Its Progress from Reimarus to Wrede*. Translated by W. Montgomery. New York: Macmillan, 1910.

Scobie, Charles H. H. *John the Baptist*. London: SCM Press, 1964.

Segal, Alan F. "Jesus and First-Century Judaism." Pages 55–57 in *Jesus at 2000*. Edited by M. J. Borg. Boulder, Colo.: Westview, 1997.

Seitz, Otto J. F. "Love Your Enemies: The Historical Setting of Matthew V. 43f.; Luke VI.27f." *NTS* 16 (1970): 39–54.

Shemesh, Aharon. "4Q271.3: A Key to Sectarian Matrimonial Law." *JJS* 49 (1998): 244–63.

———. *Halakhah in the Making: The Development of Jewish Law from Qumran*. Berkeley: University of California Press, 2009.

Shimoff, Sandra R. "Gardens: From Eden to Jerusalem." *JSJ* 26 (1995): 145–55.

Sigal, Philip. "Further Reflections on the 'Begotten' Messiah." *HAR* 7 (1983): 221–33.

———. *The Halakhah of Jesus of Nazareth according to the Gospel of Matthew*. SBL 18. Atlanta: Society of Biblical Literature, 2007.

Simon, Marcel. *Jewish Sects at the Time of Jesus*. Translated by J. H. Farley. Philadelphia: Fortress, 1967.

Slater, Thomas B. "One Like a Son of Man in First-Century CE Judaism." *NTS* 41, no. 2 (1995): 183–98.

Sloan, David B. "The τίς ἐξ ὑμῶν Similitudes and the Extent of Q." *JSNT* 36, no. 3 (2016): 339–55.
Sloan, Robert B. *The Favorable Year of the Lord: A Study of Jubilary Theology in the Gospel of Luke*. Austin: Scholars, 1977.
Smith, Daniel A. "What Difference Does Difference Make? Assessing Q's Place in Christian Origins." Pages 183–211 in *Scribal Practices and Social Structures Among Jesus Adherents: Essays in Honour of John S. Kloppenborg*. Edited by W. E. Arnal, R. S. Ascough, R. A. Derrenbacker, Jr., and P. A. Harland. BETL 285. Leuven: Peeters, 2016.
Smith, Dennis E. *From Symposium to Eucharist: The Banquet in the Early Christian World*. Minneapolis: Fortress, 2003.
Smith, Jonathan Z. *Drudgery Divine: On the Comparison of Early Christianities and the Religions of Late Antiquity*. Chicago: University of Chicago Press, 1990.
———. "In Comparison a Magic Dwells." Pages 19–35 in *Imagining Religion: From Babylon to Jonestown*. Chicago: University of Chicago Press, 1982.
Smith, Morton. "Ascent to the Heavens and Deification in 4QM.ᵃ" Pages 181–88 in *Archaeology and History in the Dead Sea Scrolls: The New York University Conference in Memory of Yigael Yadin*. Edited by L. H. Schiffman. JSPSup 8. Sheffield: JSOT, 1990.
———. "The Description of the Essenes in Josephus and the Philosophumena." *HUCA* 29 (1958): 273–313.
———. "'God's Begetting the Messiah' in 1QSa." *NTS* 5 (1958–1959): 218–24.
———. "Two Ascended to Heaven—Jesus and the Author of 4Q491." Pages 290–301 in *Jesus and the Dead Sea Scrolls*. Edited by J. H. Charlesworth. New York: Doubleday, 1992.
So, Ky-Chun. "The Sabbath Controversy of Jesus: Between Jewish Law and the Gentile Mission." Ph.D. diss., Claremont Graduate University, 1999.
———. "The Sabbath Saying (Q 14:5)." International Q Project, 11 v 98.
Sollamo, R. "War and Violence in the Ideology of the Qumran Community." Pages 341–52 in *Verbum et Calamus: Semitic and Related Studies in Honour of the Sixtieth Birthday of Professor Tapani Harviainen*. Edited by H. Juusola, J. Laulainen, and H. Palva. SO 99. Helsinki: Finnish Oriental Society, 2004.
Stacey, David. "A Reassessment of the Stratigraphy of Qumran." Pages 7–74 in *Qumran Revisited: A Reassessment of the Archaeology of the Site and Its Texts*. Edited by David Stacey and Gregory Doudna. BARIS 2520. Oxford: Archaeopress, 2013.
———. "Some Archaeological Observations on the Aqueducts of Qumran." *DSD* 14, no. 2 (2007): 222–43.
Stager, Lawrence E. "Jerusalem and the Garden of Eden." *Eretz-Israel* 26 (1999): 183–94.
Stanton, Graham. "On the Christology of Q." Pages 27–42 in *Christ and Spirit in the New Testament*. Edited by B. Lindars and S. S. Smalley. Cambridge: Cambridge University Press, 1973.

Stauffer, Ethelbert. *Jesus and the Wilderness Community at Qumran.* Translated by H. Spalteholz. Philadelphia: Fortress, 1964.
Steckoll, S. H. "Preliminary Excavation Report on the Qumran Cemetery." *RevQ* 6 (1968): 323–36.
Steenburg, David. "The Worship of Adam and Christ as the Image of God." *JSNT* 39 (1999): 95–109.
Stegemann, Ekkehard, ed. *Messias-Vorstellungen bei Juden und Christen.* Stuttgart: W. Kohlhammer, 1993.
Stegemann, H. "Der lehrende Jesus: Der sogenannte biblische Christus und die geschichtliche Botschaft Jesu von der Gottesherrschaft." *NZSTh* 24 (1982): 3–20.
———. *Die Essener, Qumran, Johannes der Täufer und Jesus: Ein Sachbuch.* Freiburg: Herder, 1993.
———. *The Library of Qumran: On the Essenes, Qumran, John the Baptist, and Jesus.* Grand Rapids: Eerdmans, 1998.
———. "The Qumran Essenes: Local Members of the Main Jewish Union in Late Second Temple Times." Pages 83–166 in *The Madrid Qumran Congress.* Edited by J. Trebolle Barrera and L. Vegas Montaner. Leiden: Brill, 1992.
Steiner, Anton. "Warum lebten die Essener asketisch?" *BZ* 15 (1971): 1–2.
Steinman, Jean. *Saint John the Baptist and the Desert Tradition.* Translated by M. Boyes. London: Longmans, Green, 1958.
Steinmüller, F. *Die Feindesliebe.* Regensburg, 1903.
Stendahl, Krister, ed. *The Scrolls and the New Testament.* New York: Harper & Brothers, 1957.
Steudel, Annette. "4QMidr Esch: 'A Midrash on Eschatology' (4Q174 + 4Q177)." Pages 2:531–41 in *The Madrid Qumran Congress: Proceedings of the International Congress on the Dead Sea Scrolls, Madrid, 18–21 March, 1991.* Edited by J. Trebolle Barrera and L. Vegas Montaner. 2 vols. Leiden: Brill, 1992.
———. *Der Midrasch zur Eschatologie aus der Qumrangemeinde (4QmidrEschata-b).* STDJ 13. Leiden: Brill, 1994.
———. "The Development of Essenic Eschatology." Pages 79–86 in *Eschatology in the Bible and in Jewish and Christian Tradition.* Edited by H. G. Reventlow. Sheffield: Sheffield Academic, 1997.
Stökl Ben Ezra, Daniel. "Old Caves and Young Caves: A Statistical Reevaluation of a Qumran Consensus." *DSD* 14 (2007): 313–33.
Stone, M. E., and J. C. Greenfield, eds. *Discoveries in the Judaean Desert XXII, Qumran Cave 4 XVII: Parabiblical Texts, Part 3.* Edited by G. Brooke, J. Collins, T. Elgvin, P. Flint, J. Greenfield, E. Larson, C. Newsom, E. Puech, L. H. Schiffman, M. Stone, and J. T. Barrera, with J. C. VanderKam. Oxford: Clarendon, 1996.
Stowers, Stanley K. *A Rereading of Romans: Justice, Jews, and Gentiles.* New Haven: Yale University Press, 1994.
Strathearn, Gaye. "4Q521 And What It Might Mean for Q 3–7." Pages 395–424 in *Bountiful Harvest: Essays in Honor of S. Kent Brown.* Edited by A. C. Skinner, D. Morgan Davis, and C. W. Griffin. Chicago: University of Chicago Press, 2012.

Strecker, G. *Der Weg der Gerechtigkeit*. Göttingen: Vandenhoeck & Ruprecht, 1971.
Streeter, B. H. "The Original Extent of Q." Pages 185–208 in *Oxford Studies in the Synoptic Problem*. Oxford: Clarendon, 1911.
Strickert, Frederick M. "Damascus Document VII, 10–20 and Qumran Messianic Expectation." *RevQ* 47 (1986): 327–49.
Strugnell, John, Daniel J. Harrington, and Torleif Elgvin. *Qumran Cave 4.XXIV: 4QInstruction (Musar leMevin): 4Q415ff*. DJD 34. Oxford: Clarendon, 1999.
Stuckenbruck, Loren T. *The Book of Giants from Qumran: Text, Translation, and Commentary*. TSAJ 63. Tübingen: Mohr Siebeck, 1997.
———. "Daniel and Early Enoch Traditions in the Dead Sea Scrolls." Pages 2:368–86 in *The Book of Daniel: Composition and Reception*. Edited by J. J. Collins and P. W. Flint. Leiden: Brill, 2002.
———. "Eschatologie und Zeit im *1 Henoch*." Pages 43–60 in *Q in Context I: The Separation between the Just and the Unjust in Early Judaism and in the Sayings Source*. Edited by M. Tiwald. BBB 172. Bonn: Bonn University Press, 2015.
Stuckenbruck, Loren T., and Gabriele Boccaccini. "1 Enoch and the Synoptic Gospels: The Method and Benefits of a Conversation." Pages 1–17 in *Enoch and the Synoptic Gospels: Reminiscences, Allusions, Intertextuality*. Edited by L. T. Stuckenbruck and G. Boccaccini. EJL 44. Atlanta: Society of Biblical Literature, 2016.
———, eds. *Enoch and the Synoptic Gospels: Reminiscences, Allusions, Intertextuality*. EJL 44. Atlanta: Society of Biblical Literature, 2016.
Stuhlmacher, Peter. "The Theme: The Gospel and the Gospels." Pages 1–25 in *The Gospel and the Gospels*. Edited by P. Stuhlmacher. Translated by J. Vriend. Grand Rapids: Eerdmans, 1991.
———. *Wie treibt man Biblische Theologie*. Biblisch-theologische Studien 24. Neukirchen-Vluyn: Neukirchener, 1995.
Suggs, M. J. *Wisdom, Christology and Law in Matthew's Gospel*. Cambridge, Mass.: Harvard University Press, 1970.
Sukenik, E. L. *The Dead Sea Scrolls of the Hebrew University*. Jerusalem: Magnes, 1955.
———. *Megillot Genuzot I*. Jerusalem: Mosad Bialik, 1948.
Sutcliffe, E. F. "Sacred Meals at Qumran?" *Heythrop Journal* 1 (1960): 48–65.
Suter, David W. *Tradition and Composition in the Parables of Enoch*. SBLDS 47. Missoula, Mont.: Scholars, 1979.
———. "Weighed in the Balance: The Similitudes of Enoch in Recent Discussion." *RSR* 7 (1981): 217–22.
Swarup, Paul. *The Self-Understanding of the Dead Sea Scrolls Community: An Eternal Planting, A House of Holiness*. LSTS 59. New York: T&T Clark, 2006.
Szekely, Edmond Bordeaux. *The Essene Gospel of Peace*. Nelson, BC: International Biogenic Society, 1981 [1928].
Tabor, James D., and Michael O. Wise. "4Q521 'On Resurrection' and the Synoptic Gospel Tradition: A Preliminary Study." Pages 151–63 in *Qumran Questions*. Edited by J. H. Charlesworth. Sheffield: Sheffield Academic, 1995.

Tait, Michael. "The End of the Law: The Messianic Torah in the Pseudepigrapha." Pages 196–207 in *The Torah in the New Testament: Papers Delivered at the Manchester-Lausanne Seminar of June 2008*. Edited by M. Tait and P. Oakes. LNTS 401. London: T&T Clark, 2009.

Talmon, Shemaryahu. "The Calendar Reckoning of the Sect from the Judaean Desert." Pages 162–99 in *Aspects of the Dead Sea Scrolls*. Edited by C. Rabin and Y. Yadin. ScrHier 4. Jerusalem: Magnes, 1965 [1958].

———. "The Community of the Renewed Covenant: Between Judaism and Christianity." Pages 3–24 in *The Community of the Renewed Covenant: The Notre Dame Symposium on the Dead Sea Scrolls (1993)*. Edited by E. C. Ulrich and J. C. VanderKam. CJA 10. Notre Dame, Ind.: University of Notre Dame Press, 1994.

———. "The Concepts of *Mashiah* and Messianism in Early Judaism." Pages 79–115 in *The Messiah: Developments in Earliest Judaism and Christianity. The First Princeton Symposium on Judaism and Christian Origins*. Edited by J. H. Charlesworth. Minneapolis: Fortress, 1992.

———. "The Emergence of Institutionalized Prayer in Israel in Light of Qumran Literature." Pages 200–243 in *The World of Qumran from Within*. Jerusalem: Magnes, 1989.

———. "The 'Manual of Benedictions' of the Sect of the Judaean Desert." *RevQ* 2 (1960): 475–500.

———. "Qumran Studies: Past, Present and Future." *JQR* 85 (1994): 1–31.

———. "The Sectarian יחד—A Biblical Noun." *VT* 3 (1953): 133–40.

———. "Waiting for the Messiah: The Spiritual Universe of the Qumran Covenanters." Pages 111–38 in *Judaisms and their Messiahs at the Turn of the Christian Era*. Edited by J. Neusner, W. Scott-Green, and E. S. Frerichs. New York: Cambridge University Press, 1987.

Tatum, W. Barnes. *John the Baptist and Jesus: A Report of the Jesus Seminar*. Sonoma, Calif.: Polebridge, 1994.

Taylor, Joan E. "Buried Manuscripts and Empty Tombs: The Qumran Genizah Theory Revisited." Pages 269–315 in *"Go Out and Study the Land" (Judges 18:2): Archaeological, Historical and Textual Studies in Honor of Hanan Eshel*. Edited by A. M. Maeir, J. Magness, and L. H. Schiffman. Leiden: Brill, 2012.

———. *The Essenes, the Scrolls, and the Dead Sea*. New York: Oxford University Press, 2012.

———. *The Immerser: John the Baptist within Second Temple Judaism*. SHJ 2. Grand Rapids: Eerdmans, 1997.

———. *Jewish Women Philosophers of First-Century Alexandria: Philo's "Therapeutae" Reconsidered*. New York: Oxford University Press, 2003.

———. "Women, Children, and Celibate Men in the *Serekh* Texts." *HTR* 104, no. 2 (2011): 171–90.

Taylor, Justin. *Where Did Christianity Come From?* Collegeville, Minn.: Liturgical, 2001.

Teeple, Howard M. *The Mosaic Eschatological Prophet*. Philadelphia: Society of Biblical Literature, 1957.

———. "Qumran and the Origin of the Fourth Gospel." *NovT* 4 (1960): 6–25.
Theisohn, Johannes. *Der auserwählte Richter: Untersuchungen zum traditiongeschichtlichen Ort der Menschensohngestalt der Bilderreden des Äthiopischen Henoch.* Göttingen: Vandenhoeck & Ruprecht, 1975.
Theissen, Gerd, and Annette Merz. "Der umstrittene historische Jesus. Oder: Wie historisch ist der historische Jesus?" Pages 3–32 in *Jesus als historische Gestalt: Beiträge zur Jesusforschung.* Göttingen: Vandenhoeck & Ruprecht, 2003.
Thiede, Carsten Peter. *The Dead Sea Scrolls and the Jewish Origins of Christianity.* Oxford: Lion, 2000.
———. *The Earliest Gospel Manuscript? The Qumran Fragment 7Q5 and Its Significance for New Testament Studies.* Carlisle, UK: Paternoster, 1992.
Thiering, Barbara. *Jesus & the Riddle of the Dead Sea Scrolls: Unlocking the Secrets of His Story.* New York: HarperSanFrancisco, 1992.
———. *The Qumran Origins of the Christian Church.* Sydney: Theological Explorations, 1983.
Thomas, J. *Le mouvement baptiste en Palestine et Syrie (150 av. J.C.–300 ap. J.C.).* Gembloux, Belgium: Duculot, 1935.
Thomas, Samuel I. *The "Mysteries" at Qumran: Mystery, Secrecy, and Esotericism in the Dead Sea Scrolls.* EJL 25. Atlanta: Society of Biblical Literature, 2009.
Tiller, Patrick A. *A Commentary on the Animal Apocalypse of 1 Enoch.* Atlanta: Scholars, 1993.
Tiwald, Markus. "Hat Gott sein Haus verlassen (vgl. Q 13,35)? Das Verhältnis der Logienquelle zum Fruhjüdentum." Pages 63–89 in *Kein Jota wird vergehen: Das Gesetzesverstandnis der Logienquelle vor dem Hintergrund frühjüdischer Theologie.* BWANT 10. Stuttgart: Kohlhammer, 2013.
Tomson, Peter J. *Paul and the Jewish Law: Halakha in the Letters of the Apostle to the Gentiles.* Assen: van Gorcum, 1990.
Tov, Emanuel. "The Orthography and Language of the Hebrew Scrolls Found at Qumran and the Origins of These Scrolls." *Textus* 13 (1986): 31–57.
Trautmann, M. *Zeichenhafte Handlungen Jesu: Ein Beitrag zur Frage nach dem geschichtlichen Jesus.* Forschung zur Bible 37. Würzburg: Echter, 1980.
Trilling, Wolfgang. "Die Täufertradition bei Matthäus." *BZ* (1959): 271–89.
Tuckett, Christopher M. *Q and the History of Early Christianity: Studies on Q.* Edinburgh: T&T Clark, 1996.
———. "Q, the Law and Judaism." Pages 90–101 in *Law and Religion.* Edited by B. Lindars. Cambridge: James Clarke, 1988.
———. *The Revival of the Griesbach Hypothesis.* Cambridge: Cambridge University, 1983.
———. "Scripture and Q." Pages 3–26 in *The Scriptures in the Gospels.* Edited by C. M. Tuckett. BETL 131. Leuven: Leuven University Press, 1997.
———. "The Son of Man and Daniel 7: Q and Jesus." Pages 371–94 in *The Sayings Source Q and the Historical Jesus.* Edited by A. Lindemann. BETL 158. Leuven: Leuven University Press, 2001.

Tukasi, Emmanuel O. *Determinism and Petitionary Prayer in John and the Dead Sea Scrolls: An Ideological Reading of John and the Rule of the Community (1QS)*. LNTS/LSTS 66. New York: T&T Clark, 2008.

Ullmann-Margalit, Edna. "The Identity, Identification and Existence of the Sects: The 'Zadokite Priests,' the Essenes, and the Scrolls." *Cathedra* 139 (2011): 31–54.

———. *Out of the Cave: A Philosophical Inquiry into the Dead Sea Scrolls Research*. Cambridge, Mass.: Harvard University Press, 2006.

Van der Kooij, Arie. "The *Yahad*—What is in a Name?" *DSD* 18 (2011): 109–28.

Van der Ploeg, J. "The Meals of the Essenes." *JSS* 2 (1957): 163–75.

Van der Woude, Adam S. "11QMelchizedek and the New Testament." *NTS* 12 (1966): 301–26.

———. *Die messianischen Vorstellungen der Gemeinde von Qumran*. Assen: Van Gorcum, 1957.

———. "Melchisedek als himmlische Erlösergestalt in den neugefundenen eschatologischen Midraschim aus Qumran Höhle XI." *Oudtestamentische Studien* 14 (1965): 354–73.

Van Henten, Jan Willem. *The Maccabean Martyrs as Saviours of the Jewish People: A Study of 2 and 4 Maccabees*. JSJSup 57. Leiden: Brill, 1997.

Van Unnik, W. C. "Die Motivierung der Feindesliebe in Lukas 6:32-35." *NovT* 8 (1966): 284–300.

VanderKam, James C. "1 Enoch, Enochic Motifs, and Enoch in Early Christian Literature." Pages 32–101 in *The Jewish Apocalyptic Heritage in Early Christianity*. Edited by James C. VanderKam and William Adler. CRINT 3/4. Minneapolis: Fortress, 1996.

———. "Adam's Incense Offering (Jubilees 3:27)." *Meghillot: Studies in the Dead Sea Scrolls* V–VI. Jerusalem: Bialik Institute, 2007.

———. "The Book of Enoch and the Qumran Scrolls." Pages 254–80 in *The Oxford Handbook of the Dead Sea Scrolls*. Edited by T. H. Lim and J. J. Collins. New York: Oxford University Press, 2010.

———. "The Dead Sea Scrolls and Christianity." Pages 181–202 in *Understanding the Dead Sea Scrolls: A Reader from the Biblical Archaeological Review*. Edited by H. Shanks. New York: Random House, 1992.

———. *The Dead Sea Scrolls Today*. Grand Rapids: Eerdmans, 1994.

———. *Enoch: A Man for All Generations*. Columbia: University of South Carolina Press, 1995.

———. *Enoch and the Growth of an Apocalyptic Tradition*. CBQMS 16. Washington, D.C.: Catholic Biblical Association of America, 1984.

———. "Identity and History of the Community." Pages 487–533 in *The Dead Sea Scrolls after Fifty Years: A Comprehensive Assessment*. Edited by P. W. Flint and J. C. VanderKam. Leiden: Brill, 1999.

———. "The People of the Dead Sea Scrolls: Essenes or Sadducees?" Pages 51–61 in *Understanding the Dead Sea Scrolls*. Edited by H. Shanks. New York: Vintage, 1993.

———. "Righteous One, Messiah, Chosen One, and Son of Man in *1 Enoch* 37–71." Pages 166–91 in *The Messiah*. Edited by J. H. Charlesworth. Philadelphia: Fortress, 1992.

———. "Sabbatical Chronologies in the Dead Sea Scrolls and Related Literature." Pages 159–79 in *The Dead Sea Scrolls in Their Historical Context*. Edited by T. H. Lim. Edinburgh: T&T Clark, 2000.

———. "Sinai Revisited." Pages 44–66 in *Biblical Interpretation at Qumran*. Edited by M. Henze. Grand Rapids: Eerdmans, 2005.

———. "Those Who Look for Smooth Things, Pharisees, and Oral Law." Pages 465–77 in *Emanuel: Studies in the Hebrew Bible, Septuagint and Dead Sea Scrolls in Honor of Emanuel Tov*. Edited by S. M. Paul, R. A. Kraft, L. H. Schiffman, and W. W. Fields. VTSup 94. Leiden: Brill, 2003.

Venturini, Karl Heinrich. *Natürliche Geschichte des großen Propheten von Nazareth*. 4 vols. Copenhagen, 1800–1802.

Vermes, Geza. "Appendix E: The Use of בר נש/בר נשא in Jewish Aramaic." Pages 310–30 in *An Aramaic Approach to the Gospels and Acts*. Edited by M. Black. 3rd ed. Oxford: Clarendon, 1967.

———. *The Authentic Gospel of Jesus*. London: Allen Lane, 2003.

———. *The Complete Dead Sea Scrolls*. New York: Penguin, 1997.

———. *The Dead Sea Scrolls in English*. 3rd ed. Sheffield: JSOT, 1987.

———. *The Dead Sea Scrolls: Qumran in Perspective*. Philadelphia: Fortress, 1977.

———. *Discovery in the Judean Desert*. New York: Desclee, 1956.

———. "Essenes and Therapeutae." *RevQ* 3 (1962): 495–504.

———. "Essenes-Therapeutae-Qumran." *DUJ* 21 (1960): 97–115.

———. "The Etymology of 'Essenes.'" *RevQ* 7 (1960): 427–43.

———. *Jesus the Jew: A Historian's Reading of the Gospels*. Philadelphia: Fortress, [1973] 1981.

———. "The Oxford Forum for Qumran Research: Seminar on the Rule of War from Cave 4 (4Q285)." *JJS* 43 (1992): 85–94.

———. "The Qumran Community, the Essenes, and Nascent Christianity." Pages 581–86 in *The Dead Sea Scrolls Fifty Years after Their Discovery: Proceedings of the Jerusalem Congress, July 20–25, 1997*. Edited by L. H. Schiffman, E. Tov, and J. C. VanderKam. Jerusalem: Israel Exploration Society, 2000.

———. "Qumran Forum Miscellanea I." *JJS* 43 (1992): 299–305.

———. "Sectarian Matrimonial Halakhah in the Damascus Rule." *JJS* 25 (1974): 197–202.

Vermes, Geza, and Martin Goodman, eds. *The Essenes according to the Classical Sources*. OCT 1. Sheffield: JSOT, 1989.

Vielhauer, Philip. "Gottesreich und Menschensohn in der Verkündigung Jesu." Pages 51–79 in *Festschrift für Günther Dehn, zum 75. Geburtstag am 18. April 1957*. Neukirchen: Kreis Moers, Verlag der Buchhandlung Erziehungsvereins, 1957.

Von Lohse, Eduard. "Jesu Wurte über den Sabbat." Pages 79–89 in *Judentum, Urchristentum, Kirche: Festschrift für Joachim Jeremias*. Edited by Walther Eltester. Berlin: Alfred Töpelmann, 1960.

Von Rad, Gerhard. "The Theological Problem of the Old Testament Doctrines of Creation." Pages 131–43 in *The Problem of the Hexateuch and Other Essays*. Edinburgh: Oliver & Boyd, 1966.

Vouga, P. *Jésus et la Loi: Selon la Tradition Synoptique*. Genèva: Labor et Fides, 1988.

Waddell, James A. *The Messiah: A Comparative Study of the Enochic Son of Man and the Pauline Kyrios*. JCT 10. London: T&T Clark, 2011.

———. "The Messiah in the Parables of Enoch and the Letters of Paul: A Comparative Analysis." Ph.D. diss., University of Michigan, 2010.

Wagner, Siegfried. *Die Essener in der wissenschaftlichen Diskussion: Vom Ausgang des 18. bis zum begin des 20. Jahrhunderts: Eine wissenschaftsgeschichtliche Studie*. Berlin: Alfred Töpelmann, 1960.

Walck, Leslie W. *The Son of Man in the Parables of Enoch and in Matthew*. JCT 9. Edinburgh: T&T Clark, 2011.

Waldmann, Michael. *Die Feindeliebe in der antiken Welt und im Christentum*. Vienna: Mayer, 1902.

Wallace, David. "The Essenes and Temple Sacrifice." *TZ* 13 (1957): 335–38.

Wapnick, Kenneth. *Absence from Felicity: The Story of Helen Schucman and Her Scribing of "A Course in Miracles."* Temecula, Calif.: FACIM, 1991.

Wassen, Cecilia. "Do You Have to Be Pure in a Metaphorical Temple? Sanctuary Metaphors and Construction of Sacred Space in the Dead Sea Scrolls and Paul's Letters." Pages 55–86 in *Purity, Holiness, and Identity in Judaism and Christianity: Essays in Memory of Susan Haber*. Edited by C. S. Ehrlich, A. Runesson, and E. Schuller. WUNT 305. Tübingen: Mohr Siebeck, 2013.

Webb, R. L. "Jesus' Baptism by John: Its Historicity and Significance." Pages 95–150 in *Key Events in the Life of the Historical Jesus: A Collaborative Exploration of Context and Coherence*. Edited by D. L. Bock and R. L. Webb. WUNT 247. Tübingen: Mohr Siebeck, 2009.

———. "John the Baptist and His Relationship to Jesus." Pages 179–229 in *Studying the Historical Jesus: Evaluations of the State of Current Research*. Edited by B. D. Chilton and C. A. Evans. Leiden: Brill, 1994.

———. *John the Baptizer and Prophet: A Socio-historical Study*. JSNTSup 62. Sheffield: JSOT, 1991.

Weinfeld, Moshe. *The Organizational Pattern and the Penal Code of the Qumran Sect: A Comparison with Guilds and Religious Associations of the Hellenistic-Roman Period*. NTOA 2. Göttingen: Vandenhoeck & Ruprecht, 1986.

———. "Prayer and Liturgical Practice in the Qumran Sect." Pages 241–58 in *The Dead Sea Scrolls: Forty Years of Research (University of Haifa, March 20–24, 1988)*. Edited by D. Dimant and U. Rappaport. Leiden: Brill, 1992.

Weiss, B. *Die Evangelien des Markus und Lukas*. Göttingen: Vandenhoeck & Ruprecht, 1901.

———. *Die Quellen der Synoptischen Überlieferung*. Leipzig: J. C. Hingischs'sche Buchhandlung, 1908.

———. *Die Quellen des Lukasevangelium*. Stuttgart & Berlin: J.G. Cotta'sche Buchhandlung Nachfolger, 1907.

Weiss, H. "The Sabbath in the Synoptic Gospels." *JSNT* 38 (1990): 13–27.
Weiss, Johannes. *Die Predigt Jesu vom Reiche Gottes*. Göttingen: Vandenhoeck & Ruprecht, 1892.
———. *Jesus' Proclamation of the Kingdom of God*. Philadelphia: Fortress, 1971.
Werline, Rodney A. "The Curses of the Covenant Renewal Ceremony in 1QS 1:16–2:19." Pages 280–88 in *For a Later Generation: The Transformation of Tradition in Israel, Early Judaism, and Early Christianity*. Edited by R. A. Argall, B. A. Bow, and R. A. Werline. Harrisburg, Pa.: Trinity International, 2000.
———. "Defining Penitential Prayer." Pages xiii–xvii in *Seeking the Favor of God, Vol. 1: The Origins of Penitential Prayer in the Second Temple Period*. Edited by M. Boda, D. K. Falk, and R. A. Werline. 3 vols. SBLEJL 22. Leiden: Brill, 2007.
Westcott, B. F., and F. J. A. Hort. *The New Testament in the Original Greek*. New York: Harper & Brothers, 1881.
Westerholm, Stephen. *Jesus and Scribal Authority*. ConBNT 10. Lund: CWK Gleerup, 1978.
Wieder, N. "The 'Law Interpreter' of the Sect of the Dead Sea Scrolls: The Second Moses." *JJS* 4 (1953): 158–75.
Wiesenberg, E. "Chronological Data in the Zadokite Fragments." *VT* 5 (1955): 284–308.
Williams, Jarvis J. *Maccabean Martyr Traditions in Paul's Theology of Atonement: Did Martyr Theology Shape Paul's Conception of Jesus's Death?* Eugene, Ore.: Wipf & Stock, 2010.
Williams, Sam K. *Jesus' Death as Saving Event: The Background and Origin of a Concept*. HDR 2. Missoula, Mont.: Scholars, 1975.
Wink, Walter. "Jesus' Reply to John: Matt 11:2-6 // Luke 7:18-23." *Forum* 5 (1989): 121-28.
———. "John the Baptist and the Gospel." Th.D. diss., Union Theological Seminary, 1963.
———. *John the Baptist in the Gospel Tradition*. Cambridge: Cambridge University Press, 1968.
———. "Neither Passivity nor Violence: Jesus' Third Way (Matt. 5:38-42 parr.)." Pages 102–5 in *The Love of Enemy and Nonretaliation in the New Testament*. Edited by W. M. Swartley. Louisville, Ky.: Westminster John Knox, 1992.
Wise, Michael. "4QFlorilegium and the Temple of Adam." *RevQ* 15 (1991): 103–32.
———. *The First Messiah: Investigating the Saviour Before Christ*. San Francisco: HarperOne, 1999.
Wise, Michael O., and James D. Tabor. "The Messiah at Qumran." *BAR* 18, no. 6 (1992): 60–65.
Wolfson, Elliott R. "Mysticism and the Poetic-Liturgical Compositions from Qumran: A Response to Bilhah Nitzan." *JQR* 85 (1994): 185–202.
Worrell, John E. "Concepts of Wisdom in the Dead Sea Scrolls." Ph.D. diss., Claremont Graduate School, 1968.
Wright, N. T. *The Climax of the Covenant: Christ and the Law in Pauline Theology*. Edinburgh: T&T Clark, 1991.

———. *Jesus and the Victory of God*. Vol. 2, *Christian Origins and the Question of God*. Minneapolis: Fortress, 1996.

———. *Simply Jesus: A New Vision of Who He Was, What He Did, and Why He Matters*. New York: HarperOne, 2011.

Xeravits, Géza G. *King, Priest, Prophet: Positive Eschatological Protagonists of the Qumran Library*. STDJ 47. Leiden: Brill, 2003.

Yadin, Yigael. "L'attitude essénienne envers la polygamie et le divorce." *RB* 79 (1972): 98–99.

———. "A Note on Melchizedek and Qumran." *IEJ* 15 (1965): 152–54.

———. *The Scroll of the War of the Sons of Light against the Sons of Darkness: Edited with Commentary and Introduction*. Oxford: Oxford University Press, 1962.

———. *The Temple Scroll*. 3 vols. Jerusalem: Israel Exploration Society, 1977.

———. *The Temple Scroll: The Hidden Law of the Dead Sea Sect*. New York: Random House, 1985.

Yang, Yong-Eui. *Jesus and the Sabbath in Matthew's Gospel*. JSNTSup 139. Sheffield: Sheffield Academic, 1997.

Yardeni, Ada. "A Note on a Qumran Scribe." Pages 287–98 in *New Seals and Inscriptions: Hebrew, Idumean, and Cuneiform*. Edited by M. Lubetski. HBM 8. Sheffield: Sheffield Phoenix, 2007.

Zerbe, Gordon Mark. *Non-retaliation in Early Jewish and New Testament Texts: Ethical Themes in Social Contexts*. JSPSup13. Sheffield: JSOT, 1993.

Zimmermann, J. *Messianische Texte aus Qumran: Königliche, priesterliche und prophetische Messiasvorstellungen in den Schriftfunden von Qumran*. WUNT 2/104. Tübingen: Mohr Siebeck, 1998.

INDEX OF AUTHORS

Abegg, M. G., 7
Albani, M., 56
Albright, William F., 51
Alexander, P. S., 56
Alexis-Baker, Andy, 126
Allegro, John M., 156
Allison, Dale C., 20, 83, 92, 96, 97, 98, 103, 106, 107, 110, 111, 116, 117
Anderson, B. W., 102
Argall, Randall A., 37
Arnal, William E., 20
Atkinson, Kenneth, 37
Avalos, Hector, 126

Back, Sven-Olav, 118
Badia, Leonard F., 13, 14
Bahrdt, Karl Heinrich, 3
Baillet, Maurice, 158
Balla, Marta, 42
Bammel, Ernst, 13
Banks, Robert, 116
Bardtke, Hans, 123

Bar-Nathan, Rachel, 41
Barrera, J. T., 29
Barrett, Charles K., 91
Barthélemy, D., 73
Basser, Herbert W., 119
Bauckham, Richard, 11, 18, 47, 166
Baumgarten, Albert I., 22, 132, 134, 135, 137
Baumgarten, Joseph M., 14, 54, 58, 76, 77, 103, 108, 109, 110, 112, 113, 138
Bazzana, Giovanni, 21
Beall, Todd S., 27, 45, 46, 47, 132
Becker, Jürgen, 129
Becker, Michael, 86, 87, 88, 89
Benoit, Pierre, 8, 10, 13, 110
Berger, Klaus, 115
Bergmeier, Roland, 37, 38, 85, 87, 89
Bergsma, John Sietze, 91
Bermejo-Rubio, Fernando, 125
Beskow, Per, 5
Betz, Otto, 10, 12, 29, 89, 165
Bilde, Per, 29, 37, 47, 107, 130, 158

INDEX OF AUTHORS

Black, Matthew, 11, 12, 110, 118, 124, 165
Blavatsky, Helena P., 5
Blenkinsopp, Joseph, 79
Bloom, Harold, 4
Boccaccini, Gabriele, 27, 30, 47, 85, 109, 161, 166
Bock, D. L., 15
Bockmuehl, Markus, 6, 121
Boda, Mark J., 62
Bond, Helen K., 150
Borg, Marcus J., 97, 101
Boring, M. Eugene, 120
Bovon, François, 114, 117
Boyarin, Daniel, 24, 154, 159
Brandt, W., 16
Braun, Herbert, 1
Braun, Willi, 34
Bredin, Mark R., 126
Breengaard, C., 107
Brin, G., 103, 104
Brodie, Thomas L., 93
Brooke, George J., 1, 8, 10, 17, 63, 75, 77, 85, 88, 90, 92, 103, 105, 143, 146, 159, 160
Broshi, Magen, 40, 47, 164
Brown, Raymond E., 8, 12, 13
Brownlee, William H., 1, 23, 33, 54, 78, 82, 157
Bruce, F. F., 8, 10, 12, 164
Bultmann, Rudolf, 92, 114, 115
Burchard, Christian, 40
Burns, Joshua Ezra, 131, 168, 169
Burrows, Millar, 5, 14, 27, 57
Busse, U., 117
Bussmann, W., 114

Callaway, Philip R., 50
Cameron, R., 150
Campbell, Jonathan, 11, 51
Cansdale, Lena, 44
Capper, Brian J., 29
Cargill, Robert R., 41, 43
Carmignac, Jean, 64
Carter, Jeffrey, 25
Casey, P. Maurice, 92

Castor, George DeWitt, 115
Catchpole, David R., 104, 107
Cayce, Edgar, 6
Chamberlain, J. V., 157
Chapman, David W., 126, 148, 149, 151
Charlesworth, James H., 1, 9, 16, 17, 39, 59, 65, 84, 85, 113, 155, 164
Chazon, Esther G., 61
Chester, Andrew, 89
Chilton, Bruce D., 14, 15, 21, 79, 80, 88, 90, 95
Cohen, Shaye J. D., 39
Coloe, M. L., 12
Collins, Adela Yarbro, 15, 130
Collins, John J., 8, 17, 18, 33, 34, 37, 47, 48, 49, 50, 51, 52, 54, 62, 65, 66, 67, 71, 72, 73, 81, 83, 84, 87, 88, 89, 94, 96, 97, 98, 109, 110, 123, 130, 137, 156, 160, 161, 167
Conybeare, F. C., 36
Conzelmann, Hans, 16
Coppens, Joseph, 108
Crawford, Sidnie White, 1, 109
Creed, J. M., 116
Cross, Frank Moore, 15, 27, 32, 34, 47, 50, 145
Crossan, J. D., 115
Crossley, James G., 20, 121
Crown, Alan David, 44
Croy, N. Clayton, 126
Cullmann, Oscar, 15, 59

Dahl, Nils Alstrup, 10, 71, 77, 130
Daly, Robert, 155
Daniel, Constantin, 34
Davidson, M. J., 58
Davies, Philip R., 28, 31, 33, 44, 50, 52, 54, 76, 97, 103, 109
Davies, W. D., 111, 116, 117, 156
De Jonge, Marinus, 71, 81, 161
De Quincey, Thomas, 4
De Vaux, Roland, 47
De Waard, J., 105
Del Medico, Henri E., 28
Deasley, Alex R. G., 55
Desjardins, M., 36

Duhaime, Jean, 123
Dibelius, Martin, 92
Dimant, Devorah, 28, 29, 146
DiTommaso, Lorenzo, 62
Dodd, C. H., 130
Doering, Lutz, 76, 102, 106, 114, 120
Donceel, Robert, 41
Donceel-Voûte, Pauline, 41
Doudna, Gregory, 44
Douglas, R. Conrad, 129
Dowling, Levi, 6
Driver, G. R., 44
Dungan, D., 106
Dunn, James D. G., 12, 17, 92, 96, 160
Dupont-Sommer, André, 11, 27, 32, 156

Ehrman, Bart D., 96, 98
Eisenman, Robert H., 7, 74, 84
Elder, Linda Bennett, 110
Elgvin, Torleif, 54, 66, 67, 68
Elior, Rachel, 28, 53, 61
Elliott, Mark A., 43
Elukin, Jonathan M., 4
Eshel, E., 34, 47, 61
Esler, Philip Francis, 114
Evans, Craig A., 1, 73, 75, 80, 85, 88, 90, 95, 96
Evans, C. F., 116

Falk, Daniel K., 62, 63
Faierstein, Morris M., 83
Fander, M., 104
Feldman, L. H., 13
Finkbeiner, Douglas P., 37, 131
Fiorenza, Elisabeth Schüssler, 146
Fischel, Henry A., 32
Fitzmyer, Joseph A., 8, 12, 17, 27, 44, 71, 73, 79, 81, 83, 84, 92, 103, 104, 115, 116, 118, 165
Fleddermann, Harry T., 115, 117
Fletcher-Louis, Crispin H. T., 33, 60, 98, 129
Flusser, David, 12, 17, 50, 79, 119, 124, 128, 130
Fraade, Stephen D., 63, 110
Frankemölle, Hubert, 80

Freedman, David N., 10, 32
Freidenreich, David M., 24
Frey, Jörg, 7, 37
Freyne, S., 61
Fritsch, Charles, 13
Furst, Jeffrey, 6

Gärtner, Bertil, 145
Gaster, Theodore H., 11, 27, 50, 65
García Martínez, Florentino, 8, 17, 27, 29, 74, 81, 84, 87, 103, 159
Gathercole, Simon, 153
Geyser, A. S., 12
Gibson, Shimon, 38
Gilders, William K., 132
Ginsburg, Christian D., 4, 5
Ginzberg, Louis, 44, 156
Glaim, Aaron, 28, 54, 153
Goff, Matthew J., 66, 67, 97
Goguel, Maurice, 92
Golb, Norman, 44, 123
Goodacre, Mark S., 20
Goodman, Martin, 29, 31, 35, 40, 45, 46, 131, 132, 154, 168
Goranson, Stephen, 33, 40
Gordis, Robert, 73
Gottstein, M. H., 44
Grabbe, Lester L., 22, 32, 33, 123
Graetz, Heinrich Hirsch, 4
Green, Dennis, 76
Green, William Scott, 71
Greenfield, J. C., 32, 34
Grossman, Maxine L., 6, 49
Grundmann, W., 117
Guillaume, A., 157
Guillaumont, Antoine, 108
Gundry, R. H., 114
Gunnweg, Jan, 42

Haas, Nicu, 109
Haber, Susan, 55
Hachlili, Rachel, 109, 110
Haenchen, Ernst, 16, 116
Hagner, Donald A., 4, 120
Hahn, Oliver, 42
Han, Kyu Sam, 61

INDEX OF AUTHORS

Hanson, R. Kenneth, 15
Harrington, Daniel J., 66, 67, 68
Havener, Ivan, 114
Hayes, John H., 50
Hays, Richard, 128
Heger, Paul, 99
Hempel, Charlotte, 28, 47, 48, 50, 51, 52, 53, 109
Hengel, Martin, 73, 114
Heschel, Susannah, 3, 4
Hezser, Catherine, 127
Himmelfarb, Martha, 59, 144, 146
Hirschfeld, Yizhar, 41
Hoffmann, Paul, 92, 115
Hogeterp, Albert I. A., 88
Hollenback, Paul W., 13
Holmén, Tom, 99, 100
Hooker, Morna D., 96
Hopkins, Jamal-Dominique, 133, 134, 139, 142, 144
Horbury, William, 80
Horsley, Richard, 1, 97
Hort, F. J. A., 116
Hübner, Hans, 108, 110
Hughes, John J., 94
Hultgren, Stephen, 51, 53, 87
Humbert, Jean-Baptiste, 42, 145
Hurtado, Larry W., 161, 162
Hutchesson, Ian, 43
Hutt, Curtis, 43

Instone-Brewer, D., 103, 119

Jackson, Bernard S., 100
Jassen, Alex P., 66, 77, 78, 79, 81, 82, 83, 122
Jaubert, Annie, 50
Jeremias, Joachim, 106, 116
Johns, Loren L., 123
Johnson, Sherman E., 10
Jokiranta, Jutta, 52
Jones, Allen H., 34
Joseph, Simon J., 2, 19, 31, 72, 93, 100, 110, 126, 127, 129, 151, 156, 160, 164

Kampen, John, 34
Kapfer, Hilary Evans, 52, 53, 140, 145
Kasper, Walter, 95
Kazen, Thomas, 100, 101, 102, 161
Kee, Howard Clark, 1, 10
Keith, Chris, 20, 101
Kendall, D., 3
Kilpatrick, G. D., 114
Kim, Seyoon, 17
King, Karen L., 24
Kirk, Alan, 21
Kirk, J. R. Daniel, 161
Kister, Menahem, 104, 141
Klassen, William, 129
Klawans, Jonathan, 28, 44, 145, 146, 147, 155, 169
Klinzing, Georg, 146
Kloppenborg, John S., 20, 91, 92, 93, 97, 105, 115, 129
Klumbies, Paul-Gerhard, 115
Knibb, Michael A., 28, 48, 50, 51, 52, 143, 146
Koester, Helmut, 95, 115
Kohler, Kaufmann, 4
Kosch, D., 104, 114, 117
Kranenborg, Reender, 5
Kugler, Robert A., 53, 142
Kuhn, Heinz-Wolfgang, 18, 113, 120, 129
Kuhn, K. G., 165
Kümmel, Werner G., 91, 92
Kvalbein, Hans, 89, 90

Labahn, Michael, 93
Lagrange, M. J., 117
Lange, Armin, 65
Lasor, William S., 12, 65
Laufen, Rudolf, 115
Leaney, Alfred C., 65
Le Déaut, R., 106
Le Donne, Anthony, 111
Lefebvre, Jean-François, 91
Lenzi, Alan, 65
Leonhardt, Jutta, 132
Levine, Amy-Jill, 104, 105
Levison, John R., 79

INDEX OF AUTHORS

Licht, Jacob, 56, 64
Lichtenberger, Hermann, 13
Lightfoot, J. B., 5
Lim, Timothy, 7, 8
Liver, Jacob, 54
Loader, William R. G., 105, 106, 108, 110, 113, 114, 121
Lönnqvist, Kenneth, 42
Lönnqvist, Minna, 42

Maccoby, Hyam, 119
Magen, Yizhak, 42
Magness, Jodi, 32, 37, 41, 42, 43, 94, 135, 145
Maier, Johann, 63
Malina, Bruce, 60
Mandell, Sara R., 50
Mann, C. S., 51
Manson, T. W., 111, 116
Marcus, Joel, 89
Marguerat, Daniel, 163
Marshall, I. H., 114, 117, 118
Martin, Dale B., 125, 128
Marx, Alfred, 108, 110
Masic, Admir, 42
Mason, Steve, 21, 22, 23, 34, 36, 37, 41, 123, 154
Matthews, Kenneth A., 140
Mayer-Haas, Andrea J., 101
McCasland, S. V., 165
McDonald, J. Ian H., 19
Meier, John P., 13, 34, 75, 92, 96, 97, 99, 100, 104, 105, 113, 114, 120, 121, 149
Mendels, Doron, 36
Mermelstein, Ari, 102
Metso, Sarianna, 51, 53, 54
Metzger, Bruce M., 116
Meurois-Givaudan, Anne and Daniel, 6
Milgrom, J., 143, 144
Milik, J. T., 17, 27, 32, 73, 80
Miller, Merrill P., 79, 150
Mimouni, Simon C., 168
Miner, Daniel F., 80
Moehring, Horst R., 108
Mowinckel, Sigmund, 71

Mroczek, Eva, 24
Mueller, J. R., 103
Müller, G. H., 115
Murphy, Catherine M., 37, 47
Murphy O'Connor, Jerome, 9, 12, 47, 50, 103

Najman, Hindy, 78
Nathan, N., 109
Neirynck, Frans, 114, 116, 117
Neufeld, Thomas R. Yoder, 126
Neusner, Jacob, 21, 22, 71, 102
Newsom, Carol A., 52, 58, 62
Newman, Hillel, 43
Newman, Judith Hood, 61
Newton, Michael, 55
Nickelsburg, George W. E., 30, 45, 97, 107, 138
Niebuhr, Karl Wilhelm, 84, 86, 87, 89
Nissen, A., 130
Nitzan, Bilhah, 58, 59, 61, 64
Nodet, Étienne, 33
Nolland, John, 134, 138
North, Robert G., 91
Notley, R. Steven, 119, 128
Novakovic, Lidija, 87, 89
Novenson, Matthew V., 71

Och, Bernard, 102
Oegema, Gerbern S., 71
Oesterreicher, J. M., 12
O'Callaghan, José, 7
O'Collins, G., 3
Ouseley, Gideon Jasper, 5

Peleg, Yuval, 42
Penner, Jeremy, 62
Petersen, D., 82
Pixner, Bargil, 38
Piper, John, 129, 130
Piper, Ronald A., 129
Pitre, Brant, 150
Polag, A., 92, 114
Pomykala, Kenneth E., 71
Powery, E. B., 106
Prideaux, Humphrey, 2, 3

Priest, John F., 73
Puech, Émile, 17, 80, 82, 84, 85, 87, 89, 159

Qimron, Elisha, 76, 109, 139

Rabin, Ira, 42
Rabinowitz, Isaac, 50
Rajak, Tessa, 136
Reed, Annette Yoshiko, 31
Reed, Jonathan L., 61
Reeves, John C., 28
Regeffe, A., 5
Regev, Eyal, 43, 50, 52, 54, 108, 139, 141, 153
Reinach, Théodore, 40
Reinhartz, Adele, 55
Renan, Ernest, 5
Reventlow, Henning Graf, 65
Riaud, Jean, 29
Richardson, H. Neil, 73
Riesner, Rainer, 10, 38, 89, 165
Riggs, John W., 150
Ringgren, H., 58, 82, 123
Rivkin, E., 22
Roberts, Colin H., 7
Robinson, James M., 93, 115, 167
Rofé, Alexander, 68
Rolland, P., 114
Rollens, Sarah E., 72, 129
Roloff, J., 107
Rost, Leonard, 123
Roth, Cecil, 44, 123
Rothschild, Clare K., 19
Rowland, Christopher, 30, 58, 97, 123, 128

Sacchi, Paolo, 30
Saldarini, Anthony J., 22, 111
Sanders, E. P., 10, 13, 65, 96, 101, 104, 106, 130, 148
Sanders, James A., 14, 80, 91, 125
Sandmel, Samuel, 16, 18
Schäfer, Peter, 107, 159
Schalit, Abraham, 123
Schenk, W., 117

Schiffman, L. H., 18, 23, 44, 54, 61, 64, 65, 66, 73, 75, 76, 77, 82, 84, 85, 99, 103, 109, 133, 138, 142
Schlatter, Adolf, 117
Schmidt, F., 56
Schofield, Alison, 24, 48, 51, 54, 108
Schonhoffer, T. Nicholas, 125, 127
Schubert, Kurt, 11, 16, 82
Schuller, Eileen M., 59, 60, 61
Schulz, Siegfried, 92, 115
Schuré, Edouard, 6
Schürer, Emil, 32
Schürmann, H., 92
Schwartz, Daniel R., 12, 15, 47, 77
Schwartz, Seth, 96
Schweitzer, Albert, 3, 96
Scobie, Charles H. H., 15
Segal, Alan F., 101
Shemesh, Aharon, 76, 103
Shimoff, Sandra R., 146
Sigal, Philip, 73, 100
Simon, Marcel, 11
Sloan, David B., 118
Sloan, Robert B., Jr., 91
Smith, Daniel A., 20
Smith, Dennis E., 150
Smith, Jonathan Z., 25
Smith, Morton, 59, 73, 124, 158
So, Ky-Chun, 114
Sollamo, R., 122, 123
Stacey, David, 42
Stager, Lawrence E., 146
Stanton, Graham, 91
Steckoll, S. H., 109
Stegemann, H., 27, 47, 50, 86, 105
Steiner, Anton, 110
Stendahl, Krister, 12, 156
Steudel, Annette, 64
Stökl Ben Ezra, Daniel, 167
Stone, M. E., 34
Stowers, Stanley K., 147, 152
Strathearn, Gaye, 94
Strecker, G., 117
Streeter, B. H., 114
Strickert, Frederick M., 82
Stuckenbruck, Loren T., 63, 161

Stuhlmacher, Peter, 80, 89
Strugnell, J., 27, 67, 68, 76, 139
Sukenik, E. L., 27
Sutcliffe, E. F., 166
Swarup, Paul, 143
Szekely, Edmond Bordeaux, 5

Tabor, James D., 84, 85, 89, 90, 93
Tait, Michael, 107
Talmon, Shermaryahu, 29, 46, 47, 54, 61, 62, 64, 65, 73, 75, 77
Taylor, Joan E., 2, 6, 15, 16, 19, 28, 29, 34, 37, 91, 108, 124, 131, 132, 133, 135, 137
Taylor, Justin, 12
Teeple, Howard M., 82
Thatcher, T., 12
Theisohn, Johannes, 161
Thiede, Carsten Peter, 7, 39
Thiering, Barbara, 7
Thomas, J., 16, 134
Thomas, Samuel I., 65, 66
Tiwald, Markus, 106
Tov, Emanuel, 85
Trautmann, M., 114
Tuckett, Christopher M., 90, 91, 107, 114, 116, 117, 119, 120
Tukasi, Emmanuel O., 60, 63

Ullmann-Margalit, Edna, 19, 28

VanderKam, James C., 8, 15, 22, 23, 27, 29, 30, 31, 33, 44, 54, 91, 144
Van der Kooij, Arie, 29
Van der Ploeg, J., 166
Van der Woude, Adam S., 79, 81, 82, 125
Van Henten, Jan Willem, 154
Vermes, Geza, 7, 8, 29, 31, 33, 35, 40, 44, 59, 65, 66, 67, 74, 81, 82, 85, 101, 103, 106, 123, 132, 140, 141, 142, 154, 166, 169

Vielhauer, Philip, 96
Von Lohse, Eduard, 116, 120
Von Rad, Gerhard, 102
Vouga, P., 117

Wagner, Siegfried, 2
Walck, Leslie W., 162
Wallace, David, 134, 135
Wapnick, Kenneth, 6
Wassen, Cecilia, 143
Webb, Robert L., 13, 15, 92, 94
Weinfeld, M., 61, 62
Weiß, B., 114, 115
Weiss, H., 114
Werline, Rodney A., 62, 63
Westcott, B. F., 116
Westerholm, Stephen, 101
Wieder, N., 82, 84
Wiesenberg, E., 50
Williams, Jarvis J., 147, 153
Williams, Sam K., 161
Wilson, S. G., 36
Wink, Walter, 92, 130
Wise, Michael O., 74, 84, 85, 89, 90, 93, 146, 157
Wolff, Timo, 42
Wolfson, Elliott R., 59, 60
Worrell, John E., 67
Wright, N. T., 97, 128, 149, 160

Xeravits, Géza G., 71, 72, 74, 80, 81, 83, 88

Yadin, Yigael, 57, 77, 79, 108
Yang, Yong-Eui, 115, 121
Yardeni, Ada, 43

Zerbe, Gordon Mark, 124
Zimmermann, J., 88

INDEX OF SUBJECTS

Adam, 31, 49, 55, 59, 111, 125, 143–46, 162
apocalypticism, 97–98
asceticism, 36, 45–46, 49, 58, 108, 110–12
atonement, 53, 55, 138, 145–46, 148, 153, 159

Beatitudes, 17

categories, 19, 23–24, 97
celibacy, 108–12
Christian origins, 9–10, 25
Christianity, 2–5, 169; and anxiety of influence, 4; as a form of Essenism, 5; and the Essenes, 164–69
communal meals, 135, 165
comparison, 19, 155; method, 23–25
criteria of authenticity, 20

Day of Atonement, 80

Dead Sea Scrolls, 1, 7–9, 23–25, 27, 31–32; discovery, 27; as Essene texts, 28, 47–48; and the Gospel of John, 12; and the letters of Paul, 12; and the "Mystery (That Is to Come)," 64–69; and the New Testament, 12; prayer, 60–63; 4QInstruction, 66–69
Dio Chrysostom, 40
divorce, 103–7

Ein-Gedi, 40–41
"End of Days," 64
Enoch tradition, 29–30, 138–39
eschatology, 12, 30, 45, 86, 96–97, 107, 120
Essenes: celibacy, 108–9; conspiracy theories, 4–5; crucifixion by an eyewitness, 5; and the Dead Sea Scrolls, 27–30; disappearance, 167–69; and the Enochic tradition, 28–32; Essene gate, 10, 38; etymology, 32–34, 85; in Galilee, 39; Gospel of

the Holy Twelve, 5; Gospel of Peace, 5; influence on early Christianity, 2–12; in Jerusalem, 10, 38–39; and John the Baptist, 12–16; marrying, 37, 45n89; New Age, 5–6; pacifism, 43; in Palestine, 39; as "philosophy," 38; and rabbinical Judaism, 167–69; and the Revolt, 167–68; Sabbath, 112–14; sacrifice, 45, 53, 131–38; as sun-worshippers, 45; survival, 168; violence, 123–25
Eucharist, 151, 166

"Gabriel's Revelation," 158
Gospel of John, 12, 121, 126
Gospel of Luke, 17

Halakhah, 25, 77, 82, 99–100, 102, 121, 148–49, 155, 163
Hasmonean, 39, 41–42, 44, 72, 75
Herod the Great, 39

Jesus, 6, 23, 127, 167; and asceticism, 110; and celibacy, 108, 110–12; death as sacrifice, 151–52, 155–56, 160–61; distinctiveness, 25; and divorce, 103–7; and the Essenes, 164; Jesus Research, 20, 25, 99, 128, 148; and the Mosaic Law/Torah, 99–101, 153–54, 163; as prophet, 96–98; and Sabbath, 112–21; and sacrifice, 148–51; as Teacher, 99–100; and the Teacher of Righteousness, 156–57; and the Temple, 126, 155–56; and violence, 125–30; and 4Q521, 84
Jewish Christian, 20, 107, 156, 167, 169
John the Baptist, 12–16; and the Essenes, 12–16
Josephus: on Essenes, 35–39; and Greco-Roman interests, 36; on sacrifice, 133–38
Jubilee, 91

Last Supper, 148, 150–51, 156, 166
letter of Jude, 31

Maccabean, 32, 38, 50, 52, 147, 153–55; martyrdom, 147, 154
Messianism, 24, 71–72, 75, 153, 162; age of healing, 95; "Branch," 75; classification, 71–75; Davidic, 72–75; diversity, 72, 72n7; and the Isaiah Scroll, 157; "Pierced Messiah" text, 74; 4Q521, 86–89; Qumran, 72–75; and the Suffering Servant, 157, 160–61; in the Talmud, 158
Moses, 22, 35, 49, 78, 81–84, 89, 100, 101, 105–7, 112, 150–51, 167

parallelomania, 16–19
Passover, 149–51, 153, 156
Pharisees, 21; and Jesus, 21; and Josephus, 21; and the Law, 22; and rabbinical Judaism, 22; as "seekers of smooth things," 22
Philo, 2, 28–29, 32–37, 44–47; on the Essenes, 34–35; on sacrifice, 131–33
Pliny the Elder: on the Essenes, 39–40
prophets, 78–80; as "anointed," 79–84, 87

Q (Sayings Source/Gospel), 20–21, 93, 115, 127, 167; existence, 20–21; and the Sabbath saying, 114–21; Two Source/Document Hypothesis, 20; and 4Q521, 90–95
Qumran, 6–7, 13, 164, 166–68; angelic fellowship, 58; calendar, 76–77; celibacy, 108–11; communality of goods, 166; daily life, 58; "Damascus," 50; destruction, 167–68; divorce, 103–7; Eschatological Prophet, 81–83; "Glory of Adam," 59; as a Hasmonean fortress, 41; holy spirit, 14, 164; initiation, 55–59; Law, 75–77; as a manor house, 42; as a manufacturing center, "men of holiness," 56; new covenant, 48–49, 65; prayer, 60–63; prophecy, 78–80; purification rites, 14; Qumran/Essene hypothesis, 19, 32–47; revelation, 77–78; Sabbath, 112–14; sacrifice, 131, 138–46,

153, 156; "Sons of Light," 57; 42; as substitute temple, 62; Teacher of Righteousness, 50–51, 53, 60, 67, 82–83, 156–58; and the Temple, 61–62; "Temple of Adam," 143–46; two eras of research, 19; Two Spirits, 56–57; violence, 122–23; "The Way," 164–65; *Yaḥad*, 48–56, 63, 94–95, 122, 153, 156

Revolt (Jewish), 36, 50, 123–25, 167–69

Sabbath, 112–21
sacrifice, 131–55
"Seekers of Smooth Things," 22

Son of Man, 120–21, 127, 151, 161–62
Son of God text, 17

Talmud, 158
Torah, 75, 77–78, 82, 98, 99–102; of creation, 102, 105–7

Urzeit-Endzeit, 102, 128

violence, 122–30

Wicked Priest, 141, 158

Zadokites, 19, 44, 50, 53, 85, 158